AN ANALYTICAL CONCORDANCE OF THE BOOKS OF THE APOCRYPHA

Volume II

Lester T. Whitelocke
Virginia Union University School of Theology

University Press of America™

Library of Congress Catalog Card Number: 78-61389

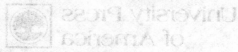

DEDICATION

This book is dedicated to the memory of
the late Mrs. Agnes (Ramsden) Helwig,
B.A., Oxon, who taught me Greek at an
early age in Jamaica, West Indies.

This book is the product of several years of research and a comparative study of the Greek language during the last two hundred years of Old Testament times, and the first one hundred years of the Christian era; for within this time span the books of the Apocrypha were written. The idea of writing a concordance of the books of the Apocrypha came to me out of desperation while I was in graduate school at Boston University in the late 1950's. What precipitated the urgency to write a volume of this magnitude was the fact that, I was required to do research in the area of the Intertestamental Period, bringing into focus the value and importance of the books of the Aprocrypha, which would lead to an understanding of certain doctrinal beliefs which prevailed during this period. Not only that, the books of the Apocrypha reflect the mode of thinking of post-exilic communities in Palestine as well as in Egypt, even though they are not completely preserved in Hebrew.

Of special interest to me was the period of the Maccabean Revolt, which focused attention on the idea of the resurrection of the dead, and placed a great deal of emphasis on feast days, sabbath observance, etc. My problem was to find references whenever I wanted them and for whatever purpose I needed them. I could not find any type of accumulative work that would help me or that would reduce my nightmare of completing my research to the satisfaction of my professors. It was then that I decided that after graduation I would write a simple concordance which would be helpful to students and laymen alike in their study of the books of the Apocrypha.

Those students of the Bible who are interested in the Greek language will enjoy comparing the Greek of the books of the Apocrypha and koine Greek, that is the original language in which the New Testament was written. For eight years, I labored laboriously at the available text with painstaking effort to make sure that this work will serve the purpose for which it is designed. I have transliterated the Greek words into English in order to facilitate those who do not know the Greek language; in this way, the work can be easily followed by almost any one who had a liking for Greek and even those who do not care too much for the language itself.

It is my hope this book will be helpful to those who will be engaged in some form of study of the books of the Apocrypha and the Bible as a whole.

L. T. Whitelocke

ABBREVIATIONS

```
esp......................................especially
I Esd........................................I Esdras
Tobit.........................................Tobit
Judith.......................................Judith
Wisd.-Sol........................Wisdom of Solomon
Eccl.............................Ecclesiasticus
Bar...........................................Baruch
Epis.-Jer.....................Epistle of Jeremiah
Song-Child..............Song of the Three Children
His.-Sus......................History of Susanna
Bel-Drag.......................Bel and the Dragon
I Macc...................................I Maccabees
II Macc................................II Maccabees
III Macc..............................III Maccabees
IV Macc................................IV Maccabees
Pr.-Mans......................Prayer of Manasseh
```

NEW TESTAMENT GREEK

LESSON I

The Alphabet

1. The Greek alphabet is as follows:

Capital Letters	Small Letters	Name	Pronunciation
A	α	Alpha	a as in *father*
B	β	Beta	b
Γ	γ	Gamma	g as in *got*[1]
Δ	δ	Delta	d
E	ε	Epsilon	e as in *get*
Z	ζ	Zeta	dz
H	η	Eta	ʽa as in *late* (ē)
Θ	θ	Theta	th
I	ι	Iota	i as in *pit*, ee as in *feet*
K	κ	Kappa	k
Λ	λ	Lambda	l
M	μ	Mu	m
N	ν	Nu	n
Ξ	ξ	Xi	x
O	o	Omicron	o as in *obey*
Π	π	Pi	p
P	ρ[2]	Rho	r
Σ	σ(ς)[3]	Sigma	s
T	τ	Tau	t
Υ	υ	Upsilon	French u or German ü
Φ	φ	Phi	ph
X	χ	Chi	German ch in *Ach*
Ψ	ψ	Psi	ps
Ω	ω	Omega	o as in *note*

[1] Before another γ or κ or χ, γ is pronounced like ng.

[2] At the beginning of a word ρ is written ῥ, rh.

[3] ς is written at the end of a word, elsewhere σ.

<u>EXPLANATORY NOTES</u>

1. Each English word used is given the Greek spelling
   as it appears in the text; nevertheless, it is
   transliterated for the benefit of the reader.

2. ē: this symbol represents the long "e" in Greek
   known as <u>Eta</u>.

3. θ this symbol represents "th" in English; the
   Greek <u>Theta</u>.

4. ϕ this symbol represents "ph" in English,
   known as <u>Phi</u> in the Greek. It is pronounced with
   an "f" sound.

5. χ this symbol represents the English "ch"; the
   Greek <u>Chi</u>.

6. ψ this symbol represents "ps" in English; the
   Greek <u>Psi</u>.

7. ō: this symbol represents the long "o" in Greek,
   known as <u>Omega</u>.

8. ' : this symbol which resembles a comma turned
   to the left over certain vowels as a, e, i, o, u;
   and over certain diphthongs as ai, ei, oi, au, eu,
   ou, ui, is known as the smooth breathing. It does
   not require an "h" sound. For instance, ὸν should
   be pronounced as "on". The rough breathing is
   represented by the symbol ', and requires an "h"
   sound when the word is to be pronounced, for ex-
   ample ὁν, should be pronounced <u>hon</u>, ὁ, <u>ho</u>, ἁ, <u>ha</u>,
   etc.

9. In the case of the diphthong, the smooth breathing
   as well as the rough breathing is placed over the
   second vowel letter, οἱ is pronounced <u>hoi</u>, υἱ, is
   written as <u>hui</u>, as in the word <u>huios</u>.

10. ῥ: this symbol represents the English "r". When-
    ever it appears with a rough breathing it is writ-
    ten "rh", as in the <u>rhema</u>. With a smooth breath-
    ing it retains its original form as "r".

11. Once the meaning of a word is given, if the same
    word appears again in the same book, the meaning
    is not repeated, unless the occasion warrants it.

x

12. Verbs are generally written in the present tense,
    even though they appear in different tense in
    the Text.

13, ² : this symbol indicates that the letter is
    long, and that it takes a smooth breathing.

14. ι: this symbol, known as Iota Subscript,
    appears at intervals under such letters as a, e,
    and o. It does not affect the pronunciation of
    the word, but it must be written.

IV Macc. 9:2, fathers, if we did not...take know-
        ledge for our

LABOUR, kopos, "toil, trouble, suffering, pain"
Wisd.-Sol. 3:11, their hope is vain, their labours
        unfruitful

    ponos, "task-work, hard work, toil"
Wisd.-Sol. 3:15, For glorious is the fruit of good
        labours: and
        5:1, great boldness...and made no account
        of...labours
        8:7, And if a man love righteousness, her
        labours are
        10:10, she...multiplied the fruit of his
        labours

    kopos
Wisd.-Sol. 10:17, to the righteous a reward of their
        labours,

    ponos
Wisd.-Sol. 15:4, deceive us, nor...the painter's
        fruitless labour

    huperesia, "hard work, hard service"
Wisd.-Sol. 15:7, fashioneth every vessel with much
        labour for our

    kopiao,"to·work hard, grow weary, tired"
Wisd.-Sol. 16:20, send them...bread prepared, with-
        out their labour

    ergon, "anything done or to be done, a deed,
        action"
Wisd.-Sol. 17:20, and none were hindered in their
        labour:

    kopos
Wisd.-Sol. 31:23, what profit have they then but
        labour?

    kopiao
Eccl. 16:27, they neither labour, nor are weary,
        nor cease from

    ponos
Eccl. 28:15, A backbiting tongue...deprived them of
        their labours

    ergazomai, "to work, labour"
Eccl. 30:25, If thou set thy servant to labour,
        thou shalt find

1

Eccl. 30:27, Send him to labour, that he be not
             idle; for idleness
      ergon
Eccl. 38:25, he get wisdom...and is occupied in their
             labours, and
      ergazomai
Eccl. 40:18, To labour, and to be content with that
             a man hath,
      kopiaō
Eccl. 51:27, your eyes, how that I have had but
             little labour,
      ergon
III Macc. 4:14, not for that hard servitude of
             labour which we
      epicheireō, "to set to work, to put one's
             hand to a thing"
III Macc. 6:24, and me your benefactor ye have
             laboured to
      ponos
IV Macc. 7:13, And what is most wonderful...though
             the labours of
      kopiaō
IV Macc. 9:12, And when they had laboured hard
             without effect in

LABOURER, ergatēs, "a labourer, a worker"
Wisd.-Sol. 17:17, whether he were husbandman...or
             a labourer in
LABOURETH, ergazomai
Eccl. 10:27, Better is he that laboureth, and
             aboundeth in all
      kopiaō
Eccl. 11:11, There is one that laboureth, and taketh
             pains, and
        34:4, The poor man laboureth in his poor
             estate; and when

LABOURING, ergatēs, "labourer, worker, a work man"
Eccl. 19:1, A labouring man that is given to
             drunkenness shall

LACEDEMONIANS, Spartiatai
I Macc. 12:2, He sent letters also to the Lace-
             monians, and to
        12:5, letters which Jonathan wrote to the

          Lacedemonians
I Macc. 12:6, Jonathan the high priest...unto the
          Lacedemonians
     12:20, Areus king of the Lacedemonians to
          Onias the high
     12:21, It is found in writing, that the
          Lacedemonians and
     14:20, the copy of the letters that the
          Lacedemonians
     14:23, to the end the people of the Lacede-
          monians might
     15:23, and to Sampsames, and the Lacedemo-
          nians,
II Macc. 5:9, Thus he...had driven many...to the
          Lacedemonians, and

LADDER, klimax, "a ladder or staircase, flight of
          steps"
I Macc. 5:30, morning...and, behold...people bearing
          ladders and
     11:59, he made captain from the place called
          The Ladder

LAMB, arnos, "a lamb, sheep"
I Esd. 1:7, that was found there...thirty thousand
          lambs and kids,
     6:29, the governor, for bullocks, and rams,
          and lambs;
     8:66, three score and twelve lambs, goats
          for a

     amnos, "a lamb"
Wisd.-Sol. 19:9, at large like horses, and leaped
          like lambs,

     arnos
Eccl. 46:16, the mighty Lord...when he offered the
          sucking lamb
     47:3, as with kids, and with bears as with
          lambs

LAMENT, threneo, "to wail, lament, mourn"
Eccl. 38:16, fall down over the head and begin to
          lament, as if
IV Macc. 16:11, But with such a lament as this
          the holy and

LAMENTABLE, penthos, "mourning, sorrow, lament"
III Macc. 4:2, their hearts, all things around being
          lamentable,

       pikros, "bitter, cruel, harsh, stern,

hateful"
III Macc. 6:31, of the cup...of a grievous and
         lamentable death

LAMENTATION, threneō, "to lament, mourn"
I Esd. 1:32, And in all Jewry they mourned for
         Josias...and...made lamentation for him

         threnos, "wailing, lamentation"
Tobit 2:6, into mourning, and all your mirth into
         lamentation

         penthos, "mourning, sorrow, lament"
Wisd.-Sol. 19:3, they were yet mourning and making
         lamentation at
Eccl. 38:17, Weep bitterly, and make great moan,
         and use lamentation, as he is worthy,
         and that

         threnos
I Macc. 1:27, Every bridegroom took up lamentation,
         and she that

         kopetos, "lamentation, a wailing, a beat-
               ing of the breast"
I Macc. 2:70, and all Israel made a great lamentation
         for him
      4:39, they rent their clothes, and made
         great lamentation
      9:20, him, and all Israel made great lamen-
         tation for him,

         threnos
I Macc. 9:41, into mourning, and...their melody into
         lamentation

         penthos
I Macc. 12:52, wherefore all Israel made great la-
         mentation

         kopetos
I Macc. 13:26, And all Israel made great lamentation
         for him, and

         odurmos, "bitter lamentation, wailing"
II Macc. 11:6, they and all the people with lamen-
         tation and tears

         kraugē, "a cry, clamour, lamentation,
               earnest supplication"
III Macc. 1:16, they filled the temple with lamen-
         tations and

kopetos
III Macc. 4:3, there...not fill with wailing and
        lamentation?
      ,
      oiktos, "expression of grief or pity,
              weeping, wailing"
III Macc. 5:49, They gave way, therefore, to la-
              mentations and

LAMENTED, threneō, "to wail, lament, mourn"
  I Esd. 1:32, Jeremy the prophet lamented for Josias,
        and the
        dakruō, "to shed tears, weep"
  IV Macc. 15:20, torture into a burying ground, thou
        lamentedst

LAMP, lampas, "a lamp, lantern, a protable lamp
  Judith 10:22, he came out before his tent with
              silver lamps going
  Eccl. 48:1, prophet as fire, and his word burned
        like a lamp

      luchnos, "a light, lamp, candle"
  I Macc. 4:50, upon the altar they burned incense,
        and the lamps

      lampas
  I Macc. 6:39, mountains glistened...and shined like
        lamps of fire

      luchnos
  II Macc. 1:8, offered also sacrifices...and lighted
        the lamps, and

LANCE, logchē, "a spear, lance"
  II Macc. 5:2, days, there were seen horsemen...
        armed with lances,

LAND, gē, "earth, land"
  I Esd. 4:2, O ye men, do not men...bear rule over
        sea and land,
        5:50, them out of the other nations of the
              land, and
        5:72, But the heathen of the land lying
              heavy upon the
        8:83, That the land, which ye enter into
              to possess as an
        8:83, peace with them...eat the good things
              of the land,
        8:87, again...to mingle...with the...nations

of the land

chōra, "a land, country, estate, farm"
Tobit 1:3, who came with me...into the land of the
        Assyrians
    1:4, And when I was in mine own country, in
        the land of

gē
Tobit 6:3, young man laid hold of the fish, and drew
        it to land
    14:4, scattered in the earth from that good
        land:
    14:5, mercy on them, and bring them again into
        the land,
Judith 1:11, But all the inhabitants of the land
        made light of
    1:12, that he would slay...the inhabitants
        of the land
    3:8, frontiers...for he had decreed to de-
        stroy...the land
    5:9, commanded them to depart...and go into
        the land of
    5:15, So they dwelt in the land of the Amorites,
        and they
agros, "a field, land, also country"
Judith 8:7, husband Manasses had left her gold...
        and lands; and

gē
Wisd.-Sol. 12:3, will to destroy...our fathers...of
        thy holy land
    12:7, that the land, which thou esteem-
        edst above all
    16:19, might destroy the fruits of an
        unjust land
    18:15, a fierce man of war into the midst
        of a land of
    19:7, where water stood before, dry land
        appear; and
    19:10, things that were done...in the
        strange land,
Eccl. 20:28, He that tilleth his land shall increase
        his heap:

xeros, "dry, parched, dry land"
Eccl. 39:22, His blessing covered the dry land as
        a river, and

6

gē
Eccl. 44:21, bless the nations...unto the utmost
           part of the land
     45:22, Howbeit in the land of the people he
           had no
     46:8, on foot, they two alone...bring them
           into...the land
Eccl. 46:9, strength also unto Galeb...so that he
           entered...the land
     47:24, that they were driven out of the land
Bar. 1:8, vessels...that were carried out of...the
           land of Juda,
     1:19, that the Lord brought our forefathers
           out of the land
     1:20, he brought our fathers out of the land
           of Egypt, to give us a land that floweth
           with milk and honey,
     2:11, that...brought thy people out of the
           land of Egypt with
     2:21, so shall ye remain on the land that I
           gave unto your
     2:32, and they shall praise me in the land of
           their
     3:10, Israel,that thou art in thine enemies'
           land...?

chōra
Epis.-Jer. 1:53, For neither can they set up a king
                 in the land,

gē
I Macc. 1:1, who came out of the land of Chettim,
             had smitten
        1:19, Thus they got the stong cities in the
              land of
        1:24, he had taken all away, he went into
              his own land,
        1:28, The land also was moved for the in-
              habitants thereof
        1:44, that they should...the laws of the
              land
        1:52, and so they committed evils in the land
        2:56, Caleb...received the heritage of the
              land
        3:24, and the residue fled into the land of
              the Philistines
        3:36, and that he should...divide their land
              by lot
        3:39, with them he sent...horsemen to go
              into the land of

7

I Macc. 3:41, a power of Syria and of the land of
               the Philistines
         4:22, they fled every one into the land of
               strangers
         5:45, Israelites...that they might come
               into the land of
         5:48, Let us pass through land to go into
               our own country
         5:65, and fought against...Esau in the
               land toward
         5:66, From thence he removed to go into the
               land of the
         5:68, So Judas turned to Azotus in the land
               of the
         6:5,   the armies that, which went against the
               land of
         6:13, I perish through great grief in a
               strange land
         7:6,   his brethren have...driven us out of
               our own land

        chōra
I Macc. 7:7,   what havock he hath made...in the king's
               land, and

        gē
II Macc. 7:10, So they departed, and came...into the
               land of Juda,
         7:22, after they had gotten the land of
               Juda into their
         7:50, Thus the land of Juda was in rest a
               little while
         8:10, and took possession of their lands,
               and pulled

        xeros
I Macc. 8:23, people of the Jews, by sea and by land
               for ever
         8:32, Justice, and fight with thee by sea
               and by land
         9:1,   Bacchides and Alcimus into the land of
               Judea, the

        gē
I·Macc. 9:57, whereupon the land of Juda was in rest
               two years
         9:72, unto him the prisoners...taken...out
               of the land of
        10:30, so that they shall not be taken out
               of the land of

I Macc. 10:33, Jews, that were carried captives out of the land of

10:37, even as the king hath commanded in the land of

10:55, the day wherein thou didst return into the land of

10:67, came Demetrius out of Crete into the land of his

10:72, have been twice put to flight in their own land

12:4, that they should bring them into the land of Judea

chōra

I Macc. 12:25, from Jerusalem, and met them in the land of

gē

I Macc. 12:52, Whereupon they all came into the land of Judea

13:1, together a great host to invade the land of Judea,

13:12, removed from Ptolemais...to invade the land of

13:20, And after this came Tryphon to invade the land,

13:24, Tryphon returned and went into his own land

13:32, and brought a great calamity upon the land

chōra

I Macc. 13:34, Simon...sent to...Demetrius, to... give land an

gē

I Macc. 14:4, As for the land of Judea, that was quiet all the

14:11, He made peace in the land, and Israel rejoiced

14:13, neither was there left in the land to fight

15:10, year went Antiochus into the land of his fathers:

15:14, he vexed the city by land and by sea, neither

15:29, thereof ye have wasted, and done... hurt in the land

15:33, We have neither taken other men's land, nor holden

16:10, Afterward he returned into the land

of Judea in
II Macc. 1:7, Jason and his company revolted from
the holy land
5:21, weening in his pride to make the
land navigable,

chōra
II-Macc. 9:24, they of the land, knowing to whom
the state was

gē
III Macc. 6:3, being doing wrongfully destroyed...
in a strange land
6:5, grievous king of Assyria...subdued
the whole land
6:15, wouldst not forget...the land of
their enemies
7:20, They departed unharmed...by land,
by sea, and by

LANGUAGE, larugx, "the larynx or upper part of the
windpipe, throat"
Eccl. 6:5, Sweet language will multiply friends:
and a

alloglossos, "of a strange tongue, foreign"
Bar. 4:15, brought a nation upon them...of a
strange language, who

phonē, "a loud clear voice, any articulate
sound, language"
I Macc. 7:8, But he answered in his own language,
and said, No.
7:21, exhorted every one of them in her own
language,
7:27, spake in her country language on this
manner;
12:37, And with that he began in his own
language, and

LASTHENES, Lasthenei
I Macc. 11:31, of the letter which we did write unto
...Lasthenes
11:32, King Demetrius unto his father
Lasthenes sendeth

LAUGH, katagelaō, "to deride, jeer, mock; hence, to
laugh at"
Eccl. 7:11, Laugh no man to scorn in the bitterness
of his soul;
20:17, How oft, and of how many shall he be
laughed to scorn

10

gelaō, "to laugh at, sneer at"
Bel-Drag. 1:19, Then laughed Daniel, and held the
          king that he

    katagelaō
I Macc. 7:34, But he mocked them, and laughed at
          them, and abused
      10:70, and I am laughed to scorn for thy
          sake, and

LAUGHING, chleuasia, "mockery, scoffing"
II Macc. 7:27, But she bowing herself toward him,
          laughing the

LAUGHINGSTOCK, épigrama, "an object of malignant joy"
Eccl. 42:11, shameless daughter, lest she make thee
          a laughingstock

LAUGHTER, gelos, "a subject of laughter"
Eccl. 21:20, A fool lifteth up his voice with
          laughter; but a

      gelaseiō, "to like to laugh, to be ready
          to laugh"
IV Macc. 5:28, but thou shalt not have this cause
          of laughter

LAW, nomos, "custom, a positive enactment, law,
          ordinance"
I Esd. 1:33, Josias...and his understanding in the
          law of
      1:48, neck, and his heart, he transgressed
          the law of God
      1:49, of the people...did many things
          against the laws, and
      5:51, of tabernacles, as it is commanded
          in the law,
      8:7, For Esdras...omitted nothing of the
          law and
      8:9, unto Esdras the priest and reader of
          the law of the
      8:12, look unto the affairs of Judea...which
          is in the law
      8:19, and the reader of the law of the most
          high God shall
      8:23, may judge...all those that know the
          law of thy God;
      8:24, And whosoever shall transgress the law
          of thy God,
      8:67, but we have turned back again to trans-

                        gress thy law,
I Esd. 8:94, decreed, and as many as do obey the
            law of the Lord
        9:39, spake unto Esdras...that would bring
            the law of Moses
        9:40, So Esdras the chief priest brought
            the law to the
        9:41, and all the multitude gave heed unto
            the law
        9:45, Then took Esdras the book of the law
            before the
        9:46, And when he opened the law, they stood
            all straight
        9:48, the Levites taught the law of the Lord,
            and read
Tobit 6:12, cannot marry her to another according
            to the law
        7:13, Behold, take her after the law of Moses,
            and lead her
        14:9, But keep thou the law and the command-
            ments, and shew
Judith 11:12, that God hath forbidden them to eat
            by his law:
Wisd.-Sol. 2:11, Let our strength be the law of
            justice: for
        2:12, he upbraideth us with our offending
            the law, and
        6:4, ye have not judged aright, nor keep
            the law,
        6:18, and love is the keeping of her laws;
            and the
        14:16, of time an ungodly custom...was
            kept as a law,
        16:6, to put them in remembrance...of thy
            law
        18:4, by whom the uncorrupt light of the
            law was to be
        18:9, of good men...with one consent made
            a holy law,
Eccl. 2:16, They that fear the Lord...shall be filled
            with the law

    dikaioma, "an act of justice, the making good a
            wrong"
Eccl. 4:17, she may trust his soul, and try him by
            her laws
        9:15, and all thy communication in the law of
            the most High

12

Eccl. 15:1, and the knowledge of the law shall
            obtain her;
      17:11, gave them knowledge, and the law of life
            for an
      19:17, give place to the law of the most High
      19:20, and in all wisdom is the performance
            of the law
      19:24, one that hath...wisdom, and transgress-
            eth the law
      21:11, He that keepeth the law of the Lord
            getteth the
      23:23, For first, she hath disobeyed the law
            of the most
      24:23, are the book of the covenant...even the
            law which
      31:8, The law shall be found perfect without
            lies: and
      32:1, He that keepeth the law bringeth offer-
            ings enough: he
      35:15, He that seeketh the law shall be filled
            therewith:

      nomos
Eccl. 36:2, A wise man hateth not the law; but he
            that is an
      36:3, A man of understanding trusteth in the
            law; and the law is faithful
      39:1, But he that giveth his mind to the law
            of the most
      39:8, He shall...glory in the law of the cove-
            nant of the
      41:8, which have forsaken the law of the most
            High God!
      42:2, of the law of the most High, and his cove-
            nant; and of
      44:20, who kept the law of the most High, and
            was in
      45:5, hear his voice...and gave him...the law
            of life and
      45:17, commandments...that he should teach
            Jacob...his laws
      46:14, By the law of the Lord he judged the
            congregation,
Bar. 2:2, to the things that were written in the law
      2:28, Moses...when thou didst command him to
            write thy law
      4:1, book of the commandments of God, and the
            law that
      4:12, my children...because they departed from

13

the law
His.-Sus. 1:3, taught their daughter according to
the law of
1:62, and according to the law of Moses
they did unto

nomimos, "conformable to usage or law, custom,
legal, lawful"
I Macc. 1:42, and every one should leave his laws:
so all the

nomizō, "to hold or own as a custom, to adopt,
practise a custom"
I Macc. 1:44, of Juda that they should follow the
strange laws

nomos
I Macc. 1:49, to the end they might forget the law,
and change
1:56, they had rent in pieces the books of
the law...they
1:57, found with any...or if any consented
to the law, the
2:21, God forbid that we should forsake the
law and the
2:26, Thus dealt he zealously for the law
of God, like as
2:27, Whosoever is zealous of the law...let
him follow me
2:42, company of Assideans who were...devo-
ted unto the law
2:48, So they recovered the law out of the
hand of the
2:50, now therefore, my sons, be ye zealous
for the law,
2:58, Elias for being zealous and fervent
for the law was
2:64, ye my sons, be valiant...in the behalf
of the law;
2:67, Take also unto you all those that observe the law,
2:68, and take heed to the commandments of
the law

nomimos
I Macc. 3:21, but we fight for our lives and our
laws
3:29, upon the land in taking away the laws
which had
3:48, and laid open the book of the law,
wherein the

14

I Macc. 3:56, every man to his own house according
          to the law
     4:42, conversation, such as had pleasure
          in the law:
     4:47, Then they took whole stones according
          to the law,
     4:53, offered sacrifice according to the law
          upon the new
     6:59, that they shall live after their laws,
          as they did

nomos
I Macc. 10:14, certain of those that had forsaken
          the law and the
     10:37, and that they live after their own
          laws, even as
     13:3, I and brethren...have done for the
          laws and the
     13:48, put all the uncleanness out of it
          ...and keep the law,and
     14:14, the law he searched out; and every
          contemner of the law and wicked per-
          son he took away
     15:21, punish them according to their own
          law
II Macc. 1:4, and open your hearts in his law and
          commandments,
     2:2, how that the prophet, having given
          them the law,
     2:3, exhorted he them, that the law should
          not depart
     2:18, as he promised in the law, will short
          ly have mercy
     2:22, city, and upheld the laws which were
          going down,
     3:1, was inhavited...and the laws were
          kept very well,

nomothetes, "to make laws, to make laws for
          oneself, to ordain by law"
II Macc. 3:15, themselves...called unto heaven upon
          him that made a law

nomos
II Macc. 4:2, Thus was he bold...and was so zealous
          of the laws

nominos
II Macc. 4:11, the governments which were according
          to the law,

15

<u>nomos</u>
II Macc. 4:17, a light thing to do wickedly against
              the laws of
        5:8, pursued of all men, hated as a for-
              saker of the laws
        5:15, with this...Menelaus, that traitor
              to the laws,
        6:1, to compel the Jews to depart from the
              laws of their
        6:5, filled with profaned things, which
              the law
        6:28, notable example...to die willingly...
              for the...laws

<u>áthemis</u>, "lawless"
II Macc. 7:1, were...compelled...against the law to
              taste swine's
        7:2, rather than to transgress the laws of
              our fathers
        7:9, who have died for his laws, unto ever-
              lasting life
        7:11, These I had from heaven; and for his
              laws I
        7:23, now regard not your own selves for
              his laws' sake
        7:24, if he would turn from the laws of his
              fathers; and
        7:30, but I will obey the commandment of the
              law that
        7:37, offer up my body and life for the
              laws of our
        8:21, and ready to die for the laws and
              the country,
        8:36, Thus...they followed the laws that
              he gave them
       10:26, adversary to their adversaries, as
              the law

<u>nomimos</u>
II Macc. 11:24, we should suffer them to live after
               their...laws

<u>nomos</u>
II Macc. 11:31, shall use their own kind of meat
               and laws, as
        12:40, to the idols...which is forbidden
               the Jews by...law
        13:10, commanded...to be put from their law,
        13:14, to fight...even unto death, for the
               laws...he

II Macc. 15:9, And so comforting them out of the
              law and the

nomimos
III Macc. 1:3, But Dositheus...afterward a renegade
               from the laws

nomos
III Macc. 1:12, Then they read the law to him; but
                he persisted
         1:23, and to die...in defence of the law
               of their

nomimos
III Macc. 3:2, was, that the Jews kept them away
               from the...law
         3:4, as they worshipped God, and observed
              his law, they
         7:10, upon those...who...transgressed...
               the law of God
         7:12, destroy those who had transgressed
               the law of God
IV Macc. 1:17, And this is contained in the education
               of the law;
         1:34, kind of food which are forbidden us
               by the law,

nomos
IV Macc. 2:5, For instance, the law says, Thou shalt
              not covet
        2:6, Now then, since it is the law, which
             has forbidden
        2:8, therefore, who regulates his course
             by the law,
        2:9, parsimonious, he is ruled by the law
             acting through
        2:10, For the law conquers even affliction
              toward
        2:13, assertion that reasoning can...of the
              law conquer
        2:23, And he gave a law to this mind, by
              living according
        4:23, if any of them lived according to the
              laws of his

eunoia, "kindness, good will, favourably"
IV Macc. 4:24, destroy his decrees the obedience
               to the law of

nomos
IV Macc. 5:16, who are persuaded that we live under
               a divine law,

17

IV Macc. 5:18, And indeed, were our law...not truly
             divine...we
      5:20, For transgression of the law, whether
             in small or
      5:21, for in either case the law is equally
             slighted
      5:25, for believing that the law was esta-
             blished by God,
      5:33, as on my account to break the law of
             my country
      5:34, I will not belie thee, O law, my in-
             structor! or

    nomothēsia, "law-giving, legislation"
IV Macc. 5:35, thee, O honoured priesthood, and
             science of the law

    nomos
IV Macc. 6:21, by not contending to the death for
             our...law
      6:27, I am slain for the sake of the law
             by tortures
      6:30, resisted in his reasoning for the
             sake of the law
      7:7, O harmonizer with the law, and sage
             devoted to a
      7:8, ought those to be who perform the
             duties of the law
      9:2, disgracing our fathers if we did not
             obey the law
      9:15, am no murderer...but a defender of
             the Divine law
    11:5, of all things, and to live according
             to his...law?
    11:12, enabling us to manifest our adherence
             to the law
    11:27, the guards not of a tyrant but of a
             divine law are
    13:9, Brother, may we die brotherly for the
             law
    13:13, our heart our souls to God...for the
             keeping of...law
    13:21, the more powerfully...and exercise
             in the law of
    13:23, For being educated in the same law,
             and practising
    15:9, Not but that...and their obedience
             to the law, her

nomimos
IV Macc. 15:10, their mother...they obeyed her by
                observing the law
         15:29, O mother of a nation, avenger of
                the law, and

nomophulax, "a guardian of the laws"
IV Macc. 15:32, so thou, the guardian of the law,
                when surrounded

nomos
IV Macc. 16:16, noble is the contest...strive for
                the laws of your
         18:1, O Israelitish children...obey this
                law, and in
         18.4, and having renewed the observance
                of the law in
         18:10, to teach you, when yet with you,
                the law and the

LAWBREAKING, paranomia, "violation of the law, trans-
                         gression"
IV Macc. 9:3, O tyrant, consellor of law-breaking,
              do not,

LAWFUL, parabaino, "to overstep or transgress"
I Esd. 1:16, it was not lawful for any to go from
             his ordinary

        themis, "agreed on by common consent or
                prescription"
II Macc. 6:20, against such things as are not lawful
               for love

LAWLESS, anomos, "lawless, violating law, wicked"
Song-Child. 1:8, didst deliver us into the hands
                 of lawless

         paranomia, "violation of the law, transgres-
                    sion"
III Macc. 2:17, Punish us not...lest the lawless
                ones should boast

         anomos
III Macc. 6:4, when that lord...was uplifted with
               lawless
          6:9, who are insulted by abhorred, lawless
               Gentiles
          6:12, are withdrawn from life...by the...
                insolence of lawless men

LAWLESSNESS, anomos, "lawless"
III Macc. 1:27, aid in the present crisis, and over-

weening lawlessness

paranomia, "violation of the law"
IV Macc. 4:19, perverted their civil customs into
all lawlessness

LAWYER, nomikos, "a lawyer, one learned in the law"
IV Macc. 5:4, seized...a priest by family, by
profession a lawyer,

LAY, anapiptō, "to fall back, recline, to throw oneself back"
His.-Sus. 1:37, who there was hid, came unto her,
and lay with

LEAD, molubdinos, "leaden, of lead"
Eccl.22:14, What is heavier than lead? and what is
the name

molibdos, "lead"
Eccl. 47:18, gather gold as tin, and...multiply
silver as lead

LEADER, hegemōn, "a leader, chieftain, a guide"
Judith 14:12, Assyrians saw them, they sent to their
leaders,
Song-Child. 1:14, there at this time prince, or...
prophet, or leader, or
I Macc. 13:8, Thou shalt be our leader instead of
Judas
II Macc. 1:13, For when the leader was come into
Persia...they were
4:40, one Anranus being the leader, a man
of war gone in

kathēgētēs, "a guide, a leader"
II Macc. 10:28, the other side making their rage
leader of their

hegemōn
IV Macc. 2:22, time He enthroned above all the holy
leader, mind,

LEADERSHIP, hegemonia, "leadership, sovereignty"
IV Macc. 13:4, it is impossible to overlook the
leadership of

LEAGUE, histemi, "to make to stand, to set forth, fix,
appoint"
I Macc. 8:1, of the Romans that they...make a league
of amity with
8:17, Judas chose Eupolemus...to make a
league of amity

20

I Macc. 10:54, now therefore let us make a league
         of amity

      diathēkē, "a will, a testament, a covenant,
             a league"
I Macc. 11:9, Come, let us make a league betwixt us,
         and I will

      summachia, "an alliance"
I Macc. 12:3, to the end ye should renew the...lea-
         gue, as in
      12:8, At which time...declaration was made
         of the league
      12:16, For this cause we chose...the former
         league
      14:18, unto him in tables of brass, to re-
         new...the league
      14:28, After this Simon sent...to confirm
         the league with
      15:17, ambassadors...came unto us to renew
         the...league,

LEAP, enallomai, "to leap in or on, to rush against"
I Macc. 3:23, as he had left off speaking, he leaped
         suddenly

LEARN, manthanō, "to learn, be taught, to comprehend"
Eccl. 8:8, the wise...for of them thou shalt learn
         instruction
      8:9, of the elders: for they also learned of
         their fathers

      pepaideuō, "to educate, instruct children,
             to be taught, learn"
Eccl. 42:8, to inform the unwise...thus shalt thou
         be truly learned

      manthanō
Bar. 3:14, Learn where is wisdom, where is strength,
         where is

LEARNING, paideia, "education, training up, instruc-
             tion"
Eccl. 30:17, for myself only, but for all them that
         seek learning
      51:28, Get learning with a great sum of money,
         and get much

LEAVES, phullas, "a heap of leaves, leafage, foliage"
Eccl. 6:3, Thou shalt eat up thy leaves, and lose
         thy fruit, and
      14:18, As for the green leaves on a thick tree,
         some fall,

LEG, skelos, "the leg"
IV Macc. 10:6, round his fingers, and his arms,
          and his legs, and

LEND, daneion, "a loan, debt"
Eccl. 8:12, lend not unto him that is mightier than
          thyself;

LENDER, daneistēs, "a lender, creditor"
Eccl. 29:28, upbraiding of houseroom, and reproaching
          of the lender

LEOPARD, pardalis, "a leopard or panther"
Eccl. 28:23, upon them as a lion, and devour them
          as a leopard

LESSON, paideia, "teaching, education, discipline"
Eccl. 9:1, and teach her not an evil lesson against
          thyself

LETTER, epistolē, "a message, commission, a letter"
I Esd. 4:47, Then Darius the king...wrote letters
          for him unto all
       4:48, He wrote letters also unto the lieute-
          nants that were
       4:61, And he took the letters, and went out,
          and came unto
       6:7, The copy of the letters which Sisinnes,
          governor of
I Macc. 1:44, For the king had sent letters by mes-
          sengers unto
       5:10, and sent letters unto Judas and his
          brethren,
       5:14, While these letters were yet being
          read, behold,
       9:60, and came with a great host, and sent
          letters
       10:3, Moreover Demetrius sent letters unto
          Jonathan with
       10:7, came Jonathan to Jerusalem, and read
          the letters in
       10:17, Upon this he wrote a letter, and sent
          it unto him,
       11:29, So the king consented, and wrote let-
          ters unto
       11:31, We send you here a copy of the
          letters which we did
       12:2, He sent letters also to the Lacedemo-
          nians, and to
       12:4, Upon this the Romans gave them letters
          unto the

I Macc. 12:5, And this is the copy of the letters
             which Jonathan
        12:7, There were letters sent in times past
             unto Onias the
        12:8, and received the letters, wherein
             declaration was
        12:17, We commanded them also to...deliver
             you our letters
        12:19, And this is a copy of the letters
             which Oniares
        14:20, And this is the copy of the letters
             that the
        15:1, Moreover Antiochus...the king sent
             letters from the
        15:15, Numenius, and his company...having
             letter to the
        16:19, and unto the tribunes he sent letters
             to come unto
II Macc. 9:18, he wrote unto the Jews the letter
             underwritten

     gramma, "a letter, a writing, book"
II Macc. 11:16, For there were letters written unto
             the Jews from

     ,
     epistolē
II Macc. 11:22, Now the king's letters contained
             these words:
        11:27, And the letter of the king unto the
             nation of the
        11:34, The Romans also sent unto them a
             letter containing
III Macc. 3:11, Now the king...wrote the following
             letter to the
        3:25, As soon, therefore, as the contents
             of this letter
        3:30, Such was the purport of the king's
             letter
        6:41, and wrote the subjoined letter, of
             magnanimous
        7:10, When they had received this letter,
             they were not

LEVI, Leut
Eccl. 45:6, Aaron...even his brother, of the tribe
            of Levi
IV Macc. 2:19, our most wise father Jacob shame
            Simon and Levi

LEVITES, Leuitēs
I Esd. 1:3, And he spake unto the Levites, the holy

23

ministers of
I Esd. 1:5, temple according to...the families of...
the Levites,
1:7, given...according as he promised...to
the Levites,
1:9, And Jeconias...gave to the Levites...
five thousand
1:10, the priests and Levites...stood in
very comely order
1:14, offered the fat until night: and the
Levites
1:16, one to go from his service...for the
Levites prepared
1:21, and the priests and the Levites, and
the Jews, held
2:8, the priests also, and the Levites, and
all they whose
4:55, and likewise for the charges of the
Levites, to be
5:46, And so dwelt the priests and the Levites
and the
5:59, and the Levites the sons of Asaph had
cymbals,
5:63, Also of the priests and Levites, and
of the chief of
7:6, children of Israel, the priests, and
the Levites, and
7:9, The priests also and the Levites stood
arrayed in
7:10, after that the priests and the Levites
were
7:11, for they were sanctified, because the
Legites were
8:22, that ye require no tax...of the priests,
or Levites,
8:96, an oath of the chief of the priests
and Levites
9:23, And of the Levites; Jozabad, and Semis,
Coius,
9:37, And the priests and Levites, and they
that were of
9:49, Then spake Attharates...to the Levites
that taught
9:53, So the Levites published all things to
the people,

LEWDNESS, áchreiotēs (áchreios), "unprofitable,
worthless, useless"
Tobit 4:13, in pride is destruction...and in lewdness is the mother

24

LIAR, pseudēs, "lying, false, untrue"
Wisd.-Sol. 10:14, that accused him, she shewed
            them to be liars,

     pseudos, "lie, falsehood, untruth, deceit"
Eccl. 20:26, The disposition of a liar is dishonour-
            able, and his
      25:2, hateth...a poor man...a rich man that
            is a liar
LIBERTY, éleutheria, "freedom, liberty"
Eccl. 7:21, a good servant, and defraud him not of
            liberty
     30:25, but if thou let him go idle, he will
            seek liberty
I Macc. 10:33, Moreover I...set at liberty every one
            of the Jews,

     áphemi, "to send away, suffer to depart,
            emit"
I Macc. 14:26, in fight their enemies, and confirmed
            their liberty
II Macc. 9:14, That the holy city...he would set at
            liberty

LIBRARY, bibliothēkē, "a book-case, library"
II Macc. 2:13, and how he founding a library gather-
            ed together
LICENCE, áphesis, "a letting go, setting free, re-
            mission, forgiveness"
Judith 11:14, to Jerusalem...to bring them a licence
            from the

     éxousia, "power or authority to do a thing"
I Macc. 1:13, Then certain of the people...gave
            them licence
      4:9, if he might have licence to set him
            up a place of

LIE, pseudē, "false, untrue, falsehood"
Wisd.-Sol. 14:28, they are mad when they be merry,
            or prophesy lies,
Eccl. 7:12, Devise not a lie against thy brother;

     pseudos, "a lie, falsehood, untruth, a fraud,
            deceit"
Eccl. 7:13, Use not to make any manner of lie:
     20:24, A lie is a foul blot in a man, yet it
            is continually
      31:8, The law shall be found perfect without
            lies:

Eccl. 41:17, Be ashamed...of a lie before a prince
             and a mighty man

    pseudē
Epis.-Jer. 1:47, For they left lies and reproaches
                  to them that

LIED, pseudo, "to cheat, defraud, be false"
His.-Sus. 1:55, And Daniel said, Very well; thou
                hast lied
          1:59, Well, thou hast also lied against
                thine own head:

LIFE, zōē, "life, subsistence, goods, means"
Tobit 12:10, but they that sin are enemies to their
             own life
      13:3, I am aged and am ready to depart out
            of this life
Judith 12:18, Judith said, I drink now, my lord,
              because my life
       16:22, her, but none knew her all the days
              of her life,
Wisd.-Sol. 1:12, Seek not death in the error of
                 your life: and

    bios, "life, the course of life, lifetime"
Wisd.-Sol. 2:1, Our life is short and tedious,
                and in the death
           2:4, shall be forgotten...and our life
                shall pass away
           2:15, for his life is not like other
                 men's, his ways
           4:9, hair unto men, and an unspotted
                life is old age
           5:4, we fools accounted his life madness,
                and his end
           7:6, For all men have an entrance into
                life, and the
           8:5, riches be a possession to be de-
                sired in this life
           8:7, labours...can have nothing more...
                in this life
    psuchē, "sign of life, life, spirit"
Wisd.-Sol. 15:8, employing his labour loosely...
                 when his life

    bios
Wisd.-Sol. 15:9, much labour, nor that his life is
                 short
           15:10, His heart is ashes...and his life
                  of less value

zōē
Wisd.-Sol. 15:12, But they counted our life a pas-
time, and our

psuchē
Wisd.-Sol. 16:9, was there found any remedy for
their life

zōē
Wisd.-Sol. 16:13, For thou hast power of life and
death:

makroemereō, "long-lived, lasting long"
Eccl. 1:12, of the Lord maketh a merry heart...and
long life
1:20, the Lord, and the branches thereof are
long life
3:6, that honoureth his father shall have a
long life;

zōē
Eccl. 4:12, He that loveth her loveth life; and they
that seek to
6:16, A faithful friend is the medicine of
life; and they

psuchē
Eccl. 10:29, who will honour him that dishonoureth
his own life?

zōē
Eccl. 11:14, Prosperity and adversity, life and
death, poverty
15:17, Before man is life and death; and
whether he liketh
16:3, Trust not thou in their life, neither
respect their
17:11, he gave them knowledge, and the law
of life for an
21:13, and his counsel is like a...fountain
of life
22:11, but the life of the fool is worse than
death
22:12, fool and an ungodly man all the days
of his life
23:1, O Lord, Father and Governor of my life,
leave me not
23:4, O Lord, Father and God of my life, give
me not a
25:2, soul hateth, and I am greatly offended
at their life

Eccl. 29:21, The chief thing for life is water,
        and bread, and

bios
Eccl. 29:22, Better is the life of a poor man in
        a mean cottage,

zoē
Eccl. 29:24, for it is a miserable life to go from
        house to house
      30:23, thou shalt end thy days, and finish
        thy life,
      31:17, he raiseth up the soul...he giveth
        health, life, and
      31:21, The bread of the needy is their life;
        he that
      34:27, Wine is as good as life to a man, if
        it be drunk
      37:18, manners of things appear: good and
        evil, life and
      37:25, The days of the life of man may be
        numbered, but the
      37:31, but he that taketh heed prolongeth his
        life

euodoō, "to put in the right way, help on the
        way, to be successful"
Eccl. 38:14, which they give for ease and remedy to
        prolong life

bios
Eccl. 38:19, and the life of the poor is the curse
        of the heart

zoē
Eccl. 39:26, things for the whole use of man's life
        are water,

psuchē
Eccl. 51:3, out of the hands of such as sought after
        my life, and

zoē
Bar. 1:11, and pray for the life of Nabuchodonosor
        king of
     3:9, Hear, Israel, the commandments of life:
    3:14, mayest know also where is length of days
        and life,
     4:1, all they that keep it shall come to life;
I Macc. 9:71, never do him harm all the days of his
        life

psuchē
I Macc. 13:5, it far from me, that I should spare
            mine own life

zōē
II Macc. 3:31, call upon the most High to grant him
               his life,
          3:33, as for his sake the Lord hath grant-
                ed thee life
          3:35, made great vows unto him that had
                saved his life,
          6:20, such things as are not lawful for
                love or life

bios
II Macc. 6:27, Wherefore now, manfully changing this
               life, I will

zōē
II Macc. 7:9, like a fury takest us out of this
              present life, but
          7:14, thee thou shalt have no resurrection
                to life
          7:22, for I neither gave you breath nor
                life, neither
          7:23, of the world...will...give you
                breath and life again
          7:36, are dead under God's covenant of
                everlasting life:

psuchē
II Macc. 7:37, But I, as my brethren, offer up my
               body and life

bios
II Macc. 14:25, he married, was quiet, and took part
                of this life

psuchē
II Macc. 14:38, of Judaism, and...jeopard his body
                and life

helikia, "a particular period of life"
II Macc. 15:30, continued his love toward his coun-
                trymen all his life,

bios
III Macc. 4:4, reflecting upon the uncertain issue
               of life,

zōē
III Macc. 5:32, Had it not been for familiar friend-
                ship...your life

bios
III Macc. 6:1, had attained to length of days, and
whose life had
6:10, If our life has during our exile
been stained

zoē
III Macc. 6:12, upon us who are being withdrawn from
life, like

pneuma, "wind, air, the breath of life, spirit"
III Macc. 6:24, ye have laboured to deprive...of...
my life

bios
IV Macc. 1:15, then, intellect accompanied by a life
of rectitude
4:1, Simon...once held the high priesthood
for life,

helikia
IV Macc. 5:6, taste the swine's flesh and save your
life;

bios
IV Macc. 5:36, my old age, nor the...stature of a
perfect life

psuchē
IV Macc. 6:29, and take my life in recompense for
theirs

bios
IV Macc. 7:7, with the law, and sage devoted to a
divine life!
7:15, O blessed old age, and...hoar head,
and life
8:7, and, conforming to the Greek mode
of life, alter
8:22, Why withdraw ourselves from a most
sweet life, and

psuchē
IV Macc. 9:25, this, he revered youth abruptly
closed his life
10:15, brethren...and the glorious life of
the pious, I
13:19, period...through the same principle
of life,

bios
IV Macc. 13:23, and reared up in a just course of
life, they

30

zōē
IV Macc. 15:3, which according to God preserves to
            eternal life
         17:12, For at that time virtue presided
            over...eternal life

   bioō, "to live, to live happily"
IV Macc. 17:18, the divine throne, and live a bles-
            sed life

zōē
IV Macc. 18:16, of Solomon, who saith, he is a tree
            of life
         18:19, This is our life, and the length of
            our days
Pr.-Mans. 1:15, I will praise thee...all the days
            of my life:

LIGHT, phōs, "light, daylight"
Judith 13:13, received them, and made a fire for a
            light,

      phōs, "light, an instrument of light"
Wisd.-Sol. 7:10, and chose to have her instead of
            light
         7:26, is the brightness of the everlasting
            light, the
         7:29, being compared with the light, she
            is found

      phlox, "a flame"
Wisd.-Sol. 10:17, for a cover by day, and a light
            of stars in

      phōstēr, "a light-giver, luminary"
Wisd.-Sol. 13:2, or wind...or the violent water, or
            the lights of

      photizō, "to shine, give light, beam"
Wisd.-Sol. 17:5, No power of the fire might give
            them light:

      phōs
Wisd.-Sol. 17:20, For the whole world shined with
            clear light,
         18:1, thy saints had a very great light,
            whose voice
         18:4, For they were worthy to be deprived
            of light,

      phōteinos, "shining bright, giving light"
Eccl. 17:31, yet the light thereof faileth: and flesh
            and blood

31

phōs
Eccl. 24:27, the doctrine of knowledge appear as
        the light, and

luchnos, "a light, lamp"
Eccl. 26:17, As the clear light is upon the holy
        candlestick: so

phos
Eccl. 36:7, one day excel another, when as all the
        light of every

photizō
Eccl. 42:16, The sun that giveth light looketh upon
        all things,

phōstēr, "an opening for light, a door or a
        window"
Eccl. 43:7, From the moon is the sign of feasts,
        and light that

photizō
Eccl. 50:7, most High, and as the rainbow giving
        light in the

phōs
Bar. 3:14, Learn where is wisdom...where is the
        light of the eyes,
     3:20, Young men have seen light, and dwelt
        upon the earth;
     3:33, he that sendeth forth light, and it goeth,
        calleth it
     3:34, and so with cheerfulness they shewed
        light unto him
     4:2, walk in the presence of the light thereof,
        that thou
     5:9, For God shall lead Israel with joy in the
        light of his
Epis.-Jer. 1:67, shew signs in the heavens...nor
        give light as the
Song-Child. 1:47, O ye light and darkness, bless ye
        the Lord:
I Macc. 1:21, sanctuary, and took away...the candle-
        stick of light
     12:29, company knew it...for they saw the
        lights burning
II Macc. 1:32, but it was consumed by the light that
        shined from

pheggos, "light, splendour"
III Macc. 4:10, deck above them barred out the light,
        and shut

phōs
III Macc. 6:7, didst bring him back again unhurt
to light

LIGHTED, haptō, "to light, kindle"
II Macc. 1:8, also sacrifices and fine flour, and
lighted the

LIGHTNING, astrapē, "lightning, lustre, brightness"
Eccl. 35:10, Before the thunder goeth lightning,
and before a
43:13, he sendeth swiftly the lightnings of
his judgment
Epis.-Jer. 1:61, In like manner the lightning when
it breaketh
Song-Child. 1:50, O ye lightnings and clouds, bless
ye the Lord:

LILY, krinon, "a lily"
Eccl. 39:14, as frankincense, and flourish as a lily,
50:8, the spring of the year, as lilies by
the rivers

LIMB, melos, "a member, limb, any part of the body"
II Macc. 2:22, he cast him upon the pavement...with
limbs
IV Macc. 9:17, cut my limbs, and burn my flesh, and
twist my
10:20, Gladly do we lose our limbs in behalf
of God
11:18, Extended upon which, with limbs
racked and

LINEN, homolinon, "made of raw flax"
Eccl. 40:4, and...unto him that is clothed with a
linen frock

LION, leōn, "a lion, a cruel adversary"
Eccl. 4:30, Be not as a lion in thy house, nor fran-
tic among thy
21:2, the teeth thereof are as the teeth of a
lion, slaying
25:16, I had rather dwell with a lion and a
dragon, than to
27:10, As the lion lieth in wait for the prey;
so sin for
27:28, but vengeance, as a lion, shall lie in
wait for him
28:23, it shall be sent upon them as a lion,
and devour them
Bar. 1:31, who cast him into the lions' den: where

he was six
Bar. 1:32, and in the den there were seven lions,
and they had
1:34, the dinner...unto Daniel, who is in the
lions' den
I Macc. 2:60, innocency was delivered from the mouth
of the lions
3:4, In his acts he was like a lion, and
like a lion's
III Macc. 6:7, as a prey to lions down below, didst
bring him
IV Macc. 16:3, And not so fierce were the lions
round Daniel, nor
16:21, And the righteous Daniel was cast
unto the lions
18:13, to glorify Daniel, who was in the
den of lions,

LIP, cheilos, "a lip, language or dialect"
Eccl. 1:23, He will hide his word for a time, and
the lips of
12:16, An enemy speaketh sweetly with his lips,
but in his
21:16, but grace shall be found in the lips of
the wise
21:25, The lips of talkers will be telling such
things as
23:27, he that keepeth it shall never be taken
in his lips
39:15, and shew forth his praise with the songs
of thy lips
50:20, to give the blessing of the Lord with
his lips,
51:2, and hast preserved my body...from the...
lips that forge

LITANY, litanos, "praying, supplicant"
III Macc. 5:9, Their litany so earnest went up to
heaven

LIVE, zaō, "to live, to be possessed of vitality"
Eccl. 3:12, age, and grieve him not as long as he
lieveth
30:5, While he lived, he saw and rejoiced in
him:
30:20, As long as thou livest and hast breath
in thee, give
31:13, The spirit of those that fear the Lord
shall live;
48:11, thee, and slept in love; for we shall

surely live
Bar. 1:12, and we shall live under the shadow of
   Nabuchodonosor
I Macc. 2:33, to the commandment of the king, and
   ye shall live
   4:35, of Judas' soldiers...how they were
   ready either to live or

poreuomaï, "to be devoted to, live in any manner"
I Macc. 10:37, be of themselves, and that they live
   after their

politeuō, "to be governed, to order one's life
   and conduct"
II Macc. 6:1, king...compel the Jews...not to live
   after the laws

zaō
III Macc. 7:6, we at length permitted them to live

epibioō, "to survive"
IV Macc. 6:20, It would be disgraceful if we should
   live on some

zaō
IV Macc. 18:18, For...I will kill and I will make
   to live

LIVER, hepar, "the liver, as the seat of passion"
Tobit 6:4, Open the fish, and take the heart and the
   liver and
   6:7, Touching the heart and the liver, if a
   devil or an
   6:16, marriage chamber, thou shalt take the
   ...liver of the
   8:2, took the ashes...and put the heart and
   liver of the

LIVES, psuchē, "breath, the life, the principle of
   animal life"
I Macc. 2:50, now therefore, my sons...give your
   lives for the
   3:21, but we fight for our lives and our laws
   9:44, Jonathan said...Let us go up now and
   fight for our lives,

LIVING, zaō, "living, to be alive"
Wisd.-Sol. 18:23, fallen down by heaps...he...parted
   ...to the living
Eccl. 42:8, truly learned, and approved of all men
   living

bios, "means of living"
II Macc. 15:4, And when they said, There is in hea-
               ven a living
IV Macc. 17:14, and the world and living men were
                the spectators

LOAVES, artos, "a loaf, esp. of wheat"
I Macc. 4:51, Furthermore they set the loaves upon
              the table, and
II Macc. 1:8, porch...and lighted the lamps, and set
              forth...loaves

LOCK, kleithron, "a bolt or bar for closing a door"
Epis.-Jer. 1:18, the priests make fast their temples
                 with...locks

LOCUST, akris, "a locust"
Judith 2:20, A great number also...came with them
             like locusts,

LODGE, koimao,"to lull to sleep, to fall asleep, to
              rest"
I Macc. 11:6, the king, where they salute one another,
              and lodged

LOFTY, hupselos, "high, lofty, elevated"
IV Macc. 5:1, sitting in public state...upon a cer-
              tain lofty place

LOIN, osphus, "the loins"
Judith 8:5, her a tent...and put on sackcloth upon
            her loins,
Eccl. 32:18, till he have smitten in sunder the loins
             of the
II Macc. 10:25, But when he drew near they...girded
                their loins
IV Macc. 11:10, at his knees...they bent down his
                loins upon the

LONGSUFFERING, makrothumia, "longsuffering, patience,
                           forbearance"
Wisd.-Sol. 15:1, our God, art gracious and true,
                 longsuffering,
Eccl. 5:4, for the Lord is longsuffering, he will
           in no wise let
Pr.-Mans. 1:7, for thou art the Lord most high...
               longsuffering,

LORD, kurios, "having power or authority over, lord,
              master"
I Esd. 1:1, feast of the passover in Jerusalem unto
            his Lord,

I Esd. 1:3, that they should hallow themselves unto
the Lord,
1:4, now therefore serve the Lord your God,
and minister
1:6, the passover according to the commandment of the Lord
1:11, according to the several dignities...
before...the Lord
1:17, things that belonged to the sacrifices
of the Lord
1:24, came to pass...the words of the Lord
rose up against
1:27, I am not sent from the Lord God against
thee;
1:28, rods of the prophet...spoken by the
mouth of the Lord
1:41, also took of the holy vessels of the
Lord, and carried
1:44, and did evil before the Lord
1:45, brought into Babylon...the holy vessels
of the Lord
1:47, and he did evil also in the sight of
the Lord, and
1:48, had made him to swear by the name of
the Lord,
1:49, also of the people...defiled the temple
of the Lord,
1:51, and, in the day that the Lord spake unto
them, they
1:54, And they took all the holy vessels of
the Lord, both
1:55, As for the house of the Lord, they burn
it, and
1:57, servants to him...to fulfil the word of
the Lord
2:1, In the first year of Cyrus...the word of
the Lord
2:2, the Lord raised up the spirit of Cyrus
the king of
2:3, The Lord of Israel, the most high Lord,
hath made me
2:5, any of you that are of his people, let
his Lord be
2:7, gifts...and other things...for the temple of the Lord
2:8, the Levites, and all they whose mind the
Lord had
2:18, Be it known to the Lord the king, that

37

the Jews that

<u>kurieuō</u>, "to be lord or master of"
I Esd. 4:3, But yet the king is more might: for he
         is lord of

<u>despotēs</u>, "master, lord, master, a despot"
I Esd. 4:60, Blessed art thou...I give thee thanks,
         O Lord of our

<u>kurios</u>
I Esd. 5:58, Levites...to advance...in the house of
         the Lord
      5:60, singing songs of thanksgiving, and
         praising the Lord
      5:61, with loud voices songs to the praise
         of the Lord,
      5:62, with a loud voice, singing songs...
         unto the Lord
      5:67, And they...did build the temple unto
         the Lord God of
      5:69, For we likewise, as ye, do obey your
         Lord, and do
      5:71, We ourselves alone will build unto the
         Lord of
      6:1, unto the Jews...in the name of the Lord
         God of Israel
      6:2, and Jesus...and began to build the house
         of the Lord
      6:5, the Jews obtained favour, because the
         Lord had
      6:8, Let all the things be know unto our lord
         the king,
      6:9, building an house unto the Lord, great
         and new, of
      6:13, us this answer, We are the servants of
         the Lord
      6:19, and that the temple of the Lord should
         be built in
      6:20, laid the foundations of the house of the
         Lord at
      6:22, found that the building of the house of
         the Lord at
      6:24, king Cyrus commanded that the house of
         the Lord at
      6:26, and that the holy vessels of the house
         of the Lord,
      6:27, elders of the Jews, to build the house
         of the Lord,
      6:28, have commanded also to have...the house

of the Lord

I Esd. 6:29, to be given...for the sacrifices of
the Lord,

6:33, The Lord therefore, whose name is there
called upon,

7:4, these things by the commandment of the
Lord God of

7:9, The priests also...in the service of the
Lord God of

7:13, And the children of Israel...sought the
Lord

7:14, the feast of unleavened bread...before
the Lord,

7:15, strengthened their hands in the works
of the Lord

8:6, and came to Jerusalem...which the Lord
gave them

8:8, Esdras the...reader of the law of the
Lord,

8:9, Artaxerxes unto Esdreas...reader of the
law of the Lord

8:12, that they may look unto the affairs...
of the Lord;

8:13, and carry the gifts unto the Lord of
Israel to

8:15, that they may offer sacrifices unto
the Lord upon the

8:47, And by the mighty hand of our Lord they
brought unto

8:50, And there I vowed...before our Lord,
to desire of

8:52, said unto the king, that the power of
the Lord

8:53, And again we besought our Lord as
touching these

8:55, and the holy vessels of the house of
our Lord,

8:58, Both ye are holy unto the Lord, and
the vessels are

8:60, Levites...brought them into the temple
of the Lord

8:61, we departed...by the mighty hand of our
Lord

8:62, was weighed was delivered in the house
of the Lord

8:65, out of captivity offered sacrifice unto
the Lord God

8:66, and twelve lambs...all of them a sacrifice to the Lord

I Esd. 8:72, that were moved at the word of the Lord
God of
8:73, fast...and stretching forth my hands
unto the Lord
8:74, I said, O Lord, I am confounded and
ashamed before
8:78, And now...O Lord, that there should be
left us a root
8:79, unto us a light in the house of the
Lord our God,
8:80, were in bondage, we were not forsaken
of our Lord;
8:81, yea, and honoured the temple of our
Lord, and raised
8:82, And now, O Lord, what shall we say,
having these
8:86, for thou, O Lord, didst make our sins
light,
8:89, O Lord of Israel, thou art true: for
we are left a
9:13, we turn away the wrath of the Lord from
us for this
9:39, that he would bring the law...of the
Lord God
9:47, hands they fell to the ground, and
worshipped the Lord
9:48, Also Jesus...taught the law of the Lord
to the
9:50, This day is holy unto the Lord;
9:52, for this day is holy unto the Lord: and
be not
9:53, This day is holy to the Lord; be not
sorrowful
Tobit 2:2, find out of our brethren, who is mindful
of the Lord;
3:11, Blessed art thou, O Lord my God, and
thine holy and
4:5, My son, be mindful of the Lord our God
all thy days,
5:19, For that which the Lord hath given us
to live with
8:7, And now, O Lord, I take not this my sister
for lust,
13:4, for he is our Lord, and he is the God of
our Father
13:11, Many nations shall come...to the name
of the Lord God
Judith 2:13, thou transgress none of the commandments
of thy lord

Judith 2:14, Holofernes went forth from the pre-
           sence of his lord,
     5:5, Let my lord now hear a word from the
           mouth of thy
     5:20, Now therefore, my lord and governor,
           if there be any
     6:13, they bound Achior...and returned to
           their lord

   despotēs
Judith 7:11, Now therefore, my lord, fight not
           against them in

   kurios
Judith 7:19, Then the children of Israel cried unto
           the Lord
     8:11, words that ye have spoken before...the
           Lord turn to
     8:23, but the Lord our God shall turn it to
           dishonour
     8:31, Therefore now pray thou for us...and
           the Lord will
     9:1, Judith fell upon her face...in the house
           of the Lord,
     9:2, O Lord God of my father Simeon, to whom
           thou gavest a

   dunastēs, "lord, master, ruler"
Judith 9:3, thou...smotest the servants with their
           lords, and the lords

   kurios
Judith 11:4, shall hurt thee...as they do the ser-
           vants of...my lord
     11:10, Therefore, O lord and governor, reject
           not his word
     11:11, And now, that my lord be not defeated
           and frustrate
     11:22, to send thee...upon them that lightly
           regard my lord
     12:4, Then said Judith...As thy soul liveth,
           my lord, thine
     12:8, And when she came out, she besought
           the Lord God of
     12:14, Who am I now, that I should gainsay
           my lord?
     12:18, So Judith said, I will drink now, my
           lord, because
     13:1, dismissed the waiters from the pre-
           sence of his lord

Judith 13:15, and the Lord hath smitten him by the
          hand of a
       13:16, As the Lord liveth, who hath kept me
          in my way that
       15:10, blessed be thou of the Almighty Lord
          for evermore
       16:2, Begin unto my God with timbrels, sing
          unto my Lord
       16:6, But the Almighty Lor, hath disappointed
          them by the
       16:12, they perished by the battle of my Lord
       16:16, but he that feareth the Lord is great
          at all times
       16:18, entered into Jerusalem, they worshipped
          the Lord
Wisd.-Sol. 1:1, think of the Lord with a good
          (heart), and in
       1:7, For the spirit of the Lord filleth
          the world:
       1:9, sound of his words shall come unto
          the Lord for
       2:13, and he calleth himself the child
          of the Lord
       3:8, They shall judge the nations...and
          their Lord
       3:10, neglected the righteous, and for-
          saken the Lord
       3:14, given...an inheritance in the temple
          of the Lord
       4:14, for his soul pleased the Lord:
          therefore hasted
       4:17, end of the wise...and what end the
          Lord hath set
       5:7, but as for the way of the Lord, we
          have not
       5:15, live for evermore; their reward....
          is with the Lord
       6:3, For power is given you of the Lord,
          and

     despotēs
Wisd.-Sol. 6:7, For he which is Lord over all shall
          fear no man's

     kurios
Wisd.-Sol. 8:21, I prayed unto the Lord, and besought
          him, and
       9:1, O God of my fathers, and Lord of
          mercy, who hast

Wisd.-Sol. 10:16, into the soul of the servant of
                  the Lord, and
           10:20, spoiled the ungodly, and praised
                  the...Lord,
           11:13, punishmeht...they had some feeling
                  of the Lord

    despotēs
Wisd.-Sol. 11:26, for they are thine, O Lord, thou
                  lover of souls

    kurios
Wisd.-Sol. 12:2, Therefore chastenest thou them...
                 O Lord

    despozō, "to be lord and master of"
Wisd.-Sol. 12:16, and because thou art the Lord of
                  all, it maketh
           13:3, let them know how much better the
                 Lord of them

    kurios
Wisd.-Sol. 16:12, but thy word, O Lord, which healeth
                  all things
           16:26, that thy children, O Lord, whom
                  thou lovest,
           19:9, at large like horses...praising
                 thee, O Lord, who
           19:22, For in all things, O Lord, thou
                  didst magnify
Eccl. 1:1, All wisdom cometh from the Lord, and is
           with him for
      1:8, There is one wise and greatly to be feared
           the Lord
      1:11, The fear of the Lord is honour, and glory
            and
      1:12, The fear of the Lord maketh a merry
            heart, and giveth
      1:13, Whoso feareth the Lord, it shall go well
            with him at
      1:14, To fear the Lord is the beginning of wis-
            dom: and it
      1:18, The fear of the Lord is a crown of wis-
            dom, making
      1:20, The root of wisdom is to fear the Lord,
            and the
      1:25, If thou desire wisdom...the Lord shall
            give her unto
      1:26, For the fear of the Lord is wisdom and
            instruction:

Eccl. 1:27, Distrust not the fear of the Lord when
           thou art poor;

      1:30, Exalt not thyself, lest...the Lord dis-
            cover thy

      2:1, My son, if thou come to serve the Lord
           God, prepare

      2:7, Ye that fear the Lord, wait for his
           mercy; and go not

      2:8, Ye that fear the Lord, believe him; and
           your reward

      2:10, did ever any trust in the Lord, and was
            confounded?

      2:11, For the Lord is full of compassion and
            mercy,

      2:14, and what will ye do when the Lord shall
            visit you?

      2:15, They that fear the Lord will not disobey
            his word;

      2:16, They that fear the Lord will seek that
            which is

      2:17, They that fear the Lord will prepare
            their hearts,

      2:18, saying, we will fall into the hands of
            the Lord, and

      3:2, For the Lord hath given the father honour
           over the

      3:6, and he that is obedient unto the Lord
           shall be a

      3:18, thou art...thou shalt find favour before
            the Lord

      4:13, and wheresoever she entereth, the Lord
            will bless

      4:28, Strive for the truth unto death, and
            the Lord shall

      5:3, for the Lord will surely revenge thy
           pride

      5:4, for the Lord is longsuffering, he will
           in no wise let

      6:16, of life; and they that fear the Lord
            shall find him

      6:17, Whoso feareth the Lord shall direct his
            friendship

      6:37, Let thy mind be upon the ordinances of
            the Lord, and

      7:4, Seek not of the Lord preeminence, neither
           of the king

      7:5, Justify not thyself before the Lord; and
           boast not of

Eccl. 7:29, Fear the Lord with all thy soul, and
          reverence his
     7:31, Fear the Lord, and honour his priest:
          and give him
     9:16, and let thy glorifying be in the fear
          of the Lord
    10:4, The power of the earth is in the hand
          of the Lord, and
    10:13, and therefore the Lord brought upon
          them strange
    10:14, The Lord hath cast down the thrones of
          proud princes,
    10:15, The Lord hath plucked up the roots of
          the proud
    10:16, The Lord overthrew countries of the
          heathen, and
    10:22, noble or poor, their glory is the fear
          of the Lord
    10:24, there none of them greater than he that
          feareth the Lord
    11:4, for the works of the Lord are wonderful,
          and his works
    11:12, yet the eye of the Lord looked upon him
          for good, and
    11:14, and adversity, life and death...come of
          the Lord
    11:17, The gift of the Lord remaineth with the
          godly, and
    11:21, but trust in the Lord and abide in thy
          labour:
    11:22, The blessing of the Lord is in the re-
          ward of the
    11:26, For it is an easy thing unto the Lord
          in the day of
    14:11, My son...do good to thyself, and give
          the Lord his due
    15:1, He that feareth the Lord will do good;
          and he that
    15:10, praise shall be uttered in wisdom, and
          the Lord will
    15:11, Say not thou, It is through the Lord,
          that I fell
    15:13, The Lord hateth all abomination; and
          they that fear
    16:2, rejoice not in them, except the fear of
          the Lord be
    16:17, Say not thou, I will hide myself from
          the Lord:

Eccl. 16:26, The works of the Lord are done in
                judgment from the
      16:29, After this the Lord looked upon the
                earth, and
      17:1, The Lord created man of the earth, and
                turned him
      17:18, but Israel is the Lord's portion
      17:20, but all their sins are before the Lord
      17:25, Return unto the Lord, and forsake thy
                sins, make thy
      17:28, the living and sound in heart shall
                praise the Lord
      17:29, How great is the lovingkindness of the
                Lord our God,
      18:2, The Lord only is righteous
      18:6, As for the wondrous works of the Lord,
                there may
      18:23, and be not as one that tempteth the
                Lord
      18:26, the evening...all things are done be-
                fore the Lord
      19:20, The fear of the Lord is all wisdom;
                and in all
      21:6, but he that feareth the Lord will repent
                from his
      23:1, O Lord, Father and Governor of my life,
                leave me not
      23:4, O Lord, Father and God of my life, give
                me not a
      23:19, such a man...knoweth not that the eyes
                of the Lord
      23:27, that there is nothing better than the
                fear of the Lord
      24:12, And I took root...in the portion of
                the Lord's
      25:10, yet there is none above him that feareth
                the Lord
      25:11, But the Love of the Lord passeth all
                things for
      26:3, is a good portion...of them that fear
                the Lord
      26:4, if he have a good heart toward the Lord,
                he shall
      26:14, A silent and loving woman is a gift of
                the Lord:
      26:28, the Lord prepareth such an one for the
                sword
      27:24, but nothing like him; for the Lord will
                hate him

Eccl. 28:1, He that revengeth shall find vengeance
           from the Lord,
      28:3, beareth hatred...and doth he seek pardon
           from the Lord
      28:23, Such as forsake the Lord shall fall
           into it;
      29:19, man transgressing the commandments of
           the Lord shall
      30:19, nor smell: so is he that is persecuted
           of the Lord
      31:13, The spirit of those that fear the Lord
           shall live:
      31:16, Blessed is the soul of him that feareth
           the Lord:
      32:3, depart from wickedness is a thing pleas-
           ing to the Lord
      32:4, Thou shalt not appear empty before
           the Lord
      32:8, Give the Lord his honour with a good
           eye, and
      32:11, For the Lord recompenseth, and will give
           thee seven
      32:16, He that serveth the Lord shall be ac-
           cepted with
      32:18, For the Lord will not be slack, neither
           will the
      33:1, Have mercy upon us, O Lord God of all,
           and behold us:
      35:14, Whoso feareth the Lord will receive
           his discipline;
      35:16, They that fear the Lord shall find
           judgment, and
      35:24, He that believeth in the Lord taketh
           heed to the
      36:1, shall no evil happen unto him that fear-
           eth the Lord;
      36:11, In much knowledge the Lord hath divided
           them, and
      36:17, O Lord, hear the prayer of thy servants,
           according to
      37:12, But be continually with a godly man...
           of the Lord,
      37:21, For grace is not given him from the Lord
           because he
      38:1, for the Lord hath created him
      38:9, My son...pray unto the Lord, and he will
           make thee
      38:12, Then give place to the physician, for
           the Lord hath

47

Eccl. 38:14, For they shall also pray unto the Lord, that he
39:5, He will give his heart to resort early to the Lord
39:6, When the great Lord will, he shall be filled with the
39:14, send forth a smell, and sing a song of praise, bless the Lord in all his works
39:16, All the works of the Lord are exceeding good, and
39:33, All the works of the Lord are good: and he will
40:26, but the fear of the Lord is above them both: there is no want in the fear of the Lord,
40:27, The fear of the Lord is a fruitful garden, and
41:3, sentence of death...for this is the sentence of the Lord
42:15, I will now remember the works of the Lord, and
42:16, that giveth light...is full of the glory of the Lord
42:17, The Lord hath not given power to the saints to
42:18, for the Lord knoweth all that can be known, and he
43:9, giving light in the highest places of the Lord
43:29, The Lord is terrible and very great, and marvellous
43:30, When ye glorify the Lord, exalt him as much as ye
43:33, For the Lord hath made all things; and to the godly
44:2, The Lord hath wrought great glory by them through his
44:16, Enoch pleased the Lord, and was translated, being an
45:16, of all men living to offer sacrifices to the Lord,
45:19, This the Lord saw, and it displeased him, and in his
45:21, for they eat of the sacrifices of the Lord, which he
45:22, for the Lord himself is his portion and inheritance
45:23, because he had zeal in the fear of the Lord,

Eccl. 46:3, for the Lord himself brought his enemies
     over to him
46:6, because he fought in the sight of the
     Lord, and he
46:9, The Lord gave strength also unto Caleb,
     which
46:10, Israel might see that it is good to
     follow the Lord
46:13, Samuel, the prophet of the Lord, be-
     loved of his Lord
46:14, By the law of the Lord he judged the
     congregation, and the Lord
46:16, He called upon the mighty Lord, when
     his enemies
46:17, And the Lord thundered from heaven, and
     with a great
46:19, And before his long sleep...the Lord...
     anointed
47:5, for he called upon the most high God;
     and he gave him
47:6, people...praised him in the blessings
     of the Lord
47:11, The Lord took away his sins, and exalted
     his horn
47:18, By the name of the Lord God, which is
     called the Lord
47:22, But the Lord will never leave off his
     mercy, neither
48:3, By the word or the Lord he shut up the
     heaven, and
48:7, Who heardest the rebuke of the Lord in
     Sinai,
48:20, But they called upon the Lord who is
     merciful, and
48:22, For Ezekias...pleased the Lord, and was
     strong in the
49:3, He directed his heart unto the Lord and
     in the time
49:12, son of Josedec...set up an holy temple
     to the Lord,
49:15, unto Joseph...whose bones were regarded
     of the Lord
50:13, and the oblations of the Lord in their
     hands,
50:17, together...fell down...to worship their
     Lord God
50:19, And the people besought the Lord, the
     most High, by

Eccl. 50:20, Then went down...to give the blessing
            of the Lord
      50:29, for the light of the Lord is his path
      51:1, I will thank thee, O Lord, and King,
            and praise thee,
      51:8, The thought I upon thy mercy, O Lord,
            and upon thy
      51:10, I called upon the Lord, the Father of
            my Lord, that
      51:12, and praise thee, and bless thy name,
            O Lord
      51:22, The Lord hath given me a tongue for
            my reward, and I
Bar. 1:5, Whereupon they wept, fasted, and prayed
          before the Lord
      1:8, when they received the vessels of the
           house of the Lord
      1:10, buy...sin offerings...and offer upon the
            altar of the Lord
      1:12, and the Lord will give us strength, and
            lighten our
      1:13, Pray for us also unto the Lord our God,
            for we have
      1:14, this book...to make confession in the
            house of the Lord
      1:15, And ye shall say, To the Lord our God
            belongeth
      1:17, for we have sinned before the Lord,
      1:18, and disobeyed...the voice of the Lord our
            God, to walk
      1:19, since the day that the Lord brought our
            forefathers
      1:20, evils cleave unto us, and curse, which
            the Lord
      1:21, we have not hearkened unto the voice of
            the Lord our
      1:22, own wicked heart...to do evil in the
            sight of the Lord
      2:1, Therefore the Lord hath made good his
           words, which he
      2:4, reproach...among all the people...where
           the Lord hath
      2:6, To the Lord our God appertaineth righteous-
           ness: but
      2:7, these plagues are come upon us, which the
           Lord hath
      2:8, Yet have we not prayed before the Lord,
           that we might

Bar. 2:9, Wherefore the Lord watched over us for evil, and the Lord hath brought it upon us:

2:11, And now, O Lord God of Israel, that hast brought thy

2:12, O Lord our God, we have sinned, we have done ungodly,

2:14, Hear our prayers, O Lord, and our petitions, and

2:15, all the earth may know that thou art the Lord our God,

2:16, O Lord, look down from thy holy house, and consider us

2:18, that is greatly vexed...will give thee praise...O Lord

2:19, make our...supplication before thee, O Lord our God,

2:21, Thus saith the Lord, Bow down your shoulders to serve

2:22, But if ye will not hear the voice of the Lord, to

2:27, O Lord our God, thou hast dealt with us after all thy

2:31, and shall know that I am the Lord their God: for I

2:33, the way of their father, which sinned before the Lord

3:1, O Lord Almighty, God of Israel, the soul in anguish,

3:2, Hear, O Lord, and have mercy; for thou art merciful:

3:6, For thou art the Lord our God, and thee, O Lord, will

3:8, Behold...thou hast scattered us...from the Lord our God

theos, "a deity, God, the true God"

Bar. 3:27, Those did not the Lord choose, neither gave he the way

4:21, Be of good cheer, O my children, cry unto the Lord,

despotēs

Epis.-Jer. 1:6, But say ye in your hearts, O Lord, we must

kurios

Song-Child. 1:2, Blessed art thou, O Lord God of our fathers:

1:19, us...and give glory to thy name,

O Lord:

Song-Child. 1:21, and let them know that thou art
Lord, the only

1:25, But the angel of the Lord came
down into the

1:28, Blessed art thou, O Lord God of
our fathers:

1:34, all ye works of the Lord, bless
ye the Lord:

1:35, O ye heavens, bless ye the Lord:
praise and

1:36, O ye angels of the Lord, bless
ye the Lord:

1:37, O all ye waters...bless ye the
Lord:

1:38, O all ye powers of the Lord, bless
ye the Lord:

1:39, O ye sun and moon, bless ye the
Lord:

1:40, O ye stars of heaven, bless ye the
Lord:

1:41, O every shower and dew, bless ye
the Lord:

1:42, O all ye winds, bless ye the Lord:

1:43, O ye fire and heat, bless ye the
Lord:

1:46, O ye nights and days, bless ye the
Lord:

1:47, O ye light and darkness, bless ye
the Lord:

1:56, all that move in the waters, bless
ye the Lord:

1:57, O all ye fowls of the air, bless
ye the Lord:

1:58, O all ye beasts and cattle, bless
ye the Lord:

1:59, O ye children of men, bless ye the
Lord:

1:60, O Israel, bless ye the Lord:

1:61, O ye priests of the Lord, bless ye
the Lord:

1:62, O ye servants of the Lord, bless
ye the Lord:

1:63, and the souls of the righteous,
bless ye the Lord:

1:64, holy and humble men of heart, bless
ye the Lord:

1:65, Ananias, Azarias, Misael, bless ye

the Lord:

Song-Child. 1:66, O give thanks unto the Lord,
because he is

1:67, O all ye that worship the Lord,
bless the God

His.-Sus. 1:2, a very fair woman, and one that fear-
ed the Lord

despotēs

His.-Sus. 1:5, two of the ancients...such as the
Lord spake of,

kurios

His.-Sus. 1:23, to fall...than to sin in the sight
of the Lord

1:35, toward heaven: for her heart trusted
in the Lord

1:44, And the Lord heard her voice

1:45, Therefore...the Lord raised up the
holy spirit of

1:53, albeit the Lord saith, The innocent
and the

Bel-Drag. 1:25, unto the king, I will worship the
Lord my God:

1:34, But the angel of the Lord said unto
Habbacuc, Go

1:35, And Habbacuc said, Lord, I never saw
Babylon;

1:36, Then the angel of the Lord took him
by the crown,

1:39, and the angel of the Lord set
Habbacuc in his own

1:41, cried the king...Great art thou O
Lord God of

I Macc. 2:53, kept the commandment, and was made lord
of Egypt;

4:10, Now therefore let us cry unto...the
Lord...and

4:24, song of thanksgiving, and praised the
Lord in

7:37, Thou, O Lord, didst choose this house
to be called

7:41, O Lord, when they that were sent from
the king of

9:25, choose the wicked men, and made them
lords of the

II Macc. 1:8, then we prayed unto the Lord and were
heard; we

1:24, prayer was after this manner: O Lord,

53

Lord God,
II Macc. 2:2, charged them not to forget...the Lord,
and that
2:8, Then shall the Lord shew them those
things, and the glory of the Lord,
2:10, And as when Moses prayed unto the
Lord, the fire
2:22, and recovered again the temple...the
Lord being

theos
II Macc. 3:22, They then called upon the Almighty
Lord to keep the

kurios
II Macc. 3:24, Now as he was there...the Lord of
spirits, and the
3:30, But they praised the Lord, that had
miraculously
3:33, for his sake the Lord hath granted
thee life:
3:35, after he had offered sacrifice unto
the Lord, and
4:38, Thus the Lord rewarded him his punishment, as he
5:20, communicated in the benefits sent
from the Lord
6:30, It is manifest unto the Lord, that
hath the holy
7:6, The Lord God looketh upon us, as Moses
in his song,
7:20, because of the hope she had in the
Lord
7:33, And though the living Lord be angry
with us a
7:40, undefiled, and put his whole trust
in the Lord
8:2, And they called upon the Lord, that
he would look
8:5, for the wrath of the Lord was turned
into mercy
8:14, that they had left, and withal besought the Lord,
8:27, gathered...yielding...praise and
thanks to the Lord
8:29, When this was done...they besought
the....Lord to be
8:35, he was through the help of the Lord
brought down

II Macc. 9:5, But the Lord Almighty, the God of
              Israel, smote
         10:1, Now Maccabeus and his company, the
              Lord guiding
         10:4, When that was done...they besought the
              Lord, that
         10:28, virtue their refuge also unto the
              Lord for a
         10:38, When this was done they praised the
              Lord with
         11:6, he besieged the holds, they...be-
              sought the Lord that
         11:10, for the Lord was merciful unto them
         12:36, Judas called upon the Lord that he
              would shew
         13:10, Judas...commanded the multitude to
              call...the Lord
         13:12, all done this...and besought the mer-
              ciful Lord with
         13:13, get the city, to go forth...by the
              help of the Lord
         13:17, This was done...because the protec-
              tion of the Lord
         14:35, Thou, O Lord of all things, who hast
              need of
         14:36, therefore now, O holy Lord of all
              holiness, keep
         15:4, And when they said, There is in hea-
              ven a living Lord
         15:7, Maccabeus had ever sure confidence
              that the Lord
         15:21, Maccabeus...called upon the Lord that
              worketh
         15:22, O Lord, thou didst send thine angel
              in the time of
         15:23, wherefore now also, O Lord of heaven,
              send a good
         15:34, So every man praised...the glorious
              Lord, saying,
         15:35, He...manifest sign unto all of the
              help of the Lord
III Macc. 2:2, O Lord, Lord, King of the heavens,
              and Ruler of
          2:3, It is thou, the Creator of all, the
              Lord of the
          5:7, They invoked the Almighty Lord, and
              ceaselessly
          5:51, sent up an exceeding great cry,
              entreating...Lord

dunastēs,"lord, master, ruler"
III Macc. 6:4, Thou destroyest Pharaoh...when that
                lord of this

despotēs
III Macc. 6:10, destroy us, O Lord, by the death
                which thou

kurios
III Macc. 6:15, Let it be shewn...that thou art
                    with us, O Lord,
IV Macc. 2:7, Since in what way is...reasoning...
                lord of the

kurieuō, "to be lord or master of"
IV Macc. 2:12, And it lords it over the love of
                parents toward

kurios
IV Macc. 7:23, For the wise and brave man only is
                lord over his

despotēs
IV Macc. 18:2, Knowing that religious reasoning is
                lord of the

kurios
Pr.-Mans. 1:1, O Lord Almighty, the God of our fa-
                thers Abraham
           1:7, For thou art the Lord most high, com-
                passionate,
           1:8, Surely thou, O Lord, the God of the
                just, hast not
           1:9, My transgressions are multiplied, O
                Lord, they are
           1:13, but I pray and beseech thee, release
                me Lord,

LOT, kleros, "a lot, casting lots, drawing lots"
  Wisd.-Sol. 2:9, for this is our portion, and our lot
                is this
  Eccl. 14:15, thou not leave...thy labours to be
                divided by lot?

Lōt, "Lot"
  Eccl. 16:8, Neither spared he the place where Lot
                sojourned, but

LOVE, phileō, "to love, regard with affection"
  I Esd. 3:22, they are in their cups, they forget
                their love both

agapaō, "to welcome, love dearly, to be well
          pleased"
Tobit 4:13, Now therefore, my son, love thy brethren,
          and despise

phileō
Tobit 6:14, for a wicked spirit loveth her, which
          hurteth no one
      6:17, when Tobias had heard these things, he
          loved her, and

agapaō
Tobit 13:14, O blessed are they which love thee,
            for they shall
      14:7, all those which love the Lord God in
          truth and

agapē "brotherly love, charity"
Wisd.-Sol. 3:9, and such as be faithful in love shall
              abide with
          6:17, and the care of discipline is love;
          6:18, and love is the keeping of her laws;
              and the

agapaō
Wisd.-Sol. 7:10, I loved her above health and beauty,
              and chose
          8:7, And if a man love righteousness, her
              labours are
          16:26, that thy children, O Lord, whom
              thou lovest,
Eccl. 1:10, flesh...and he hath given her to them
          that love him
      2:15, and they that love him will keep his
          ways
      2:16, and they that love him shall be filled
          with the law

prosphileō, "to be kindly affectioned, to love
            dearly "
Eccl. 4:7, Get thyself the love of the congregation,
          and bow thy

agapaō
Eccl. 4:10, Be as a father to the fatherless...and
          he shall love
      4:12, He that loveth her loveth life; and they
          that seek to
      7:21, Let thy soul love a good servant, and
          defraud him not
      7:30, Love him that made thee with all thy

strength, and

philios, "of or from a friend"
Eccl. 9:8, for herewith love is kindled as a fire
   27:18, so hast thou lost the love of thy
          neighbour

ạgapaō
Eccl. 30:1, He that loveth his son causeth him oft
            to feel the
   31:16, the eyes of the Lord are upon them that
          love him, he
   40:20, but the love of wisdom is above them
          both
   48:11, Blessed are they that saw thee, and
          slept in love;
Bel-Drag. 1:38, thou forsaken them that seek thee
                and love thee
I Macc. 4:33, down with the sword of them that love
              thee, and let
III Macc. 2:10, And thou didst promise, out of love
                to the house

philios
IV Macc. 2:12, And it lords it over the love of
               parents toward

philoteknos, "loving one's children or off-spring"
IV Macc. 14:13, And consider how comprehensive is
                the love of
   15:11, so many circumstances connected with
          love of
   15:25, council-room, beholding...parentage
          and love of

LOWLY, tapeinos, "low, lying low, humbled"
Eccl. 10:15, plucked up the roots...and planted the
             lowly in their

LUCIUS, Leukios
I Macc. 15:16, Lucius, consul of the Romans unto
               king Ptolemee,

LUST, porneia, "fornication,prostitution"
Tobit 8:7, And now, O Lord, I take not my sister
           for lust, but

ọveidos, "reproach, blame, a disgrace"
Wisd.-Sol. 15:5, the sight whereof, enticeth fools
                 to lust after

epithumia, "a desire, yearning, longing, lust"
Eccl. 18:30, Go not after thy lusts, but refrain
            thyself from
      23:6, Let not the greediness of the belly nor
            the lust of
His.-Sus. 1:8, walking: so that their lust was in-
            flamed toward
      1:11, For they were ashamed to declare
            their lust, that
      1:14, they acknowledged their lust: then
            appointed
      1:56, beauty hath deceived thee, and lust
            hath perverted
IV Macc. 1:3, to hold the mastery over passions...
            such as...lust,
      1:22, Before pleasure is lust; and after
            pleasure, joy
      1:31, temperance consists of a command over
            the lusts
      1:32, But of the lusts, some belong to the
            soul, others
      2:1, And what wonder? if the lusts of the
            soul, after
      2:6, reasoning is able to govern our lusts,
            just as it
      5:23, we are superior to all pleasures and
            lusts

LYDIA, Ludia
 I Macc. 8:8, and the country of India, and Media,
            and Lydia, and

LYSIAS, Lusias
 I Macc. 3:32, So he left Lysias, a nobleman, and
            one of the
      3:38, Then Lysias chose Ptolemee the son
            of Dorymenes,
      4:26, strangers that had escaped came and
            told Lysias
      4:28, In the following year therefore, Ly-
            sias gathered
      4:34, and there were slain of the host of
            Lysias about
      4:35, Now when Lysias saw his army put to
            flight...he went
      6:6, and that Lysias, who went forth first
            with a great
      6:17, Now when Lysias knew that the king
            was dead, he

I Macc. 6:55, At that time Lysias heard say, that
          Philip...had
       7:2, palace...his forces had taken Antiochus
          and Lysias
II Macc. 10:11, when he was come to the crown, he
          set one Lysias
       11:1, Not long after this, Lysias the king's
          protector
       11:12, and Lysias himself also fled away
          shamefully, and
       11:15, Then Maccabeus consented to all that
          Lysias
       11:16, letters written unto the Jews from
          Lysias to this
       11:22, King Antiochus unto his brother
          Lysias sendeth
       11:35, Whatsoever Lysias the king's cousin
          hath granted,
       12:1, When these covenants were made,
          Lysias went unto
       13:2, and with him Lysias his protector,
          and ruler of
       13:4, moved Antiochus'mind...and Lysias
          informed the king
       13:26, Lysias went up to the judgment seat,
          said as much
       14:2, country, and killed Antiochus, and
          Lysias his

MAASIAS, Maasaios
  Bar. 1:1, words of the book, which Baruch...the son
          of Maasias

MACCABEUS, Makkabaios
  I Macc. 2:4, Judas who was called Maccabeus
       2:66, As for Judas Maccabeus, he hath been
          mighty and
       3:1, Then his son Judas, called Maccabeus,
          rose up in his
       5:34, host of Timotheus, knowing that it
          was Maccabeus,
  II Macc. 2:19, Now as concerning Judas Maccabeus
          and his brethren
       5:27, But Judas Maccabeus with nine others,
          or
       8:1, Then Judas Maccabeus, and they that
          were with him,
       8:5, Now when Maccabeus had his company
          about him, he

II Macc. 8:16, So Maccabeus called his men together
              unto the
     10:1, Now Maccabeus and his company, the
              Lord guiding
    10:16, Then they that were with Maccabeus
              made supplication
    10:19, Maccabeus left Simon and Joseph, and
              Zaccheus also
    10:21, But when it was told Maccabeus what
              was done, he
    10:25, when he drew near, they that were
              with Maccabeus
    10:30, and took Maccabeus betwixt them, and
              covered him
    10:33, But they that were with Maccabeus
              laid siege
    10:35, Nevertheless...twenty young men of
              Maccabeus'
    11:6, Now when they that were with Maccabeus
              heard that
    11:7, Then Maccabeus himself first of all
              took weapons,
    11:15, Then Maccabeus consented to all that
              Lysias
    12:19, Howbeit Dositheus and Sosipater...
              Maccabeus
    12:20, And Maccabeus ranged his army by
              bands, and set
    12:26, Then Maccabeus marched forth to
              Carnion, and to
    13:24, and accepted well Maccabeus, made
              him principal
    14:6, Those of the Jews...whose captain is
              Judas Maccabeus
    14:27, that he should send Maccabeus prison-
              er in all
    14:30, Notwithstanding, when Maccabeus saw
              that Nicanor
    15:7, But Maccabeus had ever sure confidence
              that the
    15:21, Maccabeus seeing the coming of the
              multitude, and

MACEDONIAN, Makedōn
I Macc. 6:2, a very rich temple...which, Alexander...
             the Macedonian
II Macc. 8:20, And he told them of the...Macedonians
               being

MACHINATIONS, memechanemenios, "the science of
                              mechanics"
  III Macc. 6:22, converted...and he wept at his own
                   machinations

MACHINE, organon, "an instrument, implement, tool"
  IV Macc. 9:20, defiled all over...about the axles
                 of the machine

MACHMAS, Machmas
  I Macc. 9:73, but Jonathan dwelt at Machmas, and
                began to govern

MACRON, Makron
  II Macc. 10:12, For Ptolemeus, that was called
                  Macron

MADNESS, mania, "madness, frenzy"
  IV Macc. 8:4, counsel you not to share the madness
                of the old man
            10:13, Do not thou share the madness of thy
                   brethren;

            aponoia, "loss of all sense, folly, madness"
  IV Macc. 12:4, Thou seest the end of the madness of
                 thy brethren:

MAGEDDO, Mageddo
  I Esd. 1:29, but joined with him in the plain of
               Mageddo, and the

MAGIC, mageia, "the religion of the Magi, magic, art"
  Wisd.-Sol. 17:7, As for the illusions of art magic,
                   they were put

MAGNIFY, megalosune, "greatness, majesty"
  Eccl. 39:15, Magnify his name, and shew forth his
               praise with the
       43:28, How shall we magnify him? for he is
              great above all

       megaluno, "to enlarge, amplify, to magnify"
  Eccl. 43:31, Who hath seen him...and who can
               magnify him as he is?
       45:2, him like to the glorious saints, and
             magnified him
       49:11, How shall we magnify Zorobabel? he was
              even as a
  I Macc. 10:3, sent letters unto Jonathan...so...he
                magnified him

       dozazo, "to think, extol, magnify"
  II Macc. 3:2, that even the kings themselves...
                magnify the temple

MAID, paidiskē, "a young girl, maiden, damsel"
Tobit 3:7, Raguel was also approached by her father's
         maids;

     korasion, "a little girl, damsel"
Tobit 6:12, And the maid is fair and wise; now
          therefore hear me
     6:13, I have heard...that this maid hath been
          given

     paidiskē
Tobit 8:12, said unto his wife Edna, Send one of the
          maids, and

     habros, "delicate, pretty, dainty"
Judith 10:2, rose where she had fallen down, and
          called her maid,
     10:5, Then she gave her maid a bottle of wine,
          and a cruse
     10:10, they had done so, Judith went out,
          and her maid
     10:17, an hundred men to accompany her and
          her maid:

     doulos, "a slave, bondman"
Judith 12:15, So she arose...and her maid went and
          laid soft skins
     12:19, took and ate and drank before him
          what her maid had
     13:3, Now Judith had commanded her maid to
          stand without

     habros
Judith 13:9, forth, and gave Holofernes her head
          to her maid;
     16:23, more and more in honour...and made her
          maid free;

     parthemos, "a maid, maiden, virgin"
Eccl. 9:5, Gaze not on a maid, that thou fall not by
          those things

     paidiskē
Eccl. 41:22, or to be overbusy with his maid, and
          come not near

     korasion
His.-Sus. 1:15, they watched a fit time, she went
          in...with two maids only,
     1:17, Then she said to her maids, Bring
          me oil and
     1:19, Now when the maids were gone forth,
          the two

His.-Sus. 1:21, and therefore thou didst send away
               thy maids from
          1:36, the elders said...this woman came
               in with two maids

MAIMED, ạchrestos, "useless, unprofitable, unservice-
          able"
II Macc. 7:5, Now when he was thus maimed in all his
               members, he

          ạnapēros, "maimed, crippled, halt"
II Macc. 8:24, by the help of the Almighty they...
               maimed the most

MAJESTY, megalōsunē, "greatness"
Wisd.-Sol. 18:24, For in the long garment was...thy
               majesty upon
Eccl. 2:18, fall into the hands of the Lord...for
               as his majesty

          megaleios, "magnificent, splendid"
Eccl. 17:13, Their eyes saw the majesty of his glory,
               and their

          megalōsunē
Eccl. 18:5, Who shall number the strength of his
               majesty?

          timē, "dignity, the honour in which one is
               held, esteem, worship"
II Macc. 3:12, to the holiness of the place and to
               the majesty

          doxa, "glory, splendour, honour"
III Macc. 2:14, profane man seeks to dishonour...
               thy majesty

MAKED, Maked
I Macc. 5:26, many of them were shut up in Bosora...
               Maked, and

MALE, ạrrenikos, "masculine, male"
I Macc. 5:28, Hereupon Judas and his host...slew all
               the males
          5:35, This done...Judas...slew all the males
               therein, and
          5:51, who then slew all the males with the
               edge of the
IV Macc. 15:30, O thou nobler in endurance than
               males, and more

MALICE, kakia, "disgrace, dishonour, badness, base-
          ness"

Wisd.-Sol. 12:10, their malice was bred in them,
                  and...their
            12:20, whereby they might be delivered
                  from...malice
            16:14, A man...killeth through malice:
                  and the spirit

     mēnis, "wrath, anger"
Eccl. 27:30, Malice and wrath even these are abomi-
             nations; and
      28:7, Remember the commandments, and bear no
            malice to thy

     ĕchthros, "hated, hateful"
I Macc. 13:6, heathen are gathered to destroy us of
              very malice

     kakia
II Macc. 4:4, of his contention...did rage, and
              increase...malice
         4:50, remained still in authority, increas-
               ing in malice,

     kakoētheia, "badness of disposition, malicious-
                 ness"
IV Macc. 1:4, it surely also and manifestly has..
              such as malice;
         3:4, one of you may not be able to eradi-
              cate malice, but

MALICIOUS, kakotechnos, "using bad arts or mal-prac-
                        tices"
Wisd.-Sol. 1:4, For into a malicious soul wisdom
                shall not enter:

           kakoēthes, "of ill habit, ill-disposition,
                      malicious"
IV Macc. 1:25, there exists in pleasure a malicious
               disposition

MALICIOUSLY, ponereuomia, "to be evil or wicked, to
                          deal wickedly"
His.-Sus. 1:43, did such things as these men have
                maliciously
          1:62, Moses they did unto them...as they
                maliciously

MALIGNANT, kakoēthes, "of ill habits, ill-disposed,
                      malicious"
IV Macc. 2:16, temperate understand repels all these
               malignant

MALIGNED, zeloō, "to be jealous, envious, spiteful"
Eccl. 45:18, Strangers conspired against him, and

maligned him in

MALLOS, Mallōtas
II Macc. 4:30, things were in doing, they of Tarsus
          and Mallos

MAN, plusios, "a rich man"
I Esd. 3:21, and it maketh every heart rich, so
          that a man

    anēr, "a man, a husband"
Tobit 1:9, Furthermore, when I was come to the age
          of a man, I
     3:14, knowest, Lord, that I am pure from all
          sin with man

    anthrōpos, "man, mankind, man in general"
Tobit 4:14, Let not the wages of any man, which hath
          wrought for
     5:3, Seek thee a man which may go with thee,
          and I will
     5:4, Therefore when he went to seek a man, he
          found Raphael
     5:16, Go thou with this man, and God, which
          dwelleth in
     6:7, we must make a smoke thereof before the
          man
     6:8, As for the gall, it is good to anoint a
          man that hath
     7:7, Thou art the son of an honest and good man
     12:1, Tobit called his son Tobias, and said...
          the man have

    anēr
Judith 1:11, yea, he was before them as one man, and
          they sent
      2:18, and plenty of victual for every man of
          the army, and

    anthrōpos
Judith 6:3, but we his servants will destroy them as
          one man; for

    anēr
Judith 7:11, Now therefore...there shall not so much
          as one man of

    anthrōpos
Judith 8:14, For ye cannot find the depth of the heart
          of man,
      8:16, for God is not as man, that he may be
          threatened;

ánabatḗs, "a horseman"
Judith 9:7, multiplied...they are exalted with horse
        and man;

ánḗr
Judith 14:2, and go forth every valiant man out of
        the city, and

ánthrōpos
Judith 15:2, trembling fell upon them, so that there
        was no man
Wisd.-Sol. 2:1, and in the death of a man there is
        no remedy:

ánḗr
Wisd.-Sol. 5:12, or like as when an arrow is shot
        ...so that a man

ánthrōpos
Wisd.-Sol. 7:1, I myself also am a mortal man, like
        to all, and

ánḗr
Wisd.-Sol. 7:2, being compacted in blood, of the
        seed of a man,

ánthrōpos
Wisd.-Sol. 9:2, and being ordained man through thy
        wisdom, that he

ásebḗs, "an ungodly man, unholy, profane"
Wisd.-Sol. 10:6, ungodly perished, she delivered
        the righteous man

ánthrōpos
Wisd.-Sol. 13:13, and fashioned it to the image of
        a man
        14:15, mourning....when his child...was
        then a dead man,
        14:20, took him now for a god, which...
        before was...man
        15:16, For man made them, and he that
        borrowed his own
        16:14, A man indeed killeth through his
        malice: and
        16:26, not the growing of fruits that
        nourisheth man:

ánḗr
Eccl. 4:2, not a hungry soul sorrowful; neither
        provoke a man in

ánthrōpos
Eccl. 8:1, Strive not with a mighty man, lest thou
          fall into his
      8:2, Be not at variance with a rich man, lest
          he overweigh
      8:3, Strive not with a man that is full of
          tongue, and heap
      8:5, Reproach not a man that turneth from sin,
          but
      8:6, Dishonour not a man in his old age: for
          even some of
      9:13, Keep thee far from the man that hath
           power to kill:
ánēr
Eccl. 10:5, In the hand of God is the prosperity
           of man:
       10:7, Pride is hateful before God and man: and
            by both
       10:11, For when a man is dead, he shall in-
             herit creeping
       11:2, Commend not a man for his beauty: neither
            abhor a man
       11:26, an easy thing unto the Lord...to reward
             a man
       11:28, for a man shall be known in his child-
             ren
       11:29, Bring not every man into thine house:
             for the deceitful man shall be known
       11:32, a heap of coals is kindled: and a sin-
             ful man laveth
       12:9, In the prosperity of a man enemies will
            be grieved:
       13:15, Every beast loveth his like, and every
             man loveth
       13:16, consorteth according to kind, and a
             man will cleave
ánthrōpos
Eccl. 13:25, The heart of a man changeth his coun-
            tenance, whether
ánēr
Eccl. 14:1, Blessed is the man that hath not slipped
           with his
ánthrōpos
Eccl. 14:3, and what should an envious man do with
           money?
ánēr
Eccl. 14:20, Blessed is the man that doth meditate

                              good things

ánthrōpos
Eccl. 15:14, He himself made man from the beginning
              and left him
        15:17, Before man is life and death; and
              whether he liketh
        15:19, and his eyes are upon them...and he
              knoweth every work of man

ánēr
Eccl. 16:12, he judgeth a man according to his works
        16:23, He that wanteth understanding will
              think upon vain things: and a foolish
              man erring...

ánthrōpos
Eccl. 17:1, The Lord created man of the earth, and
              turned him
        17:22, The alms of a man is as a signet with
              him, and he will keep the good deeds
              of a man as the
        18:7, When a man hath done, then he beginneth;
              and when he leaveth off, then he shall
              be
        18:9, The number of a man's days at the most
              is an hundred years
        18:27, A wise man will fear in every thing,
              and in the day of sinning he will be-
              ware

ánēr
Eccl. 19:30, A man's attire, and excessive laughter,
              and gait, shew what he is
        20:6, Some man holdeth his tongue, because he
              hath not to answer
        20:7, A wise man will hold his tongue till he
              see opportunity: but a babbler and a
              fool
        20:13, A wise man by his words maketh himself
              beloved: but the graces of fools
        20:15, He giveth little and upbraideth much
              ...such an one is to be hated of God
              and man
        20:24, A lie is a foul blot in a man, yet it
        20:27, A wise man shall promote himself to
        20:31, Better is he that hideth his folly than
              a man that
        21:22, A foolish man's foot is soon in...
        23:11, A man that useth much swearing shall be
        23:15, The man that is accustomed to...words

anthrōpos
Eccl. 23:18, A man that breaketh wedlock, saying
              thus in his
        23:19, such a man only feareth the eyes of
              men, and knoweth

anēr
Eccl. 23:23, whore in adultery, and brought child-
              ren by...man
        25:20, way...so is a wife full of words to a
              quiet man
        26:1, Blessed is the man that hath a virtuous
              wife, for the
        26:28, There be two things that grieve...a
              man of war that
        27:4, one sitteth with a sieve...so the filth
              of a man is
        27:7, Praise no man before thou hearest him
              speak;

anthrōpos
Eccl. 28:3, One man beareth hatred against another,
              and doth he
        28:4, He sheweth no mercy to a man, which is
              like himself:
        28:8, for a furious man will kindle strife

anēr
Eccl. 28:9, A sinful man disquieteth friends, and
              maketh debate

anthrōpos
Eccl. 28:10, and as a man's strength is, so is his
              wrath;
        29:28, These things are grievous to a man of
              understanding;
        30:22, The gladness of the heart is the life
              of man,

anēr
Eccl. 31:1, The hopes of a man void of understanding
              are vain and
        31:9, A man that hath travelled knoweth many
              things:
        31:21, he that defraudeth him thereof is a
              man of blood
        31:26, So is it with a man that fasteth for
              his sins, and
        32:7, The sacrifice of a just man is accept-
              able, and the

anthrōpos
Eccl. 32:19, till he have rendered to every man

according to his deeds, and to the works
of men

Eccl. 34:16, Eat, as it becometh a man, those things
which are

34:19, A very little is sufficient for a man
well nurtured,

aner

Eccl. 34:20, but the pain of watching...are with an
unsatiable man

anthrōpos

Eccl. 34:27, Wine is as good as life to man, if it
be drunk

35:17, A sinful man will not be reproved, but
findeth an

aner

Eccl. 35:18, A man of counsel will be considerate;
but a strange and proud man,

36:2, A wise man hateth not the law; but he
that is an

anthrōpos

Eccl. 36:3, A man of understanding trusteth in the
law; and the

36:13, As the clay is in the potter's hand...
so man is in

36:20, A froward heart causeth heaviness: but
a man of

36:26, so (who will believe) a man that hath
no house, and

aner

Eccl. 37:12, But be continually with a godly man,
whom thou knowest

37:14, For a man's mind is sometime wont to
tell him more

37:23, A wise man instructeth his people; and
the fruits of

37:24, A wise man shall be filled with blessing; and all

37:25, The days of the life of a man may be
numbered; but

anthrōpos

Eccl. 39:26, The principal things for the whole use
of man's life

40:1, Great travail is created for every man,
and an heavy

40:8, (Such things happen) unto all fresh,
both man and

anēr
Eccl. 40:29, The life of him that dependeth on
              another man's table is not

anthrōpos
Eccl. 41:15, A man that hideth his foolishness is
              better than a man that hideth his wis-
              dom

anēr
Eccl. 42:14, Better is the churlishness of a man
              than a courteous

anthrōpos
Eccl. 46:19, any man's goods, so much as a shoe:
              and no man did
Bar. 2:3, that a man should eat the flesh of his
           own son, and the
Epis.-Jer. 1:17, For like as a vessel that a man
                  useth is nothing
          1:36, They can save no man from death,
                 neither deliver
          1:37, They cannot restore a blind man
                 to his sight, nor help any man
          1:73, Better therefore is the just man
                 that hath no idols:

anēr
His.-Sus. 1:1, There dwelt a man in Babylon, called
                Joacim:
I Macc. 2:8, Her temple is become as a man without
              glory
         2:65, I know that your brother Simon is a
                man of counsel,

anthrōpos
I Macc. 5:42, Suffer no man to remain in the camp,
               but let all

anēr
I Macc. 5:63, Howbeit the man Judas and his brethren
               were greatly
          6:54, did so prevail against them, that...
                 every man to his
          7:7, Now therefore send some man whom thou
                trustest, and
          9:29, Since thy brother Judas died, we have
                 no man like him
          10:16, he said, Shall we find another man?
                  now therefore
          13:53, And when Simon saw that John was a
                  valiant man, he made him

II Macc. 3:11, We have heard of thee, that thou
              art a man of
        3:17, For the man was so compassed with
              fear and horror
        3:32, Jews, offered a sacrifice for the
              health of the man
        4:35, the Jews...were grieved for the...
              murder of the man
        6:18, Eleazar, one of the principal scribes,
              an aged man

anthrōpos
II Macc. 7:23, the Creator...who formed the genera-
              tion of man, and
        7:34, But thou, O godless man, and of all
              other most

anēr
II Macc. 8:8, So when Philip saw this man increased
              by little and
       14:24, for he loved the man from his heart
       14:31, commanded the priests...to deliver
              him the man
       15:13, This done, in like manner there ap-
              peared a man

anthrōpos
III Macc. 7:9, we shall never have our opposite, not
              man, but the
IV Macc. 2:21, For at the time when God created man,
              He implanted

anēr
IV Macc. 4:1, For a certain man named Simon, who was
              in opposition
        6:30, Thus speaking, the holy man departed,
              noble in his torments,
        7:23, For the wise and brave man only is
              lord over his

MANASSES, Manassēs
   Judith 16:22, And many desired her...after that
               Manasses her
          16:23, buried her in the cave of her husband
               Manasses
          16:24, to all them...nearest of kindred to
               Manasses

MANDATE, entolas, "an injunction, command"
   II Macc. 4:25, So he came with the king's mandate,
                bringing

MANGLE, aikizō, "to treat injuriously, esp. by blows, to plague"
  II Macc. 7:13, man was dead also, they tormented and mangled the
           7:15, Afterward they brought the fifth also, and mangled

MANIFEST, epideiknumi, "to exhibit, to show, demonstrate"
  IV Macc. 11:12, thou bestowest upon us...enabling us to manifest

MANIFESTATION, apodeiknumi, "to point out, display, demonstrate"
  IV Macc. 13:10, Let us not be cowards in the manifestation of

MANIFOLD, polutropos, "manifold, various, in many ways"
  IV Macc. 14:11, when even a woman's mind despised more manifold

MANKIND, genos, "family, kindred, race"
  III Macc. 3:6, What all the rest of mankind said, was, however,

MANLINESS, andreia, "manliness, manly spirit"
  IV Macc. 1:4, those which are hindrances to manliness, as wrath,
           1:6, does not rule over...affections...and manliness and
           1:11, for their manliness and endurance, became the
           1:18, And the forms...are prudence, and justice, and manliness
           5:23, and it exercises us in manliness, so that we
           5:31, I am not so old and void of manliness, but that my

MANLIUS, Manlios
  II Macc. 11:34, also sent unto them...Memmius and Titus Manlius

MANLY, andreios, "belonging to a man, manly, masculine"
  IV Macc. 15:10, For they were both just, temperate, and manly,
           15:30, O thou nobler in endurance...and more manly than

MANNA, manna, "the miraculous food of the Israelites ...in the desert"
  Bar. 1:10, Behold, we have sent you money...prepare ye manna, and

74

MANNER, tropos, "a turn, direction, manner, a way"
  IV Macc. 5:14, While the tyrant excited him in this
               manner to the
        6:1, When Eleazar, had in this manner ans-
               wered the

MARDOCHEUS, Mardochaikēs
  II Macc. 15:36, day of the twelfth month...the day
               before Mardocheus' day

MARISA, Marisa
  II Macc. 12:35, A horseman...smote off his shoulder,
               so that Georgias fled unto Marisa

MARK, molops, "the mark of a blow, a stripe"
  Eccl. 28:17, The stroke of the whip maketh marks
            in the flesh:

MARKETPLACE, ágora, "any assembly, the place of as-
              sembly, a market"
  I Esd. 2:19, the Jews...come into Jerusalem...build
            the marketplaces

MARRIAGE, gamos, "a wedding, marriage, wedlock, nup-
              tial"
  Tobit 6:12, return from Rages we will celebrate the
            marriage:
      6:13, given to seven men, who all died in the
            marriage
      6:15, same night shall she be given thee in
            marriage
      6:16, And when thou shalt come into the mar-
            riage chamber
      8:20, For before the days of the marriage were
            finished,
  Wisd.-Sol. 14:24, they kept neither lives nor mar-
              riage any longer
       14:26, disquieting of good men...disorder
             in marriages,
  I Macc. 9:37, to Jonathan...that...Jambri made a
            great marriage
      9:41, Thus was the marriage turned into
            mourning, and the
     10:58, daughter Cleopatra, and celebrated
            her marriage

      gamiskō,"to give in marriage"
  II Macc. 4:6, a lamentable cry in lieu of the mar-
            riage hymn

      gamos
  IV Macc. 2:11, And it prevails over marriage, love,
            condemning it

MARRIED, gameō, "to marry, enter in marriage"
   Tobit 1:9, Furthermore...J married Anna of mine own
        kindred, and
      3:8, because that she had been married to
        seven husbands,
   II Macc. 14:25, so he married, was quiet, and took
        part of this
      16:9, Alas, of my children, some of you...
        have married to

MARRY, ekdosis, "a giving in marriage"
   Eccl. 7:25, Marry thy daughter,and so shalt thou
        have performed

      epigambreuō, "to marry a widow as her husband's
        next of kin"
   I Macc. 10:56, for I will marry my daughter to thee
        according to

MARVEL, thaumazō, "a wonder, marvel, to wonder"
   Eccl. 11:21, Marvel not at the works of sinners;
        but trust in the
      43:24, the danger...and when we hear it...we
        marvel thereat

MARVELLED, apothaumazō, "to wonder at a thing, to won-
        der much"
   Eccl. 47:17, The countries marvelled at thee for thy
        songs, and

      thaumazō
   I Macc. 1:22, a great fire kindled, so that every
        man marvelled

      ekplessō, "to strike out of, to astonish,
        amaze"
   II Macc. 7:12, Insomuch that the king...marvelled at
        the young

MARVELLOUS, thaumastos, "to be wondered at, wonderful,
        marvellous"
   Eccl. 43:2, declaring at his rising a marvellous in-
        strument,
      43:29, The Lord is terrible and very great,
        and marvellous
      48:14, life, and at his death were his works
        marvellous
   Song-Child. 1:19, Deliver us also according to thy
        marvellous
   II Macc. 7:20, But the mother was marvellous above
        all, and

MASALOTH, <u>Maisaloth</u>
    I Macc. 9:2, who went forth by the way that leadeth
                to...Masaloth,

MASON, <u>latomos</u>, "a stone-cutter, quarry-man"
    I Esd. 5:54, And they gave unto the masons and car-
                penters money,

MASPHA, <u>Massēpha</u>
    I Macc. 3:46, assembled themselves together, and
                came to Maspha,
           5:35, This done, Judas turned aside to Mas-
                pha;

MASSACRE, <u>phonoktonia</u>, "a killing slaughter, murder"
    I Macc. 1:24, when he had taken all away, he...
                made a great massacre, and spoken

MASTER, <u>despotos</u>, "a master, a despot, absolute ruler"
    IV Macc. 1:1, reasoning is the absolute master of
                the passions,

           <u>despozō</u>, "to be lord and master"
    IV Macc. 1:5, reasoning...is not also master of for-
                getfulness...?

           <u>autokrator</u>, "one's own master"
    IV Macc. 1:7, religious reasoning is the sole master
                of the
           1:13, whether reasoning be absolute master
                of the

           <u>epikrateō</u>, "to rule over, govern"
    IV Macc. 2:4, sensual indulgence...that reasoning
                is able to master

           <u>krateō</u>, "to rule, hold sway, to become master
                of"
    IV Macc. 2:15, And reasoning appear to be master of
                the more

           <u>despozō</u>
    IV Macc. 2:16, all these malignant passions...for
                it masters...this

           <u>krateō</u>
    IV Macc. 2:24, a man may say, if reasoning be mas-
                ter of the

           <u>epikrateō</u>
    IV Macc. 6:34, that...reasoning, since it masters
                external

           <u>krateō</u>
    IV Macc. 7:18, religion...these alone can master

the passions

II Macc. 7:22, it is...for the sake of religion master his passion

autokrateō, "self-rule, possessing full power"
IV Macc. 8:27, were well aware of the sufferings and masters of

autodespotos, "absolute ruler or master"
IV Macc. 13:1, on all sides that righteous reasoning is absolute master

autokrator, "self-ruler or ruler of the self, one's own master"
IV Macc. 16:1, children...confessedly religious reasoning is master

MASTERBUILDER, architektōn, "a master-builder, director of works"
II Macc. 2:29, For as the master builder of a new house must care

MASTERED, krateō, "to rule, to become master of"
IV Macc. 6:35, and I prove that reasoning has not mastered pains,

MASTERY, epikrateia, "mastery, dominion"
IV Macc. 6:32, I would have given them the witness of...mastery

pathokrateia, "ruling with passion"
IV Macc. 13:5, can we avoid according to these men mastery of

autokrateō
IV Macc. 16:2, that not only men have obtained mastery of

MASTICK, schinos, "a mastick tree"
His.-Sus. 1:54, And he said, Under the mastick tree

MATTATHIAS, Mattathias
I Macc. 2:1, In those days...Mattathias the son of John...dwelt in
         2:14, Then Mattathias and his sons rent their clothes
         2:16, when many of Israel came unto them, Mattathias...and
         2:17, Then...the king's officers...said to Mattathias...Thou
         2:19, Then Mattathias answered and spake with a loud
         2:24, Which thing when Mattathias saw, he was inflamed

I Macc. 2:27, And Mattathias cried throughout the
            city with a
        2:39, Now when Mattathias and his friends
            understood
        2:45, Then Mattathias and his friends went
            round about,
        2:49, Now when the time drew near that
            Mattathias should
       11:70, there was not one of them left, except
            Mattathias
       14:29, Simon the son of Mattathias, of the
            posterity of
       16:14, came...to Jericho with his sons,
            Mattathias and

MATTER, hulē, "matter, the stuff of which a thing is
            made"
  Wisd.-Sol. 11:17, that made the world of matter with-
            out form,

MEAT, artos, "bread, a loaf, esp. of wheat"
  Tobit 10:7, day into the way...and did eat no meat
            in the daytime

    opsopoiikos, "of or for delicate cookery"
  Judith 12:1, they should prepare for her of his own
            meats,

    trophē, "nutriment, nourishment, food"
  Judith 12:9, in the tent, until she did eat her meat
            at evening

    brōma, "that which is eaten, food"
  Judith 13:10, and she put it in her bag of meat: so
            they twain

    sarx, "flesh"
  Wisd.-Sol. 19:21, melted they the icy kind of hea-
            venly meat, that

    brōma
  Eccl. 13:7, And he will shame thee by his meat, un-
            til he have
        30:18, poured upon a mouth shut up are as
            messes of meat

    artos
  Eccl. 34:23, Whoso liberal of this meat, men shall
            speak well of
        34:24, But against him that is a niggard of
            his meat the

79

broma
Eccl. 34:29, in any dainty thing, nor too greedy
            upon meats;
      36:18, The belly devoureth all meats, yet is
             one meat
      37:30, for excess of meats bringeth sickness,
             and

artos
Eccl. 41:19, and to lean with thy elbow upon the
             meat; and of

broma
Bel-Drag. 1:11, priests said: but thou, O king set
                on the meat,
          1:14, when they were gone forth, the king
                set meat
I Macc. 1:63, that they might not be defiled with
              meats,

   trophe, "nourishment, food, victuals"
III Macc. 3:7, of the Jews with regard to their
               worship and meats
IV Macc. 1:33, that when urged on to forbidden meats,
               we reject
         4:26, every one...by tasting forbidden
               meats, to adjure

broma
IV Macc. 6:15, We will bring you some meat cooked by
               yourself,

MEDABA, Medaba
   I Macc. 9:36, But the children of Jambri came out of
                 Medaba, and

MEDDLE, praxis, "mode of acting, deeds"
   Eccl. 11:10, My son, meddle not with many matters:
                for if thou meddle much, thou shalt
                not be innocent

MEDES, Medon
   Judith 1:1, days of Arphaxad, which reigned over
               the Medes in
         16:10, Persians quaked at her boldness, and
                the Medes were
   I Macc. 1:1, Alexander...had smitten Darius king of
                the...Medes,

MEDIA, Media
   I Esd. 6:23, Ecbatana the palace, which is in the
               country of Media

Tobit 1:14, And I went into Media, and left in
   trust with Gabael,
 1:15, was troubled, that I could not go into
   Media
 3:7, the same day, that in Ecbatane a city of
   Media, Sara
 4:1, money which he had committed to Gabael
   ...of Media,
 9:2, take with thee...two camels, and go to
   Rages of Media
 11:15, and told his father the great things...
   in Media
 14:4, Go into Media, my son, for I surely believe those
 14:14, And he died at Ecbatane in Media, being
   an hundred
I Macc. 6:56, was returned to Persia and Media, and
   the king's
 8:8, and the country of India and Media,
   and Lydia, and
 14:1, gathered his forces together, and went
   into Media,
 14:2, But when Arsaces, the king of Persia
   and Media,

MEDICINE, pharmakon, "a drug"
 Eccl. 6:16, A faithful friend is the medicine of
   life:
 38:4, The Lord created medicine out of the
   earth;

MEDITATE, dianeomai, "to think over, intend, purpose"
 Eccl. 39:7, knowledge, and on his secrets shall he
   meditate

MEEK, epieikeia, "likelihood, reasonableness, natural
   mildness"
 Wisd.-Sol. 2:19, Let us examine him...that we may
   know his meekness

 praotēs, "meekness, gentleness"
 Eccl. 1:26, fear of the Lord is wisdom...and faith
   and meekness
 3:17, My son, go on with thy business in meekness;
 4:8, down...and give him a friendly answer
   with meekness
 10:28, My son, glorify thy soul in meekness,
   and give it

MEET, hupantaō, "to meet"
  Eccl. 9:3, Meet not with an harlot, lest thou fall
            into her

MELODY, melos, "a song, strain, the music to which a
            song is set"
  Eccl. 35:6, As a signet ring...so is the melody of
            music with
        40:21, The pipe and psaltery make sweet me-
            lody: but a
        47:9, before the altar, that...they might make
            sweet melody
        50:18, variety of sounds was there made sweet
            melody

  mousikos, "music or lyric poetry set and sung
            to music"
  I Macc. 9:41, turned into mourning, and...their me-
            lody into

  melōdos, "singing, musical"
  IV Macc. 10:21, speedily find you...the instrument
            of divine melody
         15:21, Not so do siren melodies, or songs
            of swans,

MEMMIUS, Memmios
  II Macc. 11:34, Quintus Memmius and Titus Manlius,
            ambassadors of

MEMORIAL, mnēmē, "remembrance, memory, recollection,
            monument"
  Wisd.-Sol. 4:1, for the memorial of thereof is im-
            mortal:
         4:19, and their memorial shall perish
         8:13, and leave behind me an everlasting
            memorial
         10:8, but also left behind them to the
            world a memorial

  mimnēskō, "to remember, recollect, call to
            mind"
  Eccl. 10:17, He...destroyed them, and hath made
            their memorial to
        24:20, For my memorial is sweeter than honey,
            and mine
        32:7, of a just man is acceptable, and the
            memorial thereof
        38:11, Give a sweet saviour, and a memorial
            of fine flour;
        39:9, his memorial shall not depart away, and
            his name shall

Eccl. 44:9, And some there be, which have no memorial; who are
      45:1, even Moses, beloved of God and men,
whose memorial is
      45:9, a noise might be heard in the temple
for a memorial
      45:11, with a writing engraved for a memorial,
after the
      45:16, He chose him out of all men...for a
memorial, to make
Bar. 4:5, Be of good cheer, my people, the memorial
of Israel
I Macc. 3:7, and made Jacob glad...and his memorial
is blessed for
      3:35, to take away their memorial from that
place
    12:53, upon them, and take away their memo-
rial from that
    14:23, the people of the Lacedemonians might
have a memorial

      mneia, "remembrance, memory"
IV Macc. 17:8, And it had been a worthy thing...as
memorial to

MEMORY, mnēmosunē, "remembrance, memory"
Eccl. 23:26, She shall leave her memory to be cursed
and her
    46:11, And concerning the judges...let their
memory be

      mnēmē, "remembrance, memory, recollection"
II Macc. 2:25, they that are desirous to commit to
memory might

MEN, anthropoi, "men in general, mankind"
I Esd. 4:2, O ye men, do not men excel in strength,
that bear

      andres, "men as opposed to women; emphatically,
men indeed"
I Esd. 4:12, O ye men, how should not the king be
mightiest...?
     4:14, O ye men, it is not the great king nor
the multitude of men, neither is it
wine,

      anthropoi
I Esd. 4:17, These also make garments for men; these
bring glory unto men;
     4:34, O ye men, are not women strong? great
is the earth,

ἀνδρες
I Esd. 8:46, and commanded them that they...should
            send men as
Tobit 7:11, I have given my daughter in marriage to
            seven men,
Judith 2:5, from my presence, and take with thee
            men that trust
       3:5, So the men came to Holofernes, and de-
            clared unto him
       6:12, and when the men of the city saw them,
             they took up
       7:2, Then the strong men removed their camps
            in that day, and the army of the men
            of war

ἀνθρωποι
Judith 8:12, ye that tempted God...among the child-
             ren of men?

ἀνδρες
Judith 10:13, losing the body or life of any one of
              his men
       10:14, Now when the men heard her words....
              they wondered
       10:17, Then they chose out of them an hundred
              men to
Eccl. 44:1, Let us now praise famous men, and our
            fathers that
      44:3, Such as did bear rule in their kingdoms,
            men renowned
      44:6, rich men furnished with ability, living
            peaceably in
      44:10, But these were men, merciful men, whose
             righteousness

ἀνθρωποι
Eccl. 44:22, did he establish likewise...the bless-
             ing of all men,
      45:1, even Moses beloved of God and men, whose
            memorial is

ἀνδρες
Eccl. 45:18, even the men that were of Dathan's and
             Abiram's side

ἀνθρωποι
Bar. 2:1, Lord has made good his word...against the
          men of Israel
     3:17, pastime with the fowls of the air...
           wherein men trust,
Epis.-Jer. 1:26, whereby they declare unto men that
                 they be

Epis.-Jer. 1:51, they are no gods, but the works
                 of men's hands,
           1:53, set up a king in the land, nor give
                 rain unto men
           1:64, neither to judge...nor to do good
                 unto men
Song-Child. 1:59, O ye children of men, bless ye
                  the Lord: praise

ǎndres

Bel-Drag. 1:20, And the king said, I see the foot-
                 steps of men,
I Macc. 1:34, And they put therein a sinful nation,
              wicked men,
        2:18, come thou first...like...the men of
              Juda also,
        2:31, told the king's servants...that cer-
              tain men...had
        2:44, So they joined their forces, and smote
              sinful men
        3:24, where were slain about eight hundred
              men,
        3:38, and Georgias, mighty men of the king's
              friends:

huioi, "a son, in respect of membership or service"
I Macc. 4:2, And the men of the fortress were his
             guides

ǎndres

I Macc. 4:6, Judas shewed himself...with three
             thousand men,
        4:8, Then said Judas to the men that were
             with him, Fear
        4:15, were slain of them as many as three
              thousand men,
        4:29, Idumea...and Judas met them with ten
              thousand men,
        4:34, were slain of the host about five
              thousand men
        4:41, Then Judas appointed certain men to
              fight against
        5:13, they have destroyed there about five
              thousand men
        5:17, Choose thee out men, and go and de-
              liver thy brethren
        5:20, Now unto Simon were given three thou-
              sand men to go
        5:34, killed of them that day about eight
              thousand men

I Macc. 5:59, Then came Georgias and his men out of city to

5:62, Moreover these men came not of the seed of those by

6:35, for every elephant they appointed a thousand men,

6:42, there were slain of the king's army six hundred men

7:1, departed from Rome, and came up with a few men

7:19, his tents in Bezeth...and took many of the men

7:28, I will come with a few men, that I may see you in

7:32, slain of Nicanor's side about five thousand men

7:40, Judas pitched in Adasa with three thousand men, and

9:5, Now Judas had...three thousand chosen men with him

9:25, Then Bacchides chose the wicked men, and made them

9:49, Bacchides' side that day about a thousand men

9:61, Wherefore they took of the men of the country

10:36, among the king's forces about thirty thousand men

10:74, So...Judas...choosing ten thousand men...went out of

10:85, Thus there were burned and slain... eight thousand men

11:43, thou shalt do well, if thou send me men to help me;

11:44, Jonathan sent him three thousand men unto Antioch:

11:74, heathen that day about three thousand men.

12:1, Now...Jonathan...chose certain men, and sent them to

12:41, went out to meet him with forty thousand men

ánthrōpoi

I Macc. 12:53, take away their memorial from among men

13:10, So then he gathered together all the men of war,

13:34, Moreover Simon chose men, and sent

                          to king
I Macc. 13:48, and placed such men there as would
               keep the law,
        14:23, And it pleased the people to enter-
               tain the men
        15:13, Antiochus against Dora...with...an
               hundred...men of
        15:26, Simon sent him two thousand chosen
               men to aid him;
        16:4, chose out of the country twenty thou-
               sand men of war
        16:6, were afraid...he went first...and then
               the men

laoi, "the people, the soldiery, host, army"
I Macc. 16:7, That done, he divided his men, and
               set the horsemen

andres
I Macc. 16:15, howbeit he hid the men there
II Macc. 4:44, Now when the king came to Tyrus, three
                men that
         5:12, and commanded his men of war not to
                spare such as
         5:13, killing of young and old, making
                away of men,
        10:29, there appeared...five comely men upon
                horses,

anthrōpoi
II Macc. 11:9, ready not only to fight with men,
                but with...beasts
III Macc. 3:2, an individious rumour was uttered...
                men who had
          3:7, they alleged that they were men un-
                sociable, hostile
          3:8, Nor was this unexpected uproar...con-
                cerning men who
         3:18, carried away by their old arrogance
                ...toward...men
          7:6, clemency which we are wont to extend
                to all men,

andres
III Macc. 7:15, slaying thus, in that day, above
                 three hundred men
IV Macc. 1:10, For their virtues...I should commend
                those men who

anthrōpoi
IV Macc. 1:11, they, winning admiration not only

                    from men in
IV Macc. 4:12, he would celebrate to all men the
               blessedness of
           11:7, thou been capable of the higher feel-
               ings of men,

ándres
IV Macc. 14:11, reasoning bore rule over those men
               in their

ánthrōpoi
IV Macc. 14:14, possess...love for their offspring
               with men

ándres
IV Macc. 16:2, I have proved them, then, that not
               only men have

ánthrōpoi
IV Macc. 17:14, and the world and living men were
               the spectators
           18:3, persons...were not only admired by
               men, but were
Pr.-Mans. 1:7, thou art the Lord...repenting of the
               evils of men

MENELAUS, Menelaos
II Macc. 4:23, Three years afterward Jason sent
               Menelaus, the
           4:27, So Menelaus got the principality: but
               as for the
           4:29, Now Menelaus left his brother Lysi-
               machus in his
           4:32, Now Menelaus, supposing that he had
               gotten a
           4:34, Wherefore Menelaus, taking Andronicus
               apart,
           4:39, had been committed...with the consent
               of Menelaus,
           4:43, therefore there was an accusation...
               against Menelaus
           4:45, but Menelaus, being now convicted,
               promised
           4:47, insomuch that he discharged Menelaus
               from the
           4:50, And so through...them that were of
               power Menelaus
           5:5, being put back, and the city...taken
               Menelaus fled
           5:15, Menelaus, that traitor to the laws,
               and to his own

II Macc. 5:23, and at Garizim, Andronicus; and
            besides, Menelaus,
      11:29, Menelaus declared unto us, that your
            desire was to
      11:32, I have sent also Menelaus, that he
            may comfort you
      13:3, Menelaus also joined himself with
            them, and with

MENSTRUOUS, haptō, "to have intercourse with, to know
            carnally"
   Epis.-Jer. 1:29, Menstruous women, and women in
            childbed eat

MERARI, Merari
   Judith 8:1, Judith heard thereof...the daughter
            of Merari, the son

MERCHANT, emporos, "a merchant, a trader"
   Eccl. 26:29, A merchant shall hardly keep himself
            from doing
      37:11, Neither consult with a...merchant con-
            cerning exchange
      42:5, and of merchants' indifferent selling;
            of much
   Bar. 3:23, that seek wisdom upon earth, the mer-
            chants of Meran
   I Macc. 3:41, And the merchants of the country,
            hearing the fame
   II Macc. 8:34, who had brought a thousand merchants
            to buy the

MERCIFUL, philanthropos, "loving mankind, humane"
   Wisd.-Sol. 12:19, taught thy people that the just
            man should be merciful,

         eleos, "mercy, compassion, pity"
   Eccl. 29:1, He that is merciful will lend unto his
            neighbour; and
      44:10, But these were merciful men, whose
            righteousness
      44:24, And he brought of him a merciful man,
            which found

         eleēmon, "merciful, pitiful, compassionate"
   Eccl. 48:20, But they called upon the Lord who is
            merciful, and
      50:19, by prayer before him that is merciful

         eleos
   I Macc. 2:57, David for being merciful possessed the

                        throne of an
                hileos, "propitious, favourable, merciful"
        II Macc. 7:37, God that he would be speedily be
                        merciful unto our

                eleēmon
        II Macc. 8:29, When this was done...they besought
                        the merciful

                hileos
        II Macc. 10:26, of the altar, and besought him to
                        be merciful

                eleēmon
        II Macc. 11:9, Then they praised the merciful God
                        all together,
                 11:10, for the Lord was merciful unto them
                 13:12, So...they besought the merciful Lord
                        with weeping
        III Macc. 5:7, invoked the...Lord...with tears their
                        merciful God

                hileos
        IV Macc. 6:28, Be merciful to thy people and be
                        satisfied with
                  9:24, our just and paternal Providence...
                        being merciful
                 12:18, call upon the God of my fathers to
                        be merciful to

                polueleos, "very merciful, very compassionate"
        Pr.-Mans. 1:7, the Lord most high, compassionate...
                        and...merciful

MERCY, eleēmosunē, "pity, compassion"
        Tobit 3:2, thou art just...and all thy ways are
                        mercy and truth,

                eleeō, "to have pity on, shew mercy"
        Tobit 8:17, praised, because thou hast had mercy
                        of two that were
                 11:17, gave thanks before them, because God
                        had mercy on him
                 13:2, For he doth scourge, and hath mercy: he
                        leadeth down
                 13:5, scourge us for our iniquities, and will
                        have mercy
                 14:5, and that again God will have mercy on
                        them, and bring

                hileos
        Judith 7:30, the Lord...may turn his mercy toward us;
                        90

Wisd.-Sol. 3:9, for grace and mercy is to his saints
            and he hath
        4:15, That his grace and mercy is with
            his saints and

éleos
Wisd.-Sol. 6:6, For mercy will soon pardon the
            meanest: but
        9:1, O God of my fathers, and Lord of
            mercy, who hast
        11:9, For when they were tried, albeit
            but in mercy
        12:22, ourselves are judged, we should
            look for mercy

éleeō
Wisd.-Sol. 15:1, longsuffering, and in mercy order-
            ing all things

éleos
Wisd.-Sol. 16:10, for thy mercy was by them, and
            healed them

aneleēmon, "unmerciful"
Wisd.-Sol. 19:1, wrath came upon them without mercy
            unto the end

éleos
Eccl. 2:7, Ye that fear the Lord, wait for his
            mercy; and go not
      2:9, Ye that fear the Lord, hope for good...
            joy and mercy

éleēmon
Eccl. 2:11, For the Lord is full of compassion and
            mercy,

éleos
Eccl. 2:18, for as his majesty is, so is his mercy
      16:12, As his mercy is great, so is his cor-
            rection also:

éleēmosunē
Eccl. 16:14, Make way for every work of mercy: for
            every man

éleos
Eccl. 18:11, patient with them, and poureth forth
            his mercy upon
      18:13, The mercy of man is toward his neigh-
            bour; but the mercy of the Lord is

éleeō
Eccl. 18:14, He hath mercy on them that receive

                     discipline

ĕxilaskomai, "to appease completely, propiti-
              ate"
Eccl. 18:20, judgment examine thyself...and thou
             shalt find mercy

     éleos
Eccl. 32:19, his deeds...and made them to rejoice
             in his mercy
      32:20, Mercy is seasonable in the time of af-
             fliction,

     éleeō
Eccl. 33:1, Have mercy upon us, O Lord God of all,
            and behold us

     éleos
Eccl. 46:7, In the time of Moses also he did a work
            of mercy, he
      47:22, But the Lord will never leave off his
             mercy, neither
Bar. 2:27, with us...according to all that great
           mercy of thine

     éleeō
Bar. 3:2, Hear, O Lord, and have mercy; for thou
          art merciful:

     éleēmosunē
Bar. 4:22, from the Holy One, because of the mercy
           which shall
      5:9, lead Israel with joy in the light of his
            ...mercy and
Epis.-Jer. 1:38, They can shew no mercy to the wi-
                 dow, nor do good

     éleos
Song-Child. 1:11, and cause not thy mercy to depart
                  from us, for
            1:14, to sacrifice before thee, and to
                  find mercy
            1:66, for his mercy endureth for ever
            1:67, for his mercy endureth for ever
I Macc. 3:44, Then the congregation...ask mercy and
              compassion

     éleaō, "to pity, have compassion, commiserate"
I Macc. 4:10, unto heaven, peradventure the Lord
              will have mercy,

     éleos
I Macc. 4:24, because it is good, because his mercy
              endureth for

éleeō, "to receive pity, experience compassion"
I Macc. 16:3, But now I am old, and ye, by God's
mercy, are of a

hileos
II Macc. 2:7, gather his people...and receive them
unto mercy

éleeō
II Macc. 2:18, promised in the law, will shortly
have mercy upon

éleos
II Macc. 6:16, And therefore he never withdraweth
his mercy from
7:23, Creator of the world...will also of
his own mercy

éleeō
II Macc. 7:29, that I may receive thee again in
mercy with thy

éleos
II Macc. 8:5, for the wrath of the Lord was turned
into mercy
8:27, unto that day, which was the beginning of mercy
9:13, vowed also unto the Lord, who now...
have mercy upon

épieikeia, "reasonableness, equity, clemency"
II Macc. 10:4, him...he himself would chasten them
with mercy;

éleos
Pr.-Mans. 1:6, the mercy of thy promise is both im-
measurable and
1:14, all thy benevolence...according to
thy great mercy

MESOPOTAMIA, Mesopotamia
Judith 2:24, went over Euphrates, and went through
Mesopotamia,
5:7, and they sojourned heretofore in Mesopotamia, because
5:8, from the face of their gods, and they
fled into Mesopotamia
8:26, Remember...what happened to Jacob in
Mesopotamia of

MESSAGE, apaggellō, "to declare plainly, to announce
formally"
I Macc. 15:32, the glory of Simon...and told him

                    the king's message

MESSENGER, aggelos, "a messenger, envoy"
  I Esd. 1:50, the God of their fathers sent by his
                    messenger to
          1:51, But they had his messengers in deri-
                    sion; and, in the
  I Macc. 1:44, For the king sent letters by messen-
                    gers unto
          5:14, were yet being read...there came other
                    messengers
          7:10, came...into...Juda, where they sent
                    messengers to

          presbeia, "ambassadors"
  I Macc. 13:14, Now...Tryphon...sent messengers unto
                    him, saying,

          presbuterion, "a council of elders"
  I Macc. 13:21, Now they that were in the tower sent
                    messengers

          theoros, "a spectator, observer, and am-
                    bassador"
  II Macc. 4:19, this ungracious Jason sent special
                    messengers from

MIDST, mesos, "middle, midway between, moderate"
  Eccl. 42:12, everybody's beauty, and sit not in the
                    midst of
          50:6, He was as the morning star in the midst
                    of a cloud,

MIGHTY, krataios, "mighty, strong, resistless"
  I Esd. 8:47, And by the mighty hand of our Lord they
                    brought unto
          8:61, we...came to Jerusalem by the mighty
                    hand of our Lord

          dunastes, "potentate, sovereign, prince"
  Eccl. 4:27, underling...neither accept the person
                    of the mighty

          dokimasia, "proving, examination"
  Eccl. 6:21, She will lie upon him as a mighty stone
                    of trial

          dunastes
  Eccl. 7:6, at any time thou fear the person of the
                    mighty
          8:1, Strive not with a mighty man, lest thou
                    fall into his
          11:6, Many mighty men have been greatly

                          94

disgraced; and the

dunesteia, "power, lordship, sovereignty"
Eccl. 15:18, the wisdom of the Lord is great, and
he is mighty in

dunastēs
Eccl. 16:11, he is mighty to forgive and to pour
out displeasure

dunesteia
Eccl. 31:16, For the...Lord is their mighty protec-
tion and strong

dunastēs
Eccl. 41:17, and of a lie before a prince and a
mighty man;

krataios
Eccl. 46:6, and with hailstones of mighty power he
made the battle

dunastēs
Eccl. 46:16, He called upon the mighty Lord when
his enemies

dunatos, "able, powerful, having power"
Eccl. 47:5, strength in his right hand to slay the
mighty warrior
Bar. 1:9, Nabuchodonosor...carried away...the
mighty men, and the

krataios
Bar. 2:11, brought thy people out of...Egypt with a
mighty hand,

ischuros, "mighty, strong, powerful"
Epis.-Jer. 1:36, neither deliver the weak from the
mighty
I Macc. 1:4, And he gathered a mighty strong host,
and ruled over
2:42, a company of Assideans, who were
mighty men of
2:66, As for Judas Maccabeus, he hath been
mighty and
3:15, made him ready to go up...with him a
mighty host of

dunatos
I Macc. 3:38, Then Lysias chose Ptolemee...and
Georgias, mighty men

ischuros
I Macc. 4:30, And when he saw that mighty army, he
prayed and

krataia
I Macc. 5:6, the children of Ammon, where he found
            a mighty power

ischuros
I Macc. 6:41, the noise...for the army was very
             great and mighty

dunatos
I Macc. 8:1, heard of the fame of the Romans, that
            they were mighty
        9:11, in the foreward were all mighty men

dunastes
II Macc. 15:3, wretch demanded, if there were a
              mighty one in
         15:4, There is in heaven a living Lord,
              and mighty, who
         15:5, Then said the other, And I also am
              mighty upon

megalokrator, "far-ruling"
III Macc. 6:2, O King, mighty in power, most high,
              Almighty God,

MILITARY, strategos, "the leader or commander of an
                     army, a general"
IV Macc. 4:2, Whence coming to Apollonius, the mili-
             tary governor

MILK, gala, "milk"
Eccl. 39:26, for the whole use of man's life are
             water...milk, and
      46:8, bring them...unto the land that floweth
           with milk and
Bar. 1:20, to give us a land that floweth with milk
          and honey
III Macc. 5:49, their breasts, which drew what seem-
               ed...last milk

galaktopotes, "a milk-drinker"
IV Macc. 13:20, and having sucked the milk from the
               same

MIND, pneuma, "breath, spirit, life"
I Esd. 2:8, and all they whose mind the Lord had
            moved to go up,

dianoia, "thought, intellect, mind, intention"
I Esd. 3:19, it maketh the mind of the king and of
            the fatherless

nous, "mind"
Wisd.-Sol. 4:12, of naughtiness...doth undermine
                 the simple mind

dianoia
Wisd.-Sol. 4:15, This people...this in their minds,
                 That his grace

nous
Wisd.-Sol. 9:15, corruptible body...weighed down
                 the mind that

psuche, "the soul, mind, reason, spirit, life"
Eccl. 5:2, Follow not thine own mind and thy
           strength, to walk in
      6:32, be taught: and if thou wilt apply thy
            mind, thou

dianoia
Eccl. 6:37, Let thy mind be upon the ordinances of
            the Lord, and

psuchē
Eccl. 7:26, Hast thou a wife after thy mind? for-
            sake her not
     23:16, a hot mind is as a burning fire, it will
            never be
     27:16, loseth his credit; and shall never find
            friend to his mind

dianoia
Eccl. 29:17, and he that is of a unthankful mind
             will leave him

psuchē
Eccl. 34:29, drunken with excess maketh bitterness
             of the mind
     37:6, Forget not thy friend in thy mind, and
           be not
     37:12, But...keep the commandments of the
            Lord, whose mind
     37:14, for a man's mind is sometime not wont
            to tell him

kardia, "heart, to speak from the heart"
Eccl. 38:26, He giveth his mind to make furrows;
             and is diligent

psuchē
Eccl. 39:1, But he that giveth his mind to the law
            of the most

nous
His.-Sus. 1:9, And they perverted their own mind,
                and turned away

psuchē
I Macc. 3:31, Wherefore being greatly perplexed in
                mind, he
II Macc. 1:3, all an heart...to do his will with...
                a willing mind

dianoia
II Macc. 2:2, charged them...that they should not
                err in...minds,

psuchē
II Macc. 3:16, countenance...declared the inward
                agony of his mind
          5:11, whereupon removing out of Egypt in
                a furious mind,

kardia
II Macc. 5:21, all haste...such was the haughtiness
                of his mind

nous
III Macc. 1:25, the king strove...to divert his
                haughty mind
IV Macc. 3:17, For the temperate mind has power to
                conquer the

enthumesis, "cognition, reflection, the act of
            thought"
IV Macc. 5:13, For bear in mind, that if there be
                any power which

enthumeomai, "to ponder in one's mind, meditate"
IV Macc. 8:20, And let us bear in mind that we shall
                be dying as

nous
IV Macc. 16:13, But as one possessed with an adapt-
                able mind, and

MINES, metallon, "a mine, quarry"
I Macc. 8:3, they had done in...Spain for the win-
                ning of the mines

MINISTER, doulos, "a servant, a bond-man, slave"
I Esd. 1:3, And he spake unto the Levites, the holy
                minister of

therapeuō, "to wait on, attend, serve"
I Esd. 1:4, now therefore serve the Lord your God,

and minister

latreuō, "to work for hire, to serve, be
bound or enslaved"
I Esd. 4:54, concerning...the priests' vestments
wherein they minister

doulos
I Esd. 8:5, certain of the children of Israel...and
ministers of
8:22, that ye require no tax...of the ministers of the

didomi, "to give oneself up, devote oneself"
Tobit 1:7, I gave to the sons of Aaron, who minis-
tered at

huperetēs, "a lictor, officer, an attendant,
or servant"
Wisd.-Sol. 6:4, Because, being ministers of his
kingdom, ye have

leitourgos, "a minister or servant"
Eccl. 4:14, They that serve her shall minister to
the Holy One:
7:30, with all thy strength, and forsake not
his ministers
10:42, be released because they appertain to
the...minister

leitourgeō, "to perform public duties, to
minister as a priest"
Eccl. 45:15, Moses consecrated him...that they
should minister

MINISTRY, leitourgia, "a public service, divine service"
Wisd.-Sol. 18:21, man...bringing the shield of his
proper ministry

MIRTH, euphrosunē, "joy, gladness, rejoicing"
Bar. 2:23, I will cause to cease...the voice of
mirth, and the
I Macc. 4:59, ordained...the month Casleu, with
mirth and gladness
III Macc. 5:36, king arranged...and proclaimed an
invitation to mirth

MISAEL, Misaēl
Song-Child. 1:65, O Ananias, Azarias, and Misael,
bless ye the

I Macc. 2:59, Ananias, Azarias, and Misael, by
          delivering were
IV Macc. 16:3, the lions round Daniel, nor the
          furnace of Misael
       16:21, And the righteous Daniel...and
          Misael, were slung
       18:12, to tell you of the zealous...
          Azarias, and Misael

MISCHIEF, poneros, "causing pain, distress, sorrow,
          plight"
I Macc. 1:15, themselves to the heathen, and were
          sold to do mischief

       kakia, "badness, baseness, wickedness"
I Macc. 7:23, Now when Judas saw all the mischief
          that Alcimus
       9:61, that country, that were authors of
          that mischief,
II Macc. 4:41, Menelaus...who...was the cause of
          all the mischief
       6:3, The coming in of this mischief was
          sore and
       7:31, thou, that hast been the author of
          all mischief

MISERABLE, deilos, "miserable, cowardly, wretched,
          worthless"
Bar. 4:31, Miserable are they that afflicted thee,
          and rejoiced
       4:32, Miserable are the cities which thy child-
          ren served:
IV Macc. 16:7, fruitless givings of suck, and miser-
          able nursings

MISERY, kakos, "misery, affliction, suffering"
I Macc. 3:42, Now when Judas and his brethren saw
          that miseries

       talaiporia, "hard work, severe labor, afflic-
          tion, suffering"
II Macc. 6:9, Then might have a man seen the pre-
          sent misery

       algedon, "sense of pain, pain, grief"
IV Macc. 9:28, but he bearing with firmness this
          misery, said

MIST, homichle, "a mist, fog, cloud"
Eccl. 43:22, A present remedy of all is a mist
                        100

coming speedily:

MITHRIDATES, Mithridatēs
   I Esd. 2:11, king of the Persians...delivered them
                to Mithridates
           2:16, Artaxerxes king of the Persians
                Belemus, Mithridates

MOAB, Moab
   Judith 7:8, the chief...and all the governors of
               the people of Moab

MOAN, kopos, "trouble, uneasiness, wearisome"
   Eccl. 38:17, Weep bitterly and make great moan and
                use lamentation

        goos, "a weeping, groaning, wailing"
   III Macc. 5:49, gave way, therefore, to lamentations
                   and moans:

MOCK, gelaō, "to laugh at, sneer at"
   Tobit 2:8, But my neighbours mocked me, and said,
              This man is not

        empaigmos, "mocking, scoffing, scorn"
   Wisd.-Sol. 12:25, thou didst send a judgment to
                     mock them

        mukterizō, "to turn up the nose or sneer at"
   I Macc. 7:34, But he mocked them, and laughed at
                 them, and abused
   II Macc. 7:39, him worse than all the rest, and...
                  he was mocked

MOCKERY, empaiymos, "mocking, scoffing, scorn"
   Eccl. 27:28, Mockery and reproach are from the proud
                but

           empaigmonē, "mocking, scoffing, derision"
   II Macc. 8:17, of the city whereof they made a mock-
                  ery,

MOCKING, empaigmos, "mocking, scoffing, scorn"
   II Macc. 7:7, brought the second to make him a
                 mocking stock:
            7:10, After him was the third made a
                  mocking stock:

MODIN, Modin
   I Macc. 2:1, a priest...from Jerusalem, and dwelt in
               Modin

I Macc. 2:15, while the king's officers...came into
                the city Modin
          2:23, to sacrifice on the altar which was
                at Modin,
          2:70, him in the sepulchre of his fathers
                at Modin,
          9:19, buried him in the sepulchre...in
                Modin
         13:25, bones of Jonathan...and buried them
                in Modin
         13:30, This is the sepulchre which he made
                at Modin, and
         16:4, men of war...who rested that night at
                Modin
II Macc. 13:14, to the Creator of the world...he
                camped by Modin

MOLTEN, cheō, "to pour, melt, dissolve"
  Epis.-Jer. 1:24, for neither when they were molten
                did they feel

MOMENT, stigmē, "moment, instant, a point of time"
  II Macc. 9:11, being plagued...his pain increasing
                every moment

MONEY, argurios, "silver, anything made of silver,
                money"
  Tobit 4:1, In that day Tobit remembered the money
             which he had
        5:2, but how I receive the money, seeing I
             know him not?
        9:2, take with thee a servant...and bring me
             the money, and
       10:2, detained...there is no man to give me the
             money?
       10:11, and gave him Sara his wife, and...ser-
              vants...and money
       12:3, for he hath brought me...the money, and
             likewise healed

       chrēma, "goods, money"
  Eccl. 14:3, and what should an envious man do with
              money?
        21:8, He that buildeth his house with other
              men's money is
        29:5, and for his neighbour's money he will
              speak
        29:6, if not, he hath deprived him of his
              money, and he hath

arǵurios
Eccl. 29:10, Lose thy money for thy brother and thy
            friend, and
      51:25, and said, Buy her for yourselves with-
            out money
      51:28, Get learning with a great sum of money,
            and get much
Bar. 1:6, They made also a collection of money ac-
          cording to every
     1:10, And they said, Behold we have sent you
          money to buy

   chalkos, "brass or copper, anything made of
           brass or metal"
Epis.-Jer. 1:35, like manner, they can neither give
                riches or money

   arǵurios
I Macc. 3:29, Nevertheless, when they saw that the
            money of his
       3:31, being greatly perplexed in mind, he
            ...gather...money
       8:26, they give any thing unto them...or
            aid them with...money
       8:28, victuals be given to them...or weapons,
            or money,
      13:15, Jonathan thy brother in hold, it is
            for money that he
      13:17, Hereupon Simon...sent he the money
            and the children,
      13:18, Because I sent him not the money and
            the children,

   nomisma, "the current coin of a state"
I Macc. 15:6, I give thee leave also to coin money
             for thy

   chrēma
II Macc. 1:14, For Antiochus...would...receive
             money in name of a
        3:6, the treasury in Jerusalem was full
            of...money,
        3:7, to the king, and had shewed him...the
            money whereof
        4:1, speak afore, having been a betrayer
            of the money,
       4:23, Jason sent Menelaus...to bear the
            money unto the
       4:27, but as far as the money that he had
            promised...he

II Macc. 4:45, promised Ptolemee...to give him much
        money,

  phoros, "that which is brought in, tribute,
        paid by foreigners"
II Macc. 8:10, So Nicanor undertook to make much
        money of the

  argurios
II Macc. 8:20, were persuaded for money through
        certain

  prosodos, "income, rent, esp. the public re-
        venue"
III Macc. 3:16, So, having bestowed considerable
        sums of money

  chrema
IV Macc. 3:20, Nicanor, the king of Asia assigned
        them money for
        4:6, of the king that he should take the
        private money,

MONSTER, kētos, "any sea-monster or huge fish"
III Macc. 6:8, pining away in the belly of the sea-
        bred monster,

MONTH, mēn, "a month"
I Esd. 1:1, passover...the fourteenth day of the
        first month;
        1:35, reigned in Judea and in Jerusalem three
        months: and
        1:44, and reigned but three months and ten
        days in
        5:47, But when the seventh month was at hand
        ...the children
        5:57, of God in the first day of the second
        month,
        7:5, in the three and twentieth day of the
        month Adar,
        7:10, passover, the fourteenth day of the
        first month,
        8:61, Thereas we departed the twelfth day of
        the first month
        9:5, at Jerusalem the twentieth day of the
        ninth month
        9:16, and in the first day of the tenth
        month they sat
        9:17, to an end in the first day of the first
        month
        9:40, the law...in the first day of the

                    seventh month
Judith 2:1, And in the eighteenth year...of the
            first month, there
       3:10, and Scythopolis, and...tarried a whole
             month,
       8:4, Judith was widow in her house three
            years and four months
       16:20, in Jerusalem...for the space of three
              months,

     chronos, "time, period, season, space of time"
Wisd.-Sol. 7:2, fashioned to be flesh in the time
                of three months

     mēn
Eccl. 43:8, The month is called after her name, in-
            creasingly
Bar. 1:2, the fifth year, and in the seventh day of
          the month
I Macc. 1:58, by their authority unto the Israelites
              every month,
        1:59, Now the five and twentieth day of the
              month, they
        4:52, on the five and twentieth day of the
              ninth month,
        7:43, So the thirteenth day of the month
              Adar the hosts
        9:3, Also the first month of the hundredth
             fifty and
        10:21, So in the seventh month of the hun-
               dred and sixtieth
        13:51, it the three and twentieth day of the
               second month,
        16:14, Now Simon...came down himself...in
               the eleventh month
II Macc. 1:9, And now see that ye keep the feast...
              in the month
         6:7, And in the day of the king's birth
              every month they
         7:27, have pity upon me that bare thee
               nine months in my
         15:36, ordained all...the thirteenth day of
                the...month,

MOON, _noumenia_, "the new moon, the time of the moon"
   I Esd. 1:52, and after that...the sacrifice...of
                the new moons, and
   Judith 8:6, and the sabbaths, and the eyes of the
               new moons,

     selēnē, "moon"
Eccl. 27:11, always with wisdom: but a fool changeth

as the moon

dichomenos, "in the middle of the month, at of
the full moon"
Eccl. 39:12, for I am filled as the moon at the full

selēnē
Eccl. 43:6, He made the moon also to serve in her
season for a
43:7, From the moon is the sign of feasts,
a light that
50:6, in the midst of a cloud, and as the
moon at the full:
Epis.-Jer. 1:60, For sun, moon, and stars, being
bright, and sent
1:67, shine as the sun...nor give light
as the moon
Song-Child. 1:39, O ye sun and moon, bless ye the
Lord: praise

MORNING, prōios, "early, early day, at morn"
I Esd. 1:11, dignities of the fathers...did they in
the morning

eōthinos, "in the morning, early"
Judith 12:5, arose when it was toward the morning
watch

orthros, "the dawn, the morning"
Judith 14:2, And as soon as the morning shall appear, and the sun
14:11, And as soon as the morning arose,
they hanged the

orthrinos, "of or belonging to the morning,
morning"
Wisd.-Sol. 11:22, world before thee is...as a drop
of the morning

prōios
Eccl. 18:26, From the morning till the evening the
time is

orthros
Eccl. 24:32, I will yet make doctrine to shine as
the morning,

proi, "in the morning, early"
Eccl. 47:10, feasts...that the temple might sound
from morning

eōthinos
Eccl. 50:6, He was as the morning star in the midst

106

of a cloud,

proi
Bel-Drag. 1:16, In the morning betime the king
arose, and Daniel
I Macc. 3:58, Judas said...ye be in readiness
against the morning,

eōthinos
I Macc. 5:30, And betimes in the morning they looked up, and,

prōios, "early at morn, early in the season"
I Macc. 9:13, They also of Judas' side...continued
from morning
10:80, in the host, and cast darts...from
morning till

proi
I Macc. 12:29, Jonathan and his company knew it not
till...morning
16:5, And whereas they rose in the morning,
and went into

orthrios, "at day-break, in the morning"
III Macc. 5:23, The morning cock had just crowed,
and Hermon,

MORTAL, thnētos, "mortal, obnoxious death"
Wisd.-Sol. 7:1, I myself also am a mortal man, like
to all and
15:17, For being mortal, he worketh a
dead thing with
II Macc. 9:12, subject to God, and that a man that
is mortal

MOSES, Mōusē
I Esd. 1:11, dignities...as it is written in the
book of Moses:
5:49, sacrifices...as it is...commanded in
book of Moses
7:6, added unto them...according to the...
book of Moses
7:9, Levites stood array...according to the
book of Moses
8:3, as a scribe, being very ready in the
law of Moses,
9:39, Esdras the reader, that he would bring
the law of Moses,
Tobit 6:12, her to another according to the law of
Moses
7:12, Behold take her after the law of Moses

Eccl. 24:23, are the book of...the law which Moses
                commanded for
      45:1, even Moses, beloved of God and men,
                whose memorial is
      45:15, Moses consecrated him, and anointed
                him with holy
      46:1, valiant...and was the successor of Moses
                in prophecies
      46:7, In the time of Moses he did a work of
                mercy, he and
Bar. 1:20, which the Lord appointed by Moses his
                servant
      2:2, to the things that were...in the law of
                Moses;
      2:28, as thou spakest by thy servant Moses in
                the day when
His.-Sus. 1:3, their daughter according to the law
                of Moses
        1:62, and according to the law of Moses
                they did unto
II Macc. 1:29, thy people again in thy holy place,
                as Moses hath
      2:4, also contained in the same writing...
                where Moses
      2:8, them these things...as it was shewed
                unto Moses,
      2:10, And as when Moses prayed unto the
                Lord, the fire
      2:11, And Moses said, Because the sin
                offering was not
      7:6, The Lord looketh upon us...as Moses
                in his song
      7:30, commandment of the law that was given
                unto...Moses

    Mōusē
IV Macc. 2:17, Thus Moses, when angered against
                Dathan and Abiram
      17:19, For Moses saith, And all the saints
                are under thy
      18:18, For he did not forget the song which
                Moses taught,

MOST HIGH, hupsistos, "highest, the Most High"
   Eccl. 32:6, The offering of the righteous...is be-
                fore the most High
      32:10, Give unto the most High according as
                he hath

Eccl. 32:17, and will not depart until the most
           High shall behold
    36:15, So look upon the works of the most
           High; and there
    37:15, And above all this pray to the most
           High, that he
    38:2, For of the most High cometh healing,
           and he shall
    39:1, giveth his mind to the law of the most
           High...will
    39:5, He will give his heart to...the most
           High, and will
    41:4, why art thou against the pleasure of
           the most High?
    41:8, which have forsaken the law of the most
           High...?
    42:2, of the law of the most High, and his
           covenant; and of
    43:2, it appeareth, declaring...the work of
           the most High:
    43:12, with...and the hands of the most High
           have bended it
    44:20, who kept the law of the most High, and
           was in
    46:5, He called upon the most high Lord, when
           the enemies
    47:5, for he called upon the most high Lord;
           and he gave
    48:5, raise up a dead man, by the word of the
           most High:
    49:4, for they forsook the law of the most
           High, even the
    50:7, and the sun shining upon the temple of
           the most High,
    50:14, he might adorn the offering of the
           most high Almighty
    50:16, and made a great noise...before the
           most High
    50:17, worship...their Lord God Almighty, the
           most High
    50:19, And the people besought the Lord, the
           most High, by
    50:21, they bowed themselves down to worship
           ...the most High
Pr.-Mans. 1:7, for thou art the Lord most high,
           compassionate,

MOTHER, mētēr, "a mother, a parent, city"
  Tobit 1:8, I gave unto them...as Debora my father's

                              mother had
Tobit 4:3, when I am dead, bury me: and despise not
                thy mother,
      4:13, for lewdness is the mother of famine
      5:17, But Anna his mother wept, and said to
                Tobit, Why hast
      10:8, Let me go, for my father and my mother
                look no more to
      11:17, hath brought thee unto us, and blessed
                ...thy...mother
      14:10, And bury me decently, and thy mother
                with me;
Judith 8:26, when he kept the sheep of...his mother's
                brother
Wisd.-Sol. 7:2, and in my mother's womb was fashion-
                ed to be flesh
      7:12, and I knew not that she was the
                mother of them
Eccl. 3:2, the Lord...hath confirmed the authority
                of the mother
      3:4, and he that honoureth his mother is as
                one that layeth
      3:6, obedient unto the Lord shall be a comfort
                to...mother
      3:8, Honour thy father and mother both in word
                and deed,
      3:9, but the curse of the mother rooteth out
                foundations
      3:11, and a mother in dishonour is a reproach
                to the
      3:16, and he that angereth his mother is cur-
                sed of God
      4:10, fatherless, and instead of a husband
                unto...mother
      7:27, with thy whole heart, and forget not...
                thy mother
      15:2, and as a mother shall she meet him, and
                receive him as
      23:14, Remember thy father and thy mother when
                thou sittest
      40:1, the day they go out of their mother's
                womb
      41:17, Be ashamed of a whoredom before father
                and mother:
      49:7, who was a prophet, sanctified in his
                mother's womb,

goneis, "the parents"
His.-Sus. 1:30, So she came with her father and
                mother...and all

meter
I Macc. 13:28, he set up seven pyramids, one against
                another, for his father and his
                mother,
II Macc. 7:1, that seven brethren with their mother
               were taken,
          7:4, the utmost parts of the body...his
               mother looking on
          7:5, dispersed, they exhorted one another
               with the mother
          7:20, But the mother was marvellous above
                all, and
          7:25, But...the king called his mother,
                and exhorted her
          7:41, Last of all the sons and the mother
                died
III Macc. 1:20, New born babes were deserted by
                 their mothers or
IV Macc. 1:8, prove it with...seven brethren, and
               their mother
          1:10, commend those men who died with their
                mother
          8:2, seven brethren were brought...with
               their...mother
          8:3, Whom, when the tyrant beheld, encir-
               cling their mother, handsome, and
          8:19, compassion upon our age...the years
                of...mother
          10:2, But he cried out and said...and the
                same mother bare
          12:6, having thus exhorted him, he sent for
                the mother of
          12:7, And he, after his mother had urged
                him on in the

metroos, "of or belonging to a mother"
IV Macc. 13:18, and has engendered through the
                 mother's womb

meter
IV Macc. 14:12, For the mother of these seven youths
                 endured the
          14:20, with her children did not turn aside
                 the mother
          15:1, sons...and religion more desirable
                to a mother

111

IV Macc. 15:2, The mother, when two things were set
                before her,
        15:4,   especially through the greater sym-
                pathy of mothers
        15:5,   for by how much mothers are by na-
                ture weak in
        15:6,   And of all mothers the mother of the
                seven was the

    philimēter, "loving one's mother"
IV Macc. 15:10, they were both just...and so fond
                of their mother

    mētēr
IV Macc. 15:11, And yet...with love of children to
                draw...a mother
        15:14, and roasting of each one...the ob-
                servant mother
        15:16, O thou mother, who wast tried at
                this time with
        15:21, O voices of children, calling upon
                your mother in
        15:22, and what manner of torments was the
                mother
        15:24, the destruction of seven children,
                the...mother
        15:29, O mother of a nation, avenger of the
                law, and
        16:1,   woman, and that an aged one, and the
                mother of
        16:4,   But with the reasoning of religion
                the mother
        16:6,   having born seven sons, have become
                the mother of
        16:11, as this the holy and God-fearing
                mother bewailed

    heptamētōr, "mother of seven"
IV Macc. 16:24, With these arguments, the mother of
                seven,

    mētēr
IV Macc. 17:2, O thou mother...who together with
                seven children
        17:4,   Be of good cheer, therefore, O holy-
                minded mother!
        17:7,   would not shudder at beholding the
                mother of seven
        17:13, and the mother of the seven child-
                ren entered the
        18:7,   And the righteous mother of the seven

                        children
    IV Macc. 18:23, But the children of Abraham, with
                    their...mother,

MOUNT, MOUNTAIN, óros, "mountain, hill"
    I Esd. 4:4, against the enemies, they go, and break
                ...mountains,
    Tobit 1:21, and they fled into the mountains of
                Ararath;
    Judith 1:15, He took also Arphaxad in the mountains
                 of Ragau, and
          5:14, and brought them to mount Sina, and
                Cades-Barne, and
          6:4, tread them under foot, and their moun-
               tains shall be
          7:4, for neither the high mountains, nor the
               valleys, nor
          7:10, of Israel...trust...in the height of
                the mountains
          7:12, which issueth forth of the foot of
                the mountain:
          7:13, Bethulia...shall go up to the tops of
                the mountains
          10:10, after her, until she was gone down the
                 mountain,
          11:2, if thy people that dwelleth in the
                mountains had not
          13:10, passed the camp, they...went up the
                 mountain of
          14:11, by bands unto the straits of the moun-
                 tain
          15:3, They also that had camped in the moun-
                tains round
          15:7, that were in the mountains and in the
                plain, gat many
          16:4, Assur came out of the mountains from
                the north, he
          16:15, For the mountains shall move from their
                 foundations
    Eccl. 16:19, The mountains also and foundations of
                 the earth
          24:13, was exalted like...a cypress tree upon
                 the mountains
          43:4, a furnace is in...heat, but the sun
                burneth...mountains
          43:16, At his sight the mountains are shaken,
          43:21, It devoureth the mountains, and burn-
                 eth the

Eccl. 50:26, they that sit upon the mountains of
    Samaria and they
Epis.-Jer. 1:39, like the stones that be hewn out
     of the mountain
Song-Child. 1:52, O ye mountains and little hills,
     bless ye the
I Macc. 2:28, So he and his sons fled into the
    mountains, and
   4:5, no man there, he sought them in the
    mountains:
   4:18, Georgias and his host are here by us
    in the mountain
   4:19, there appeared a part of them...in
    the mountain:
   4:38, desolate...as in a forest, or in one
    ...mountains
   4:46, and laid up the stones in the moun-
    tain of the
   4:60, At that time they builded mount Sion
    with high
   6:39, Now when the sun shone upon the...
    mountains...and
   6:40, the king's army being spread upon the
    ...mountains,
   6:48, and...pitched...against Judea, and
    against mount Sion
   6:62, Then the king entered into mount Sion:
    but when he
   7:33, After this went Nicanor up to mount
    Sion, and there
   9:15, and pursued them unto the mount Azotus
   9:38, went up themselves under the covert
    of....mountains
  10:11, the workmen to build and walls and
    the mount Sion
  10:70, thou vaunt thy power against us in the
    mountain?
  11:37, and set upon the holy mount in a...
    place
  11:68, laid men in ambush for him in the
    mountains,
II Macc. 2:4, same writing...as he went forth into
    the mountain,
   5:27, withdrew himself...and lived in...
    mountains
   9:8, weigh the high mountains in a balance,
   9:28, died a miserable death...in the
    mountains

II Macc. 10:6, whereas they wandered in the moun-
          tains and dens

MOURN, __pentheō__, "to lament, be sad, mourn"
I Esd. 1:32, And in all Jewry they mourned for
          Josias, yea,
     48:24, he...comforted them that mourned in
          Sion
I Macc. 2:39, his friends understood thereof, they
          mourned for

MOURNING, __penthos__, "mourning, sorrow, grief"
Wisd.-Sol. 19:3, For whilst they were yet mourning
          ...they added
Eccl. 22:6, A tale out of season (is as) music in
          mourning:
     41:11, The mourning of men is about their
          bodies:
Bar. 4:9, God hath brought upon me great mourning;
     4:11, but sent them away with weeping and
          mourning
     4:23, For I sent you out with mourning and
          weeping: but God
     4:34, rejoicing...and her pride shall be turn-
          ed in mourning
     5:1, Put off, O Jerusalem, the garment of thy
          mourning and
I Macc. 1:25, Therefore there was great mourning
          in Israel in
     1:39, laid waste...her feasts were turned
          into mourning
     1:40, glory...her excellency was turned
          into mourning
     9:41, Thus was the marriage turned into
          mourning, and the

MOUTH, __stoma__, "mouth"
I Esd. 1:28, words...of Jeremy spoken by the mouth
          of the Lord
     1:57, word of the Lord spoken by the mouth
          of Jeremy;
     2:1, that he had promised by the mouth of
          Jeremy:
     4:19, letting those things go...and even
          with open mouth
     4:31, the king gaped and gazed upon her,
          with open mouth:
     4:46, that thou make good the vow...with
          thine own mouth

Judith 2:2, communicated with them...his secret...
out of his...mouth
    2:3, that did not obey the commandment of
his mouth
    5:5, Let my lord now hear a word from the
mouth of thy
    8:21, shall require the profanation thereof
at our mouth
  11:19, dog shall not so much as open his mouth
at thee:
Wisd.-Sol. 1:11, and the mouth that belieth slayeth
the soul
    8:12, they shall lay their hands upon
their mouth
  10:21, For wisdom opened the mouth of
the dumb, and
Eccl. 13:24, Riches are good...and poverty is evil
in the mouth
  14:1, is the man that hath not slipped with
his mouth, and
  15:5, of the congregation shall she open his
mouth
  20:15, upbraideth much; he openeth his mouth
like a crier;
  20:20, be rejected when it cometh out of a
fool's mouth
  20:24, yet it is continually in the mouth of
the untaught
  20:29, blind the eyes of the wise, and stop
his mouth
  21:5, A prayer out of a poor man's mouth
reacheth to the
  21:17, They enquire at the mouth of the wise
man in the
  21:26, The heart of fools is in their mouth:
but the mouth
  22:22, If thou hast opened thy mouth against
thy friend,
  23:7, Hear, O ye children, the discipline
of the mouth:
  23:9, Accustom not thy mouth to swearing;
neither use
  23:13, Use not thy mouth to intemperate
swearing, for
  24:2, of the most High shall she open her
mouth, and
  24:3, I came out of the mouth of the most
High, and covered

Eccl. 26:12, She will open her mouth, as a thirsty
              travellor when
      27:23, sweetly...but at the last he will
              writhe his mouth,
      28:12, If thou blow the spark, it shall burn
              ...thy mouth
      28:25, balance, and make a door and bar for
              thy mouth
      29:24, thou art a stranger, thou darest not
              open thy mouth
      30:18, and wisdom is perfection to a faithful
              mouth
      37:22, fruits of understanding are commend-
              able in his mouth
      39:5, He will...open his mouth in prayer,
              and make
      39:17, stood as an heap, and at the words of
              his mouth,
      39:35, praise ye the Lord with the whole
              heart and mouth,
      40:30, Begging is sweet in the mouth of the
              shameless: but
      51:25, I opened my mouth, and said, Buy her
              for yourselves
I Macc. 2:60, for his innocency was delivered from
              the mouth of
        9:55, for his mouth was stopped, and he was
              taken with a
III Macc. 2:20, broken hearted may praise thee with
              their mouth
          4:16, His erring heart far from the truth,
              and his profane mouth, gave glory
IV Macc. 5:36, Mouth! Thou shalt not pollute my
              old age, nor the

MULE, hemionos, "a half-ass, a mule"
  Judith 15:11, and she took it, and laid it on her
              mule; and made

MULTIFORM, polutropos, "manifold, turning many ways"
  IV Macc. 1:25, there exists in pleasure...the most
              multiform of

MULTITUDE, plēthos, "a great number, a throng, a
                      crowd"
  Judith 5:3, Tell me now...what is the multitude of
              their army...?
        5:10, down into Egypt...and became there a
              great multitude

117

laos, "the people, the soldiery, host, army,
      common men"
Judith 6:6, shall the sword of mine army, and the
      multitude of

plēthos
Judith 7:4, children of Israel, when they saw the
      multitude of
      9:11, For thy power standeth not in multi-
            tude, nor thy
      16:4, came out of the mountains...with...the
            multitude, whereof

ochlos, "a throng of people, a mob, a multi-
        tude"
Judith 8:10, sake I shall have estimation among the
      multitude,

plēthos
Judith 8:15, I shall be found among the multitude,
      and valiant in
      11:15, thou didst send a multitude of...
            beasts upon them
      11:17, wanted not means to send among them a
            multitude of
      14:20, And so the multitude, allured by the
            grace of the
      18:5, thou tookest away the multitude of their
            children,
      19:10, and how the river cast up a multitude
            of frogs
Eccl. 6:34, Stand in the multitude of the elders,
            and cleave unto
      7:7, Offend not against the multitude of a
            city, and then
      7:9, Say not, God will look upon the multi-
            tude of my
      7:14, Use not many words in a multitude of
            elders, and make
      7:16, Number thyself among the multitude of
            sinners, but
      16:1, Desire not a multitude of unprofitable
            children,
      16:3, thou in their life, neither respect their
            multitude:
      26:5, the gathering together of an unruly mul-
            titude, and a
      32:18, till he have taken away the multitude
            of the proud,

Eccl. 42:11, lest she make thee...ashamed before
        the multitude
    51:3, and hast delivered me, according to the
        multitude of

    poluochlos, "a great number of people, a large
        crowd"
Epis.-Jer. 1:5, in no wise...see the multitude be-
        fore them and

    plēthos
Song-Child. 1:18, and according to the multitude of
        thy mercies

    ochlos
I Macc. 1:17, Wherefore he entered into Egypt with
        a....multitude,
    1:20, Antiochus...went up against Israel...
        with a....multitude
    1:29, came to Jerusalem with a great multi-
        tude

    athroisis, "a gathering"
I Macc. 3:13, say that Judas had gathered unto him
        a multitude

    plēthos
I Macc. 3:17, we be able...to fight against so
        great a multitude...?
    4:8, Fear ye not their multitude, neither
        be ye afraid of
    6:41, all that heard the noise of their mul-
        titude, and
    9:6, who seeing the multitude of the other
        army to be so
    15:3, old estate, and...gathered a multitude
        of foreign
II Macc. 2:21, but a few, they overcame the whole
        ...multitudes,
    3:6, and told him...that the multitude of
        their riches
    3:21, a man to see the falling down of the
        multitude
    5:3, and troops of horsemen in array...and
        multitude of
    5:26, And he...slew great multitudes
    8:16, them not to...fear the great multi-
        tude
    9:2, whereupon the multitude running to
        defend themselves

sunathroisis, "an assembly, a gathering together"
II Macc. 10:24, Now Timotheus...had gathered a
great multitude of

plēthos
II Macc. 12:27, And he had put to flight...a great
multitude of
13:10, he commanded the multitude to call
upon the Lord

ŏchlos
II Macc. 14:43, the multitude also rushing within
the doors,

plēthos
II Macc. 15:21, Maccabeus seeing the coming of the
multitude, and
III Macc. 1:24, During this time the multitude kept
on praying
2:7, he made pursuit with chariots, and
with multitude
4:5, A multitude of aged hoary-headed
men, were driven
4:17, brought word to the king that the
multitude of
Pr.-Mans. 1:7, and in the multitude of thy kindness
thou hast
1:9, transgressions are multiplied...for
the multitude

MURMURING, goggusmos, "muttering"
Wisd.-Sol. 1:10, and the noise of murmurings is not
hid
1:11, Therefore beware of murmuring,
which is
Eccl. 46:7, he did a work of mercy...and appeased
the wicked murmuring

MUSIC, mousikos, "music, song, a muse"
Eccl. 22:6, A tale out of season (is as) music in
mourning:
35:3, Speak thou, that art the elder...and
hinder not music
35:5, A concert of music in a banquet of wine
is as a
35:6, As a signet of an emerald...so is the
melody of music
40:20, Wine and music rejoice the heart: but
the love of

Eccl. 49:1, it is sweet as honey in all mouths,
          and as music at a
I Macc. 9:39, meet them with...instruments of music,
          and many

MUSICAL, mousikos, "music, a singer"
  Eccl. 44:5, such as found out musical tunes, and
          recited verses

MYRRH, smurna, "myrrh, the resinous gum of an Arabian
          tree, used for embalming the dead"
  Eccl. 24:15, and I yielded a pleasant odour like
          the best myrrh

NABATHITES, Nabataioi
  I Macc. 9:25, where they met with the Nabathites,
          who came unto
          9:35, to pray his friends the Nabathites,
          that they

NABUCHODONOSOR, Nabouchodonosor
  I Esd. 1:40, Wherefore against him Nabuchodonosor
          ...came up and
          1:41, Nabuchodonosor also took of the holy
          vessels of the
          1:45, So after a year Nabuchodonosor sent
          and caused him
          1:48, And after that Nabuchodonosor had
          ·made him to swear
          2:10, forth the holy vessels which Nabucho-
          donosor
          6:15, them over into the power of Nabuchodo-
          nosor
  Judith 1:1, the twelfth year of the reign of
          Nabuchodonosor, who
          1:5, Even in those days Nabuchodonosor made
          war with king
          1:11, made light of all the commandment of
          Nabuchodonosor
          1:12, Therefore Nabuchodonosor was very
          angry with all
          2:1, there was talk in the house of Nabucho-
          donosor king of
          2:4, And when he had ended his counsel,
          Nabuchodonosor
          2:19, all his power to go before king Nabu-
          chodonosor
          3:8, that all nations worship Nabuchodonosor
          only,

Judith 6:4, for they shall utterly perish, saith
Nabuchodonosor
11:1, hurt any that was willing to serve
Nabuchodonosor,
11:7, As Nabuchodonosor king of all the earth
liveth...who
11:23, shalt dwell in the house of...
Nabuchodonosor
12:13, which serve in the house of Nabuchodonosor
14:18, brought shame upon the house of...
Nabuchodonosor
Bar. 1:9, After that Nabuchodonosor...carried away
Jechonias, and
1:11, and pray for the life of Nabuchodonosor
king of
1:12, shall live under the shadow of Nabuchodonosor
Epis.-Jer. 1:2, shall be led away captives...by
Nabuchodonosor

NADABATHA, Nadabath
I Macc. 9:37, word to Jonathan...that...the bride
from Nadabatha

NAIL, passalos, "a peg"
Eccl. 27:2, As a nail sticketh fast between the
joinings of the

NAKED, gumos, "naked, unclad, defenceless"
Tobit 4:16, and of thy garments to them that are
naked

NAME, ŏnoma, "a name"
I Esd. 1:48, Nabuchodonosor had made them to swear
in the name of
5:4, And these are the names of the men
which went up
8:49, hundred and twenty, the catalogue of
whose names
9:16, the priest chose unto him the principal...all by name
Tobit 3:15, and that I never polluted thy name, nor
the name of
5:11, unto him, I would know, brother, thy
kindred and name
8:5, God of our fathers, blessed is thy holy
...name for ever
13:11, nations shall come from far to the name
of the Lord

122

Judith 14:7, Blessed art thou in...Juda...which
bearing thy name
16:2, him a new psalm: exalt him, and call
upon his name
Wisd.-Sol. 2:4, and our name shall be forgotten in
time, and no
10:20, Therefore the righteous...praised
thy holy name,
14:21, tyranny...ascribe unto stones...
the...name
19:18, as in a psaltery notes change the
name of the
Eccl. 6:1, for (thereby) thou shalt inherit an ill
name, shame,
6:22, For wisdom is, according to her name,
and she is not
15:6, gladness, and she shall...inherit an
everlasting name
17:9, and they shall praise his holy name,
that they may
17:14, What is heavier than lead? and what
is the name
23:10, so he that sweareth and nameth God
continually shall
37:1, there is a friend, which is only a
friend in name
39:9, his memorial shall not depart away, and
his name shall
39:11, If he die, he shall leave a greater
name than a
39:15, Magnify his name, and shew forth his
praise with the
40:19, and the building of a city continue a
man's name:
41:11, an ill name of sinners shall be blotted
out
41:12, Have regard to thy name; for that shall
continue with
41:13, A good life hath but few days: but a
good name
43:8, The mouth is called after her name, increasing
44:8, There be of them that have left a name
behind them,
44:14, Their bodies are buried in peace; but
their name
45:15, of the priesthood, and bless the people
in his name

```
Eccl. 46:1, son of Nave was valiant...who accord-
            ing to his name was
       46:12, Let their bones flourish...and let
            the name of them
       47:10, their feasts...that they might praise
            his holy name,
       47:13, for God made...him...build an house
            in his name
       47:16, Thy name went far unto the islands;
            and for thy peace
       47:18, By the name of the Lord God, which is
            called the Lord
       50:20, blessing of the Lord...and to rejoice
            in his name
       51:1, I will thank thee...and give praise
            unto thy name:
       51:3, delivered me, according to the...great-
            ness of thy name
       51:11, I will praise thy name continually,
            and will sing
       51:12, and I give thanks...and bless thy name,
            O Lord
Bar. 2:11, O Lord God of Israel...hast gotten thy-
            self a name,
       2:15, Israel and his posterity is called by
            thy name
       2:26, And the house which is called by thy
            name hast thou
       2:32, and they shall praise me...and think
            upon my name
       3:5, but think upon thy power and thy name
            now at this time
       3:7, put thy fear...that we should call upon
            thy name,
       4:30, for he that gave thee that name will
            comfort thee
       5:4, For thy name shall be called of God for
            ever, The peace
Song-Child. 1:2, thy name is worthy to be praised
            and glorified
       1:10, Yet deliver us not up wholly, for
            thy name's
       1:19, to thy...works, and give glory
            to thy name,
       1:29, And blessed is thy glorious and
            holy name:
His.-Sus. 1:2, and he took a wife, whose name was
            Susanna, the
```

His.-Sus. 1:45, the Lord raised up...a youth, whose
                name was
I Macc. 2:51, shall ye receive great honour and an
              everlasting name
        3:14, he said, I will get me a name and
              honour in the
        4:33, let all those that know thy name
              praise thee with
        5:57, Wherefore they said, Let us also get
              us a name, and
        5:63, were greatly renowned...wheresoever
              their name was
        6:17, know that the king was dead...and his
              name he called
        6:44, himself in jeopardy...and get him a
              perpetual name
        7:37, Thou, O Lord, didst choose this house
              to be called by thy name,
        8:12, insomuch as all that heard of their
              name
       14:10, He provided victuals...so that his
              honourable name
       14:43, and that all...writings...be made in
              his name
II Macc. 8:4, infants, and the blasphemies...against
              his name
       12:13, and the name of it was Caspis
III Macc. 2:9, thou didst make this place sacred to
               thy name,
         2:14, consecrated out of the earth to the
               name of thy
         4:14, Every individual was to be speci-
               fied by name;
Pr.-Mans. 1:3, abyss and sealed it with thy...
               glorious name

NANEA, Nanaias
II Macc. 1:13, the temple of Nanea by the deceit of
               Nanea's
         1:15, Which when the priests of Nanea had
               set forth, and

NAPHTHAR, Nephthar
II Macc. 1:36, And Neemias called this thing Naph-
               thar, which is

NASOR, Nasōr
I Macc. 11:67, the morning they gat them to the
               plain of Nasor

NATHAN, Nathan
  Eccl. 47:1, And after him rose up Nathan to pro-
            phesy in the time

NATHANIEL, Nathanaēl
  I Esd. 1:9, And Jeconias, and Samaias, and Nathan-
            iel his brother,

NATION, éthnos, "a nation, people, a company, body
            of men"
  I Esd. 1:49, governors...passed all the pollutions
             of all nations,
         5:50, were gathered unto them out of the
             other nations of
         8:69, The nation of Israel, the princes,
             the priests, and

       genos, "descendant, a race, a nation"
  Tobit 1:17, and if I saw any of my nation dead, or
            cast about the
        2:3, again, and said, Father, one of our
            nation is

       éthnos
  Tobit 3:4, delivered us...for a reproach to all the
            nations
        4:19, for every nation hath not counsel, but
            the Lord
        13:5, scourge us...and will gather us out of
            all nations,
        13:11, Many nations shall come from far to
            the name of the
        14:6, And all nations shall turn, and fear the
            Lord God
  Judith 1:8, and to those among the nations that
            were of Carmel,
         3:8, he did cast down their frontiers...that
            all nations

       genos
  Judith 5:10, Egypt...so that one could not number
            their nation

       éthnos
  Judith 5:21, But if there be no iniquity in their
            nation, let my

       demos, "the common people, country-district"
  Judith 6:1, said unto Achior and all...the company
            of other nations

       genos
  Judith 6:5, face no more...until I take vengeance of

this nation

Judith 6:19, Lord God of heaven...pity the low estate of our nation

8:20, he will not despise us, nor any of our nation.

8:32, I will do a thing...to the children of any nation

éthnos

Judith 9:14, And make every nation and tribe to acknowledge that

genos

Judith 11:10, for our nation shall not be punished, neither can

éthnos

Judith 12:3, for there be none with us of thy nation

laos, "the people, the soldiery, host, army"

Judith 13:20, because thou hast not spared...our nation

éthnos

Judith 14:7, thou in all the tabernacle of Juda, and in...nations,

genos

Judith 15:9, thou art the great rejoicing of our nation:

éthnos

Judith 16:17, Woe to the nations that rise up against my kindred!

Wisd.-Sol. 3:8, They shall judge the nations, and have dominion

6:2, ye that rule the people, and glory in the...nation

8:14, I shall set the people in order, and the nations

10:5, Moreover the nations in their wicked conspiracy

10:15, people, and blameless seed from the nation

12:12, or who shall accuse thee for the nations that

17:2, unrighteous men thought to oppress the...nation;

I Macc. 2:18, commandment, like as all other nations have

2:19, Though all the nations that are under the king's

I Macc. 3:25, brethren...to fall upon the nations
          round about
      3:58, yourselves...that ye may fight with
          these nations,
      5:1, Now when the nations round about
          heard that the altar

   laos
I Macc. 6:24, for which cause they of our nation
          besiege the

   ethnos
I Macc. 6:58, therefore, let us be friends...with
          all their nation
      10:20, ordain thee to be the high priest of
          thy nation,
      11:30, unto his brother Jonathan, and unto
          the nation of
      11:42, I will greatly honour thee and thy
          nation,
      12:6, the high priest, and the elders of
          the nation, and
      13:6, Doubtless I will avenge my nation,
          and the
      13:36, unto Simon...and...unto the elders
          and nation of the
      14:4, for he sought the good of his nation
          in such wise,
      14:6, and enlarged the bounds of his nation,
          and
      14:28, congregation of the priests...and
          rulers of...nation,
      14:29, Jarib...resisting the enemies of their
          nation
      14:30, (For after Jonathan, having gathered
          his nations...)
      14:32, time Simon rose up, and fought for
          his nation, and
      14:35, what glory he thought to bring his
          nation,
      15:2, the high priest and prince of his
          nation,
      15:9, obtained our kingdom, we will honour
          ...thy nation,
      16:3, be ye instead of me...go and fight
          for our nation,
II Macc. 4:2, him a traitor...and tendered his own
          nation,
       4:35, cause, not only the Jews, but many
          ...other nations,

homoethnēs, "the same nation"
II Macc. 5:6, his own citizens...not considering
...his own nation

genos
II Macc. 5:22, And he left governors to vex the
nation: at
6:12, discouraged...for a chastening of
our nation

ethnos
II Macc. 6:14, For not as with other nations, whom
the Lord
6:31, death for an example...unto all his
nation

genos
II Macc. 7:16, yet think not that our nation is
forsaken of God

ethnos
II Macc. 7:37, God that he...be merciful unto our
nation;

genos
II Macc. 7:38, wrath of the almighty...is...upon
all our nation

ethnos
II Macc. 8:9, he sent him...twenty thousand of all
nations under
10:4, they might not be delivered unto...
barbarous nations
10:8, those days should be kept of the whole
nation of the
11:25, Wherefore our mind is, that this
nation shall be
11:27, And the letter of the king unto the
nation of the
13:11, the people...to be in subjection to
the...nations

genos
II Macc. 14:8, for all our nation is in no small
misery through
14:9, O king...be careful for our country,
and our nation

ethnos
II Macc. 14:34, him that was over a defender of
their nation
III Macc. 1:11, when they told him that...none of
the nation...in

III Macc. 3:19, us, they alone among the nations
             lift up
        6:5, him and...shew forth thy might to
             many nations
        6:15, Let it be shewn to all the nations
             that thou art
IV Macc. 1:11, means of the destruction...against
             their nation,
        4:7, And the nation, indignant at his
             proclamation, and
        4:18, he committed to him the...rulership
             over the nation
        4:24, could by no means destroy...the law
             of the nation,
        9:24, paternal Providence, becoming mer-
             ciful to...nation,
        15:29, O mother of a nation, avenger of
             the law, and
        16:16, you being called as a witness for
             the nation
        17:8, worthy thing...as a memorial to those
             of the nation
        17:10, These also avenged their nation,
             looking unto God,
        17:20, These, therefore...did not overcome
             our nation;
        17:22, they became the antipoise to the
             sin of the nation
        18:4, And the nation through them obtained
             peace...in

NATIONAL, politeia, "citizenship, the state of being
             a citizen"
  IV Macc. 8:6, receive places...if you forsake your
             national

NATIVITY, genesis, "an origin, source: birth, race,
             descent"

  Wisd.-Sol. 6:22, her out from the beginning of her
             nativity,

        tokos, "a bringing forth, birth, offspring"
  Eccl. 23:14, Be not forgetful...and curse the day
             of thy nativity

NATURAL, phusis, "native, natural frame"
  IV Macc. 16:3, were the lions...as that natural
             love of children

130

NATURE, phusis, "the nature, inborn quality, one's
                nature"
   IV Macc. 5:8, It seems senseless...to reject the
                boons of nature
           5:25, by God...the Creator...sympathises
                with our nature
           13:26, And yet, although nature and inter-
                course...increased
           15:13, O holy nature and parental feeling,
                and...unconquerable...affection

NAVE, Nauē
   Eccl. 46:1, Jesus the son of Nave was valiant in
                the wars, and

NAVY, stolos, "an equipment for warlike purposes, an
                army, fleet"
   I Macc. 1:17, Wherefore he entered into Egypt with
                ...a great navy
   II Macc. 12:9, the Jamnite also by night, and set
                fire on...navy
           14:1, entered by the haven...with great
                power and navy

NAZARITES, Nazaraioi
   I Macc. 3:49, brought also the priest's garment...
                and the Nazarites

NEBAT, Nabat
   Eccl. 47:23, There was also Jeroboam the son of
                Nebat, who caused

NECESSITY, anagkē, "by force, violence, necessity"
   IV Macc. 8:21, pardon us if we fear the king through
                necessity
           8:23, Let us not oppose necessity, nor
                seek vain-glory

NECK, trachēlos, "neck"
   I Esd. 1:48, And hardening his neck and his heart,
                he transgressed
           3:6, be clothed in purple...and a chain about
                his neck
   Tobit 11:13, and when he saw his son, he fell upon
                his neck
   Judith 13:8, And she smote twice upon his neck with
                all her
           16:9, eyes...and the fauchion passed through
                his neck
   Eccl. 6:24, and put thy feet into fetters, and thy
                neck into her

Eccl. 30:12, Bow down his neck in his youth
    30:26, A yoke and a collar do bow the neck:
         so are tortures
    51:26, Put your neck under the yoke, and let
         your soul
Bar. 4:25, shalt see destruction, and shalt tread
         upon his neck
I Macc. 1:61, And they hanged the infants about
         their necks, and

    auchē, "neck, throat"
III Macc. 4:8, instead of crowns wore halters
         round their necks;

    trachēlos
III Macc. 4:9, unyielding chains...some had their
         necks thrust
    5:49, of kin to each other hung about one
         another's neck

NEEMIAS, Neemios
Eccl. 49:13, And among the elect was Neemias, whose
         renown is
II Macc. 1:18, Therefore whereas...Neemias offered
         sacrifice,
    1:20, after many years, when it pleased
         God, Neemias
    1:21, and when the sacrifices were laid
         on, Neemias
    1:31, Now when the sacrifice was consumed,
         Neemias
    1:33, So when this matter was known...
         Neemias had
    1:36, And Neemias called this thing Naph-
         thar which is
    2:13, things also were reported in the
         writings...Neemias

NEIGHBOUR, plēsion, "one's neighbour, near, hard by"
Tobit 2:8, But my neighbours mocked me, and said,
         This man is not
    7:4, multitude...and said every one to his
         neighbour,
    10:19, because of her, and every one said to
         his neighbour,
    15:2, there was no man...in the sight of his
         neighbour,
Eccl. 6:17, feareth the Lord...for as he is, so
         shall his neighbour
    9:14, As near as thou canst, guess at thy
         neighbour, and

Eccl. 10:6, Bear not hatred to thy neighbour for
       every wrong;
  17:14, gave every man commandment concerning
       his neighbour
  18:13, The mercy of a man is toward his neigh-
       bour: but the
  19:17, Admonish thy neighbour before thou
       threaten him; and
  22:23, Be faithful to thy neighbour in his
       poverty, that
  25:1, the unity of brethren, the love of
       neighbours, a man
  25:18, Her husband shall sit among his neigh-
       bours; and when
  27:18, so hast thou lost the love of thy
       neighbour
  27:19, letteth a bird go...so hast thou let
       thy neighbour go
  28:2, Forgive thy neighbour the hurt he hath
       done unto thee,
  28:7, commandments, and bear no malice to thy
       neighbour:
  29:1, He that is merciful will lend unto his
       neighbour;
  29:2, Lend to thy neighbour in time of his
       need, and pay
  29:5, and for his neighbour's money he will
       speak
  29:20, Help thy neighbour according to thy
       power, and
  31:22, He that taketh away his neighbour's
       living slayeth
  34:15, Judge of thy neighbour by thyself:
       and be discreet
  34:31, Rebuke not thy neighbour at the wine,
       and despise

    paroikos, "dwelling beside, neighbouring"
Bar. 4:24, Like as now the neighbours of Sion have
       seen your

    plēsion
His.-Sus. 1:62, did unto them...as...to their neigh-
       bours:

    ásturgeitōn, "near or bordering on a city, a
       neighbour"
II Macc. 6:8, Moreover there went out a decree to
       the neighbouring

133

geitōn, "a neighbour"
II Macc. 9:25, the princes that are...neighbours
unto my kingdom

plēsion
III Macc. 1:6, the king decided to proceed to the
neighbouring

geitōn
III Macc. 3:10, Some of the neighbours, friends,
and fellow

plēsion
IV Macc. 2:5, Thou shalt not covet thy neighbour's
wife,

NEPHI, Nephthaei
II Macc. 1:36, called this thing Naphthar...but
many call it Nephi

NERIAS, Nerios
Bar. 1:1, And these are the words which Baruch the
son of Nerias

NICANOR, Nikanora
I Macc. 3:38, chose Ptolemee the son of Dorymenes,
and Nicanor,
7:26, Then the king sent Nicanor, one of
his honourable
7:27, So Nicanor came to Jerusalem with a
great force:
7:31, Nicanor also, when he saw that this
counsel was
7:32, and there were slain of Nicanor's
side about five
7:33, After this went Nicanor up to mount
Sion, and there
7:39, So Nicanor went out of Jerusalem, and
pitched his
7:43, but Nicanor's host was discomfited,
and he himself
7:44, Now when Nicanor's host saw that he
was slain, they
7:47, and the prey, and smote off Nicanor's
head,
9:1, Furthermore when Demetrius heard that
Nicanor and
II Macc. 8:9, Then forthwith choosing Nicanor the
son of
8:10, So Nicanor undertook to make so much
money of the

II Macc. 8:12, when word was brought unto Judas of
             Nicanor's
      8:14, that they had left...and the wicked
             Nicanor before
      8:23, the first band, he joined battle
             with Nicanor
      8:24, they...maimed the most part of
             Nicanor's host,
      8:34, And for that most ungracious Nicanor,
             who had
      9:3, was brought him what had happened un-
             to Nicanor
     12:2, places, Timotheus, Apollonius...and
             beside...Nicanor
    14:12, And forthwith calling Nicanor...and
             making him
    14:14, Then the heathen...came to Nicanor
             by flocks,
    14:15, Now when the Jews heard of Nicanor's
             coming...they
    14:17, Judas' brother, had joined battle
             with Nicanor,
    14:18, Nevertheless Nicanor, hearing of the
             manliness of
    14:23, Now Nicanor abode in Jerusalem, and
             did no hurt,
    14:26, But Alcimus...told him that Nicanor
             was not well
    14:27, Then the king...wrote to Nicanor
             signifying that
    14:28, When this came to Nicanor's hearing,
             he was much
    14:30, Notwithstanding...Nicanor began to
             be churlish
    14:37, Now was there accused unto Nicanor
             one Razis, one
    14:39, So Nicanor, willing to declare the
             hate that he
    15:1, But Nicanor, hearing that Judas and
             his company
    15:6, So Nicanor in exceeding pride and
             haughtiness...set
    15:25, Then Nicanor and they that were with
             him came
    15:28, Now when the battle was done...Ni-
             canor lay dead in
    15:30, And Judas...commanded to strike off
             Nicanor's head

II Macc. 15:32, and shewed them vile Nicanor's head,
and the hand
15:33, cut out the tongue of that ungodly
Nicanor, he
15:35, He hanged also Nicanor's head upon
the tower, an
15:37, Thus went it with Nicanor: and from
that time
IV Macc. 3:20, For at that time...Seleucus Nicanor,
the king of

NIGGARD, poneros, "causing pain or hardship, knavish,
wicked"
Eccl. 34:24, But against him that is a niggard of
his meat the

NIGHT, aoria, "untimely fate or death, an unseasonable time"
I Esd. 1:14, For the priests offered the fat until
night: and

nux, "night-season or a night"
Tobit 2:9, The same night also I returned from the
burial, and
6:15, for this same night shall she be given
thee in
7:11, in marriage to seven men, who died,
that night
8:9, So they slept both at night. And Raguel
arose, and
10:7, every day into the way...and ceased not
whole nights to
Judith 6:21, they called on the God of Israel all
that night for
8:33, Ye shall stand this night in the gate,
and I will go
11:3, be of good comfort, thou shalt live
this night, and
11:5, him...I will declare no lie to thee
this night
11:17, and serveth the God of heaven day and
night
12:7, in the camp three days, and went out in
the night
13:14, God...for he...hath destroyed our
enemies by...night
Wisd.-Sol. 7:30, For after this cometh night: but
vice shall not
10:17, and a light of stars in the night
season;

Wisd.-Sol. 17:2, being...fettered with the bonds
of a long night,
17:5, give them light...to lighten that
horrible night
17:14, But they sleeping the same sleep
that night,
17:21, over them only was spread a heavy
night, and an
18:6, Of that night were our fathers
certified afore,

nuktōr, "by night"
Eccl. 38:27, carpenter and workmaster, that laboureth night and
40:5, Wrath and envy...rest upon his bed his
night sleep, do

nux
Bar. 2:25, heat of the day, and to the frost of the
night
Song-Child. 1:46, O ye nights and days, bless ye
the Lord: praise
Bel-Drag. 1:15, Now in the night came the priests
with their wives
I Macc. 4:1, thousand footmen...and removed out of
the camp by night
4:5, In the mean season came Georgias by
night into the
5:29, From whence he removed by night, and
went till he
5:50, pitched, and assaulted the city...all
that night,
9:58, saying...who shall take them all in
one night
12:26, He sent spies also unto their tents
...in the night
12:27, Jonathan commanded his men to watch
...all the night
13:22, Tryphon made ready all his horsemen
to come...night
II Macc. 8:7, But specially took he advantage of the
night for
12:6, God the righteous Judge he...burnt the
haven by night
12:9, he came upon the Jamnites also by
night, and set
13:15, young men he went into the king's
tent by night
III Macc. 5:19, explained that he had done his bid-
ding over night

III Macc. 5:22, Nor did they employ the night in
              sleep, so much

NINEVE, Nineuē
  Tobit 1:10, And when we were carried away captives
             to Nineve...all
        1:17, my nation dead, or cast about the walls
              of Nineve,
        1:22, Achiacharus intreating for me, I re-
              turned to Nineve
        11:1, went on his way till they drew near un-
              to Nineve
        11:17, was joy among all his brethren which
               were at Nineve
        14:4, those things...which the prophet spake
              of Nineve
        14:8, And now, my son, depart out of Nineve,
              because that
        14:15, he died, he heard of the destruction of
               Nineve
  Judith 1:1, the reign of Nabuchodonosor, who reign-
              ed in Nineve
         2:21, And they went forth of Nineve three
               days' journey

NINTH, énnea, "nine"
  I Macc. 4:52, Now on the five and twentieth day of
               the ninth

NOAH, Nōe
  Eccl. 44:17, Noah was found perfect and righteous:
              in the time
  IV Macc. 15:31, For as the ark of Noah, bearing
                  the world...bore

NOBLE, éndoxos, "held in repute, honoured"
  Eccl. 10:22, Whether he be rich, noble or poor,
              their glory is

             dunatos, "powerful, strong, mighty, able"
  Bar. 1:4, and in hearing of the nobles, and of the
            king's sons,
  I Macc. 8:2, It was told him also of their wars and
              noble acts
          9:22, things concerning Judas and his wars,
                and the noble

             andragathia, "the character of a brave good
                          man, bravery"
  I Macc. 10:15, it was told him of the battles and
                noble acts

138

eugenēs, "well-born, of high rank, honourable"
IV Macc. 6:5, But Eleazar, the highminded and truly
noble, as one

gennaios, "noble both in mind and blood"
IV Macc. 6:10, and like a noble athlete, the old
man, when struck

eugenēs
IV Macc. 6:30, Thus speaking, the holy man departed,
noble in his
9:13, And the noble youth, extended upon
this, became
9:27, whether he would eat...they heard
his noble
10:3, I abjure not the noble relationship
of my brethren
10:15, my brethren...I will not repudiate
the noble

gennaios
IV Macc. 15:24, the destruction of seven children,
the noble mother
16:16, O sons, noble is the contest: to
which you being
17:24, And they proved to be to him noble
and brave for

NOBLEMAN, endoxos, "notable, memorable, gorgeous"
I Macc. 3:32, So he left Lysias, a nobleman, and
one of the blood

NOBLENESS, gennaiotēs, "nobleness of character"
IV Macc. 17:2, O thou mother, who...exhibit the
nobleness of faith

NOBLER, gennaiotes, "nobility, nobleness of character"
IV Macc. 11:12, thou bestowest upon us...by means
of nobler

NOBLY, eugenēs, "well-born, of noble race, of high
descent"
IV Macc. 9:22, transformed by fire into immortality,
he nobly
13:11, And one said, Courage brother; and
another, nobly

gennaios, "noble, high-born"
IV Macc. 15:32, so thou, guardian of the law...
didst bear up nobly

NOISE, echē, "sound, the tumultuous noise of a crowd"
Wisd.-Sol. 17:4, but noises (as of waters) falling
down sounded

phōenē, "sound, tone, a loud clear voice"
I Macc. 6:41, Wherefore all that heard the noise
of their
9:41, marriage turned into mourning, and
the noise of

tarachē, "confusion, commotion, tumult"
II Macc. 5:29, Then they made a great shout and a
noise, praising

NOMADES, Nomades
II Macc. 12:11, so that the Nomades of Arabia, being overcome,

NOON, mesembria, "midday, noon"
Eccl. 43:3, at noon it parcheth the country, and
who can abide

mesos, "middle, midday"
His.-Sus. 1:7, Now when the people departed away at
noon, Susanna

NOSTRIL, hris, "the nose"
Wisd.-Sol. 2:2, for the breath in our nostrils is
as smoke, and
15:15, which neither have the use of...
noses to draw

muktēr, "nose, snout; the nostrils"
IV Macc. 6:25, instruments they...poured...fluids
...into his nostrils
15:19, Nor when thou didst behold...their
nostrils

NOTION, logismos, "a computation, a thought, cognition"
IV Macc. 5:11, and give up the folly of your notion;
and regaining

NUMBER, arithmos, "number, a number, amount, size"
Eccl. 42:7, Deliver all things in number and weight;
and put all
45:11, twisted scarlet...for a memorial after
the number of
I Macc. 6:30, So that the number of his army was
an hundred
Pr.-Mans. 1:9, for I have sinned above the number
of the sand of

NUMENIUS, Noumenion,
I Macc. 12:16, For this cause we chose Numenius the
son of

I Macc. 14:22, Numenius son of Antiochus, and Anti-
              pater son of
         14:24, After this Simon...Numenius to Rome
              with a great
         15:15, In the mean season came Numenius
              and his company

NURSE, tithēnē, "nurse"
III Macc. 1:20, babes were deserted by their
              mothers or nurses

NURSING, tithnos, "nursing"
IV Macc. 16:7, seven useless childbirths...and
              miserable nursings

OATH, horkos, "an oath, a vow"
Judith 8:11, that ye have spoken...are not right,
              touching...oath
        8:30, But the people...compelled us...to
              bring an oath upon
Wisd.-Sol. 18:6, knowing unto what oaths they had
              given credence
           18:22, alleging the oaths and covenants
              made with the
Eccl. 44:21, Therefore he assured him by an oath,
              that he would

     omnuō, "to promise with an oath"
I Macc. 6:61, Also the king and the princes made
              an oath unto
        6:62, he saw the strength of the place, he
              brake his oath
        7:18, for they have broken the covenant and
              oath that

     horkos
II Macc. 4:34, apart...gave him his right hand with
              oaths;
         7:24, Now Antiochus...assured him by oaths,
              that he
        15:10, shewing them...the falsehood...and
              the breach of oaths
III Macc. 5:42, He swore a fruitless oath and de-
              termined
IV Macc. 5:29, nor will I transgress the sacred
              oath of my

OBEDIENCE, eupeithēs, "ready to obey, obedient"
IV Macc. 15:9, excellent disposition of her sons,
              and...obedience

OBEDIENT, ákouō, "to hear, obey"
  Bar. 2:5, against the Lord...and have not been
            obedient unto his
  I Macc. 5:61, children of Israel, because they were
            not obedient
         8:16, and that...all were obedient to that
            one, and there
  IV Macc. 7:15, and reverend hoar head, and life
            obedient to the

        eupeithēs, "obedient, tractable"
  IV Macc. 12:6, the hope of safety, to render the
            survivor obedient

OBEY, eupeithēs, "easily persuaded, pliant"
  IV Macc. 8:5, but of doing good to those who obey
            them

        peithō, "to persuade, convince, influence by
            persuasion"
  IV Macc. 8:16, and calls us to his bounty, should
            we not obey him

        eupeithēs
  IV Macc. 9:2, be disgracing our fathers if we did
            not obey the

        peithē
  IV Macc. 12:5, But if you obey, you shall be my
            friend, and have
          15:10, and temperate...even unto death
            they obeyed her

OBLATION, dōron, "a gift, present, a votive offering"
  Eccl. 7:9, God will look upon the multitude of my
            oblations, and

        prospheros, "serviceable, useful, profit-
            able"
  Eccl. 50:13, sons of Aaron in their glory, and the
            oblations of
  Song-Child. 1:14, at this time prince...or oblation,
            or incense,

OBSTINATE, sklera, "hard, harsh, stubborn, stern"
  Eccl. 3:27, An obstinate heart shall be laden with
            sorrows;

OBTAIN, metalambanō, "to get, obtain, find"
  IV Macc. 16:18, Remember that through God ye ob-
            tained existence,

142

OCHIEL, 'Ocheilos
I Esd. 1:9, And Jeconias...and Ochiel, and Joram,
          captains over

ODIUM, phainō, "to be denounced, informed against,
          impeach"
III Macc. 3:4, Hence some persons held them in
          odium

          psogos, "blame, censure"
III Macc. 3:7, men unsociable...they brought much
          odium upon them

ODOLLAM, 'Odollam
II Macc. 12:38, gathered his host, and came into
          the city of Odollam

ODONARRES, 'Odoarhrēs
I Macc. 9:66, And he smote Odonarres and his breth-
          ren, and the

OFFENCE, prosochthizō, "to be angry with, to be of-
          fended at"
Pr.-Mans. 1:10, have provoked thy anger...and mul-
          tiplying offences

OFFER, prospherō, "to offer in sacrifice, to present"
I Esd. 8:65, come out of the captivity offered
          sacrifice unto the
Eccl. 32:2, He that requiteth a good turn offereth
          fine flour;

          anapherō, "to offer sacrifices"
I Macc. 4:53, and offered sacrifice according to
          the law upon the

          prospherō, "to bring near to, to offer, tender"
I Macc. 4:56, of the altar...and offered burnt of-
          ferings,

          prosagō, "to lead or conduct to, bring, to
          bring near"
I Macc. 5:54, they went up to mount Sion...where
          they offered

OFFERING, prospheros, "serviceable, useful, profit-
          able"
Eccl. 31:18, of a thing wrongfully gotten, his of-
          fering is
     31:19, The most High is not pleased with the

offerings of

thusia, "sacrificing, the mode of sacrificing"
Eccl. 31:20, Whoso bringeth an offering of the
goods of the poor

prospheros
Eccl. 32:1, He that keepeth the law bringeth offerings enough:
32:6, The offering of the righteous maketh
the altar fat,
38:11, Give a sweet savour...and make a fat
offering, as not
50:14, at the altar, that he might adorn the
offering

holokautoma, "a whole burnt-offering"
IV Macc. 18:11, slaying of Abel and Cain, and the
offering up of

OFFICE, leitougeō, "to serve public offices, to minister as a priest"
Eccl. 45:15, Moses consecrated him...to...execute
the office of the

chreia, "service, advantage, business"
Epis.-Jer. 1:60, and stars, being bright, and sent
to their offices,
III Macc. 5:32, familiar friendship, and the claims
of your office

OFFICERS, leitougos, "performing public duties, serving the state"
Eccl. 10:2, of the people is himself, so are his
officers;

chreia, "a necessary business, affair"
I Macc. 10:41, And all the overplus, which the officers paid out
13:37, peace with you...and to write unto
our officers,

OFFSPRING, genesis, "successive generation, descent,
lineage"
Wisd.-Sol. 3:13, Their offspring is cursed. Wherefore blessed is
7:1, a mortal man, like to all, and the
offspring of
18:12, for in one moment the noblest
offspring of them

144

<u>philoteknon</u>, "loving one's child, duly paren-
tal"
IV Macc. 14:13, consider how comprehensive is the
love of offspring,

<u>teknon</u>, "descendant, posterity"
IV Macc. 14:17, and save their offspring in whatever manner they

<u>philoteknon</u>
IV Macc. 15:5, much mothers are by nature...proli-
fic in offspring,

<u>teknon</u>
IV Macc. 18:7, mother of the seven...spake...to her
offspring

OIL, <u>élaion</u>, "olive oil, oil"
Judith 10:5, gave her maid a bottle of wine, and a
cruse of oil,
11:13, spend the firstfruit...and the tenths
of wine and oil
Eccl. 39:26, principal things...are...the blood of
grape, oil,
45:15, consecrated him, and anointed him
with holy oil;
His.-Sus. 1:17, Then she said to her maids, Bring
me oil and

OINTMENT, <u>muron</u>, "ointment, unusually perfumed,
unguent"
Judith 10:3, and anointed herself with precious
ointment,
16:8, For...she anointed her face with ointment, and bound
Wisd.-Sol. 2:7, fill ourselves with costly wine
and ointments:

OLD, <u>árchaion</u>, "ancient, former"
Eccl. 9:10, Forsake not an old friend; for the new
is not

<u>helikia</u>, "time of life, age,manhood, prime of
life"
IV Macc. 11:14, brothers, but in understanding I am
as old

OLD MAN, <u>gerōn</u>, "an old man"
Eccl. 25:5, O how comely is the wisdom of an old
man, and
26:6, Much experience is the crown of old men

                              and the fear
     IV Macc. 6:6, high to heaven, the old man's flesh
                      was stripped
              6:10, and like a noble athlete, the old
                      man when struck,
              7:13, And, what is most wonderful, though
                      an old man...he
              7:16, If, then, an old man, through reli-
                      gion, despised
              7:25, when the tyrant...being unable to
                      force the old man
              8:4, counsel you...to share the madness
                      of the old man
             16:17, For it were disgraceful that this
                      old man should

OLIVE, élaia, "an olive tree, an olive"
     Judith 15:13, And they put a garland of olive upon
                      her and her
     Eccl. 24:14, exalted like a palm tree...and as a
                      fair olive tree

OLYMPIUS, 'Olumpios
     II Macc. 6:2, Jerusalem, and to call it the temple
                      of...Olympius;

ONAIRES, Onaires
     I Macc. 12:19, the copy of the letters which Oniares
                      sent.

ONIAS, 'Onios
     Eccl. 50:1, Simon the high priest, the son of Onias,
                      in his life
     I Macc. 12:7, There were letters sent in times
                      past unto Onias
             12:8, At which time Onias entreated the
                      ambassador that
             12:20, Areus king of the Lacedemonians to
                      Onias the high
     II Macc. 3:1, peace...because of the godliness of
                      Onias the high
              3:5, And when he could not overcome Onias,
                      he gat him to
              3:31, certain of Heliodorus' friends pray-
                      ed Onias, that
              3:33, saying, Give Onias the high priest
                      thanks,
              3:35, So Heliodorus after he had...salu-
                      ted Onias,
              4:1, This Simon now...slandered Onias, as
                      if he had

II Macc. 4:4, Onias, seeing the danger of this
contention, and
4:7, Jason the brother of Onias laboured
...to be high
4:33, Which when Onias knew of a surety,
he reproved him
4:34, apart, prayed him to get Onias into
his hands;
4:36, Jews that were in the city...com-
plained because Onias
4:38, where he had committed impiety
against Onias,
15:12, And this was his vision: That Onias,
who had been
15:14, Then Onias answered saying, This is
a lover of the
IV Macc. 4:1, man named Simon...was in opposition
to Onias, who
4:13, Onias the high priest, induced by
these words
4:16, Who having deposed Onias from the
high priesthood,

OPPRESS, katadunasteuō, "to oppress"
Wisd.-Sol. 2:10, Let us oppress the poor righteous
man, let us

adikeō, "to injure, wrong"
Eccl. 32:13, He...will hear the prayer of the oppressed

katadouloō, "to reduce to absolute servitude,
make a slave of"
I Macc. 8:18, the kingdom of the Grecians did oppress Israel

katadunasteuō
II Macc. 1:28, Punish them that oppress us, and
with pride do us

OPPRESSED, kataponeō, "to exhaust by labour or suffering, oppress"
III Macc. 2:2, give ear to us who are oppressed by
a wicked and

OPPRESSION, adikeō, "to be injured or oppressed"
III Macc. 3:8, yet to aid them...since was oppression around; but

OPPRESSOR, adikos, "vicious, iniquitous, unjust"
Eccl. 4:9, that suffereth wrong from the hand of
the oppressor;

ORCHARD, arneon, "the bird market"
Epis.-Jer. 1:71, wood...are like to a white thorn
        in an orchard,

ORDAIN, graphō, "to command or enact in writing"
Tobit 1:6, often to Jerusalem at the feasts, as it
        was ordained

        kataskeuazō, "to prepare, put in readiness"
Wisd.-Sol. 9:2, and ordained man through thy wis-
        dom, that he

        graphō
Eccl. 48:10, who wast ordained for reproofs in their
        times, to

        kathistēmi, "to appoint, constitute, set"
I Macc. 3:55, And after this Judas ordained captains
        over the

        histēmi, "to set forth, appoint, to fix"
I Macc. 4:59, and the whole congregation of Israel
        ordained that
        6:35, beside this for every beast were
        ordained five
        7:49, Moreover they ordained to keep yearly
        this day,

        kathistēmi
I Macc. 10:20, Wherefore now this day, we ordain
        thee to be the
        13:52, He ordained also that that should
        be kept

        psēphizomai, "to vote, to decide by vote"
II Macc. 10:8, They ordained also by a common
        statute and decree,
        15:36, And they ordained all with a common
        decree in no

ORDINANCE, dikaioma, "an act of justice, the making
        good a wrong"
I Esd. 8:7, so that he...taught all Israel the or-
        dinances

        prostagma, "an order, command"
Eccl. 6:37, Let thy mind be upon the ordinances of
        the Lord, and

        dikaioma
Bar. 2:12, Lord our God, we have sinned...in all
        thine ordinances
I Macc. 1:13, gave them license to do after the
        ordinances of the

I Macc. 1:49, might forget the law, and changed all
            the ordinances
        2:21, that we should forsake the law and
            the ordinances

prostagma
III Macc. 7:11, bellies' sake transgressed the
            ordinances of God,
IV Macc. 8:6, in me...if you forsake your national
            ordinance,

ORGAN, organon, "an instrument, tool, implement"
IV Macc. 10:18, But he said, Even...you take away
            the organ of

ORNAMENT, kosmos, "order, good order"
Eccl. 43:9, the glory of the stars, an ornament of
            giving light
        45:7, he beautified him with comely ornament,
            and clothed

kauchēma, "a glorying, boasting, laudatory
            testimony"
Eccl. 51:12, mitre...wherein was engraven Holiness,
            an ornament

kosmos
I Macc. 1:22, and the golden ornaments that were
            before the
        2:11, All her ornaments are taken away; of
            a free woman
II Macc. 2:2, forget...when they see images...with
            their ornaments
        5:3, horsemen in array...and glittering
            of...ornaments

ORPHAN, orphanos, "without a father or a mother,
            fatherless"
Tobit 1:8, I gave unto them...because I was left
            an orphan
II Macc. 8:28, sabbath...they had given...spoils to
            the...orphans
        8:30, Moreover of those...who fought...and
            maimed, orphans

ORTHOSIAS, 'Orthosiada
I Macc. 15:37, mean time fled Tryphon by ship unto
            Orthosias

OVEN, kaminos, "an oven"
Song-Child. 1:25, angel of the Lord came down into
            the oven

OVERSEER, épiskopos, "overseer"
  I Macc. 1:51, wrote he to his whole kingdom, and
            appointed overseers,

      árchōn, "one invested with power, a prince,
            magistrate, ruler"
  I Macc. 10:37, I will that their overseer and gover-
            nors be of

OVERWEENING, huperephanos, "magnificent, extravagant"
  IV Macc. 9:30, Thinkest thou not...thy overweening
            conception of

OX, 'Ox
  Judith 8:1, Now at that time Judith heard...of Ox
            the son of

OXEN, bous, "an ox, a bull or cow"
  Eccl. 38:25, How can he get wisdom that...driveth
            oxen, and is

OZIAS, 'Ozias
  Judith 6:21, And Ozias took him out of the assembly
            unto his

PACHON, Paschos
  III Macc. 6:38, being enrolled from the twenty-
            fifth of Pachon to

PACIFY, pletho, "to be filled mentally, fill, be
            under full influence"
  Eccl. 31:19, neither is he pacified for sin by the
            multitude of

PAIN, ponos, "pain, misery, anguish, travail"
  Eccl. 38:7, such doth he heal (men) and taketh a-
            way their pains

      kopos, "vexation, trouble, travail"
  I Macc. 10:15, promises Demetrius...sent to Jona-
            than...and...the pains...endured

      ponos
  II Macc. 7:35, our brethren who now have suffered
            a short pain,
            9:18, But for all this his pains would not
            cease: for
  IV Macc. 1:4, which are hindrances to manliness as
            wrath, and pain
            1:9, For all these, contemning pains even
            unto death,

IV Macc. 1:20, Of the passions, pleasure and pain are the two

1:21, attendant affections surrouding pleasure and pain

1:23, And before pain is fear; and after pain, sorrow

1:28, As pleasure and pain are, therefore, two growths

algedōn, "a sense of pain, pain, grief"
IV Macc. 3:18, and wrestle down the pains of the body, however

6:7, his body having no power to support the pains,

ponos
IV Macc. 6:9, But he endured the pains, and despised the cruelty,

algedōn
IV Macc. 8:27, were well aware of the sufferings... of the pains

ponos
IV Macc. 11:20, brothers have been called to the contest of pain

algedōn
IV Macc. 14:1, urged them...not only despised pains themselves,

14:9, undergoing it preserved...through the pains of fire

14:11, when even a woman's mind despised ...pains

ōdis, "the pain of childbirth, travail"
IV Macc. 15:7, and through her many pains undergone in connection

algedōn
IV Macc. 16:17, disgraceful that this old man should endure pains

ponos
IV Macc. 18:3, persons giving up their bodies to pains for the

PAINFUL, epalgeō, "to grieve over"
IV Macc. 14:10, And what could be more painful? for the power of

PAINFULLY, pikrotēs, "bitterness, harshness, cruelty"
IV Macc. 6:16, And Eleazar, as though the advice more painfully

PALACE, oikos, "a house, dwelling, any place to live
            in"
   I Macc. 7:2, And as he entered into the palace of
            his ancestors,

       aulē, "an open court before the house, a
            courtyard"
   III Macc. 5:46, the city was now filled...he enter-
            ed the palace

PALATE, pharugx, "the throat, a gulf, cleft"
   Eccl. 36:19, As the palate tasteth divers kinds of
            venison: so

PALM TREE, phoinix, "the palm, date-palm"
   Eccl. 24:14, I was exalted like a palm tree on the
            sea shore, and
        50:12, with his brethren round about...as
            palm trees
   II Macc. 10:7, they bare branches, and fair boughs,
            and palms also

PALSY, paralutikos, "affected with palsy, paralytic"
   I Macc. 9:55, was stopped, and he was taken with a
            palsy, so that

PAN, lebēs, "a caldron, kettle, cinerary urn"
   I Esd. 1:12, roasted the passover with fire...in
            brass pots and pans,
   II Macc. 7:3, Then the king being in rage, comman-
            ded pans and
   IV Macc. 8:12, And when the spearman brought...pans,
            and

       tēgenon, "a pan"
   IV Macc. 12:10, And he, running up to the pans,
            said,
        12:20, prayed, he hurled himself into the
            pans; and so

PANGS, ōdis, "the pain of childbirth, pangs or throws
            of labour"
   Eccl. 34:20, Sound sleep cometh...but the...pangs
            of the belly, are

       ponos, "toil, labour, hard work, pain, suffer-
            ing"
   IV Macc. 15:16, who was tried at times with bitter-
            er pangs than

       ōdis
   IV Macc. 16:8, Vainly for your sakes...I have

endured many pangs,

PAPER, chartēs, "a leaf of paper, made from...papyrus"
III Macc. 4:20, They said, and proved, that paper
and pens had

PARABLE, parabolē, "a placing one thing by the side
of another, a comparing"
Eccl. 3:29, The heart of the prudent will understand a parable;
6:35, and let not the parables of understanding escape thee
38:33, and they shall not be found where parables are spoken
47:15, the whole earth, and thou fillest it
with...parables,
47:17, marvelled at thee for thy songs...and
parables,

PARATHONI, Pharathoni
I Macc. 9:50, returned Bacchides...and Thamnatha,
and Parathoni

PARCHETH, anaxērrainō, "to dry up"
Eccl. 43:3, at noon it parcheth the country, and
who can abide

PARDON, charis, "favour, acceptance"
Wisd.-Sol. 18:2, they thanked them, and besought
them pardon,

exilaskomai, "to appease completely, propitiate"
Eccl. 20:28, and he that pleaseth great men shall
get pardon for
28:5, flesh nourish hatred, who will intreat
for pardon...?

suggnōmē, "pardon, concession, leave, permis-
sion"
IV Macc. 5:13, it will pardon you for all transgressions of the

sugginōskō, "to pardon, to agree in judgment"
IV Macc. 8:21, And Divine Justice will pardon us
if we fear the

PARENT, gennēma, "what is born or produced, progeny,
offspring"
Wisd.-Sol. 4:6, beds are witnesses...against their
parents

Eccl. 3:7, and will do service unto his parents,
        as to his

goneus, "a father, pl. parents"
His.-Sus. 1:3, Her parents also were righteous,
        and taught their
I Macc. 10:9, of the tower...delivered them unto
        their parents
II Macc. 12:24, fell into the hands...of the Jews'
        parents,

PARENTAL, philoteknos, "loving one's children or off-
        spring"
IV Macc. 15:23, her courage...enabled her to fore-
        go...parental love

PARSIMONIOUS, pheidomenos, "parsimoniously, sparing-
        ly"
IV Macc. 2:9, and should a man be parsimonious, he
        is ruled by

PARTAKER, koinonia, "partnership, fellowship"
IV Macc. 7:6, O priest...the clean and lawful a
        partaker of

PARTURITION, ponos, "labour, misery, travail, anguish"
IV Macc. 15:16, who was tried at this time with
        bitter...parturition

PASSION, pathos, "an affection, passion, suffering"
IV Macc. 1:3, appears to hold the mastery over the
        passions which
        1:7, religious reasoning is sole master
        of the passions;
        1:9, that reasoning has command over the
        passions
        1:13, whether reasoning be absolute master
        of passions
        1:14, What is reasoning? and what is pas-
        sion? and how
        1:19, these...is that reasoning rule over
        the passions
        1:20, Of the passions, pleasure and pain
        are the two
        1:28, are, therefore...many offshoots of
        these passions
        1:30, but it is the sole ruler of the
        passions
        2:3, he abrogated...the stimulus of his
        passion
        2:7, that reasoning is lord of the passions?

IV Macc. 2:9, it is reasoning that conquers his
        passions
    2:15, reasoning appears to be the master
        of...passions,
    2:16, temperate understanding repels...
        malignant passions
    2:18, mind is able...to be superior to the
        passions, and
    2:24, if reasoning be master of the pas-
        sions has it no
    3:5, an eradicator, but an antagonist of
        the passions
    3:17, has power to conquer the pressure of
        the passions,
    3:18, to abominate all the assaults of the
        passions
    6:31, religious reasoning is master of the
        passions
    6:32, For had the passions been superior
        to reasoning, I
    6:33, But now, since reasoning conquered
        the passions,
    7:1, like a first-rate pilot...in the sea
        of passions,
    7:5, broke the raging waves of the passions
        as with a
    7:10, man of more power...greatest king
        over...passions,
    7:16, religious reasoning is the ruler of
        the passions
    7:17, some might say, It is not all who
        conquer passions
    7:18, meditated upon religion...master the
        passions of
    7:20, have weak reasoning are governed by
        their passions
    7:22, thing...for the sake of religion,
        master his passion
    7:23, the wise and brave man only is lord
        over...passions

  peripathos, "concerning passion, violent pas-
        sion"
IV Macc. 8:1, Then, indeed, vehemently swayed with
        passion, he

  pathos
IV Macc. 13:1, that...reasoning is...master over
        the passions

IV Macc. 13:2, For just as if, had they as slaves
to the passions
13:3, which is praised...they mastered
their passions
13:4, for it gained the victory over both
passions and
13:7, right-reasoning...conquered the intemperance of passion
15:1, O reasoning of the sons, lord over
the passions,
15:32, surrounded on every side by the
flood of passions
16:1, religious reasoning is master even
of the passions
16:2, not only men have the mastery of
the passions, but
16:4, reasoning of religion the mother
quenched passions
18:2, That religious reasoning is lord of
the passions,

PASSOVER, <u>pascha</u>, "the Passover, paschal lamb, the
time of the feast of the Passover"
I Esd. 1:1, And Josias held the feast of the passover in Jerusalem
1:6, offer the passover in order, and make
ready the
1:8, gave to the priests for the passover...
three hundred
1:9, gave to the Levites for the passover...
seven hundred
1:12, And they roasted the passover with
fire, as
1:17, accomplished in that day, that they
might hold the passover,
1:19, So the children of Israel...held the
passover at that
1:21, all the kings of Israel held not such
a passover as
1:22, year of his reign Josias was this
passover kept
7:10, of Israel that were in captivity...
held the passover

PATERNAL, <u>patrios</u>, "a father, coming or inherited
from a father"
IV Macc. 9:24, by which means our just and paternal
Providence,
16:20, shuddered not at the sign of his own
paternal hand

PATH, ichnos, "a track, footstep, mark"
Eccl. 50:29, for the light of the Lord is his path

    tribos, "a beaten track, a road, highway"
Bar. 3:21, nor understood the paths thereof, nor
    laid hold of it:
    3:23, these have known the way of wisdom, or
    remembered her paths
    3:31, No man knoweth her way, nor thinketh of
    her path
    4:13, They know not his statutes...nor trod
    in the paths of

PATIENCE, anexikakos, "enduring or patient under
                 evils and injuries"
Wisd.-Sol. 2:19, may know his meekness and prove
    his patience

        suggnōmē, "to agree in judgment, concession"
Eccl. 3:13, And if his understanding fail, have
    patience with him

        hupomonē, "patient endurance"
Eccl. 16:13, and the patience of the godly shall
    not be frustrated
    17:24, return, and comforted those that
    failed in patience
    41:2, to him that despaireth, and hath lost
    patience!
IV Macc. 9:30, art tortured more than I, finding...
    by our patience

PATRIARCH, patriarchēs
IV Macc. 16:25, to God; as Abraham...and Jacob, and
    all the patriarchs

PATROCLUS, Patroklos
II Macc. 8:9, forthwith choosing Nicanor the son
    of Patroclus...he

PAVEMENT, edaphos, "the bottom or base of anything,
              the ground floor"
Eccl. 3:18, To slip upon a pavement is better than
    to slip with
Bel-Drag. 1:19, Behold now the pavement, and mark
    well whose
III Macc. 2:22, to and fro...he cast him upon the
    pavement,

PAY, apodidōmi, "to give back, to sell, restore"
Eccl. 18:22, Let nothing hinder thee to pay thy vow
    in due time,

PAYMENT, óphliskanō, "to incur a debt, to pay"
  Bar. 3:8, a curse, and to be subject to payments,
          according to

PEACE, eirēnē, "time of peace, to keep peace, re-
          pose"
  I Esd. 8:85, Moreover ye shall never seek to have
          peace with them

        sigē, "silence, being silent"
  Tobit 10:6, To whom Tobit said, Hold thy peace,
          take no care, for

        eirēnē
  Tobit 13:14, they which love thee, for they shall
          rejoice in peace
        14:4, and that for a time peace shall be in
          Media

        eirēnikos, "of or for peace, peaceful"
  Judith 3:1, they sent ambassadors unto him to
          treat of peace,
        7:24, have not required peace of the child-
          ren of Israel

        eirēnē
  Wisd.-Sol. 3:3, to be utter destruction: but they
          are in peace
        14:22, those so great plagues called
          they peace
  Eccl. 1:18, fear of the Lord is crown of wisdom,
          making peace and
        6:6, Be in peace with many: nevertheless
          have but one

        eireneuō, "to make peace, to live peaceably"
  Eccl. 28:9, sinful man...maketh debate among them
          that be at peace
        28:13, whisperer...for such destroyed many
          that were at peace

        eirēnē
  Eccl. 38:8, and from him is peace over all the
          earth
        41:14, My children keep discipline in peace:
          for wisdom
        45:24, Therefore was there a covenant of
          peace made with
        47:16, Thy name went far unto the islands;
          and for thy peace
        50:23, He grant us joyfulness of heart, and
          and that peace may

Bar. 3:13, way of God, thou shouldest have
            dwelled in peace
      3:14, Learn where is wisdom, where is strength
            ...and peace
      4:20, I have put off the holding of peace, and
            put upon me
      5:4, called of God for ever, The peace of
           Righteousness,
I Macc. 5:54, one...was slain until they had re-
              turned in peace
       6:49, But with them that were in Bethsura
             he made peace:
       6:58, now let us...make peace with them,
             and with all
       6:60, wherefore he sent unto them to make
             peace;
       7:13, among the children of Israel that
             sought peace
       7:28, come with a few men, that I may see
             you in peace
       8:20, with his brethren...have sent us...
             to make...peace with
       8:22, the senate wrote...that...they might
             have...peace
      10:4, For said he, Let us first make peace
            with him, before

      eirēnikos
I Macc. 10:47, because he was the first that en-
               treated of...peace
       10:66, Jonathan returned to Jerusalem with
              peace and

      sigē, "silence"
I Macc. 11:5, but the king held his peace

      dexias, "right, as opposed to left"
I Macc. 11:50, Grant us peace, and let the Jews
               cease from

      eirēnē
I Macc. 11:51, that they cast away their weapons,
               and made peace;
       13:37, we have received: and...make a stead-
              fast peace
       13:40, who are meet among you...and let
              there be peace

      dexias
I Macc. 13:45, loud voice, beseeching Simon to
               grant them peace

I Macc. 14:8, Then did they till their ground in
              peace, and the
        14:11, He made peace in the land, and
               Israel rejoiced with
        16:10, he returned into the land of Judea
               in peace
II Macc. 1:1, that are throughout Egypt, health
              and peace
         1:4, hearts to his law and commandments,
              and send you peace
         3:1, Now when the holy city was inhabited
              with all peace

     eirēnekos
II Macc. 5:25, who coming to Jerusalem, and pre-
               tending peace, did
        10:12, For Ptolemeus...endeavoured to
               continue peace with

     esuchia, "stillness, quiet, at rest"
II Macc. 12:2, would not suffer them...to live in
               peace

     eirēnē
II Macc. 12:4, accepted of it...as being desirous
               to live in peace
        12:12, Then Judas...granted them peace;
               whereupon they

     eustatheia, "goodness of health"
II Macc. 14:6, war...and will not let the realm be
               in peace

     eirēnē
III Macc. 2:20, Grant us peace, that the cast down
                and broken
          6:27, the unjust bonds; send them to
                their homes in peace,
          7:19, They were accordingly brought
                back in peace,
IV Macc. 4:20, fathers were in possession of undis-
               turbed peace

     eirēneō, "to keep peace, live peaceably"
IV Macc. 18:4, And the nation through them obtained
               peace, and

PEACEABLE, eirēneokos, "peaceful, peaceable"
  Eccl. 47:13, Solomon reigned in a peaceable time,
               and was
  I Macc. 1:30, and spake peaceable words unto them,
                but all was

I Macc. 11:2, he took his journey into Syria in
         peaceable manner,

PEACEABLY, eireneuō, "to bring to peace, live peace-
         ably"
  Eccl. 44:6, rich men furnished with abiltiy,
         living peaceably in
  I Macc. 7:15, So he spake unto them peaceably,
         and sware unto

         eirēnē, "rest, repose"
  I Macc. 12:4, the Romans...bring them into the
         land...peaceably
        12:52, they all came into the land of Judea
         peaceably,

PEACE-OFFERING, prosphera, "an offering, an act of
                  offering up or sacrific-
                  ing"
  Eccl. 32:1, He that keepeth the law...offereth a
         peace-offering

PEAK, akra, "the highest point, the top of the hill,
         peak"
  Eccl. 43:19, hoarfrost as salt...congealed, it
         becometh...peaks

PEN, kalamos, "a writing reed used as a pen; general-
         ly a pen"
  III Macc. 4:20, They said, and proved, that paper
         and pens had

PENTECOST, pentekostē, "Pentecost or the Feast of
              Weeks"
  Tobit 2:1, I was come home again...in the feast
         of Pentecost,

PEOPLE, ethnos, "a nation, people, race, tribe"
  I Esd. 1:4, serve the Lord your God, and minister
         unto his people

         laos, "the people"
  I Esd. 1:7, And unto the people that was found
         there Josias gave
        1:11, several dignities of the fathers, be-
         fore the people
        1:13, and set them before all the people;
         and afterward

         ethnos
  I Esd. 1:24, that sinned...against the Lord above
         all people
        1:34, And the people took Joachaz the son

of Josias, and

laos
I Esd. 1:49, And the governors also of the people
and of the

ethnos
I Esd. 1:52, so far forth, that he being wroth
with his people

laos
I Esd. 2:10, So all his people and his armies obey
him:
4:15, Women have borne the king and all the
people that
5:65, might not be heard for the weeping
of the people;

ethnos
I Esd. 8:14, with that also which is given of the
people for the
8:67, and they honoured the people and the
temple of God
8:69, have not put away from them the
strange people of
8:70, their sons have married...with the
strange people of

plethos, "a crowd, a mass, a great number of
persons"
I Esd. 9:47, And all the people answered, Amen:
and lifting up

demos, "plebians, common people, the commons"
I Esd. 9:53, So the Levites published all things
to the people,

laos
Tobit 4:13, in thy heart thy brethren, the sons...
of thy people,
14:7, So shall the nations praise the Lord,
and his people
Judith 5:5, I will declare...the truth concerning
this people,
5:6, This people are descended of the
Chaldeans:
5:20, if there be any error in this people,
and
5:22, finished these sayings, all the
people standing
5:23, for, lo, it is a people that have no
strength nor

Judith 6:16, all the ancients...in the midst of
            their people,

      6:18, Then the people fell down and worship-
            ped God, and

      7:1, The next day Holofernes commanded...
            all his people

      7:7, of war...and he himself removed toward
            his people

      7:8, came unto him all...the governors of
            the people of

      7:23, Then all the people assembled to
            Ozias, and to the

      7:26, call them unto you, and deliver...the
            people of

      7:32, And he dispersed the people, every
            one to their own

      8:9, Now when she heard the evil words of
            the people

      8:11, for your words that ye have spoken
            before the people

      8:29, but from the beginning of thy days
            all the people

        éthnos
Judith 9:14, there is none other that protecteth
            the people

        laos
Judith 10:19, Who would despise this people, that
            have among them

      11:2, Now therefore, if thy people that
            dwelleth in the

      11:13, things it is not lawful for any of
            the people

      11:22, done well to send thee before the
            people,

      12:8, the Lord...to the raising up of...
            her people

      13:17, Then all the people were wonderfully
            astonished,

      14:6, and saw...the assembly of the people,
            he fell down

      14:8, Judith declared unto him in the midst
            of the people

      14:9, And when she had left off speaking,
            the people

      15:10, Almighty Lord for evermore. And all
            the people said

      15:11, And the people spoiled the camp the
            space of

Judith 15:13, and she went before all the people
      in the dance,
    16:3, God breaketh the battles...in the
      midst of the people
    16:18, and as soon as the people were
      purified, they
    16:19, dedicated all the stuff...which the
      people had given
    16:20, So, the people continued feasting
      in Jerusalem
    16:22, was dead, and was gathered to his
      people
Wisd.-Sol. 3:8, the nations, and have dominion over
      the people,

   plēthos
Wisd.-Sol. 6:2, Give ear, ye that rule the people,
      and glory in

   laos
Wisd.-Sol. 6:21, O ye kings of the people, honour
      wisdom, that ye

   dēmos
Wisd.-Sol. 6:24, and a wise king is the upholding
      of the people

   laos
Wisd.-Sol. 8:14, I shall set the people in order,
      and the nations
    10:15, She delivered the righteous people
      and blameless
    12:19, But by such works hast thou taught
      thy people
    16:2, dealing graciously with thine own
      people,
    16:20, whereof thou feddest thine own
      people with
    18:7, So thy people was accepted both
      the salvation of
    19:5, and thy people might pass through
      a wonderful way
    19:22, thou didst magnify thy people,
      and glorify them,

   ochlos, "a throng of people, a mob, multitude"
Eccl. 7:7, against the multitude of a city, and...
      among the people

   laos
Eccl. 10:1, A wise judge will instruct his people;
      and the

Eccl. 10:2, As the judge of the people is himself,
            so are his
      10:3, An unwise king destroyeth his people;
            but through the

ethnos
Eccl. 10:8, the kingdom is translated from one
            people to another
      16:9, He pitieth not the people of perdition,
            who were taken
      16:17, I shall not be remembered among so
             many people: for
      24:1, and shall glory in the midst of her
            people
      24:6, sea, and in all the earth, and in every
            people
      24:12, And I took root in an honourable peo-
             ple, even in the
      30:18, Hear me, O ye great men of the people,
             and hearken

laos
Eccl. 33:9, and let them perish that oppress the
            people
      34:9, for wonderful things hath he done among
            his people
      36:17, hear the prayer of thy servants...
             over thy people
      37:23, A wise man instructeth his people;
             and the fruits of
      37:26, A wise man shall inherit glory among
             his people, and
      41:18, of iniquity before...a congregation
             of people
      42:11, lest she make thee...a reproach among
             the people
      44:4, leaders of the people by their counsels,
            and by their
      44:15, The people will tell of their wisdom,
             and the
      44:19, Abraham was a great father of many
             people: in glory
      45:3, gave him a commandment for his people,
            and shewed him
      45:6, Aaron...and gave him the priesthood
            among the people;
      45:9, in the temple for a memorial to...his
            people
      45:15, of the priesthood, and bless the people
             in his name,

Eccl. 45:22, Howbeit in the land of the people he
           had no
      45:23, stood up with courage...when the
           people were turned
      45:26, give you wisdom in your heart to
           judge his people in
      46:7, he did a work of mercy...and withheld
           the people from
      46:13, a kingdom, and anointed princes over
           his people
      47:4, and did he not take a reproach from
           the people, when
      47:5, most high Lord...and set up the horn
           of his people
      47:23, behind him...the foolishness of the
           people,
      48:15, For all this the people repented not,
           neither
      49:2, himself uprightly in the conversion of
           the people
      49:15, there a man born like unto Joseph...
           a stay of...people
      50:5, How he honoured him in the midst of
           the people in his
      50:17, Then all the people together hasted
           to worship their
      50:19, And the people besought the Lord, the
           most High, by
      50:26, and that foolish people that dwell in
           Sichem
 Bar. 1:3, Baruch did read the words...in the ears
           of all...people
      1:4, in the hearing of the nobles...and of
           all the people,
      1:7, they sent it to Jerusalem...and to all
           the people which
      1:9, Nabuchodonosor...carried away...the
           people of the land
      2:4, to be as a reproach...among all the
           people
      2:11, O Lord God of Israel, that hast brought
           thy people out
      2:30, not hear me, because it is a stiffnecked
           people
      4:5, Be of good cheer, my people, the memorial
           of Israel
His.-Sus. 1:5, appointed two of the ancients of the
           people to be

His.-Sus. 1:7, Now when the people departed away
                at noon, Susanna
          1:28, came to pass the next day when the
                people were
          1:29, and said before the people, Send
                for Susanna, the
          1:34, two elders stood in the midst of
                the people, and
          1:41, them, as those were the...judges
                of the people,
          1:50, Wherefore all the people turned
                again in haste,
          1:64, in great reputation in the sight
                of the people
I Macc. 1:13, Then certain of the people were
                forward herein,
          1:30, fell suddenly upon the city...and
                destroyed the people
          1:41, whole kingdom, that all should be
                one people,
          1:51, the selfsame manner wrote he...to all
                the people,
          1:52, Then many of the people were gathered
                unto them, to
          2:7, was I born to see this misery of my
                people, and of

anthrōpos, "a man, men in general, mankind"
I Macc. 2:38, they slew them...to the number of a
                thousand people

laos
I Macc. 2:66, be your captain, and fight the battle
                of the people
          2:67, law, and avenge ye the wrong of your
                people
          3:3, So gat his people great honour, and
                put a breastplate
          3:5, pursued the wicked...and...those that
                vexed his people
          3:42, king had given commandment to de-
                stroy the people,
          3:43, Let us restore the decayed estate of
                our people, and
          3:55, this Judas ordained captains over
                the people,

ethnos
I Macc. 3:59, than to behold the calamities of our
                people

<u>laos</u>

I Macc. 4:17, and said unto the people, Be not
             greedy of the
        4:31, shut up this army in the hand of thy
              people Israel,
        4:55, Then all the people fell upon their
              faces, worshipping and praising the
              God of heaven,
        4:58, was there very great gladness among
              the people
        4:61, set up there a garrison...that the
              people might have
        5:2, and...began to slay and destroy the
             people
        5:4, children of Baean, who had been an
             offence unto the people,
        5:6, passed over to the children of Ammon
             ...and...people
        5:16, Now when Judas and the people heard
              these words,
        5:18, left Joseph...and Azarias, captains
              of the people,
        5:19, gave commandment, saying, Take ye
              charge of...people
        5:30, they looked up, and, behold...an
              innumerable people
        5:42, he caused the scribes of the people
              to remain
        5:43, he went first over unto them, and all
              the people
        5:53, those that came behind, and exhorted
              the people
        6:19, purposing to destroy them, called all
              the people
        6:44, in jeopardy, to the end he might de-
              liver his people
        7:6, and they accused the people to the
             king, saying,
        7:18, the fear and dread of them fell upon
              all the people
        7:19, Jerusalem...and took many of the
              men...and...people
        7:22, unto him resorted all such as trou-
              bled the people,
        7:26, sent Nicanor...with commandment to
              destroy...people
        7:33, mount Sion, and...certain of the
              elders of...people

I Macc. 7:48, For this cause the people rejoiced
                    greatly, and

   plēthos
I Macc. 8:20, Maccabeus with his brethren, and the
                    people of the

   éthnos
I Macc. 8:23, Good success be to the Romans, and
                    to the people of
            8:25, the people of the Jews shall help
                    them, as the time

   ánthrōpos
I Macc. 9:2, who went forth...and...slew much
                    people

   óchlos
I Macc. 9:35, sent his brother John, a captain of
                    the people,

   éthnos
I Macc. 10:5, the evils that we have done against
                    ...his people
            10:7, the letters in the audience of all
                    the people,
            10:25, King Demetrius unto the people of
                    the Jews sendeth

   laos
II Macc. 10:46, Now when Jonathan and the people
                    heard these words
            10:80, compassed in his host, and cast
                    darts at...people,
            10:81, But the people stood still, as
                    Jonathan had

   éthnos
I Macc. 11:21, ungodly persons, who hated their
                    own people, went
            11:25, And though certain ungodly men of
                    the people had
            11:33, We are determined to do good to the
                    people of the
            11:42, Jonathan, saying...do this for thee
                    and thy people,
            12:3, went unto Rome...and said...the
                    people of the Jews,

   dēmos
I Macc. 12:6, and the elders...and the other people
                    of the Jews,

169

laos
I Macc. 12:35, again, and calling the elders of
      the people
    12:44, Why hast thou put all this people
      to so great
    13:2, and saw that the people was in great
      trembling and
    13:7, Now as soon as the people heard these
      words, their
    13:17, procured unto himself great hatred
      of the people
    13:42, Then the people of Israel began to
      write in their
    14:14, Moreover he strengthened all those
      of his people

dēmos
I Macc. 14:20, Lacedemonians, with...the residue
      of the people of
    14:21, The ambassadors that were sent unto
      our people
    14:22, things that they spake in the coun-
      cil of the people
    14:23, And it pleased the people to enter-
      tain the men
    14:25, Whereof when the people heard, they
      said, What

laos
I Macc. 14:28, the great congregation of the
      priests, and people,
    14:30, (...gathered his nation together...
      added to his people...)
    14:35, The people therefore, seeing the
      acts of Simon,
    14:44, it should be lawful for none of the
      people or

éthnos
I Macc. 15:1, from the isles...unto Simon...and
      to all the people

dēmos
I Macc. 15:17, sent from Simon...and from the
      people of the Jews:

laos
I Macc. 15:39, host toward Judea...and to war
      against the people
    15:40, came to Jamnia, and began to provoke

the people,
I Macc. 16:6, So he and his people pitched over
           against them:
II Macc. 1:29, Plant thy people again in the holy
            place, as Moses
         2:7, it shall be unknown until...God
            gathered his people
         2:17, hope also, that the God, that de-
            livered his people

   dēmos
II Macc. 4:48, the matter for the city, and for
            the people, and

   óchlos
II Macc. 6:3, of this mischief was sore grievous
            to the people:

   laos
II Macc. 6:16, adversity, yet doth he never forsake
            his people
         8:2, that he would look upon the people
            that was trodden
         10:21, Maccabeus what was done, he called
            ...the people

   óchlos
II Macc. 11:6, with Maccabeus heard...they and all
            the people

   dēmos
II Macc. 11:34, Titus Manilus...send greeting unto
            the people of

   éthnos
II Macc. 12:13, to a certain strong city...and in-
            habited by people

   laos
II Macc. 13:11, and that he would not suffer the
            people...to be in
         14:15, supplication to him that establish-
            ed his people

   óchlos
II Macc. 14:33, but sent away the people that came
            flocking unto

   laos
II Macc. 15:14, This is a lover...who prayeth much
            for the people,
         15:24, those be stricken...that come
            against thy...people

III Macc. 2:6, Pharaoh, the enslaver of thy people
...pass through

anthrōpos
III Macc. 3:8, unexpected uproar and sudden conflux
of people

ēthnos
III Macc. 3:20, endeavoured to...return treating
all people in
7:4, hatred borne by the Jews to all
other people

plēthos
III Macc. 7:13, saluted him with good wishes, and
all the people

ēthnos
IV Macc. 4:1, named Simon...could not injure him
with the people
4:19, he both changed the manner of living
of the people

laos
IV Macc. 4:26, therefore his decrees were disre-
garded by the people, he himself...
adjure the Jewish religion

ēthnos
IV Macc. 6:28, Be merciful to thy people, and be
satisfied with

PERDITION, ampoleia, "destruction, state of being
destroyed, perdition"
Eccl. 16:9, He pitied not the people of perdition,
who were taken

PERFECT, teleioō, "to make perfect, complete, consecrate"
Eccl. 31:8, The law shall be found perfect without
lies:

holokleros, "complete in all parts, entire,
sound"
IV Macc. 15:17, O thou only woman who hast brought
forth perfect

PERFECTED, telesphoreō, "to bring to maturity"
IV Macc. 13:19, In which these brothers...having
been perfected

PERFECTION, teleios, "complete, perfect, without
lies"
Eccl. 31:8, and wisdom is perfection to a faithful

mouth

PERFUME, <u>thumiama</u>, "incense, any odoriferous sub-
                        stance burnt in religious worship"
  Tobit 6:16, And...thou shalt take the ashes of per-
                    fume, and shalt
          8:2, And as he went...he...took the ashes of
                    perfumes and put
  Eccl. 49:1, of Josias is like the composition of
                    the perfume
  Epis.-Jer. 1:43, also with cords about them...
                    burn bran for perfume

PERIL, <u>kindunos</u>, "peril, danger"
  II Macc. 1:11, God hath delivered us from great
                    perils, we thank

PERIOD, <u>chronos</u>, "a certain time, season, space of
                        time"
  IV Macc. 18:8, I remained with my husband during
                    the period of my
           18:9, blessed was he...he was not grieved
                    with a period

PERISH, <u>exapollumi</u>, "to be destroyed, removed from
                        or out of"
  Wisd.-Sol. 10:6, When the ungodly perished, she
                        delivered the
             12:12, shall accuse thee for the nations
                        that perish,

         <u>apollumi</u>, "to kill, to be destroyed, to put
                        to death, perish"
  Wisd.-Sol. 14:6, old time also, when the proud
                        giants perished,

         <u>diaphtheireo</u>, "to corrupt or destroy utterly,
                        to decay"
  Wisd.-Sol. 16:5, For whom...they perished with
                        the stings of

         <u>apollumi</u>
  Wisd.-Sol. 18:19, foreshew this, lest they should
                        perish,

         <u>kakoo</u>, "to treat badly, destroy, maltreat"
  Eccl. 3:26, evil at the last; and he that loveth
                    danger shall perish

         <u>sunapollumi</u>, "to perish or be destroyed with
                        others"
  Eccl. 8:15, to his own will, and thou shalt perish

with him

apollumi

Eccl. 17:28, Thanksgiving perisheth from the dead,
as from one

37:31, By surfeiting have many perished;
but he that taketh

41:6, The inheritance of sinners' children
shall perish,

44:9, there be, which have no memorial, who
are perished,

Bar. 3:3, For thou endurest for ever, and we perish
utterly

3:28, but they were destroyed...and perished
through their

I Macc. 3:9, he received unto him such as were
ready to perish

6:13, I perceive...and, behold, I perish
through great

II Macc. 5:9, driven many out of their country
perished in a

8:19, how...under Sennacherib an hundred
...perished

thnēskō, "to die, to be dead"

IV Macc. 12:4, having been miserably tormented, will
yourself perish prematurely

PERJURY, epiorkos, "swearing falsely"
Wisd.-Sol. 14:25, in all men without exception...
tumults, perjury,

PERSECUTE, diōkō, "to pursue with malignity, persecute"
Wisd.-Sol. 16:16, strange rains, hails, and showers,
were...they persecuted,

elaunō, "to drive, urge forward, spur on"
Wisd.-Sol. 16:18, might see and perceive that they
were persecuted

diōkō, "to follow hard upon, follow
perseveringly"
Bar. 4:25, for thine enemy hath persecuted thee;
but shortly thou

PERSECUTION, kakos, "wickedness, distress, evil, vice"
I Macc. 2:43, Also all they that fled for persecution joined

PERSEPOLIS, Persepolis
II Macc. 9:2, For he had entered the city called

Persepolis, and

PERSEUS, _Persea_
  I Macc. 8:5, how they discomfited...Philip, and
           Perseus, king of

PERSIA, _Persikos_
  I Esd. 3:1, a great feast...unto all the princes
           of Media and Persia
        3:9, and said that...the three princes of
           Persia shall
        3:14, sending forth he called all the
           princes of Persia
        7:4, consent of Cyrus, Darius, and Artaxerxes
           ...of Persia
        8:80, he made us favoured before the kings
           of Persia, so
  Judith 1:7, sent unto all that dwelt in Persia,
           and to all
  Bel-Drag. 1:1, gathered to his fathers, and Cyrus
           king of Persia
  I Macc. 3:31, in his mind, he determined to go into
           Persia,
        6:1, heard say, that Elymais in...Persia
           was a city
        6:5, came one who brought him tidings into
           Persia, that
        6:56, was returned out of Persia and Media,
           and the king's
        14:2, But when Arsaces, the king of Persia
           ...heard that
  II Macc. 1:13, For when the leader was come into
           Persia, and the
        1:19, For when our fathers were led into
           Persia, the
        1:20, God, Neemias, being sent from the
           king of Persia,
        1:33, matter was known, it was told the
           king of Persia,
        9:1, came Antiochus...out of the country
           of Persia
        9:21, As for me, I was...returning out of
           Persia, and

PERSIAN, _Persikos_, "Persian"
  I Esd. 1:57, servants to him and his children,
           till the Persians
        2:1, In the first year of Cyrus king of the
           Persians, that

I Esd. 2:2, up the spirit of Cyrus the king of
          the Persians,
    2:3, saying, Thus saith Cyrus king of the
          Persians; the
    2:16, in the time of Artaxerxes king of the
          Persians
    2:30, the second year...of Darius king of
          the Persians
    5:55, it was commanded...by Cyrus king of
          the Persians
    5:71, according as Cyrus the king of the
          Persians hath
Judith 16:10, The Persians quaked at her boldness,
          and the Medes
I Macc. 1:1, had smitten Darius king of the Persians
          and the Medes,
IV Macc. 18:6, from Jerusalem, he made war against
          the Persians

PERSON, prosōpon, "a person, face, visage, counte-
          nance"
Eccl. 4:22, Accept no person against thy soul, and
          let not the
    4:27, foolish man; neither accept the person
          of the mighty
    7:6, lest at any time thou fear the person
          of the mighty,
    8:11, at the presence of an injurious person,
          lest he lie
    10:5, and upon the person of the scribe shall
          he lay
    20:22, and by accepting of person overthrow-
          eth himself
    32:12, with him is no respect of persons
    32:13, He will not accept any person against
          a poor man,
    42:1, Of these things be thou ashamed, and
          accept no person

      anēr, "man, man as opposed to woman"
I Macc. 11:21, Then certain ungodly persons, who
          hated their own
II Macc. 8:32, They slew also Philarches, that
          wicked person, who

      sōma, "a person, individual"
II Macc. 12:26, and there slew five and twenty
          thousand persons
III Macc. 2:29, who were registered, were to be
          marked on...person

III Macc. 6:20, And a cold shudder came over the
              person of the
         17:1, herself upon the pile rather than
              ...touch her person
         18:3, Whence those persons giving up
              their bodies to

PERVERT, ékklinō, "to deflect, deviate, turn away
              from"
  Eccl. 8:2, for gold hath destroyed many, and per-
            verted the hearts

PESTILENCE, ponēros, "malignity, wicked deeds, bad
              condition"
  Bar. 2:25, And lo...they died in great miseries...
            and by pestilence

PESTILENT, loimos, "pestilence, plague"
  I Macc. 10:61, At that time certain pestilent
                fellows of Israel,
           15:3, Forasmuch as certain pestilent men
                have ursurped
          15:21, If therefore there be any pestilent
                fellows, that

           álastoros, "under the influence of an
                       avenger"
  IV Macc. 18:22, Wherefore divine retribution
                  pursued...the pestilent

PETITION, deēsis, "entreaty, prayer, supplication"
  Bar. 2:14, Hear our prayer, O Lord, and our peti-
            tions, and
  I Macc. 7:37, to be a house of prayer and petition
               for thy people

           prosagō, "to induce to do a thing, induce,
                     approach"
  III Macc. 7:10, They petitioned the king to be al-
                  lowed to inflict

PHALARIS, Phalaris
  III Macc. 5:20, then with a barbarity exceeding
                  that of Phalaris,
            5:42, The king, just like another Phala-
                  ris, a prey to

PHARAOH, Pharaō
  I Esd. 1:25, all these acts of Josias it came to
              pass that Pharaoh
  I Macc. 4:9, were delivered in the Red Sea, when
              Pharaoh pursued

III Macc. 2:6, make known thy power when thou
              causest...Pharaoh
         6:4, Thou destroyedst Pharaoh, with his
              host of

PHASELIS, Phaselis
I Macc. 15:23, all the countries, and to Sampsames
              ...and Phaselis,

PHASIRON, Phasiron
I Macc. 9:66, he smote Odonarres...and the child-
              ren of Phasiron in

PHENICE, Phoinikē
I Esd. 2:24, thou shalt...have no passage into...
             Phenice
        2:27, king...reigned and exacted tributes
              in...Phenice
II Macc. 3:5, to Apollonius...governor of Celosyria
              and Phenice
         3:8, of visiting the cities of Celosyria
              and Phenice,
         4:4, being the governor of Celosyria and
              Phenice, did
         4:22, received of Jason...afterward went
              ...unto Phenice
         8:8, saw that...the governor of Celosyria
              and Phenice
        10:11, appointed him chief governor of
               Celosyria and Phenice

PHILARCHES, Phularchēs
II Macc. 8:32, They slew also Philarches, that
               wicked person, who

PHILIP, Philippos
I Macc. 1:1, it happened, after that Alexander
             son of Philip
        6:2, which Alexander the son of Philip...
             had left there
        6:14, Then called he for Philip, one of
              his friends, whom
        6:55, At that time Lysias heard say, that
              Philip...had
        6:63, returned unto Antiochia, where he
              found Philip
        8:5, Beside this, how they had discomfited
             in battle Philip
II Macc. 5:22, vex the nations: at Jerusalem,
               Philip, for his
         6:11, And others...being discovered to

Philip, were all
II Macc. 8:8, So when Philip saw that this man
increased by little
9:29, And Philip, that was brought up
with him, carried
13:23, heard that Philip who was left over
the affairs in

PHILISTINES, Phulistiem
Eccl. 46:18, of the Syrians, and all the princes
of...Philistines
47:7, and brought nought to the Philistines
his adversaries
50:26, mountains of Samaria, and...dwell
among...Philistines
I Macc. 3:24, residue fled into the land of the
Philistines
3:41, also of Syria and of the land of the
Philistines
5:66, he removed to go into the land of
the Philistines,
5:68, turned to Azotus in the land of the
Philistines,
IV Macc. 3:7, For after David had been attacking
the Philistines

PHILOMETOR, Philomētora
II Macc. 9:29, of Antiochus went into Egypt to
Ptolemeus Philometor
10:13, and called a traitor...Philometor
had committed

PHILOPATER, Philopator
III Macc. 1:1, Now Philopater, on learning from
those who came
3:12, King Ptolemy Philopater, to the
commanders...in
7:1, King Ptolemy Philopater to the
commanders

PHILOSOPHER, Philosophos, "a lover of science, a
systematic philosopher"
IV Macc. 5:6, and you appear to me to be no
philosopher
5:35, I will not put thee to shame, O
philosopher Reason

PHILOSOPHICAL, philosophia, "a love of science, a
systematic philosophy"
IV Macc. 1:1, going to demonstrate a most philosophical

PHILOSOPHY, philosophia, "love of knowledge, and
                        wisdom fondness of studious
                        pursuit"
    IV Macc. 5:11, Will you not awake from your tri-
                   fling philosophy?
            5:22, But thou deridest our philosophy,
                  as though we
            7:9, father, hast...made credible the
                 words of philosophy
            7:21, walking religiously by the...rule
                  of philosophy...?
            7:24, that even boys, imbued with philo-
                  sophy of

PHINEES, Phinees
    Eccl. 45:23, The third in glory is Phinees the son
                 of Eleazar,
    I Macc. 2:26, he zealously for the law of God,
                  like as Phinees
            2:54, Phinees our father in being zealous
                  and fervent

PHINEHAS, Phinees
    IV Macc. 18:12, used to tell you of the zealous
                    Phinehas; and

PHOENICIA, Phoinikē
    III Macc. 3:15, nurse the inhabitants of Coele-
                    Syria and Phoenicia
    IV Macc. 4:2, the military governor of Syria and
                  Phoenicia, and

PHRYGIAN, Phruga
    II Macc. 5:22, at Jerusalem, Philip, for his
                   country a Phrygian,

PHUD, Phoud
    Judith 2:23, and destroyed Phud and Lud, and
                 spoiled all the

PHYSIC, therappeuma, "service done, medical treat-
                     ment, nurture"
    Eccl. 18:19, Learn before thou speak, and use
                 physic or ever thou

PHYSICIAN, iatros, "a physician"
    Tobit 2:10, and I went to the physicians, but they
                helped me not:
    Eccl. 10:10, The physician cutteth off a long di-
                 sease: and he
            38:1, Honour a physician with the honour due
                  unto him for

Eccl. 38:3, The skill of the physician shall lift
up his head:
38:12, Then give place to the physician, for
the Lord hath
38:15, let him fall into the hand of his
physician

PIETY, eusebeia, "reverent, pious, devout"
III Macc. 2:31, abhorring any approach to the city
of piety...gave
IV Macc. 5:24, and it teaches us piety, so that we
worship the
6:2, old man adorned...with the comeliness
of piety
7:1, like...steering the vessel of piety
in the sea
7:3, in no way shifted the rudder of
piety till it sailed
13:8, For having arranged a holy choir of
piety, they
13:10, us not be cowards in the manifestation of piety
13:12, Isaac endured to be slain for the
sake of piety
14:3, concert of the seven brethren as concerning piety

PILE, pur, "fire, a funeral-pyre"
IV Macc. 17:1, she threw herself upon the pile,
rather than

PILLAR, kanon, "a cane, a measure, rule"
Judith 13:6, Then she came to the pillar of the
bed, which was at

stulos, "a pillar"
Judith 13:9, bed, and pulled down the canopy from
the pillars;

stele, "of or like a block or pillar"
Wisd.-Sol. 10:7, and a standing pillar of salt is
a monument of

stulos
Wisd.-Sol. 18:3, Instead whereof thou gavest them
a burning pillar
Eccl. 24:4, in high places, and my throne is in a
cloudy pillar
26:18, As the golden pillars are upon the
sockets of silver
36:24, a help like unto himself, and a pillar

of rest
Epis.-Jer. 1:59, Therefore it is better to be...a
                pillar of wood
I Macc. 13:29, he made cunning devices...he set
               great pillars

stēlē
I Macc. 14:27, which they set upon pillars in
               mount Sion:
III Macc. 2:27, wherefore he erected a pillar at
                the tower-porch,

stulos
IV Macc. 17:3, as a house bravely build upon the
               pillar of thy

PILLOW, proskephalaion, "a cushion for the head,
                pillow"
I Esd. 3:8, sentence...and laid it under the pillow
            of...Darius

PIOUS, eusebēia, "reverence toward the gods, piety"
IV Macc. 17:22, antipoise to the nation...by the
                blood of those pious ones,

PIPE, aulos, "any wind instrument, a flute, pipe"
Eccl. 40:21, The pipe and the psaltery make sweet
             melody; but a
IV Macc. 3:45, and joy was taken from Jacob, and
               the pipe with

PIT, lakkos, "any hollow, a hole, pit"
Wisd.-Sol. 10:13, she went down with him into the
                  pit,

bothros, "a pit, well, a cistern"
Eccl. 12:16, An enemy...imagineth how to throw
             thee into a pit
       21:10, with stones, but at the end...is the
              pit of hell
       27:26, Whoso diggeth a pit shall fall there-
              in: and he that

phrear, "a well, cistern, a pit"
I Macc. 7:19, this...Bacchides...cast them into
              the great pit

koilia, "a cavity, the belly, a hollow place"
II Macc. 1:19, took the fire of the altar...and
               hid it in...a pit

lakkos
II Macc. 10:37, and killed Timotheus, that was hid

in a certain pit, and

PITCH, pissa, "pitch, pitchy"
  Eccl. 13:1, He that toucheth pitch shall be defiled
            therewith;
  Bel-Drag. 1:25, Then Daniel took pitch, and fat,
            and hair, and

        paraballō, "to cast or to throw aside"
  I Macc. 3:57, So the camp removed, and pitched
            upon the south
        5:39, hired the Arabians...and they have
            pitched their

        paremballō, "to throw in by the way, inter-
            polate"
  I Macc. 5:50, So the soldiers pitched and assaulted
            the city all
        6:31, These went through Idumea, and pitch-
            ed against

        paraballō
  I Macc. 6:32, Upon this Judas removed from the
            tower and pitched

        paremballō
  I Macc. 7:19, removed Bacchides from Jerusalem,
            and pitched his

        paraballō
  I Macc. 7:39, So Nicanor went out of Jerusalem,
            and pitched his
        7:40, But Judas pitched in Adasa with three
            thousand men,

        paremballō
  I Macc. 9:2, Who went forth...and pitched their
            tents before
        9:5, Now Judas had pitched his tents at
            Eleasa, and three
        9:33, Then Jonathan, and Simon his brother
            ...pitched their

        paraballō
  I Macc. 10:75, he pitched his tents against Joppe:
            but they shut
        11:67, As for Jonathan and his host, they
            pitched at the

        paremballō
  I Macc. 13:13, But Simon pitched his tents at
            Adida, over against

PITY, éleeō, "to have pity on, shew mercy upon"
  Eccl. 12:13, Who will pity a charmer that is bit-
                ten with a
  Bar. 3:2, Hear, O Lord...and have pity upon us,
            because we have

        oikteirō, "to pity, have pity or compassion
                   upon"
  II Macc. 8:2, and also pity the temple profaned
                of ungodly men

        dikteirmos, "pity"
  IV Macc. 6:24, against misery, and not changing
                 at their pity,

        éleeō
  IV Macc. 9:3, O tyrant...pity us more than we pity
                ourselves

        éleos, "pity, showing mercy"
  IV Macc. 9:4, For we account your pity of us on
                the terms of

PITYING, katoiktisis, "a pitying, compassion"
  IV Macc. 12:2, whom the tyrant pitying, though he
                 had been

PLACE, diaspora, "dispersion"
  Judith 5:19, and are come up from the places where
               they were

        topos, "a place, spot, position"
  Wisd.-Sol. 19:22, and...assist them in every time
                    and place,

        érēmos, "a lonely place, desert"
  Eccl. 8:16, man, and go not with him into a soli-
              tary place:
        9:7, of the city, neither wander thou in...
             solitary places

        tapeinos, "low lying place"
  Eccl. 10:15, nations, and planted the lowly in
               their place

        topos
  Eccl. 12:12, Set him not by thee, lest...he stand
               up in thy place;

        paroikia, "a dwelling in a place, as paroikos,
                   sojourning"
  Eccl. 16:8, Neither spared he the place where Lot
              sojourned, but

hupselos, "a highland country"
Eccl. 24:4, I dwelt in high places, and my throne
          is in a cloudy

stasis, "position, post, station"
Eccl. 36:12, them hath he cursed and...turned out
           of their places

topos
Eccl. 38:12, Then give place to the physician, for
           the Lord hath
      41:19, and of theft in regard of the place
           where thou

hodos, "a path, way, road, a pathway, an en-
       trance"
Eccl. 48:5, from death, and his soul from the
          place of the dead,

topos
Eccl. 49:10, let their bones flourish again out
           of their place:
Bar. 2:24, bones of our kings...should be taken
          out of their places
     3:15, Who hath found out her place? or who
          hath come into
     3:24, how large is the place of his possession!

kriterion, "a court of judgment, tribunal, place
           of judgment"
His.-Sus. 1:49, Return again to the place of judg-
               ment: for they

topos
Bel-Drag. 1:39, angel of the Lord set Habacuc in
               his own place
I Macc. 1:8, And his servants bare rule every one
            in his place
        1:25, there was great mourning in Israel,
             in every place

eremos²
I Macc. 2:31, man...were gone down into the secret
             places in the
        2:36, army...to take away their memorial
             from that place;
        3:46, for in Maspha was the place where
             they prayed
        4:43, and bare out the defiled stones into
             an...place
        4:46, and laid up the stones...in a con-
             venient place until

I Macc. 5:49, that every man should pitch his tent
                in the place
          6:54, to disperse themselves, every man to
                his own place
          6:57, and our victuals are but small, and
                the place we
          6:62, Then the king entered into...the
                place...that he had
          9:45, water of Jordan on this side...
                neither is there place

        topos
I Macc. 10:13, for it was their place of refuge
        10:40, I give...of the king's accounts
                from the places
        10:73, the plain, where is neither stone...
                nor place to
        11:38, sent away all his forces...to his
                own place,
        11:69, they that lay in ambush rose out
                of their places,
        12:4, them letters unto the governors of
                every place,
        13:20, Simon and his host marched against
                him in...place,
        15:29, thereof ye have wasted, and done
                great hurt in...many places,
        15:30, ye have taken, and the tributes
                of the places
II Macc. 1:14, he would marry her, he came into
                the place,
          1:19, priests...took the fire...and hid
                it in a hollow place
          1:29, Plant thy people again in thy holy
                place, as Moses
          1:33, told the king of Persia, that in
                the place, where
          1:34, Then the king, enclosing the place,
                made it holy,
          2:7, As for that place, it shall be un-
                known until the
          2:8, Then shall the Lord shew them...that
                the place might
          2:18, will....gather us together...into
                the holy place
          3:2, even the kings themselves did honour
                the place, and
          3:18, flocking out of their houses...be-
                cause the place

II Macc. 3:30, praised the Lord, that had...honour-
ed his own place

3:38, for that place, no doubt, there is
an especial

palaistra, "a wrestling school, generally, a
school"

II Macc. 4:14, of the unlawful allowance in the
place of exercise

topos

II Macc. 4:36, And when the king was come again
from the places

4:38, he took away Andronicus...unto that
very place,

5:16, by other kings to the...honour of
the place,

5:17, Antiochus...that his eye was not
upon the place

5:19, God did not choose the people for
the place's sake

5:20, And therefore the place itself, that
was partaker

6:2, also the temple...as they did desire
...in the place

8:17, their eyes the injury...done to the
holy place,

8:31, together, they laid them...in convenient places,

10:7, branches...and sang psalms...in
cleansing his place

12:2, But of the governors of several
places...and beside

12:18, as for Timotheus they found him not
in the places:

13:4, kings moved Antiochus...as the manner
is in that place

13:5, Now was there in that place a tower
of fifty cubits

13:23, heard that Philip...dealt kindly
with the place

15:1, Judas and his company were in the
strong places

III Macc. 1:1, Antiochus had made himself master
of the places,

1:9, Jerusalem, sacrificed...to the sanctity of the place

1:10, struck with the exact magnificence
of the place,

III Macc. 1:23, they created a great uproar in
      the place,

  naos, "the dwelling of a god, the temple"
III Macc. 2:1, Simon bowed his knees over against
      the holy place,

  topos
III Macc. 2:9, thou didst make this place sacred
      to thy name
    2:14, this...man...dishonour this thy
      holy place,
    2:16, seemed good to thee...thou didst
      sanctify thie place
    4:3, What home, or city, or place, at
      all inhabited
    4:18, left in the land, and others...in
      various places,
    5:44, arranged their forces in...conven-
      ient places of
    6:30, should keep a gladsome festival
      in the...place
    7:20, when they had dedicated the place
      of their
IV Macc. 4:9, throw his shield over the holy, and
      despised place,
    4:12, would celebrate...the blessedness
      of the holy place
    5:1, Antiochus, sitting...upon a certain
      lofty place

PLAGUE, kakia, "malice, malignity, depravity, calam-
      ity"
  Wisd.-Sol. 14:22, war of ignorance, those so great
      plagues,

    mastix, "a scourge, ship, a scourge of di-
      sease"
  Eccl. 23:11, useth much swearing shall be filled
      with...plague

    plēgē, "a blow, stroke, affliction, plague,
      calamity"
  Eccl. 25:13, (Give me) any plague, but the plague
      of the heart:

    kaka, "disgrace, dishonour, evil"
  Bar. 2:2, to bring upon us great plagues, such as
      never happened
    2:7, For all these plagues are come upon us,
      which the Lord

Bar. 3:4, for the which cause these plagues cleave
          unpon us
     4:29, For he that hath brought these plagues
           upon you shall
Epis.-Jer. 1:48, For when there cometh any war or
                 plague upon
           1:49, they...can neither save themselves
                 ...from plague?

     plēgē
I Macc. 3:29, in the country were small, because
              of the...plague,

     mastix
II Macc. 7:37, and thou by torments and plagues
               mayest confess,

     plēgē
II Macc. 9:5, God of Israel, smote him with an in-
              curable...plague

PLAGUED, plēssō, "to strike, to smite, plague"
I Macc. 9:55, to put down, even at that time was
              Alcimus plagued
II Macc. 9:11, He therefore being plagued, he be-
               gan to leave off

PLAIN, pedion, "a plain, flat, open country"
I Esd. 1:29, but joined battle with him in the
             plain of Mageddo,
Judith 1:5, made war with...Arphaxad in the great
            plain,
      1:8, the nations...and Galaad...and the
           great plain of
      6:11, and brought him out of the camp into
            the plain,
      15:2, upon them...they fled into every way
            of the plain,
      15:7, that were in the mountains and in the
            plain, gat many

     hosios, "sanctioned or approved by the law
             of nature, the property of gods"
Eccl. 39:24, As his ways are plain unto the holy;
             so are they

     pedion
I Macc. 3:24, from the going down of Bethhoron
              unto the plain,
       4:6, Judas shewed himself in the plain
            with three
       4:15, the hindermost of them were slain...

                          unto the plains
    I Macc. 4:21, therefore they perceived these things
                     ...in the plain
             5:52, went they over Jordan into the great
                     plain before
            10:73, thou shalt not be able to abide...in
                     the plain,
            11:67, they...they gat them to the plain of
                     Nasor
            12:49, Tryphon an host of footmen...into
                     the great plain,
            13:13, pitched his tents at Abida, over
                     against the plain
            16:5, rose in the morning, and went into the
                     plain, behold
            16:11, Moreover in the plain of Jericho was
                     Ptolemeus the
    IV Macc. 18:8, destroyer of the desert, (or) ravish-
                     er of the plain

PLANK, <u>puknos</u>, "close, solid, thick"
    III Macc. 4:10, The planks of the deck above them
                     barred out the

PLANT, <u>phuton</u>, "a plant, that which has grown, a tree,
                     fruit-tree"
    Wisd.-Sol. 7:20, the diversities of plants and
                       virtues of roots
              10:7, to this day...waste land...and
                     plants bearing fruit
    Eccl. 3:28, for the plant of wickedness hath taken
                 root in him
         24:14, palm tree on the sea shore, and as a
                 rose plant in

         <u>kataphuteuō</u>, "to plant firmly"
    Eccl. 49:7, and that he might build up also, and
                 plant

PLANTED, <u>phuteuo</u>, "to plant trees or plants"
    Eccl. 10:15, The Lord hath...planted the lowly in
                 their place

PLATE, <u>arguroma</u>, "silver-plate"
    Judith 12:1, he commanded to bring her in where
                 his plate was set
          15:11, unto Judith Holofernes his tent, and
                 all his plate,

         <u>perimetros</u>, "above measure, very large, im-
                 mense"
    Eccl. 50:3, to receive water...was covered with

plates of brass:

PLEASURE, hedonē, "pleasure, gratification"
IV Macc. 1:20, Of the passions, pleasure and pain
            are the two most
         1:21, are many attendant affections sur-
            rounding pleasure
         1:22, Before pleasure is lust; and after
            pleasure, joy
         1:25, And there exist in pleasure a mali-
            cious disposition
         1:28, As pleasure and pain are, therefore,
            two growths
         5:23, it instructs us in temperance...to
            all pleasures
         9:31, For I lighten my suffering by the
            pleasures which

PLOUGH, aretron, "a plough"
Eccl. 38:25, How can he get wisdom that holdeth the
            plough, and

PLOWETH, aretriaō, "to plough"
Eccl. 6:19, Come unto her as one that ploweth and
            soweth, and

PLUCK, exairō, "to remove, eject, to lift up out of"
Eccl. 10:15, The Lord hath plucked up the roots of
            the proud
II Macc. 14:46, when as his blood was now quite
            gone, he plucked

      ekkoptō, "to cut out, remove"
IV Macc. 5:30, No, not if you pluck out my eyes,
            and consume my

POISON, pharmakon, "a medicine, drug, remedy, a medi-
            cine for disease"
Wisd.-Sol. 1:14, and there is no poison of destruc-
            tion in them,

POISONED, pharmakeuō, "to administer a drug, to purge"
II Macc. 10:13, he was so discouraged, that he
            poisoned himself

POLISH, kosmeō, "to adorn, decorate, embellish"
Eccl. 38:28, sitting by the anvil...watcheth to
            polish it perfectly

POLLUTE, akatharsia, "uncleanness"
I Esd. 8:83, ye enter into to possess...is a land
            polluted with

miainō, "to pollute, to stain, defile"
Tobit 2:9, I returned from the burial...being polluted, and my

molunō, "to stain, defile, corrupt, to seduce
a woman"
Tobit 3:15, and that I never polluted my name, nor
the name of my

miainō
Judith 9:8, for they have purposed to defile thy
thy sanctuary, and to pollute the
tabernacle

bebeloō, "to pollute, to profane"
Eccl. 47:20, Thou didst stain thy honour, and pollute thy seed:

miainō
I Macc. 1:46, and pollute the sanctuary and holy
people:
14:36, For in his time...the heathen...pol-
luted all about

miarō, "to be defiled with blood, polluted,
abominable"
II Macc. 5:16, and taking the holy vessels with
polluted hands,

molunō, "to defile, contaminate"
II Macc. 6:2, and to pollute also the temple in
Jerusalem, and to

miainō
III Macc. 7:14, destroyed with ignominy every polluted Jew that
IV Macc. 5:36, Mouth! thou shalt not pollute my
old age, nor the
7:6, thou didst not pollute thy sacred
teeth;

POLLUTETH, alisgema, "a pollution"
Eccl. 40:29, for he polluteth himself with other
men's meat:

POLLUTION, akatharsia, "uncleanness"
I Esd. 1:49, the people...passed all the pollutions
of all nations
9:69, have not put away...their pollutions
from the

miasmos, "pollution"
Judith 9:4, with zeal, and abhorred the pollution
of their blood,

miasma, "a stain, defilement, a pollution"
I Macc. 13:50, thence, he cleansed the tower from
pollutions

mulosmos, "defilement, pollution"
II Macc. 5:27, lest they should be partakers of
the pollution

POMP, doxa, "honour, splendour, glory"
I Macc. 11:6, Then Jonathan met the king with great
pomp at Joppe

POOL, lakkos, "any hollow, hole, or pit"
I Macc. 9:13, pitched their tents by the water pool
Asphar

POOR, ptochos, "a beggar, poor, mean, sorry"
Tobit 4:7, substance...neither turn thy face from
any poor,

penes, "poor, needy"
Wisd.-Sol. 2:10, Let us oppress the poor righteous
man, let us

ptochos
Eccl. 4:1, My son, defraud not the poor of his
living, and make
4:4, neither turn thy face from a poor man
4:8, not grieve thee to bow down thine ear
to the poor, and
7:32, And stretch out thine hand unto the
poor, that thy
10:22, Whether he be rich, noble or poor,
their glory is the
10:23, It is not meet to despise the poor
man that hath
10:30, The poor man is honoured for his
skill, and the rich

penes
Eccl. 11:21, of the Lord on the sudden to make a
poor man rich

ptochos
Eccl. 13:3, the poor man is wronged, and he must
entreat also

penes
Eccl. 13:18, and what peace between the rich and
the poor?

ptochos
Eccl. 13:19, so the rich eat up the poor

Eccl. 13:20, hate humility: so doth the rich abhor
            the poor
      13:21, but a poor man being down is thrust
            also away by his
      21:5, A prayer out of a poor man's mouth
            reacheth to the
      25:2, a poor man that is proud, as rich man
            that is a liar,
      26:4, Whether a man be rich or poor, if he
            have a good

    penēs
Eccl. 29:9, Help the poor for the commandment's
            sake, and turn

    ptōchos
Eccl. 29:22, Better is the life of a poor man in a
            mean cottage,
      30:14, Better is the poor, being sound and
            strong of constitution, than a rich
            man
      31:20, Whoso bringeth an offering of the
            goods of the poor
      32:13, He will not accept any person against
            a poor man,
      34:4, The poor laboureth in his poor estate:
            and when he
      38:19, and the life of the poor is the curse
            of the heart
Epis.-Jer. 1:28, the things that are sacrificed...
            unto the poor

PORTER, thurōros, "a door keeper, porter"
  I Esd. 1:16, Moreover the porters were at every
            gate; it was not
        5:46, and the Levites...the singers also
            and the porters,
        7:9, the Levites stood arrayed...and the
            porters at every
        8:5, up with him...certain of...the holy
            singers, porters,
        8:22, ye require no tax...of the priests...
            or porters,
        9:25, Of the porters, Salumus, and Talbanes

PORTION, kleros, "a part, portion, share"
    Eccl. 44:23, his blessing, and...divided his por-
            tions; among the

        meris, "a part, a division of a country, a
            portion"

IV Macc. 18:3, persons...were deemed worthy of a
         divine portion

POSIDONIUS, _Posidonios_
II Macc. 14:19, Wherefore he sent Posidonius, and
         Theodotus, and

POSSESSION, _plousios_, "rich, opulent, wealthy"
Wisd.-Sol. 8:5, If riches be a possession to be
         desired in this

         ktēnos, "property, property in animals"
Eccl. 28:24, Look that thou hedge thy possession
         about with

         ktēma, "a possession, property, estate"
Eccl. 51:21, troubled...therefore have I gotten a
         good possession
Bar. 3:24, O Israel, how great is...is the place
         of his possession

         kleros, "an allotment, portion"
I Macc. 10:89, also Accron with the borders thereof
         in possession

POSTERITY, _sperma_, "offspring, descent, family"
Eccl. 45:24, and that he and his posterity should
         have the
         45:25, that...the king should be to his
         posterity alone:
         47:22, But the Lord will never leave off...
         the posterity of

         genos, "descendant, generation"
Bar. 2:15, all the earth may know that...Israel
         and his posterity

         ékgenos, "put out from one's family, with-
         out king"
I Macc. 1:20, Neemias...did send of the posterity
         of those priests

POT, _chalkeion_, "a copper vessel, caldron, a smith's
         shop"
I Esd. 1:12, as for the sacrifices, they sod them
         in brass pots,

POTENTATE, _dunastes_, "a lord, master, ruler"
Eccl. 10:24, Great men, and judges, and potentates,
         shall be

POTTAGE, _hepsēsis_, "a boiling, generally cookery"
Bel-Drag. 1:33, prophet, called Habbacuc, who had
         made a pottage,

POTTER, keramos, "a potter"
  Wisd.-Sol. 15:7, For the potter, tempering soft
                earth, fashioneth
    Eccl. 27:5, The furnace proveth the potter's ves-
             sels; so the
        36:13, As the clay in the potter's hand...so
             man is in the
        38:29, So doth the potter sitting at his
             work, and turning

POURETH, ekcheo, "to pour out"
    Eccl. 18:11, Therefore God is patient with them,
             and poureth

POVERTY, ptocheia, "begging, beggar"
    Eccl. 10:31, He that is honoured in poverty, how
             much more in
        11:12, there is another that is slow...and
             full of poverty;
        11:14, Prosperity and adversity, life and
             death, poverty
        18:25, and when thou art rick, think upon
             poverty and need
        22:23, Be faithful to thy neighbour in his
             poverty, that
        26:28, a man of war that suffereth poverty;
             and men of

        kenos, "idle, vain, fruitless, empty-handed"
    Eccl. 29:9, poor...and turn him not away because
             of his poverty

POWER, dunamis, "power, might, strength, ability"
  Judith 5:3, multitude of their army, and wherein
             is their power...?
        5:23, people that have no strength nor
             power for a strong

        kratos, "strength, might, force, violence,
             power"
  Judith 6:3, He will send his power, and will de-
             stroy them from

        exousia, "power or authority to do a thing"
  Judith 8:15, For if he will not help us...he hath
             power to defend

        dunamis
  Judith 9:7, For the Assyrians are multiplied in
             their power; they
        9:8, Throw down their strength in thy power,
             and bring

kratos
Judith 9:9, send thy wrath...give into my hand...
            the power

dunamis
Judith 9:14, that thou art the God of all power
            and might,

kratos
Judith 11:7, king of all the earth liveth, and as
            his power

dunamis
Judith 13:4, Judith...said...O Lord God of all
            power, look at this

kratos
Judith 13:11, even our God, is with us, to shew
            his power yet in

ischus, "strength, force, might, a force of
            soldiers"
Judith 13:19, depart from...men, which remember the
            power of God

dunamis
Wisd.-Sol. 1:3, thoughts separate from God: and
            his power, when

kratos (krateo), "strength, might"
Wisd.-Sol. 6:3, For power is given you of the Lord,
            and

pantodunamis, "having all power, strength,
            might"
Wisd.-Sol. 7:23, man, steadfast, sure...having all
            power,

dunamis
Wisd.-Sol. 7:25, For she is the breath of the
            power of God, and a

exousia
Wisd.-Sol. 10:14, till she brought the...power
            against those that
          11:20, scattered...through the breath
            of thy power:

kratos
Wisd.-Sol. 11:21, and who may withstand the power
            of thine arm?

dunamis
Wisd.-Sol. 12:15, thinking it is not agreeable with
            thy power to

197

ischus
Wisd.-Sol. 12:16, For thy power is the beginning
                 of righteousness

dunamis
Wisd.-Sol. 12:17, will not believe that thou art
                 of a full power,

ischos, "powerful, strong, mighty"
Wisd.-Sol. 12:18, But thou, mastering thy power,
                 judgest with

dunamis
Wisd.-Sol. 13:4, But if they were astonished at
                 their power and
           14:31, For it is not the power of them
                 by whom they

kratos
Wisd.-Sol. 15:2, For if we sin, we are thine,
                 knowing thy power:
           15:3, yea to know thy power is the root
                 of immortality

exousia
Wisd.-Sol. 16:13, For thou hast power of life and
                  death: thou

dunamis
Wisd.-Sol. 16:19, another time it burneth...above
                  the power of

ischus
Wosd.-Sol. 19:20, The fire had power in the water,
                  forgetting his

dunasteia, "power, lordship, sovereignty"
Eccl. 3:20, For the power of the Lord is great,
            and he is

dunamis
Eccl. 6:26, whole heart, and keep her ways with
            all thy power
      8:13, Be not surety above thy power: for if
            thou be surety

exousia
Eccl. 9:13, Keep thee far from the man that hath
            power to kill:
      10:4, The power of the earth is in the hand
            of the Lord, and

ischuros, "strongly, vehement, exceedingly"
Eccl. 13:2, Burden not thyself above thy power while

thou livest;

Eccl. 15:18, For the wisdom of the Lord is great,
and he is mighty in power, and

exousia
Eccl. 17:2, gave them few days, and a short time,
and power also

dunamis
Eccl. 17:32, He vieweth the power of the height
of heaven; and

ischus
Eccl. 19:28, And for want of power he be hindered
from sinning,

dunamis
Eccl. 24:2, High shall she...triumph before his
power

exousia
Eccl. 24:11, in the beloved city he gave me rest
...and power

dunamis
Eccl. 29:20, Help thy neighbour according to thy
power, and

exousia
Eccl. 30:19, Give not thy son and wife...power over
thee while

dunasteia
Eccl. 33:3, against the...nations, and let them
see thy power

ischus
Eccl. 43:15, By his great power he maketh the clouds
fly forth as

dunasteia
Eccl. 43:29, terrible and very great, and marvellous in his power

dunamis
Eccl. 44:3, great glory by them through his great
power

kratos
Eccl. 46:6, And with hailstones of mighty power
he made the

keras, "the wing of an army or fleet"
Eccl. 49:6, for they gave their power unto others,
and their

dunatos, "strong, mighty, powerful"
Bar. 1:6, a collection of money according to every
         man's power:

dunamis
Bar. 2:11, brought thy people out...of Egypt...
           with great power,

cheir, "hand, one's power"
Bar. 3:5, but think upon thy power and thy name
          now at this time
      4:21, and he shall deliver you from the power
            and hand of

epideiknumi, "to show forth, demonstrate, to
             show one's self"
Epis.-Jer. 1:59, better to be a king that sheweth
                 his power,

dunamis
Epis.-Jer. 1:63, these are like unto them neither
                 in shew nor power

dunasteia
Song-Child. 1:20, and let them be confounded in all
                  their power

kratos
II Macc. 11:4, not at all considering the power of
               God, but

dunamis
II Macc. 13:2, his protector...having...a Grecian
               power of footmen,

ischuros
II Macc. 14:1, Demetrius...having entered...Tripo-
               lis with a...power,

kratos
III Macc. 1:27, officers...joined the Jews who has
                all power to
          2:6, Thou didst make known thy power
               when thou causest
          3:11, with his prosperous fortune, and
                ...superior power

alke, "bodily strength, force, prowess"
III Macc. 3:18, refrained from exercising our power
                upon them

dunastes
III Macc. 5:7, Almighty Lord...Ruler of all, Lord
               of every power

  dunamis
III Macc. 5:51, entreating the Lord of all power
                to reveal
         6:13, heathen cower before thy invincible
                ...power to
         6:16, the king came along...with wild
                beasts, and...power

  thumos, "of any vehement passion, courage"
IV Macc. 2:20, For if reasoning did not possess
                the power of

  dunamis
IV Macc. 5:13, For, bear in mind, that if there
                be any power

  exousia
IV Macc. 5:15, And having received power to speak,
                he began thus

  kratos
IV Macc. 6:34, we should allow, that the power be-
                longs to

  dunamis
IV Macc. 8:5, for I possess the power, not only
                of punishing
        14:10, for the power of fire, being sharp
                and quick,

POWERFUL, megaslosthenos, "powerful, great, mighty"
  III Macc. 5:13, fixed...to display the power of
                  his powerful hand

         ischuros, "strongly, vehemently, exceed-
                ingly"
  IV Macc. 9:17, he answered, not so powerful, O
                 accursed ministers

POWERLESS, adunamia, "want of strength, weakness,
                poverty"
  III Macc. 2:13, holy King how...we...are become
                  weak and powerless

PRAISE, eulogeo, "to speak well of, praise"
  Tobit 8:15, Then Raguel praised God, and said, O
              God, thou art worthy to be praised

        8:16, Thou art to be praised, for thou hast
              made me joyful;

        eulegetos, "blessed"
  Tobit 8:17, Thou art to be praised, because thou
              hast had mercy

eulogeō
Tobit 12:17, But he said unto them, Fear not...
                praise God
        12:18, For not of any favour of mine...where-
                fore praise him

exomologeō, "to agree, confess, make full ac-
                knowledgement for, praise"
Tobit 13:8, Let all men speak, and let all praise
                him for his
        13:10, Give praise to the Lord, for he is
                good: and praise

eulogētos
Tobit 13:18, And all her streets shall...praise
                him, saying,

exomologeō
Tobit 14:2, increased in the fear of the Lord...
                and praised him

aineō, "to speak in praise of, praise, approve"
Judith 13:14, Then he said to them...Praise, praise
                God, praise
        16:1, all the people sang after her this
                song of praise

hymneō, "to sing, praise, sing of, tell of"
Wisd.-Sol. 10:20, Therefore the righteous...
                praised thy holy name,

aineō
Wisd.-Sol. 18:9, men...should be...singing out the
                songs of praise

ainesis, "a praising, praise"
Eccl. 32:2, requiteth a good turn...giveth alms
                sacrificeth praise
        39:14, as frankincense...and sing a song of
                praise
        39:15, Magnify his name, and shew forth his
                praise with the

epainos, "approval, commendation"
Eccl. 44:8, a name behind them, and their praises
                might be
        44:15, and the congregation will shew forth
                their praise

ainesis
Eccl. 51:1, I will thank thee, O Lord and King,
                and praise thee,
        51:12, I will praise thy name continually,

and will sing praise with thanksgiving;
Eccl. 51:22, tongue for my reward, and I will
praise him
51:29, in his mercy, and be not ashamed of
his praise

doxa, "glory, splendour, credit, honour"
Bar. 2:17, in the graves...will give unto thee
neither praise nor
2:18, soul that is greatly vexed...will give
thee praise and
2:32, and they shall praise me in the land
of their
3:6, the Lord our God, and thee, O Lord, will
we praise

eulogeō
Song-Child. 1:2, thy name is worthy to be praised
and glorified

doxazō, "to sing, extol, magnify, praise,
adore, worship"
Song-Child. 1:27, Then the three, as out of one
mouth, praised,
1:33, Blessed art thou...and above all
to be praised
1:37, praise and exalt him above all
for ever
1:38, O all ye powers of the Lord...
praise and exalt
1:40, O ye stars of heaven...praise
and exalt him

eulogeō
Song-Child. 1:46, O ye nights and days...praise
and exalt him
1:49, O ye frost and snow...praise and
exalt him
1:57, O all ye fowls of the air...
praise and exalt him
1:58, O all ye beasts and cattle...
praise and exalt
1:59, O all ye children of men...
praise and exalt him
1:60, O Israel...praise and exalt him
above all for
1:61, O ye priests of the Lord...
praise and exalt him
1:62, O ye servants of the Lord...

                         praise and exalt him
Song-Child. 1:63, O ye spirits and souls of the
                         righteous...praise
                  1:64, O ye holy and humble men...
                         praise and exalt him
                  1:67, O all ye that worship the Lord...
                         praise him and

        aineō
I Macc. 4:56, days...and sacfificed the sacrifice
              of...praise

        eulogeō
II Macc. 3:30, But they praised the Lord, that had
               miraculously
         10:38, When this was done, they praised
                the Lord with
         11:19, Then they praised the merciful God
                all together,

        aineō
III Macc. 2:20, that the cast down and broken
                hearted may praise

        ainos, "that which is said to one's praise,
               praise"
III Macc. 7:16, Uttering exclamation of joy, with
                songs of praise

        aretē, "goodness, excellence"
IV Macc. 1:2, For reason is necessary...it embrace
              the praise of

        epaineō, "to praise, commend, applaud"
IV Macc. 2:2, on this ground...the temperate
              Joseph is praised in
         13:3, but by means of the reasoning which
               is praised by

        ainesis
Pr.-Mans. 1:15, and I will praise thee continually
                all the days

PRAY, proseuchomai, "to offer prayers or vows"
  Tobit 3:1, grieved did weep, and in my sorrow pray-
             ed, saying,

        boaō, "to utter a cry for assistance, to call
              to one, call on"
  Tobit 6:17, shalt come to her, rise up both of you,
              and pray to

204

proseuchomai
Tobit 8:4, Tobias rose out of the bed, and said...
    let us pray that
    12:12, Now therefore, when thou didst pray,
    and Sara thy

deomai, "to ask, need, want"
Judith 8:31, Therefore now pray thou for us, be-
    cause thou art a

proseuchomai
Judith 11:17, and I will pray unto God, and he will
    tell me when

deomai
Wisd.-Sol. 8:21, Nevertheless, when I perceived
    that...I prayed

entugchanō, "to intercede with, to converse with"
Wisd.-Sol. 16:28, it might be known...and at the
    dayspring pray

proseuchomai
Eccl. 7:14, Use not many words...when thou prayest

euchomai, "to pray to, pray for or beseech one"
Eccl 18:23, Before thou prayest, prepare thyself;
    and be not as

deomai
Eccl. 28:2, shall thy sins also be forgiven when
    thou prayest

euchomai
Eccl. 31:24, When one prayeth, and another curseth,
    whose voice

deomai
Eccl. 37:15, And above all this pray to the most
    High, that he

euchomai
Eccl. 38:9, My son...pray unto the Lord, and he
    will make thee

deomai
Eccl. 39:5, He will give his heart to...the Lord...
    and will pray

proseuchomai
Bar. 1:11, and pray for the life of Nabuchodonosor
    king of
    1:13, Pray for us also unto the Lord our God,
    for we have

Bar. 2:8, Yet have we not prayed before the Lord,
    that we might
I Macc. 3:44, congregation gathered together...
    that they might pray
    3:46, for in Maspha was the place where
    they prayed
    4:30, And when he saw that mighty army,
    he prayed and

parakaleō, "to call on, to invoke the gods, to
    invite"
I Macc. 9:35, Now Jonathan sent his brother...to
    pray his friends

proseuchomai
I Macc. 11:71, clothes, and cast earth upon his
    head, and prayed
II Macc. 2:10, And as when Moses prayed unto the
    Lord, the fire

parakaleō
II Macc. 9:26, Therefore I pray and request you to
    remember the

iketeuō, "to supplicate, entreat, beseech"
II Macc. 10:25, But when he drew near, they...
    pray unto God, and

parakaleō
II Macc. 12:3, Joppe also did such an ungodly deed:
    they prayed

proseuchomai
II Macc. 12:44, hoped...it had been superfluous and
    vain to pray

parakaleō
II Macc. 14:25, He prayed him also to take a wife,
    and to beget

kateuchomai, "to pray earnestly, to pray to one"
II Macc. 15:12, holding up his hands prayed for
    the whole body of

proseuchomai
III Macc. 6:1, cease to cry out to the holy God,
    and prayed thus:

kateuchomai
IV Macc. 12:20, Thus having prayed, he hurled him-
    self into the

deomai
Pr.-Mans. 1:13, but I pray and beseech thee,

                         release me, Lord,
PRAYER, proseuchē, "a place of prayer, prayer"
  Tobit 3:16, So the prayers of them both were heard
              before the
        12:8, Prayer is good with fasting and alms
              and righteousness
        12:12, Now, therefore thou didst pray, and
               Sara thy daughter
        12:15, seven angels, which present the prayers
               of the saints
        13:1, Tobit wrote a prayer of rejoicing and
              said,
  Judith 12:6, that thine handmaid may go forth unto
               prayer
         13:3, Now Judith...said she would go forth
               to her prayers,

        proseuchomai, "to pray, to offer prayers"
  Wisd.-Sol. 13:17, Then maketh he prayers for his
                    goods, for his

        proseuchē
  Wisd.-Sol. 18:21, shield of his proper ministry,
                    even prayer, and
  Eccl. 3:5, and when he maketh prayer, he shall be
             heard

        deēsis, "an entreating"
  Eccl. 4:6, for if he curse thee...his prayer shall
             be heard of him
        7:10, Be not fainthearted when thou makest
              thy prayer, and

        deomai
  Eccl. 17:25, Return unto the Lord, and...make thy
               prayer before

        deēsis
  Eccl. 21:5, A prayer out of a poor man's mouth
              reacheth to the

        proseuchē
  Eccl. 31:26, who will hear his prayer? or what
               doth his humbling
        31:26, with a man that fasteth...who will
               hear his prayer?

        deēsis
  Eccl. 32:13, against a poor man, but will hear the
               prayer of the
        32:16, shall be accepted...and his prayer
               shall reach unto

Eccl. 32:17, The prayer of the humble pierceth
            the clouds:
      36:17, O Lord hear the prayer of thy servants,
            according to

proseuchē
Eccl. 39:6, and give thanks unto the Lord in his
            prayer
      50:19, And the people besought the Lord...
            by prayer before

deēsis
Eccl. 51:11, I will praise thy name...and so my
            prayer was heard:
      51:13, was yet young...I desired wisdom
            openly in my prayer
Bar. 2:14, Hear our prayers, O Lord, and our peti-
            tions, and
      3:4, O Lord Almighty...hear now the prayers
            of the dead

deēsis
Bar. 4:20, of peace, and put on the sackcloth of
            my prayer:

proseuchē
I Macc. 5:33, So he went forth behind them...and
            cried with prayer
      7:37, didst choose this house...to be a
            house of prayer and
      12:11, at all times...do remember you...in
            our prayers, as

deēsis
II Macc. 1:5, and hear your prayers, and be at one
            with you, and
      10:27, So after the prayer they took their
            weapons, and

épikaleō, "to call on, appeal to, adjure"
II Macc. 15:22, therefore in his prayer he said
            after this manner

deēsis
III Macc. 1:21, Various were the prayers offered
            by those who
      1:23, Calling out to...elders to the
            station of prayer
      2:10, thou didst promise...thou wouldest
            hear our prayer

litanos, "praying, supplicant"
III Macc. 2:21, And at that time, God...heard that
prayer so

proseuchē
III Macc. 6:16, Now, at that time Eleazar had ended
his prayer,
7:20, registered as sacred upon a pillar
...one of prayer

PRAYETH, proseuchomai, "to offer prayers or vows"
II Macc. 15:14, This is a lover of the brethren,
who prayeth

PRAYING, euchomai, "to pray to"
II Macc. 15:27, So that fighting with their hands,
and praying

PRECIOUS, polutumos, "costly, of great price, precious"
Eccl. 45:11, with twisted scarlet...with precious
stones graven

PREFERREST, proaireomai, "to prefer, choose"
III Macc. 6:10, deliver us...O Lord, by death
which thou preferrest

PRESENCE, prosōpon, "face, countenance, visage, face
to face"
Judith 13:1, servants...dismissed the waiters from
the presence of

katenantion, "over against, opposite,
fronting"
Bar. 4:2, Turn thee, O Jacob...walk in the presence
of the light

enopion, "in the presence of"
Bel-Drag. 1:14, throughout all the temple in the
presence of the

PRESENTS, xania, "hospitality"
Eccl. 20:29, Presents and gifts blind the eyes of
the wise, and

PRESERVATION, sotēria, "a saving, preservation"
IV Macc. 15:26, the other for the preservation of
her children,

PRESERVES, sozō, "to save, to rescue"
IV Macc. 15:3, the religion which according to God
preserves to

PREVAIL, ischuō, "to be strong, to prevail, be valid"
I Macc. 10:49, the two kings had joined battle...

Alexander...prevailed

PREY, pronomē, "a foraging, foray, to forage"
  I Esd. 8:77, with our brethren...were given up...
          for a prey with
  Judith 9:4, and hast given their wives for a prey,
          and their
      16:5, burn up the borders...and make infants
          as a prey, and

      thera, "the beast, the game, quarry"
  Eccl. 27:10, As the lion lieth in wait for the
          prey; so sin for
  I Macc. 3:4, and like a lion's whelp roaring for
          its prey

      pronomē
  I Macc. 7:47, Afterward they took the spoils and
          the prey, and

      thera
  III Macc. 6:7, hurled, through slander...and as a
          prey to lions

PRICE, ktaomai, "to get for oneself, gain, acquiring,
          procuring"
  Eccl. 30:30, as thyself, because thou hast bought
          him with a price

      timē, "price, cost, worth of a thing"
  Epis.-Jer. 1:25, there is no breath are bought for
          a...high price

PRICK, nussō, "to prick, spur, pierce, puncture"
  Eccl. 22:19, He that pricketh the eye will make
          tears to fall:

PRIDE, huperēphania, "haughtiness, arrogance"
  Wisd.-Sol. 5:8, What hath pride profited us? or
          what good hath

      ekdikos, "lawless, without law, an avenger"
  Eccl. 5:8, for the Lord will surely revenge thy
          pride

      huperēphania
  Eccl. 10:7, Pride is hateful before God and man:
          and by both
      10:12, The beginning of pride is when one
          departeth from
      10:13, For pride is the beginning of sin, and
          he that hath
      10:18, Pride was not made for men, nor furious

                              anger for
Eccl. 15:8, For she is far from pride, and men that
            are liars
       16:8, where Lot sojourned, but abhorred them
            for...pride
       22:22, mouth...fear not...except for up-
            braiding, or pride,

       gauriaō, "to bear oneself proudly, pride
              oneself"
Eccl. 43:1, The pride of the height, the clear
            firmament, the
Bar. 4:34, the rejoicing of her great multitude,
            and her pride,

       huperēphania
I Macc. 2:49, Now have pride and rebuke gotten
              strength, and the
        3:20, They come against us in much pride
              and iniquity to
II Macc. 7:36, God, shalt receive just punishment
              for thy pride
         9:7, from jis bragging, but still filled
              with pride,
         9:11, plagued, he began to leave off his
              great pride,

       agerōchos, "high-minded, brace"
III Macc. 2:3, It is thou...who...judgest all who
              act with pride

       huperēphania
III Macc. 2:17, Punish us not, nor chastise us...
              in exuberant pride

       alaxōn, "braggart, making false pretense, an
              imposter"
IV Macc. 4:15, to the kingdom: a man of haughty
              pride and
         8:18, brethren...this vain-glory and de-
              structive pride?

PRIEST, hiereus, "priest, sacrificer"
I Esd. 1:2, having set the priests according to
            their daily
       1:7, allowance, according...to the priests
            and to the
       1:8, Helkias, Zacherias, and Syelus...gave
            to the priests
       1:10, And when these things were done, the
            priests and

I Esd. 1:14, For the priests offered the fat until
              night;
       1:21, held not such a passover as Josias,
              and the priests
       2:8, of the families of Judea...stood up;
              the priests also
       4:53, went from Babylon to build the city
              ...and all the priests
       4:54, also concerning the charges, and the
              priests'
       5:5, The priests the sons of Phinees, the
              sons of Aaron:
       5:46, And so dwelt the priests and the
              Levites and the
       5:48, the son of Josedec, and his brethren
              the priests, and
       5:56, in the second month...began Zorobabel
              ...and the priests
       5:63, Also of the priests and Levites, and
              of the chief of
       6:30, and also corn...according as the
              priests that be in
       7:6, And the children of Israel, the priests,
              and the
       7:9, The priests also and the Levites stood
              arrayed in
       8:2, the sons of Zadduc...the son of Aaron
              the chief priest
       8:5, certain of the children of Israel, of
              the priests, of
       8:19, that whatsoever Esdras the priest and
              the reader
       8:42, But when I found there none of the
              priests and

       hierateia, "the priest's office, priesthood"
I Esd. 8:46, to send such men as might execute the
              priests' office

       hiereus
I Esd. 8:54, separated the twelve of the chief of
              the priests,
       8:69, The nation of Israel, the princes,
              the priests and
       8:77, we with our brethren...and our priests
              were given up
       8:96, and took an oath of the chief of the
              priests and
       9:18, And of the priests that were come to-
              gether, and had

212

I Esd. 9:37, And the priests and the Levites, and
            they that were
Judith 11:13, which they had sanctified...for the
             priests
       15:8, Then Joacim the high priest, and the
             ancients of the
Eccl. 7:29, the Lord with all thy soul, and re-
            verence his priests
      7:31, Fear the Lord and honour the priest:
            and give him
      50:1, Simon the high priest, the son of Onias,
             who in his
      50:12, When he took up the portions out of the
              priests' hands
Bar. 1:16, kings, and to our princes, and to our
           priests, and to
Epis.-Jer. 1:10, Sometimes also the priests convey
                 from their
           1:18, the doors are made sure...even so
                 the priests
           1:28, sacrificed unto them, their priests
                 sell and
           1:31, And the priests sit in their
                 temples, having
           1:33, The priests also take off their
                 garments, and
           1:48, or plague upon them, the priests
                 consult with
           1:55, Where upon when fire falleth...
                 their priests will
Bel-Drag. 1:8, So the king was wroth and called
               for the priests,
          1:10, Now the priests of Bel were three
                score and ten,
          1:15, Now in the night came the priests
                with their
          1:21, and took the priests with their
                wives and children
I Macc. 2:1, arose Mattathias...son of Simeon, a
             priest of the
        3:49, They brought also the priest's
              garments, and the
        3:51, For thy sanctuary is trodden down...
              and thy priests
        4:42, So he chose priests of blameless con-
              versation, such
        5:67, At that time certain priests, desir-
              ous to shew

213

I Macc. 7:14, for said they, One that is a priest
of the seed of

7:33, went Nicanor up to mount Sion, and
...certain priests

7:36, Then the priests entered in, and
stood before the

10:42, things...appertain to the priests
that minister

11:23, certain of the elders of Israel, and
the priests,

12:6, Jonathan the high priest, and the
elders of the

14:28, in the great congregation of the
priests, and

14:41, also that the Jews and priests were
well pleased

14:44, lawful for none of the people or
priests to break

15:1, sent letters...unto Simon the priest,
and the prince

II Macc. 1:10, the people...sent greeting...unto
the...priests,

1:13, Which when the priests of Nanea had
sent forth,

1:19, our fathers were led into Persia,
the priests that

1:20, did send of the posterity of those
priests

1:21, Neemias commanded the priests to
sprinkle the wood

1:23, And the priests made a prayer whilst
the sacrifice

1:30, And the priests sung psalms of thanksgiving

1:33, that in the place, where the priests
that were led

3:15, But the priests, prostrating themselves before the

4:14, that the priests had no courage to
serve any more

14:31, But the other...commanded the priests
that were

14:34, Then the priests lifted up their
hands toward

15:31, called them...and set the priests
before the altar,

III Macc. 1:11, none of the nation, no, nor even
the priests in

III Macc. 1:16, And when the priests fell down in
               their sacred
        6:1, And Eleazar, an illustrious priest
               of the country,
        7:13, Their priests, then, as it was
               meet, saluted him
IV Macc. 4:9, And the priests, with the women and
               children,
        5:4, Eleazar, a priest by family, by pro-
               fession a lawyer
        7:6, O priest, worthy of the priesthood!
               thou didst
       17:9, Here an aged priest, and an aged
               woman, and seven

PRIESTHOOD, <u>hierateia</u>, "the priest's office, priest-
               hood"
   Eccl. 45:7, covenant he made with him, and gave
               him the priesthood
       45:15, by an everlasting covenant, and to...
               the priesthood
       45:24, that he...should have the dignity of
               the priesthood

          <u>hierōsunē</u>, "the office of priest, priest-
               hood, a priest's salary"
   I Macc. 2:54, obtained the covenant of an everlast-
               ing priesthood
        7:21, But Alcimus contended for the high
               priesthood

          <u>archierōsunē</u>, "high priesthood"
   I Macc. 11:57, saying, I confirm thee in the high
               priesthood,
       16:24, are written in the chronicles of
               his priesthood,

          <u>hierateuma</u>, "the priesthood, body of
               priests"
   II Macc. 2:17, that God...gave them all...the priest-
               hood, and the

          <u>archierōsunē</u>
   II Macc. 4:24, the presence of the king...got the
               priesthood to
        4:29, brother Lysimachus in his stead in
               the priesthood:
        11:3, gain of the temple, as of...the
               priesthood to sale
        14:7, Therefore I, being deprived of...the
               high priesthood

215

IV Macc. 4:1, man named Simon...once held the high
                priesthood
          4:18, And he committed to him the high
                priesthood and

          hierōsunē
IV Macc. 5:35, I will not...deny thee, O honoured
                priesthood, and
          7:6, O priest, worthy of the priesthood!
                thou didst

PRINCE, árchōn, "ruler, chief, captain, the chief
                magistrate"
I Esd. 1:29, with him in the plain of Megiddo,
                and the princes

          megistos, "greatest in honour"
I Esd. 3:1, he made a great feast...unto all the
                princes of Media
          3:9, and of whose side the king and the
                three princes of
          3:14, and sending forth he called all the
                princes of
          4:33, Then the king and the princes looked
                one upon
          8:55, which the king...and the princes, and
                all Israel, had
          8:69, The nation of Israel, the princes, the
                priests and

          árchōn
Judith 5:2, he was very angry, and called all the
                princes of Moab
          6:17, and declared...in the midst of the
                princes of Assur
          8:35, Then said Ozias and the princes unto
                her, Go in peace
          9:10, of my lips the servant with the prince,
                and the prince with the servant
Eccl. 10:14, The Lord hath cast down the thrones
                of proud princes

          hegemon, "a leader, a chieftain, prince"
Eccl. 39:4, serve among great men, and appear be-
                fore princes:
          41:17, father and mother: and of a lie before
                a prince

          árchōn
Eccl. 46:13, beloved of his Lord...anointed princes
                over his

216

Eccl. 46:18, of the Syrians, and all the princes
of the Philistines
48:12, whilst he lived, he was not moved...
of any prince,
Bar. 1:9, had carried away...the princes, and the
captives,
1:16, and to our kings, and to our princes,
and to our
2:1, Lord hath made good his word...against
our princes, and
3:16, Where are the princes of the heathen,
and such as
Song-Child. 1:14, Neither is there at this time
prince, or
I Macc. 3:13, Now when Seron, a prince of the army
of Syria, heard
6:60, So the king and the princes were
content:
6:61, Also the king and the princes made
an oath unto
7:26, sent Nicanor, one of his honourable
princes, a man
9:30, we have chosen thee this day to be
our prince and

megistos
I Macc. 9:37, from Nadabatha...daughter of one of
the great princes

archōn
I Macc. 10:63, him sit by himself, and said unto
his princes, Go
12:24, Now when Judas heard that Demetrius'
princes were
14:2, sent one of his princes to take him
alive

ethnarchēs, "a ruler of a nation, prefect, an
ethnarch"
I Macc. 15:1, unto Simon the priest and prince of
the Jews,
15:2, Antiochus to Simon the high priest
and prince of

dunastēs, "a lord, master, ruler"
II Macc. 3:24, the Lord of spirits, and the Prince
of all power,
9:25, Again, considering how that the
princes that are

217

PRINCIPALITY, archē, "a principality, prince of
                spiritual existence, magistrate"
   II Macc. 4:27, So Menelaus got the principality:
                but as for the
          5:7, Howbeit for all this he obtained not
                the principality

PRINCIPLE, logismos, "consideration, reasoning, con-
                clusion"
   IV Macc. 15:11, the various tortures able to per-
                vert her principle

PRISON, eirktē, "a prison, an enclosure"
   Wisd.-Sol. 17:16, there fell down was...shut up
                in a prison

          katakleiō, "to close, shut fast, shut up,
                confine"
   II Macc. 13:21, when they had gotten him, they put
                him in prison

PRISONER, desmos, "bonds, imprisonment, binding with
                a spell"
   Wisd.-Sol. 17:2, they shut them up in...houses,
                the prisoners of

          aichmalosia, "captivity, state of captivity"
   I Macc. 9:70, sent an ambassador...and deliver
                them the prisoners
          9:72, therefore he had restored unto him
                the prisoners
          15:40, invade Judea, and to take the people
                prisoners,

          desmos
   II Macc. 14:33, If ye will not deliver me Judas as
                a prisoner, I

          dorialotos, "captive of the spear, taken
                in war"
   III Macc. 1:5, and that many of them were taken
                prisoners

PRIVILY, lathra, "secretly"
   I Macc. 9:60, and sent letters privily to his ad-
                herents in Judea,
   II Macc. 1:19, the priests...took the fire of the
                altar privily,

          lanthanō, "to escape or elude without being
                seen"
   II Macc. 8:1, Then Judas Maccabeus...went privily
                into the towns,

PRIVY, airetos, "chosen, elected, preferable"
  Wisd.-Sol. 8:4, For she is privy to the mysteries
                  of the knowledge
  Bel-Drag. 1:13, for under the table they had made
                  a privy

        kruptē, "a vault or closet, a cell"
  II Macc. 1:16, and opening a privy door of the
                  roof, they threw

        epiboulē, "a purpose or design against any
                   one, conspiracy, plot"
  II Macc. 8:7, he advantage of the night for such
                 privy attempts,

PROCLAMATION, kerugma, "proclamation, proclaiming"
  I Macc. 5:49, Wherefore Judas commanded a proclama-
                 tion to be made
        10:63, Also he made...proclamation, that no
               man complain
        10:64, that he was honoured according to the
               proclamation,

            logos, "conversation, expression, that
                    which is said or expressed"
  IV Macc. 4:7, And the nation indignant at this
                 proclamation, and

PROFANATION, bebelos, "not connected with religion;
                       unholy; a despiser, scorner"
  I Macc. 1:48, uncircumcised...with all manner of...
                 profanantion

PROFANE, bebēlos, "profane, not religious, unholy"
  I Macc. 1:43, the Israelites consented...and pro-
                 faned the sabbath
        1:45, and that they should profane the
              sabbaths and
        1:63, that they might not profane the holy
              covenant:
        2:12, behold, our sanctuary...the Gentiles
              have profaned
        2:34, But they said, We will not...profane
              the sabbath day
        3:51, For thy sanctuary is trodden down
              and profaned,
        4:38, the sanctuary desolate, and the altar
              profaned, and
        4:44, what to do with the altar...which
              was profaned

I Macc. 4:54, At that time and day the heathen had
              profaned it,
II Macc. 5:16, polluted hands, and with profane
              hands, pulling

     athemitos, "unlawful, criminal, wicked"
II Macc. 6:5, The altar was also filled with pro-
              fane things,

     bebēlō, "to profane, pollute"
II Macc. 8:2, that he would...pity the temple pro-
              faned of ungodly
         10:5, upon the same day that the strangers
              profaned the

     bebēlos
III Macc. 2:2, who are oppressed by a wicked and
              profane one,
         2:14, this bold and profane man seeks to
              dishonour this

     bebēlō
III Macc. 4:16, heart, far from the truth, and his
              profane mouth,

PROFANITY, bebēlō, "to profane, pollute, violate"
    III Macc. 2:17, Punish us not by means...of their
              profanity

PROFITLESS, matēn, "fruitlessly, withou profit"
    IV Macc. 16:7, useless childbirths, and seven pro-
              fitless periods

PROGENITOR, patrōos, "hereditary, transmitted from
              one's father"
    IV Macc. 16:20, Abraham was forward to sacrifice
              Isaac our progenitor,

PROLIFIC, polugonos, "producing many, prolific"
    IV Macc. 15:5, are by nature weak in disposition
              and prolific in

PROMISE, epaggelia, "order, announcement, promise,
              assurance"
    I Esd. 1:7, king's allowance, according as he
              promised

     epaggellō, "to promise, undertake, declare"
II Macc. 2:18, as he promised in the law, will
              shortly have mercy

     epaggelia
IV Macc. 12:9, And they rejoicing exceedingly at
              the promise of

                        220

Pr.-Mans. 1:6, the mercy of thy promise is both
      immeasureable and

PROPHECY, prophetia, "the gift of interpreting the
      will of the gods, preaching"
  Tobit 2:6, remembering the prophecy of Amos, as
      he said, Your
  Eccl. 24:33, I will yet pour out doctrine of pro-
      phecy, and leave

PROPHESIED, propheteia, "the gift of expounding of
      scripture, preaching"
  I Esd. 6:1, prophesied unto the Jews in Jewry and
      Jerusalem in
  Eccl. 46:20, And after his death he prophesied and
      shewed the
     48:13, him; and after his death his body
      prophesied.

PROPHESY, propheteuo, "to interpret the word"
  Eccl. 47:1, And after him rose up Nathan to prophesy
      in the time

PROPHET, prophetes, "one who speaks for another"
  I Esd. 1:28, chariot...not regarding the words of
      the prophet
     1:32, mourned for Josias, yea, Jeremy the
      prophet lamented
     1:52, in derision...they made a sport of
      his prophets
     6:1, Darius...the son of Addo, the prophet,
      prophesied,
     6:2, Then stood up Zorobabel...and Jesus...
      the prophets of
     8:82, thy commandments, which thou gavest...
      the prophets,
  Tobit 14:4, I will believe those things which Jonas
      the prophet
     14:8, because that those things which the
      prophet Jonas
  Wisd.-Sol. 7:27, she maketh them friends of God,
      and prophets
     11:1, there works in the hand of the holy
      prophet
  Eccl. 1:1, things have been delivered unto us by
      the...prophets,
     36:15, Give testimony unto those that...raise
      up prophets
     46:13, Samuel, the prophet of the Lord, be-
      loved of his Lord,

Eccl. 46:15, By his faithfulness he was found a
            true prophet, and
      48:1, Then stood up Elias the prophet as
            fire, and his word
      48:8, who anointedst kings to take revenge,
            and prophets to
      48:22, the thing that pleased the Lord...as
            Esay the prophet,
      49:7, entreated him evil, who nevertheless
            was a prophet,
      49:10, And of the twelve prophets, let the
            memorial be
Bar. 1:16, to our kings, and to our princes...and
           to our prophets,
     1:21, have not hearkened unto...the words of
           the prophets,
     2:20, as thou hast spoken by thy servants the
           prophets,
     2:24, But we would not hearken unto...the
           prophets...that the
Song-Child. 1:14, is there at this time prince,
                  or prophet, or
Bel-Drag. 1:33, Now there was in Jewry a prophet,
                called Habbacuc
I Macc. 4:46, until there should come a prophet
              to shew
       9:27, not since the time that a prophet
             was not seen
       9:54, he pulled down also the works of
             the prophets
       14:41, priest for ever, until there should
              arise a...prophet
II Macc. 2:1, records, that Jeremy the prophet
              commanded them
        2:4, in the same writing that the prophet
             being warned
        2:13, were reported in the writings...and
              the prophets,
        15:9, comforting them out of the law and
               the prophets,
        15:14, Then Onias answered...Jeremias the
                prophet of God
IV Macc. 18:10, when yet with you, the law and the
                prophets

PROPITIATION, exilaskomai, "to appease completely,
                          propitiate"
Eccl. 5:5, Concerning propitiation, be not without
           fear to add

PROPITIATORY, hilasterios, "propitiatory"
   IV Macc. 17:22, the blood of the pious ones, and
           their propitiatory death

PROSPER, euodoō, "cause to prosper or be successful"
   I Macc. 2:47, proud men, and the work prospered
           in their hand
       14:36, For in his time things prospered in
           his hands, so

PROSPERITY, agathos, "good, profitable, beneficent"
   Eccl. 11:14, Prosperity and adversity, life and
           death...come of

          euodoō, "to be furthered, to prosper"
   Eccl. 11:17, with the godly, and his favour
           bringeth prosperity

          agathos
   Eccl. 11:25, In the day of prosperity there is a
           forgetfulness of
       12:8, In the prosperity of a man enemies will
           be grieved:
      13:26, cheerful countenance is a token...of...
           prosperity
      22:23, that hou mayest rejoice in his pro-
           sperity
      37:4, a companion, which rejoiceth in the
           prosperity of a

          eirēnē, "tranquility, felicity, every
              kind of blessing and good"
   I Macc. 12:22, shall do well to write unto us of
           your prosperity

          agathos
   IV Macc. 12:11, Impious tyrant...having received
           prosperity and a

PROTECTOR, epitrophos, "an agent, manager, a steward,
             an overseer or guidian"
   II Macc. 11:1, after this, Lysias the king's pro-
           tector and cousin
       14:2, country, and killed Antiochus, and
           Lysias...protector
   III Macc. 6:9, And now...thou who art the protector
           of all things;

PROUD, huperephanos, "conspicuous above, hgughty,
             arrogant"
   Eccl. 11:30, partridge taken...in a cage, so is
           the heart of the proud

Eccl. 21:4, Thus the house of proud men shall be
          made desolate
     23:4, Father and God of my life, give me not
          a proud look
     23:8, both the evil speaker and the proud
          shall fall
     25:2, a poor man that is proud, a rich man
          that is a liar,
     27:28, Mockery and reproach are from the
          proud; but
     35:12, and do what thou wilt; but sin not by
          proud speech

PROUDLY, huperēphaneia, "arrogance, haughtiness,
                    contempt for a person or
                    thing"
  I Macc. 1:24, taken all away...having...spoken very
          proudly
       7:47, and...right hand, which he stretched
          out so proudly,

PROVE, peiazō, "to make proof or trial of, put to
          the proof"
  Wisd.-Sol. 3:5, God proved them, and found them
                    worthy,

    apodeiknumi, "to point out, display, to prove"
  IV Macc. 16:2, I have proved, then, that not only
          men have

PROVERB, parabolē, "a sentiment, pattern, adage, an
                    enigmatic saying"
  Tobit 3:4, delivered us for a spoil...and for a
          proverb of
  Wisd.-Sol. 5:3, we had sometimes in derision and
                    a proverb of
  Eccl. 8:8, wise, but acquaint thyself with their
          proverbs:
     47:17, marvelled at thee for thy songs, and
          proverbs,

    legō, "to tell, declare, narrate, propound"
  IV Macc. 18:16, He declared the proverbs of
                    Solomon, who saith,

PROVIDE, kataskeuazō, "to prepare, put in readiness"
  I Macc. 10:20, So in the seventh month...Jonathan
                    ...provided much

PROVIDENCE, pronoia, "providence, provision"
  Wisd.-Sol. 17:2, men...lay (there) exiled from the
                    eternal providence

boēthos, "a Helper"
III Macc. 4:21, Now this was the active interfer-
             ence of...Providence

pronoia
III Macc. 5:30, fierce anger...for by the Providence
             of God
IV Macc. 9:24,which means our just and paternal
             Providence,
         13:18,which the...all-wise Providence has
             imparted
         17:22,became antipoise...and the Divine
             Providence saved

PROVINCE, satrapeia, "a satrapy, the office or pro-
             vince of a satrap"
I Esd. 3:2, captains...in the hundred twenty and
         seven province

PROVISION, brōma, "food"
I Macc. 9:52, and put forces in them, and provision
         of victuals

PROVOKE, paroxunō, "to provoke, incite, stir up,
             irritate"
Eccl. 4:2, Make not a hungry soul sorrowful;
         neither provoke a
Bar. 4:7, For ye provoked him that made you by
         sacrificing unto

    deiknumi, "to inform against, to bring to
             light, display"
I Macc. 6:34, To the end they might provoke the
         elephants to

    orgilos, "to prone to anger, passionate"
IV Macc. 8:8, For if you provoke me by your dis-
         obedience, you will

PRUDENCE,phronēsis, "good sense, practical wisdom,
             prudence"
Wisd.-Sol. 8:6, And if prudence work: who of all
             that are is a
         8:7, love righteousness...temperance
             and prudence,

    sunesis, "understanding, intelligence,
             judgment"
Eccl. 10:3, destroyeth his people; but through the
         prudence of

    phronēsis
Eccl. 19:22, wisdom, neither...the counsel of

sinners prudence
Eccl. 25:9, Well is he that hath found prudence,
and he that

sunesis
Eccl. 31:10, but he that hath travelled is full
of prudence

phronesis
IV Macc. 1:2, For reason is...the praise of prudence, the highest
1:6, does not rule over...temperance, and
prudence,
1:18, And the forms of wisdom are prudence,
and justice,
1:19, The leading one of these is prudence;
by whose

PRUDENT, sunetos, "intelligent, discerning, sagacious,
wise"
Eccl. 3:29, The heart of the prudent will understand a parable;

panourgos, "crafty, cunning, wily"
Eccl. 6:32, thou shalt be taught and...thou shalt
be prudent

sunetos
Eccl. 10:1, and the government of a prudent man is
well ordered

PSALTERY, psalter, "a harper"
Wisd.-Sol. 19:18, elements were changed...like as
in a psaltery

PTOLEMAIS, Ptolemaidos
I Macc. 5:15, saying that they of Ptolemais, and
Tyrus, and Sidon
5:22, And he pursued them unto the gate
of Ptolemais; and
5:55, Jonathan were in...Galaad, and Simon
...before Ptolemais
10:1, Epiphanes, went up and took Ptolemais:
for the
10:39, As for Ptolemais, and the land pertaining thereto,
10:56, meet me therefore at Ptolemais, that
we may see one
10:58, Cleopatra, and celebrated her marriage at Ptolemais
10:60, Who thereupon went honourably to
Ptolemais, where

I Macc. 11:22, Whereof when he heard...he came to
                Ptolemais, and
         11:24, and took silver and gold...and went
                to Ptolemais unto
         12:45, now home...and come thou with me to
                Ptolemais, for
         12:48, Now as soon as Jonathan entered into
                Ptolemais, they of Ptolemais shut
         13:12, So Tryphon removed from Ptolemais
                with a great
II Macc. 13:24, made him principal governor from
                Ptolemais unto
         13:25, came to Ptolemais: the people were
                grieved for
III Macc. 7:17, Having arrived at Ptolemais, called
                from the

PTOLEMEE, Ptolemaios
I Macc. 1:18, and made war against Ptolemee king
              of Egypt:
        3:38, Then Lysias chose Ptolemee the son
              of Dorymenes,
        10:51, Afterward Alexander sent ambassadors
               to Ptolemee
        10:55, Then Ptolemee the king gave answer,
               saying, Happy
        10:57, So Ptolemee went out of Egypt with
               his daughter
        11:3, Now as Ptolemee entered into the
              cities, he set in
        11:8, King Ptolemee therefore, having gotten
              the dominion
        11:13, Then Ptolemee entered into Antioch,
               where he set
        11:15, heard of this, he came to...king
               Ptolemee
        11:17, took off Alexander's head, and sent
               it unto Ptolemee
        11:18, King Ptolemee also died the third
               day after, and
        15:16, Lucius, consul of the Romans unto
               king Ptolemee,
        16:16, and his sons had drunk largely,
               Ptolemee...rose up,
        16:18, Then Ptolemee wrote these things,
               and sent to the
II Macc. 4:45, but Menelaus, being now convicted,
               promised Ptolemee...to give him much
               money,

II Macc. 4:46, Whereupon Ptolemee taking the king
                aside into a
          6:8, went out a decree...by the suggestion
                of Ptolemee,

PTOLEMEUS, Ptolemaios
I Macc. 16:11, Moreover in the plain of Jericho
                was Ptolemeus the
II Macc. 1:10, sent greeting...unto Aristobulus...
                Ptolemeus' master
          4:21, for the coronation of king Ptolemeus
                Philometor,
          8:8, So when Philip saw that...he wrote
                unto Ptolemeus,
          9:29, For Ptolemeus, that was called
                Macron, choosing

PTOLEMY, Ptolemaios
III Macc. 1:2, armed men...committed to his trust
                by Ptolemy,
          1:3, But Dositheus...by birth a Jew...
                conveyed Ptolemy
          3:12, King Ptolemy Philopater, to the
                commanders and
          7:1, King Ptolemy Philopater to the
                commanders
IV Macc. 4:22, For being at war with Ptolemy in
                Egypt, he heard

PUBLIC, hupsēlos, "high, lofty, stately, proud"
IV Macc. 5:1, Antiochus, therefore sitting in
                public state

PUNISH, kolazō, "to prune, correct, chastise, punish"
Wisd.-Sol. 11:16, wherewithal a man sinneth...shall
                he be punished
I Macc. 7:7, and let him punish them with all them
                that aid them

        enochos, "held in, bound, liable or subject
                to a penalty, liable to accused of
                a crime"
I Macc. 14:45, shall do other wise...he should
                be punished

        ekdikazō, "to avenge, punish"
I Macc. 15:21, deliver them to Simon...that he may
                punish them

        basanizō, "to afflict, torment"
II Macc. 1:28, Punish them that oppress us...and
                with pride do us

ἐπιτιμιος, "penalty, rebuke, punishment"
II Macc. 6:13, are not suffered any longer, but
          forthwith punished

kolazō
II Macc. 6:14, other nations, whom the Lord...fore-
          beareth to punish

ἐκδικαζō
III Macc. 2:17, Punish us not by means of the un-
          cleanness of their

kolazō
III Macc. 7:3, malice vehemently urge us to punish
          the Jews

ἐμπιπτō, "to fall upon, to break, rushing in
          violently"
III Macc. 7:14, Then they punished and destroyed
          with ignominy

kolazō
IV Macc. 2:12, the love of parents...for they
          punish them for vice

timōreo, "an avenger, to punish"
IV Macc. 9:24, paternal Providence...will punish
          the pestilent
     12:19, But thee, both living and dead, he
          will punish
     17:21, and that the tyrant was punished
          and their

kolazō
IV Macc. 18:5, And the tyrant Antiochus was both
          punished upon

PUNISHMENT, kolasis, "a pruning, punishing, chasten-
          ing"
  Wisd.-Sol. 11:13, For when they heard by their
          own punishments
       16:24, against the unrighteous for their
          punishment
       19:4, they might fulfil the punishment
          which was

timōria, "punishment"
Wisd.-Sol. 19:13, And punishments came upon the
          sinners not

ἐπαπαγογē, "an invasion, an attack"
Eccl. 3:28, In the punishment ōf the proud there
          is no remedy:

229

'epitimia, "a punishment"
Eccl. 8:5, remember that we are all worthy of
        punishment

zemia, "loss, damage, penalty; hence,
        punishment"
II Macc. 4:48, the matter...did soon suffer unjust
        punishment

timōria
II Macc. 6:12, but that they judge those punish-
        ments not to be

kolasis, "chastisement, punishment, tor-
        ment"
III Macc. 3:26, For by the punishment of them in
        one body we

kindunos, "danger, trial, hazard"
III Macc. 6:26, Who has thus consigned to unmerited
        punishment

timōria
III Macc. 7:3, with the affliction of a montruous
        punishment
        7:10, to be allowed to inflict fitting
        punishment upon

dikē, "judicial punishment, vengeance"
IV Macc. 4:13, Apollonius was slain by...Divine
        punishment

katakrinō, "to give judgment against,
        condemn, to place in a guilty
        light"
IV Macc. 4:25, a precipice...knowing beforehand
        of the punishment

timōria
IV Macc. 5:10, moreover, be despising me to your
        own punishment

dikē
IV Macc. 6:28, and be satisfied with the punishment
        of me

kolasis
IV Macc. 8:8, compel me to destroy you...with ter-
        rible punishments

'olethros, "perdition, destruction"
IV Macc. 10:15, and the eternal punishment of the
        tyrant

timōria
IV Macc. 11:3, that you may owe heavenly vengeance
                a punishment

PURIFICATION, katharismos, "purification, ceremonial
                             cleansing"
  II Macc. 1:18, now purposed to keep the purifica-
                 tion of the
         2:16, about to celebrate the purification,
               we have
         2:19, Maccabeus, and his brethren, and
               the purification
  IV Macc. 6:29, Let my blood be a purification for
                 them, and take

PURIFY, kathairō, "to cleanse, to cleanse from sin"
  Judith 16:18, entered into Jerusalem...the people
                were purified,

        agnizō, "to purify morally, reform, to
                purify"
  II Macc. 1:33, matter was known...Neemias had puri-
                 fied the

        kathairō
  II Macc. 2:18, promised in the law...he hath...
                 purified the place
         17:21, tyrant was punished, and their
                country purified

PURPLE, porphura, "a purple garment, robe of purple"
  Judith 10:21, bed...which was woven with purple,
                and

        huakinthos, "hyacinth, resembling the hya-
                    cinth in colour"
  Eccl. 6:30, ornament upon her, and her bands are
              purple lace
       40:4, from him that weareth purple and a
             crown, unto him
       45:10, with a holy garment...and purple, the
              work of the

        porphura
  Epis.-Jer. 1:12, though they be covered with pur-
                   ple raiment

        huakinthos
  I Macc. 4:23, where they got much gold...and purple

        porphura
  I Macc. 8:14, none of them wore a crown, or was

                    clothed in purple
    I Macc. 10:62, to take off his garments, and clothe
                    him in purple:
            10:64, his accusers saw that he was...
                    clothed in purple,
            11:58, to be served in...and to be clothed
                    in purple, and
            14:43, beside this...he should be clothed
                    in purple, and
            14:44, it should be lawful...to be clothed
                    in purple, or
    II Macc. 4:38, forthwith he took away Andronicus
                    his purple,

PURSUE, diokō, "to pursue, to follow, to follow
                eagerly"
    Wisd.-Sol. 19:2, to depart...they would repent and
                    pursue them
                19:3, mourning...they...pursued them as
                    fugitives,
    I Macc. 2:47, They pursued also after the proud men,
                    and the work
            3:24, And they pursued them from the going
                    down of
            4:9, Remember how...Pharaoh...pursued them
                    with an army
            4:15, were slain...for they pursued them
                    unto Gazera,
            5:22, And he pursued them unto the gate of
                    Ptolemais; and
            5:60, Joseph and Azarias were...pursued
                    unto the borders
            7:45, Then they pursued after them a day's
                    journey, from
            9:15, Who discomfited the right wing, and
                    pursued them

        katadiokō, "to follow hard upon, to track"
    I Macc. 12:30, Then Jonathan pursued after them,
                    but overtook

        diokō
    I Macc. 15:11, Wherefore being pursued by king
                    Antiochus, he fled
    II Macc. 8:25, that came to buy them, and pursued
                    them far:

        katatrechō, "to run down"
    II Macc. 8:26, sabbath, and...they would no longer
                    pursue them

PURVEYOR, agorastēs, "the slave who had to buy pro-
                    visions, the purveyor"
  Tobit 1:13, High gave me grace...so that I was his
                    purveyor

PYRAMID, puramis, "pyramid"
  I Macc. 13:28, Moreover he set up seven pyramids,
                    one against

QUAIL, ortux, "a quail"
  Wisd.-Sol. 19:12, For quails came up unto them
                    from the sea for

QUAKE, saleuō, "to make to shake, to stir up"
  I Macc. 4:32, and cause...them to quake at their
                    destruction

QUARRELLING, antipiptō, "to fall upon; hence to re-
                    sist by force, strive against"
  Eccl. 34:29, bitterness of the mind, with brawling
                    and quarrelling

QUARTER, horios, "border, bound, goal, frontier"
  I Macc. 3:36, place strangers in all their quarters,
                    and divide
        5:9, themselves...against the Israelites...
                    in their quarters

QUENCH, aposbennumi, "to extinguish, to destroy, blot
                    out, quench"
  Eccl. 3:30, Water will quench a flaming fire; and
                    alms maketh an

        sbennumi, "to quench, put out"
  Eccl. 28:23, the Lord...it shall burn in them, and
                    not be quenched
  IV Macc. 3:17, temperate mind has power to conquer
                    ...and to quench
        9:20, blood, and the hot ashes were
                    quenched by...gore,

        katasbennumi, "to put out, quench, extinguish"
  IV Macc. 16:4, reasoning of religion the mother
                    quenched passions

QUICK, tachus, "quick, swift"
  IV Macc. 14:10, for the power of fire, being sharp
                    and quick,

QUICKLY, tachus, "fleet, swift, quick"
  III Macc. 2:20, Let thy mercies quickly go before
                    us...Grant us

spoudē, "hastily, quickly"
III Macc. 3:1, he gave orders that they should
            be quickly collected
        6:9, appear quickly to those of the
            race of Israel,
IV Macc. 4:5, and getting authority about it, and
            quickly
        4:22, For being at war...he quickly
            marched against them

QUINTUS, Kointos
    II Macc. 11:34, The Romans also sent unto them...
            Quintus Memmius

RABSACES, Hrapsaken
    Eccl. 48:18, In his time Sennacherib came up, and
            sent Rabsaces,

RACE, ktisis, "framing, creation, the human creation,
            a creature"
    Eccl. 43:25, be strange and wondrous works...the
            race of whales

        ethnos, "a nation, people"
    III Macc. 2:27, purpose was to inflict a public
            stigma upon our race;

        genos, "offspring, family, kindred, nation,
            people"
    III Macc. 3:2, a rumour was uttered...to injure
            the Jewish race
        6:4, Shedding the beams of thy mercy
            upon the race of
        6:9, And now...thou art the protector
            of...the race of
        6:13, who hast all power to save the
            race of Jacob
        7:10, they inflict fitting punishment
            upon those of their race

        ethnos
    IV Macc. 2:19, irrationally slain the whole race
            of the Shechemites
        4:26, compelled by means of tortures every
            one of this race,

        genos
    IV Macc. 12:18, God of my fathers to be merciful
            to my race

RACKING, strebloō, "instrument of torture, a wrench,
            rack"

IV Macc. 14:12, seven youths endured the rackings
                of...her children
         15:14, At the rackings and the roasting
                of each one of
         15:25, love of her children, and the
                racking of her

RAGAU, Ragau
   Judith 1:15, He took Arphaxad in the mountains of
                Ragau, and

RAGE, thumos, "vehement passion, anger, wrath"
   II Macc. 4:25, having the fury of a cruel tyrant,
                 and the rage of

     orgē, "any violent emotion or passion, anger"
   II Macc. 4:40, the common people...being filled
                 with rage...began

     ekthumos, "very spirited, ardent, frantic"
   II Macc. 7:3, Then the king being in rage, com-
                manded pans and

     thumos
   III Macc. 2:17, lest the lawless ones should boast
                  in their rage,

RAGES, Ragos
   Tobit 9:2, with thee...two camels, and go to Rages
              of Media

RAGUEL, Ragouēl
   Tobit 6:10, Brother, today we shall lodge with
               Raguel,
         7:1, And he came to the house of Raguel, and
              Sara met him:
         7:2, Then said Raguel to Edna his wife, How
              like is this
         7:3, And Raguel asked them, From whence are
              ye, my brethren
         7:6, Then Raguel leaped up, and kissed him,
              and wept,
         7:9, communicated the matter with Raguel:
              and Raguel said
         7:12, And Raguel said, Then take her from
               henceforth
         7:16, After Raguel called his wife Edna, and
               said unto her,
         8:9, So they slept both that night. And
              Raguel arose, and
         8:15, Then Raguel praised God, and said, O
               God, thou art

Tobit 8:20, For before the days of the marriage...
           Raguel had said
     10:7, went out...to bewail her son...which
           Raguel had sworn
     14:2, But Tobias departed with his wife...
           to Raguel

RAILING, loidoros, "reviling, railing"
    Eccl. 29:6, he prevail...he payeth him with curs-
                ing and railings;

RAIMENT, himation, "a garment, the upper garment,
                    mantle"
    Epis.-Jer. 1:12, gods save themselves...with
                     purple raiment
    I Macc. 11:24, and took silver and gold, and rai-
                   ment, and divers

RAIN, huetos, "rain"
    Judith 8:31, and the Lord will send us rain to
                 fill our cisterns,
    Wisd.-Sol. 16:16, For the ungodly...were scourged
                      ...with...rains,
               16:22, and sparking in the rain, did
                      destroy the
    Eccl. 1:2, Who can nunber the sand of the sea, and
               the drops of rain, and the days of
         1:19, Wisdom raineth down skill and knowledge
               of understanding, and exalteth them
        32:20, in the time of affliction as clouds
               of rain in the
        40:13, shall be dried up...like a great thun-
               der in rain
         49:9, of the enemies under the figure of the
               rain, and
    Epis.-Jer. 1:53, set up a king in the land, nor
                     give rain unto

RAINBOW, toxon, "a bow"
    Eccl. 43:11, Look upon the rainbow, and praise him
                 that made it;
         50:7, shining upon the temple...and as the
               rainbow giving

RAISE, anistēmi, "to cause to stand up or rise,
                  to raise up"
    II Macc. 7:14, he said...It is good...to be raised
                   up again

RAM, krios, "a ram, abattering-ram"
    Tobit 7:8, and after that they had killed a ram of

the flock, they
Song-Child. 1:16, Like as the burnt offerings
of rams and

RAMPART, charax, "a military palisade, rampart, a
stake"
IV Macc. 3:12, his body-guards...got over the ram-
parts of the

RAPHAEL, Raphaēl
Tobit 3:17, And Raphael was sent to heal them both,
that is, to
5:4, Therefore...he found Raphael that was
an angel
8:2, And as he went, he remembered the words
of Raphael,
9:1, Then Tobias called Raphael, and said
unto him,
9:5, Raphael went out, and lodged with
Gabael
11:2, Then Raphael said to Tobias, Dost thou
not know...?
11:7, Then said Raphael, I know, Tobias, that
thy father
12:5, I am Raphael, one of the seven holy
angels,

RAPHIA, Raphia
III Macc. 1:1, marched out as far as the parts of
Raphia,

RAPHON, Raphōn
I Macc. 5·37, gathered Timotheus another host...
against Raphon

RASSES, Rassis
Judith 2:23, Phud and Lud, and spoiled the children of Rasses,

RATHUMUS, Hrathumus
I Esd. 2:25, Then the king wrote back again to
Rathumus the

RATIONAL, logismos, "consideration, reasoning, reflection"
IV Macc. 5:31, I am not so old...but...my rational
powers are

RAY, bolē, "a throw, stroke; bolai heliou, sun-beams"
III Macc. 5:26, The sun's rays were not yet shed
abroad, and the

RAZIS, Razis
  II Macc. 14:37, Now was there accused unto Nicanor
               one Razis, one

READ, anaginoskō, "to read, to gather up knowledge
              of"
  I Esd. 2:26, I have read the epistle which ye
             have sent unto me:
         2:30, The king Artaxerxes his letters being
             read...began
  I Macc. 10:7, Jonathan to Jerusalem, and read
             the letters in the

READER, anagnostēs, "a reader"
  I Esd. 9:39, and they spake unto Esdras the priest
             and reader,
         9:42, And Esdras the priest and reader of
             the law stood up
         9:49, Attharates unto Esdras the chief priest
             and reader,

REALM, basileia, "a kingdom, dominion"
  I Macc. 1:16, Antiochus...thought...he might have
             ...two realms
          3:27, and gathered together all the forces
             of his realm,
          6:14, for Philip...whom he made ruler over
             all his realm
         10:43, let them be at liberty...in my realm
         10:52, For as much as I am come again to my
             realm, and am
         11:51, and in the sight of all that were in
             his realm
         15:28, withhold Joppe and Gazara...cities
             of my realm
  II Macc. 10:11, he set Lysias over the affairs of
             his realm,
          14:6, are seditious, and will not let the
             realm be in
  III Macc. 7:3, did of malice...punish the Jews of
             our realm

REAP, therizō, "to gather in harvest, reap"
  Eccl. 7:3, furrows of unrighteousness, and thou
             shalt not reap

REAPERS, theristēs, "one who gathers in the harvest,
             a reaper"
  Bel-Drag. 1:33, going into the field, for to bring
             it to...reapers

238

REASON, épistemé, "scientific knowledge, skill, wis-
           dom"
  IV Macc. 1:2, For reason is necessary to every
                 one as a step to

REASONING, logismos, "a computation, act of computing,
              a device"
  IV Macc. 1:1, going to demonstrate...that religious
                 reasoning is
          1:3, If, then, reasoning appears to hold
                 the mastery
          1:5, How, then, is it...that reasoning,
                 if it rule the
          1:6, For reasoning does not rule over its
                 own affections
          1:7, I might prove to you...that religious
                 reasoning is
          1:9, For all these...demonstrated that
                 reasoning has
          1:13, The question, therefore is, whether
                 reasoning be
          1:14, Let us determine, then, What is
                 reasoning? and
          1:15, Reasoning is, then, intellect accom-
                 panied by a
          1:19, The leading one of these...is that
                 reasoning bears
          1:29, And reasoning, the universal husband-
                 man, purging
          1:30, For reasoning is the leader of the
                 virtues, but it
          1:32, and over each of these classes the
                 reasoning
          1:33, Is it not because reasoning is able
                 to command the
          1:34, we withhold ourselves through the
                 mastery of reasoning
          1:35, of our appetite...are reined in by
                 reasoning
          2:2, the temperate Joseph is praised in
                 that reasoning,
          2:3, intercourse, he abrogated by reason-
                 ing the stimulus
          2:4, stimulus of sexual indulgence...that
                 reasoning is
          2:6, Now, then...reasoning is able to
                 govern our lusts,
          2:7, it be clear that reasoning is lord
                 of the passions?

IV Macc. 2:9, he is ruled by the law...through
               reasoning;
         2:13, And think it not strange assertion
               that reasoning
         2:15, And reasoning appears to be master
               of the more
         2:17, Thus Moses...regulated his anger by
               reasoning
         2:20, For if reasoning did not possess
               the power of
         2:24, How, then, a man may say, if reason-
               ing be master
         3:1, argument is exceedingly ridiculous:
               for reasoning
         3:2, may not be able to root out desire,
               but reasoning
         3:4, may not be able to eradicate malice,
               but reasoning
         3:5, For reasoning is not an eradicator,
               but an
         3:16, Wherefore setting up reasoning in
               opposite to his
         3:18, the body...the excellency of reason-
               ing...abominate
         3:19, invites us to give an illustration
               of...reasoning
         6:7, ground...he yet kept his reasoning
               upright and
         6:30, and even to...death resisted in his
               reasoning
         6:31, Confessedly, therefore, religious
               religious reasoning is
         6:32, For had the passions been superior
               to reasoning, I
         6:33, But now, since reasoning conquered
               the passions,
         6:34, should allow, that the power belongs
               to reasoning,
         6:35, and I would prove that reasoning has
               not only
         7:1, The reasoning of our father Eleazar,
               like a
         7:4, move his besiegers through the reli-
               gious reasoning
         7:12, descendant of Aaron...did not give
               up his reasoning
         7:14, By the spirit of reasoning, and the
               reasoning of

IV Macc. 7:16, confessedly religious reasoning is
            ruler of the
         7:17, But perhaps some might say, It is
            not...reasoning
         7:20, that some who have weak reasoning,
            are governed by
         7:24, imbued with the philosophy of reli-
            gious reasoning,

   eulogistos, "easy to reckon, prudent,
            rightly reckoning"
IV Macc. 8:14, and through their good reasoning
            destroyed his

   logizomai, "to count, reckon, calculate,
            reason"
IV Macc. 8:15, Now let us consider the matter...
            what reasonings

   logismos
IV Macc. 9:17, is your wheel, as to stifle my
            reasoning; cut my
         10:19, for that shalt thou extirpate our
            reasoning
         11:25, is not your inability to overrule
            our reasoning,
         11:27, through this we keep our reasoning
            unconquered
         13:1, If then...reasoning is absolute mas-
            ter over the
         13:3, now it is not so: but by means of
            the reasoning

   eulogistos
IV Macc. 13:5, avoid according to these men...
            right reasoning...?
         13:15, therefore, in the abegnation of
            divine reasoning
         14:2, O reasonings more royal than a king,
            and freer
         14:11, And think it not wonderful that
            reasoning

   logismos
IV Macc. 15:1, O reasonings of the sons, lord over
            the passions,
         15:23, But religious reasoning, having
            strengthened her
         16:1, endured...confessedly religious
            reasoning is master

IV Macc. 16:4, But with the reasoning of religion
the mother
18:2, Knowing that religious reasoning is
lord of the

REBELLED, aphistēmi, "to withdraw, induce to revolt"
I Esd. 1:48, to swear...he forswore himself and
rebelled

REBELLIOUS, apostatikos, "rebellious"
I Esd. 2:22, and thou shalt find...that that city
was rebellious,
2:23, and that the Jews were rebellious,
and raised always

REBUKE, epitimia, "a punishment, rebuke"
Eccl. 11:7, understand first, then rebuke

elegmos, "reproof, rebuke, chastisement"
Eccl. 48:7, who heardest the rebuke of the Lord in
Sinai, and in
I Macc. 2:49, Now have pride and rebuke gotten
strength, and the

RECEIVE, lepsis, "**taking**, receiving, receipt"
Eccl. 42:7, in writing that thou givest out, or
receivest in

dechomai, "to receive, admit, approve"
I Macc. 2:51, so shall ye receive great honour and
an everlasting

sunagō, "to bring together, collect, gather"
I Macc. 3:9, so that he was renowned...and he received unto him

apodechomai, "to receive kindly, embrace"
I Macc. 10:46, Now...Jonathan...received them, because they

lambanō, "to take, seize, to assume"
I Macc. 11:53, him according to the benefits which
he had received

apodechomai
I Macc. 12:43, but receive him honourably, and commended him unto

lambanō
II Macc. 1:14, For Antiochus...came into the place
...to receive

episunagō, "to gather together again, collect
    and bring to a place"
II Macc. 1:26, receive the sacrifice for thy whole
    people Israel,

komizō, "to receive, obtain, recover"
II Macc. 7:11, and from him I hope to receive them
    again

lambanō
II Macc. 8:20, help that they had from heaven,
    and so received a
III Macc. 7:10, When they had received this letter,
    they were not
IV Macc. 12:11, Impious tyrant...having received
    prosperity and a

hupodechomai, "to receive as a guest, enter-
    tain"
IV Macc. 13:16, thus, Abraham, and Isaac, and Jacob
    will receive

apolambanō, "to take or receive from another"
IV Macc. 18:23, But the children of Abraham...
    received pure and

RECOMPENCE, antapodoma, "requital, recompence"
Eccl. 12:2, to the godly man, and thou shalt find
    a recompence;
    17:23, will rise up and reward them, and
    render their recompence;
    20:10, and there is a gift whose recompence
    is double

antopodosis, "recompense, reward"
Eccl. 32:11, For the Lord recompenceth, and will
    give thee seven

RECOMPENSE, antapodosis, "recompense, reward"
Eccl. 36:20, heaviness: but a man of experience
    will recompense
Epis.-Jer. 1:34, evil...or good, they are not able
    to recompense it
I Macc. 2:68, Recompense fully the heathen, and
    take heed to the

antapodidomi, "to repay, requite, recom-
    pense"
I Macc. 10:27, still to be faithful...and we will
    recompense you

RECONCILE, epanorthoō, "to set up again, to amend,
    improve"

II Macc. 5:20, And therefore...being reconciled,
it was set up

katallassō, "to change from enmity to
friendship, reconcile"
II Macc. 8:29, they besought the merciful Lord
to be reconciled

RECONCILEMENT, diallassō, "to be reconciled to
another"
Eccl. 27:21, up; and after reviling there may be
reconcilement

RECONCILIATION, exilaskomai, "to appease completely,
propitiate"
Eccl. 45:16, chose him out of all men living...to
make reconciliation for his people
45:23, The third in glory...made reconciliation for Israel
II Macc. 12:45, Whereupon he made a reconciliation
for the dead,

RECORD, bibliophulakios, "a written volume or roll,
book, catalogue"
I Esd. 6:23, commanded king Darius to seek among
the records at

apographē, "a copy of an indictment, a list,
register"
II Macc. 2:1, It is also found in the records, that
Jeremy the

RECOUNT, prosanalegizomai, "to calculate, consider,
enumerate"
II Macc. 8:19, Moreover he recounted unto them
what helps their

REDEEMER, hrustēs, "redeemer" (verb, hruomai: "to
redeem, rescue")
III Macc. 7:23, Blessed be the Redeemer of Israel
unto

REFRACTORY, acharisteō, "to be ungrateful"
IV Macc. 9:10, the tyrant was...against them as
being refractory

REFUSE, skubalon, "refuse"
Eccl. 27:4, As when one sifteth with a sieve, the
refuse

REGISTER, apographō, "to register for one's own use,
to have a thing registered"
III Macc. 6:34, out as for death...had registered
them with joy,

REGISTERING, ápographē̂, "registration, register, inventory"
  III Macc. 4:15, The registering of these men was carried on

REGISTRAR, grammateus, "a secretary, clerk, scribe"
  III Macc. 4:17, above-mentioned interval of time, the registrars

REIGN, basileuō, "to reign, rule, rule over a people"
  I Esd. 1:43, And Joacim his son reigned in his stead:
      1:57, became servants to him...till the Persians reigned,
  Tobit 1:15, was dead, Sennacherib his son reigned in his stead:
      1:21, days...and Sarchedonus his son reigned in his stead;
  Judith 1:1, In the twelfth year of the reign of Nabuchodonosor, who reigned in Nineve,
  Wisd.-Sol. 3:8, judge the nation...and their Lord shall reign for
      6:21, thrones...honour wisdom, that ye may reign for

      épimignumi, "to mix in with, to mingle with"
  Wisd.-Sol. 14:25, So that there reigned in all men without

      basileuō
  Eccl. 47:13, Solomon reigned in a peaceable time, and was
  I Macc. 1:1, And it happened, after that Alexander ...reigned in
      1:7, So Alexander reigned twelve years, and then died
      1:10, out of them a wicked root...and he reigned in the
      1:16, before Antiochus, he thought to reign over Egypt,
      6:2, the Macedonian king, who reigned first among the
      6:17, was dead, he set up Antiochus...to reign in his
      7:1, hundred...and fiftieth year Demetrius ...reigned there
      8:7, and covenanted that he and such as reigned after him
      8:13, whom they would help to a kingdom, those reign;

I Macc. 10:1, the people had received him...where-
                of he reigned
           11:9, Demetrius, saying...thou shalt reign
                in thy father's
           11:19, By this means Demetrius reigned in
                the hundred...and
           11:40, and lay sore upon him...that he
                might reign in his
           11:54, After this returned Tryphon...who
                reigned, and was
           12:7, sent...unto Onias...from Darius,
                who reigned then
           13:32, And he reigned in his stead, and
                crowned himself
II Macc. 1:7, What time as Demetrius reigned, in
                the hundred...and

RELEASE, luō, "unfasten, loosen"
III Macc. 6:29, These things he said: and they,
                released the

           apallassō, "to set free, set at liberty,
                remove"
IV Macc. 9:16, that you may be released from your
                tortures,

           apoluō, "to release, to loose, remit"
IV Macc. 12:8, Release me, that I may speak to the
                king and all

           aniemi, "to unbind, loose, slacken, unfasten"
Pr.-Mans. 1:10, by many iron bonds...and there is
                no release
           1:13, but I pray...release me, Lord,
                release me, and

RELIGION, latreia, "hired labour, service, esp. ser-
                vice of the gods"
I Macc. 1:43, of the Israelites consented to his
                religion, and
           2:19, every one from the religion of their
                fathers,
           2:22, to the king's words, to go from our
                religion

           threskos, "religious worship, religion,
                piety"
IV Macc. 5:13, be any power which watches over
                this religion of

           eusebēia, "piety, devotion, godliness,

religion"

IV Macc. 5:18, have no right...to destroy our
sense of religion

5:31, powers are youthful in defence of
our religion

5:38, shalt not laud it over my thoughts
about religion,

7:18, But they who have meditated upon
religion with

7:22, thing to endure all...for the sake
of religion

9:6, the Hebrews have died in the cause
of religion

9:7, tyrant; and...puttest us to death
for our religion

9:23, fight the holy and honourable fight
of religion

9:29, sweet is every form of death for
the religion of

9:30, by our patience in behalf of...
religion?

11:20, O Period...in which for the sake
of religion,

12:14, dying, fulfilled their religion
towards God

13:7, right-reasoning...securing the harbour of religion

13:25, For acting along with religion,
made their

13:26, who were left...were illused for
their religion

14:6, holy youths agreed unto death for
religion's sake

14:7, for as the seven days of creation,
about religion

15:1, reasoning of sons, lord over the
passions, and religion

15:2, The mother...set before her, religion
and the safety

15:3, rather elected the religion which
according to God

15:12, separately and all together to
death for religion

15:14, one...the observant mother was prevented by religion

15:29, avenger of the law, and defender of
religion,

15:32, bear up nobly against the storms

against religion

IV Macc. 16:4, But with the reasoning of religion
the mother

16:13, she...exhorted them to death in
behalf of religion

16:14, O woman, soldier of God for religion, thou aged

16:23, unreasonable that they who know
religion should

17:5, thy sons whom thou didst illuminate
with religion

17:7, as on a tablet...the mother...en-
during for...religion

18:3, up their bodies to pains for the
sake of religion,

RELIGIOUS, eusebēia, "reverence towards the gods,
piety, religion"

III Macc. 2:32, the majority to cling to their
religious

eusebēs, "pious, religious, reverent"

IV Macc. 1:1, As I am about to demonstrate...reli-
gious reasoning

eusebēia

IV Macc. 7:4, move his besiegers through the religious reasoning

7:24, imbued with the philosophy of religious reasoning,

11:8, thou makest war against those who are
religious

eusebēs

IV Macc. 15:23, But religious reasoning, having
strengthened her

18:1, obey this law, and in every way be
religious

REMEMBER, mnēmoneuō, "to remember, recollect, call
to mind"

I Esd. 3:20, every thought into jolity...so that
a man remembereth

3:21, spend his life with his wife, and
remembereth neither

4:43, Then said he unto the king, Remember
thy vow, which

hupomimnēskō, "to call to mind, recollect,
remember"

Wisd.-Sol. 16:11, they were pricked, that they

should remember

mnēmoneuō.
Eccl. 7:36, Whatsoever thou takest in hand, remember the end, and
8:5, Reproach not a man that turneth from
sin, but remember
8:7, the greatest enemy being dead, but
remember that we

epiginōskō, "to discern, detect, perceive"
Eccl. 9:13, remember that thou goest in the midst
of snares, and
12:12, Set him not by thee...and thou at last
remember my

mnēmoneuō
Eccl. 14:12, Remember that death will not be long
in coming, and
16:17, Say not thou...shall any remember me
from above?
18:25, When thou hast enough remember the
time of hunger:
23:14, Remember thy father and thy mother,
when thou sittest
23:18, what need I fear? the most High will
not remember my
28:6, Remember thy end, and let not thy
enmity cease;
28:7, Remember thy commandments, and bear no
malice to thy
33:8, Make the time short, remember the
covenant, and let
34:13, Remember that a wicked eye is an evil
thing:
38:20, drive it away, and remember the last
end
38:22, Remember his judgment: for thine also
shall be so;
41:3, Fear not the sentence of death, remember them that
42:15, I will not remember the works of the
Lord, and

ginōskō, "to know, perceive, understand"
Bar. 2:30, For I know that they would...remember
themselves,

mnēmoneuō
Bar. 3:5, Remember not the iniquities of our fore-
father:

Bar. 3:23, these have known the way of wisdom,
           or remembered her
     4:14, Let him that dwell about Sion, and
           remember he the
     4:27, Be of good comfort...for ye shall be
           remembered of him
His.-Sus. 1:9, that they might not...remember just
               judgment
Bel-Drag. 1:38, And Daniel said, Thou hast remem-
                bered me, O God:
I Macc. 4:9, Remember how our forefathers were
             delivered in the
        4:10, peradventure the Lord will...remember
              the covenant,
        5:4, Also he remembered the injury of the
             children of

   mimnēskō, "to remind, to remember, call to
              mind"
I Macc. 6:12, But now I remember the evils that I
              did at

   mnēmoneuō
I Macc. 9:38, Therefore they remembered John their
              brother, and
        10:5, else he will remember all the evils
              that we have
II Macc. 1:2, God be gracious unto you, and remem-
              ber his covenant
         8:4, and remember the wicked slaughter of
              harmless
         9:21, I was weak, or else I would have
               remembered kindly
IV Macc. 13:12, And another, Remember of what stock
                ye are; and
         15:28, But this daughter of Abraham re-
                membered his holy

   anamimnēskō, "to remind, cause to remember"
IV Macc. 16:18, Remember that through God ye ob-
                tained existence,

REMEMBRANCE, mnēmē, "remembrance, recollection"
   Wisd.-Sol. 11:12, and a groaning for the remembrance
                     of things
   Eccl. 11:25, and in the day of affliction there is
                no remembrance
        38:23, When the dead is at rest, let his
               remembrance rest;

mnēmosunon, "a record, memorial, honourable remembrance"
Eccl. 50:16, and made a great noise...for a remembrance before the

mneia, "remembrance, recollection"
Bar. 5:5, thy children...rejoicing in the remembrance of God

mnēmoneuō
I Macc. 2:51, Call to remembrance what acts our
fathers did in

REMIT, eleutheros, "free, in a state of freedom"
I Macc. 10:33, liberty every...Jew...and all my
officers remit the

REMNANT, kataleimma, "a remnant, a small residue"
Eccl. 44:17, therefore was he left as a remnant
unto the earth,
47:22, wherefore he gave a remnant unto
Jacob, and out of

epiloipos, "remaining, still left"
I Macc. 5:18, So he left Joseph...with the remnant
of the host in
6:38, As for the remnant of the horsemen,
they set them

loipos, "remaining, the rest, remainder"
I Macc. 9:18, Judas also was killed, and the remnant fled

epiloipos
I Macc. 9:40, made a slaughter of them...and the
remnant fled into

loipos
II Macc. 8:31, the remnant of the spoils they
brought to Jerusalem

RENT, diarreynumi, "to break, rend, tear, burst"
I Macc. 3:47, Then they fasted that day...and rent
their clothes
4:39, they rent their clothes, and made
great lamentation
5:14, other messengers from Galilee with
their clothes rent,

REPAY, apotinō, "to pay off, to repay, refund, make
good"
Eccl. 20:12, There is that buyeth much for a little,
and repayeth

REPENT, metanoeō, "to make a change of principle and
            practice, reform, repent"
  Wisd.-Sol. 19:2, how that having given them leave
            ...repent and
  Eccl. 17:24, But unto them that repent, he granted
            them return,

            epistrephō, "to turn towards, to turn round,
            convert"
  Eccl. 21:6, He that hateth reproof...will repent
            from his heart

            metamelomai, "to change one's mind and pur-
            pose, regret"
  Eccl. 35:19, and when thou hast once done, repent
            not

            metanoeō
  Eccl. 48:15, For all this the people repented not,
            neither

            metamelomai
  I Macc. 11:10, For I repented that I gave my
            daughter unto him,

REPENTANCE, metanoia, "a change of mood of thought
            and feeling, repentance"
  Wisd.-Sol. 12:10, thou gavest them place of repen-
            tance,
            12:19, hope that thou givest repentance
            for sins
            44:16, wast translated, being an example
            of repentance

            metamelomai
  III Macc. 2:24, this severe check caused no re-
            pentance within him

            metanoia
  Pr.-Mans. 1:8, thou, O Lord...hast not appointed
            repentance for

REPENTING, metanoeō, "to reform, to undergo a change
            in mind and feeling"
  Wisd.-Sol. 5:3, And they repenting and groaning
            for anguish of
  Pr.-Mans. 1:7, for thou art the Lord most high...
            repenting of the

REPLENISH, methuskō, "to make drunk with wine, to
            intoxicate"
  Eccl. 35:13, made thee, and hath replenish thee
            with his good

REPROACH, ỏneidos, "reproach, disgrace"
  Eccl. 6:1, of a friend...thou shalt inherit...shame,
      and reproach

      ỏneidizō, "to upbraid, censure"
  Eccl. 8:5, Reproach not a man that turneth from
      sin, but remember
      41:7, will complain...because they will be re-
      proached for his
      42:11, shameless daughter, lest she make thee
      ...a reproach

      ỏneidismos, "reproach, reviling, censure"
  Eccl. 42:14, of a man than...a woman...which
      bringeth...reproach
      47:4, and did he not take away reproach from
      the people...?
  Bar. 2:4, Moreover he hath delivered them...to be
      as a reproach
  Epis.-Jer. 1:47, For they left lies and reproaches
      to them that
  I Macc. 4:59, great gladness among the people, for
      that the reproach

REPROOF, élegchō, "to put to proof, test, reprove,
      rebuke"
  Wisd.-Sol. 11:7, for a manifest reproof of that
      commandment,
      19:31, There is a reproof that is not
      comely: again,
      21:6, He that hateth reproof is in the
      way of sinners:
      48:10, who wast ordained for reproofs
      in their times,

REPROVE, élegchō, "to refute, reprove, rebuke"
  Eccl. 18:13, he reproveth, and nurtureth, and
      teacheth, and
      20:1, It is much better to reprove, than to
      be angry

      élegmos, "reproof, confutation"
  Eccl. 20:29, the eyes of the wise...that he cannot
      reprove

REQUITETH, ántapodidōmi, "requite, recompense, repay"
  Eccl. 3:31, And he that requiteth good turns is
      mindful of that
      30:6, that shall requite kindness to his
      friends
      32:2, He that requiteth a good turn offereth
      fine flour; and

RESIDUE, <u>loipos</u>, "remainder, remaining, the rest"
  I Macc. 3:24, were slain eight hundred men...and
          the residue fled

RESURRECTION, <u>anatasis</u>, "to cause to rise up or stand
                    up, to raise up as the dead"
  II Macc. 7:14, as for thee, thou shalt have no
          resurrection to

REVEALED, <u>apokalupto</u>, "to disclose, to set forth,
                      announce"
  Eccl. 1:6, To whom hath the root of wisdom been
          revealed? or who

REVEALER, <u>delos</u>, "clearly visible, plain, manifest"
  Eccl. 45:10, with a holy garment, with gold...with
          the revealers of

REVEALING, <u>apokalupsis</u>, "disclosure, revelation,
                     manifestation"
  Eccl. 42:1, and of revealing of secrets; so shalt
          thou be truly
      42:19, declaring the things that are past...
          and revealing

REVELLING, <u>komos</u>, "a festive procession, a merry-
               making"
  Wisd.-Sol. 14:23, children...or made revellings of
          strange rites;
  II Macc. 6:4, for the temple was filled riot and
          revelling

REVENGE, <u>ekdikeo</u>, "to execute right and justice, re-
               venge a person"
  Eccl. 5:3, for the Lord will surely revenge thy
          pride

REVERED, <u>hieropreptes</u>, "beseeming what is sacred, be-
                 .coming holy persons"
  IV Macc. 9:25, And saying this, the revered youth
          abruptly closed

REVERENCE, <u>entrope</u>, "reverence"
  Eccl. 4:22, and let not the reverence of any man
          cause thee to
      7:29, Fear the Lord with all thy soul, and
          reverence his

          <u>theosebeia</u>, "the worship or fear of God"
  IV Macc. 17:15, And reverence for God conquered,
          and crowned her

REVEREND, <u>semnos</u>, "august, venerable, honourable,

reputable"
IV Macc. 7:15, O blessed old age, and reverend
hoar head, and

REVOLT, automolēsis, "desertion"
I Macc. 7:24, into all the coasts...of them that
had revolted

automoleō, "to desert"
I Macc. 9:24, In those days...the country revolted,
and went with

aphistēmi, "to revolt, to depart from or to
go away"
I Macc. 11:14, those that dwelt in those parts had
revolted from
13:16, send an hundred talents...that...
he may not revolt
II Macc. 5:11, this that was done...he thought
Judea had revolted:

REWARD, diaphora, "excellence, advantage, profit"
I Esd. 4:39, With her there is no accepting of persons or rewards

geras, "a gift of honour, prize"
Wisd. -Sol. 2:22, hoped they for the wages of...a
reward

euergeteō, "to do well or good"
Wisd.-Sol. 3:5, little chastised; they shall be
greatly rewarded

misthos, "wages, pay, hire"
Wisd.-Sol. 5:15, But the righteous live for ever-
more; their reward
10:17, rendered to the righteous a reward
of their
Eccl. 2:8, Ye that fear the Lord...your reward
shall not fail
11:18, waxeth rich...and this is the portion
of his reward
11:22, The blessing of the Lord is in the reward of the
11:26, thing unto the Lord in the day of death
to rewards

antapodosis, "a giving back in turn, repay-
ment, reward"
Eccl. 17:23, Afterwards he will rise up and reward
them, and

misthéō, "to be hired for pay, farm out"
Eccl. 36:16, Reward them that wait for thee, and
         let thy prophets

misthos
Eccl. 51:22, The Lord hath given me a tongue for
          my reward, and I
     51:30, and in time he will give you your
          reward

doma,   "a gift"
I Macc. 10:28, will grant you many immunities,
          and give you rewards

antapodidōmi, "to repay, requite, recompence"
I Macc. 11:53, Nevertheless, he...neither rewarded
          according to

doma
I Macc. 16:19, sent letters...that he might give
          them...rewards

athlos, "tax contending for a prize, endurance,
          suffering"
IV Macc. 9:8, shall bear off the rewards of virtue

tropheia,   "pay or recompence, wages"
IV Macc. 15:13, O holy nature and parental feeling,
          and reward of

RHODOCUS, Rhodokos
II Macc. 13:21, But Rhodocus, who was in the Jews'
          host, disclosed

RIB, pleura, "a rib, the side of the body"
IV Macc. 18:7, spake also...I took care of the
          built-up rib

RICH, euporeō, "easy, abounding in easy circumstances,
          prosperous, enjoy plenty"
Wisd.-Sol. 10:10, knowledge of holy things, made
          him rich in his
          10:11, him she stood by him, and made
          him rich
Eccl. 10:22, Whether he be rich, noble or poor,
          their glory is
     10:30, honoured for his skill, and the rich
          man is honoured

plousios, "rich, opulent, wealthy"
Eccl. 11:21, in the sight of the Lord...to make a
          poor man rich
     13:3, A rich man hath done wrong, and yet he

threatened

Eccl. 13:18, and what peace between the rich and the poor?

13:19, is the lion's prey...so the rich eat up the poor

13:20, As the proud hate humility: so doth the rich abhor

13:21, A rich man beginning to fall is held up of his

13:22, When a rich man is fallen, he hath many helpers:

13:23, When a rich man speaketh, every man holdeth his

18:25, and when thou art rich, think upon poverty and need

25:2, a poor man that is proud, a rich man that is a liar,

26:4, Whether a man is rich or poor, if he have a good

30:14, sound and strong...than a rich man that is satisfied

34:3, The rich hath great labour in gathering riches

34:8, Blessed is the rich that is found without blemish,

44:6, rich men furnished with ability, living peaceably in

45:8, and strengthened him with rich garment, with breeches

His.-Sus. 1:4, Now Joacim was a very rich man, and had a fair

RICHES, ploutos, "riches, wealth, opulence"

Wisd.-Sol. 5:8, or what hath riches with our vaunting brought us?

7:11, things together came to me with... riches in her

7:13, I learned diligently, and...I do not hide...riches

8:5, If riches be a possession to be desired in this

8:18, in the works of her hands are infinite riches;

chrēma, "a thing that one uses or needs, money"

Eccl. 10:8, Because of unrighteous dealings...and riches got by

ploutos

Eccl. 10:30, for his skill, and the rich man...for his riches

10:31, that is honoured in poverty, how much more in riches

11:14, life and death, poverty and riches, come of the Lord

13:24, Riches are good unto him that hath no sin, and

14:3, Riches are not comely for a niggard: and what should

21:4, To terrify and do wrong will waste riches:

24:17, and my flowers are the fruit of honour and riches,

28:10, and according to his riches his anger riseth; and

30:16, There is no riches above a sound body, and no joy

34:1, Watching for riches, consumeth the flesh, and the

chrēma

Eccl. 34:6, and be not unmindful of him thy riches

40:26, Riches and strength lift up the heart: but the fear

Epis.-Jer. 1:35, In like manner, they can neither give riches nor

I Macc. 4:23, the tents, where they got...silver ...and...riches

6:1, say, that Elymais...was...renowned... for riches

II Macc. 3:6, treasury...was full of...multitude of their riches,

RIGHTEOUS, dikaios, "just, equitable, fair"

Tobit 13:9, have mercy again on the sons of the righteous

Wisd.-Sol. 2:10, Let us oppress the poor righteous man, let us

2:12, Therefore let us lie in wait for the righteous;

3:1, But the souls of the righteous are in the hand of

4:7, But though the righteous be prevented with death,

4:16, Thus the righteous that is dead shall condemn

5:1, Then shall the righteous man stand

in great

Wisd.-Sol. 5:15, But the righteous live for ever-
more; their

10:5, their wicked conspiracy...found
out the righteous

10:6, ungodly perished, she delivered
the righteous man

10:10, When the righteous fled from   his
brother's wrath

10:13, When the righteous was sold, she
forsook him not

10:15, She delivered the righteous people
and blameless

10:20, Therefore the righteous spoiled
the ungodly, and

12:9, bring the ungodly under the hand
of the righteous

12:15, Forsomuch then as thou art righteous thyself

16:17, for the world fighteth for the
righteous

16:23, forget his own strength that the
righteous might

18:17, was accepted both the salvation
of the righteous

18:20, Yea, the tasting of death touched
the righteous

19:17, stricken...at the doors of the
righteous man

dikaioō, "to make or render right or just"

Eccl. 18:2, The Lord only is righteous

27:29, They that rejoice at the fall of the
righteous shall

32:6, The offering of the righteous maketh
the altar fat,

34:17, Noah was found perfect and righteous;

Bar. 2:9, the Lord is righteous in all his works
which he hath

Song-Child. 1:3, for thou art righteous in all
things that thou

1:63, O ye spirits and souls of the
righteous

His.-Sus. 1:3, Her parents also were righteous,
and taught their

1:53, albeit the Lord saith, The innocent
and righteous

II Macc. 1:24, after this manner...O Lord...fearful
and...righteous

II Macc. 12:6, Calling upon the righteous Judge,
he came against
12:41, All men therefore praising the Lord,
the righteous

dikaios
III Macc. 2:3, Creator of all...who art the righteous Governor,
2:22, by a righteous judgment deprived
of the faculty

eusebēs, "pious, reverent, devout"
IV Macc. 13:1, If then...the righteous reasoning
is absolute master

dikaios
IV Macc. 16:21, And the righteous Daniel was cast
unto the lions;
18:7, And the righteous mother of the
seven children
Pr.-Mans. 1:1, fathers Abraham...Jacob and of their
righteous seed

RIGHTEOUSNESS, dikaiosunē,   "fair and equitable deal-
ing, justice, rectitude"
Tobit 12:8, is good with fasting and alms and righteousness
14:11, consider what alms doeth, and how
righteousness doth
Wisd.-Sol. 1:1, Love righteousness,ye that be
judges of the
1:15, (for righteousness is immortal:)

krisis, "justice, equity"
Wisd.-Sol. 2:22, hoped they for the wages of
righteousness
5:6, and the light of righteousness hath
not shined
5:18, He shall put on righteousness as
a breastplate,
8:7, And if a man love righteousness,
her labours are
14:7, For blessed is the wood whereby
righteousness
15:3, For to know thee is perfect righteousness:
Eccl. 26:28, and one that returneth from righteousness to sin:
27:8, If thou followest righteousness, thou
shalt obtain

dikaioō, "to make or ender right or
            just"
Eccl. 44:10, But these were merciful men, whose
            righteousness

dikaiosunē
Eccl. 45:26, you wisdom...to judge his people in
            righteousness
Bar. 1:15, say, To the Lord our God belongeth
            righteousness,
    2:6, To the Lord our God appertaineth right-
            eousness:
    2:17, give unto the Lord neither praise nor
            righteousness
    2:18, vexed...will give thee praise and right-
            eousness,
    2:19, humble supplication...for the righteous-
            ness of our
    4:13, in the paths of...discipline in his
            righteousness
    5:2, Cast about thee a double garment of the
            righteousness
    5:4, thy name shall be called...The peace
            of righteousness,
    5:9, God shall lead Israel in the light of...
            righteousness
I Macc. 2:52, faithful...and it was imputed unto
            him for righteousness?
      7:18, people...There is neither truth nor
            righteousness
IV Macc. 8:13, Fear, young man, and the Righteous-
            ness which ye

RINGLEADER, muscharē, "a ringleader"
II Macc. 5:24, He sent also that detestable ring-
            leader

RIOT, asotia, "recklessly debauched, profligacy"
II Macc. 6:4, for the temple was filled with riot
            and revelling

RIOTOUSLY, truphē, "luxury, delicate living"
Eccl. 14:4, by defrauding...shall spend his good
            riotously

RISE, exanastasis, "a removal, an uprising from, re-
            surrection"
Eccl. 17:23, Afterwards he will rise up and reward
            them, and

RITE, thesmos, "a rule, law, rite"
Wisd.-Sol. 14:23, children...or made revelling of

strange rites;

RIVER, potamos, "a river, stream"
I Esd. 8:61, And from the river Theras we departed
the twelfth
Tobit 6:1, went on their journey, they came...to
the river Tigris,
6:2, wash himself, a fish leaped out of the
river,
Judith 1:9, and to all that were in Samaria...and
the river of
2:8, shall fill their valleys...and the
river shall be
2:24, destroyed all the high cities...upon
the river
Wisd.-Sol. 11:6, instead of a fountain of a per-
petual running river troubled with
foul blood,
Eccl. 4:26, thy sins; and force not the course of
the river
24:30, I also came out to a brook from a
river, and as a
24:31, and lo my brook became a river, and my
river became a
39:22, His blessing covered the dry land as
a river, and
40:13, goods of the unjust shall be dried up
like a river,
44:21, that he would...exalt his seed as...the
river unto the
50:8, and as the...lilies by the rivers of
waters, and as the
Song-Child. 1:55, O ye seas and rivers, bless ye
the Lord:
I Macc. 3:32, to oversee the affairs of the king
from the river
5:41, but if he be afraid, and camp beyond
the river, we
7:8, the king chose Bacchides...who ruled
beyond the river
11:7, Jonathan, when he had gone with the
king to the river
12:30, Then Jonathan pursued after him...
over the river
III Macc. 7:20, departed unharmed...by land, by
sea, and by river,

ROAST, optaō, "to roast or broil meat"
Tobit 6:5, So the young man...roasted the fish,

they did eat it:

ROASTING, phlegō, "to burn, flame, kindle"
   IV Macc. 15:14, At the racking and roasting of each
               one of them,

ROBBERS, lēstēs, "a robber, plunderer"
   Epis.-Jer. 1:18, locks...lest their gods be spoiled
              with robbers
          1:57, those gods...able to escape from
              thieves or robbers

ROBE, stolē, "equipment, dress, a long garment, flow-
     ing robe"
   Eccl. 6:31, Thou shalt put her on as a robe of
            honour, and shalt
      27:8, thou...shalt put her on, as a glorious
            long robe

     poderēs, "a robe that falls over the feet"
   Eccl. 45:8, He put upon him...rich garments...with
            a long robe, and

     stolē
   Eccl. 50:11, When he put on the robe of honour, and
            was clothed
   I Macc. 6:15, And gave him the crown, and his robe,
            and his
      10:21, seventh month...Jonathan put on the
            holy robe, and

ROCK, lithos, "a stone, a tablet of stone"
   Wisd.-Sol. 11:4, water was given them out of the
            flinty rock

     petra, "a rock, stony ground, clefts"
   Eccl. 40:15, of the ungodly...are as unclean roots
            upon a rock
   II Macc. 14:45, of the throng; and standing upon
            a steep rock,

ROE, dorkas, "an antelope, gazelle"
   Eccl. 27:20, Follow after him...for he is...as a
            roe escaped out of

ROMAN, Romaios
   I Macc. 8:1, Now Judas had heard of the fame of
            the Romans, that
      8:21, So that matter pleased the Romans well
      8:23, Good success be to the Romans, and
            to the people of
      8:24, If there come first any war upon the
            Romans or any

I Macc. 8:26, neither shall they give anything
unto...the Romans:

8:27, In the same manner also..the Romans
shall help them

8:28, ships, as it hath seemed good to the
Romans;

8:29, According to these articles did the
Romans make a

12:16, Numenius...and Antipater...and sent
them unto the Romans

14:40, For he had heard say, that the Romans
had called the

15:16, Lucius, consul of the Romans unto king
Ptolemee,

II Macc. 8:19, much money...which the king was to
pay to the Romans

8:36, Thus he, that took upon him to make
good to the Romans, their tribute
by means of

11:34, The Romans also sent unto them a
letter containing

ROME, Rōmē
I Macc. 1:10, them wicked root...who had been a
hostage at Rome

7:1, and one...year Demetrius...departed
from Rome,

8:17, consideration of these things, Judas
...sent them to Rome,

8:19, They went therefore to Rome, which
was a very great

12:1, that...he chose certain men, and sent
them to Rome,

12:3, So they went unto Rome, and entered
into the Senate,

14:16, Now when it was heard at Rome, and
as far as Sparta

14:24, After this Simon sent Numenius to
Rome with a

15:15, season came Numenius and his company
from Rome,

II Macc. 4:11, the Jews by the means of John...
ambassador to Rome,

ROOF, kruptē, "a covered place, vault, crypt"
II Macc. 1:16, And opening a privy door of the roof,
they threw

ROOM, oikema, "a dwelling place, a chamber in a house"
Tobit 2:4, I took him up into a room until the going

264

down of the
Wisd.-Sol. 13:15, and when he had made a convenient
room for it,

ROOT, <u>hriza</u>, "root, that from which anything springs,
the root or origin of anything"
Wisd.-Sol. 3:15, the fruit of good labours: and
the root of
Eccl. 1:6, To whom hath the root of wisdom been
revealed?
1:20, The root of wisdom is to fear the Lord,
and the
3:28, for the plant of wickedness hath taken
root in him
10:15, The Lord hath plucked up the roots of
the proud
23:25, Her children shall not take root, and
her branches
24:12, And I took root in an honourable
people, even in the
40:15, The children of the ungodly...are as
unclean roots
47:22, a remnant unto Jacob, and out of him
a root unto
I Macc. 1:10, And there came out of them a wicked
root, Antiochus

ROSEBUD, <u>kalux</u>, "the cup or calyx of a flower, a
flower-bud"
Wisd.-Sol. 2:8, Let us crown ourselves with rosebuds, before they

ROYAL, <u>genos</u>, "family, lineage, kindred"
I Macc. 3:32, Lysias, a nobleman, and one of the
blood royal, to

<u>basileia</u>, "a prince, a lady of royal blood"
I Macc. 3:37, the half of the forces...from Antioch,
his royal city

<u>basilikos</u>, "royal, regal, a person attached
to the king"
I Macc. 6:43, Eleazar also...armed with royal
harness, was higher
IV Macc. 6:43, O reasonings more royal than a king,
and freer

RULE, <u>krateō</u>, "to be strong, to be superior to any
one, apprehend, seize"
Wisd.-Sol. 6:2, Give ear, ye that rule the people,
and glory in

kurieuō, "to be lord over, to be possessed of
        mastery over"
Eccl. 44:3, Such as did bear rule in their kingdom,
        men renowned

archō, "to be first, to govern"
Eccl. 47:21, divided, and out of Ephraim ruled a
        rebellious

kurieuō
Bar. 3:16, the heathen, and such as ruled the
        beasts upon the

archō
I Macc. 1:4, a mighty strong host, and ruled over
        countries, and
        8:16, their government to one man...who
        ruled over all
        14:17, heard that his brother Simon...ruled
        the country,

krateō
II Macc. 4:10, he had gotten into his hand the rule,
        he forthwith

kurieuō
IV Macc. 1:4, it surely also and manifestly has
        the rule over the

krateō
IV Macc. 1:5, How, then, is it...that reasoning,
        if it rule the

epikrateō, "to rule over, govern, to have power"
IV Macc. 1:19, by whose means...reasoning bears
        rule over the

krateō
IV Macc. 2:9, he is ruled by the law acting through
        reasoning;

kanon, "a measure, a rule"
IV Macc. 7:21, walking religiously by the whole
        rule of

perikrateō, "to become master of, overpowering"
IV Macc. 14:11, not wonderful that reasoning bore
        rule over

RULER, archōn, "one invested with power and dignity,
        chief, ruler, prince"
Judith 9:3, wherefore thou gavest their rulers to
        be slain, so

égemōn, "a leader, a guide, a chieftain, a
        Roman provincial governor"
Eccl. 9:17, For the hand of the artificer...and
        the wise ruler of
    10:2, officers; and what manner of man the
        ruler of the city
    30:18, and hearken with your ears, ye rulers
        of the

        archōn
Eccl. 33:10, Smite in sunder the heads of the
        rulers of the
    41:18, of an offence before a judge and ruler;
        of iniquity
    46:18, And he destroyed the rulers of the
        Tyrians, and all
    48:15, yet there remained a small people,
        and a ruler in
I Macc. 2:17, Thou art a ruler, and an honourable
        and great man in

        kathistemi, "to appoint, to set, make"
I Macc. 6:14, Then called he for Philip...who he
        made ruler over

        archōn
I Macc. 11:57, wrote...Jonathan, saying, I...appoint
        thee ruler over
    14:20, The rulers of the Lacedomonians,
        with the city,
    14:28, of the priests...and people, and
        rulers of the
II Macc. 4:27, albeit Sostratus the ruler of the
        castle required

        dunastēs, "a potentate, sovereign, prince"
III Macc. 5:7, They invoked the Almighty Lord...
        Ruler of all, Lord

        despotēs, "lord, master, sovereign"
III Macc. 7:9, but the highest God, the ruler of
        all might

        archōn
IV Macc. 1:30, For reasoning...is absolute ruler
        of the passions

        égemōn
IV Macc. 7:16, confessedly religious reasoning is
        ruler of the

SABAT, Sabat
  I Macc. 16:14, the cities...in the eleventh
              month, called Sabat:

SABBATH, sabbaton, "cessation from labour, rest,
              the Jewish sabbath"
  Judith 8:6, save the eves of the sabbaths, and
              the sabbaths,
       10:2, the house, in the which she abode
             in the sabbath
  I Macc. 1:39, feasts were turned into mourning,
              her sabbaths into
       1:43, sacrificed unto idols, and profaned
             the sabbath
       1:45, that they should profane the sab-
             baths and festivals
       2:32, and made war against them on the
             sabbath day
       2:38, they rose up against them in battle
             on the sabbath,
       2:41, to make battle with us on the sab-
             bath day, we will
       9:34, came near to the Jordan...upon the
             sabbath day
       9:43, he came on the sabbath day unto the
             banks
      10:34, I will that all the feasts, and
             sabbaths, and new
  II Macc. 5:25, did forbear till the holy day of
             the sabbath
       5:26, that were gone to the celebrating
             of the sabbath,
       6:6, Neither was it lawful for a man to
             sabbath
       8:26 for it was the day before the sab-
             bath, and
       8:27, together...they occupied themselves
             about the sabbath
       8:28, And after the sabbath, when they
             had given part of
      12:38, into the city of Odollam...and kept
             the sabbath
      15:1, without any danger to set upon them
             on the sabbath
      15:3, commanded the sabbath day to be
             kept
  IV Macc. 2:8, A man...cancelling the debt of the
             incoming sabbath

SACKCLOTH, __sakkos__, "sackcloth, a mourning garment"
  Judith 8:5, made her a tent upon the top of her
           house, and put on sackcloth
       9:1, fell upon her face...and uncovered
           the sackcloth
      10:3, and pulled off the sackcloth which
           she had on, and
  Eccl. 25:17, woman changeth her...and darkeneth
           her...like sackcloth
  Bar. 4:20, I have put...upon me the sackcloth of
           my prayer:
  I Macc. 2:14, and his sons rent their clothes,
           and put on sackcloth,
       3:47, Then they fasted that day, and put
           on sackcloth and
  II Macc. 3:19, And the women, girt with sackcloth
           under their

SACRIFICE, __thusia__, "sacrificing, the mode of sacri-
           ficing, the victim"
  I Esd. 1:6, passover in order, and make ready the
           sacrifices for
       1:12, passover with fire...as for the sa-
           crifices, they sod
       1:17, Thus were the things that belonged
           to the sacrifices
       1:18, offer sacrifices upon the altar of
           the Lord,
       5:50, and they offered sacrifices accord-
           ing to the time,
       5:51, the feast of tabernacles...and offer-
           ed sacrifices
       5:52, the continual oblations, and the
           sacrifice of the

           __thuō__, "to kill in sacrifice"
  I Esd. 5:69, we likewise...do obey your Lord,
           and do sacrifice
       8:15, to the end that they may offer sacri-
           fices unto the
       8:65, come out of the captivity offered
           sacrifice unto the

           __thusia__
  Judith 16:16, For all the sacrifice is too little
           for a sweet

           __teletē__, "any religious rites, a festival,
           celebration of mysteries"
  Wisd.-Sol. 12:4, doing...odious works...and wicked
           sacrifices;

269

Wisd.-Sol. 14:15, those that were under him cere-
monies and sacrifices
14:23, they slew their children in
sacrifices, or used

thusia
Eccl. 7:31, give him...the first fruits...and the
sacrifice of
31:19, not...pacified for sin by the multitude of sacrifices
32:7, with gifts...and trust not to unrighteous sacrifices;
45:14, Their sacrifices shall be wholly consumed every day
45:16, him out of all men living to offer
sacrifices to the
45:21, for they eat of the sacrifices of the
Lord, which he
Epis.-Jer. 1:29, women in childbed eat their
sacrifices:
Song-Child. 1:14, at this time prince, or prophet
...or sacrifice,
1:16, so let our sacrifice be in thy
sight
I Macc. 1:45, and forbid burnt offerings, and
sacrifice, and
4:53, and offered sacrifice according to
the law upon the
4:56, altar...and sacrificed the sacrifice
of deliverance

holokautos, "burnt whole, burnt offering"
I Macc. 7:33, him peaceably, and to shew him the
burnt sacrifice

thusia
II Macc. 1:8, we offered also sacrifices and fine
flour, and
1:18, Therefore...Neemias offered sacrifice, after he had
1:21, then commanded he them...when the
sacrifices were
1:23, And the priests made a prayer
whilst the sacrifice
1:26, receive the sacrifice for thy whole
people Israel,
1:31, Now when the sacrifice was consumed,
Neemias
1:33, that Neemias had purified the sacrifices therewith

II Macc. 2:9, that being wise offered the sacrifice of dedication
3:3, Asia...bare all the costs...of the
sacrifices
3:6, of riches, which did not pertain to
...the sacrifices
3:32, So the high priest....offered a
sacrifice for the
3:35, So Heliodorus, after he had offered
sacrifice unto
4:14, courage to serve...and neglecting
the sacrifices,
4:19, sent special messengers...to the
sacrifice of
4:20, then...was appointed to the sacrifice of Hercules

splagchnismos, "a feeding the inwards of
a victim"
II Macc. 6:7, by bitter constraint to eat of the
sacrifices;
6:8, that they should observe...their
sacrifices

thusia
II Macc. 6:21, did eat of the flesh taken from
the sacrifice
9:16, with goodly gifts...belonging to
the sacrifices:
10:3, temple...and offered a sacrifice
after two years,
13:23, all equal conditions...and offered
sacrifice,
14:31, Judas' policy...were offering their
usual sacrifices

thuō, "to kill in sacrifice, sacrifice"
III Macc. 2:28, refused to all those who would
not sacrifice;

thusia
III Macc. 5:43, and prevent sacrifices even after
being offered

SACRIFICE, thuō, "to offer, to kill in sacrifice,
sacrifice"
Tobit 1:4, chosen out...that all the tribes
should sacrifice
Wisd.-Sol. 18:9, righteous children of good men
did sacrifice

Eccl. 31:18, He that sacrificeth of a thing
                      wrongfully gotten, his

          thusia, "the act of sacrificing"
Epis.-Jer. 1:28, As for the things that are sacri-
                      ficed unto them,

          thuō
I Macc. 1:43, consented to his religion, and
                      sacrificed unto idols
          1:47, and chapels of idols, and sacrificed
                      swine's flesh,
          1:51, commanding the cities of Juda to
                      sacrifice
          1:59, twentieth day of the month they did
                      sacrifice upon
          2:15, came into the city of Modin, to make
                      them sacrifice
          2:23, there came one of the Jews...to sa-
                      crifice on the
          2:25, commissioner, who compelled men to
                      sacrifice, he
          4:56, And so they kept the dedication...
                      and sacrificed the sacrifice of
                      deliverance
         11:34, appertaining unto them, for all such
                      as do sacrifice

SAIL, ploion, "a vessel, ship, bark"
  Wisd.-Sol. 14:1, Again, one preparing himself to
                      sail, and about

          pleō, "to sail"
  Eccl. 43:24, They that sail on the sea tell of the
                      danger thereof

SAINT, hagios, "devoted to the gods, separate from
                      common condition and use, pure, holy"
  Tobit 8:15, therefore let thy saints praise thee
                      with all thy
       12:15, I am Raphael...which present the
                      prayers of the saints

          eklektos, "chosen out, selected"
  Wisd.-Sol. 3:9, for grace and mercy is to the
                      saints
            4:15, That his grace and mercy is with
                      his saints, and

          hagios
  Wisd.-Sol. 5:5, children of God, and his lot among

                        the saints!

                hosios, "pious, devout, religious"
        Wisd.-Sol. 18:1, Nevertheless thy saints had a
                        very great light,
                18:5, determined to slay the babes of
                        the saints, one

                theios, "godlike, superhuman, holy, sacred"
        Wisd.-Sol. 18:9, made a holy law, that the
                        saints should be

                hagios
        Eccl. 42:17, The Lord hath given power to the
                        saints to declare
                45:2, He made him like to the glorious
                        saints, and magnified

                hosios
        I Macc. 7:17, The flesh of thy saints have they
                        cast out, and

                hagiazo, "to separate, consecrate, regard
                        as holy"
        IV Macc. 17:19, For Moses saith, And all the saints
                        are under thy

SALOM, Salom
        I Macc. 2:26, as Phinees did unto Zambri the son
                        of Salom.

SALT, hals or halos, "salt, a fisherman"
        Wisd.-Sol. 10:7, and a standing pillar of salt is
                        a monument of an
        Eccl. 22:15, Sand, and salt, and a mass of iron,
                        are easier to
                39:26, for the whole use of man's life are
                        ...salt, flour of
                43:19, The hoarfrost also as salt he poureth
                        on the earth,
        I Macc. 10:29, And now do I free you...and from
                        the custom of salt

SALUTE, aspazomai, "to salute, greet, welcome"
        Eccl. 41:20, and of silence before them that
                        salute thee; and to
        I Macc. 11:6, great pomp at Joppe, where they
                        saluted one another
                12:17, also to go unto you, and to salute
                        you, and to

SALVATION, soteria, "saving, deliverance, means of
                        safety"

                            273

Judith 8:17, Therefore let us wait for salvation
    of him, and call
Wisd.-Sol. 5:2, see it, they...shall be amazed
    at...his salvation
    16:6, they were troubled...having a
    sign of salvation,
    18:7, So of thy people was accepted both
    the salvation
Bar. 4:24, Sion...shall they see shortly your
    salvation from your
    4:29, these plagues...shall bring you...
    everlasting...salvation
I Macc. 3:6, the wicked shrunk for fear...because
    salvation
III Macc. 6:31, who were before...partook of the
    cup of salvation,
    7:22, with perfectness wonders for their
    salvation
IV Macc. 11:7, and possessed the hope of salvation
    from God
    15:8, God, she neglected the temporary
    salvation
Pr.-Mans. 1:7, thou hast decreed for sinners...
    salvation

SAMAIAS, Samaias
  I Esd. 1:9, And Jeconias, and Samaias, and
    Nathanael his brother,

SAMARIA, Samareia
  I Esd. 2:25, back again to Rathumus...and dwellers
    in Samaria and
  Eccl. 50:26, they that sit upon the mountain of
    Samaria, and they
  I Macc. 3:10, the Gentiles...and a great host out
    of Samaria,
    5:66, of the Philistines, and passed
    through Samaria.
    10:30, governments which are added there-
    unto...Samaria,
    10:38, governments that are added to Judea
    ...from Samaria,
    11:28, the king that he would make...the
    country of Samaria
    11:34, governments...that are added unto
    Judea from...Samaria
  II Macc. 15:1, Judas and his company were....
    about Samaria,

SAMOS, Samos
  I Macc. 15:23, all the countries...and to
                Sampsames...and Samos,

SAMPSAMES, Sampsames
  I Macc. 15:23, and to all the countries, and to
                Sampsames, and

SAMUEL, Samouel
  I Esd. 1:20, was not kept in Israel since the
               time of...Samuel
  Eccl. 46:13, Samuel, the prophet of the Lord,
               beloved of his Lord

SANABASSARUS, Sabanassaros
  I Esd. 6:20, Then the same Sanabassarus, being
               come hither, laid

SANCTIFICATION, hagiasmos, "sanctification, moral
                            purity, sanctity"
  Eccl. 7:31, his portion...and the sacrifice of
              sanctification,

SANCTIFIED, hagiazō, "to separate, cleanse, purify,
                      sanctify"
  I Esd. 1:49, the temple of the Lord, which was
               sanctified in
         7:10, the priests and the Levites were
               sanctified,
         7:11, for they were sanctified, because
               the Levites were
  Judith 6:19, look upon the face of those that are
               sanctified unto
        11:13, spend the firstfruits...which they
               had sanctified,
  Eccl. 33:4, As thou wast sanctified among them:
              so be thou
        36:12, Some of them hath he...sanctified,
               and set near
        45:4, He sanctified him in his faithfulness
              and meekness,
        49:7, For they entreated him evil, who...
              was...sanctified in

          kathagizō, "to devote or dedicate by
                      fire, devour"
  II Macc. 2:8, that the place might be honourably
                sanctified

          hagiazō
  III Macc. 6:3, look upon the seed of Abraham...
                 they sanctified Jacob, thy

                    sanctified inheritance,
  IV Macc. 17:20, These therefore, having been sanc-
                    tified through

SANCTIFY, hagiazō, "to consecrate, sanctify, rever-
                    ence as holy"
  II Macc. 1:25, things...didst choose the fathers,
                    and sanctify
  III Macc. 2:16, it seemed good to thee..thou didst
                    sanctify this

SANCTITY, semnotēs, "majesty, dignity, seriousness"
  II Macc. 3:12, impossible...to the majesty and
                    inviolable sanctity

           poiesis, "an acting, doing, observance
                    of a law"
  III Macc. 1:9, offered thank-offering...to the
                    sanctity of the

SANCTUARY, hagios, "of persons, pious, pure: as
                    substance, a sanctuary"
  Judith 8:21, if we be taken so, all Judea...and
                    our sanctuary
      8:24, their hearts depend upon us, and the
                    sanctuary, and
      9:8, for they have purposed to defile thy
                    sanctuary, and
      16:20, continued feasting in Jerusalem be-
                    fore the sanctuary
  Eccl. 45:24, that he should be the chief of the
                    sanctuary
      47:13, reigned in peaceable time...and pre-
                    pare his sanctuary

           hagiosmos, "moral purity, sanctity, sanc-
                    tification"
  Eccl. 49:6, They burnt the chosen city of the
                    sanctuary, and made

           oikos, "a house, a temple"
  Eccl. 50:5, midst of the people in his coming out
                    of the sanctuary

           hagiosmos
  I Macc. 1:21, and entered proudly into the sanc-
                    tuary and took
      1:36, was a place to lie in wait against
                    the sanctuary
      1:37, innocent blood on every side of the
                    sanctuary, and
      1:39, Her sanctuary was laid waste like a

I Macc. 1:46, and pollute the sanctuary, and holy
         people:
      2:7, born to see this misery...and the
         sanctuary into the
      2:12, And, behold, our sanctuary, even
         our beauty and our
      3:43, one to another, Let us restore...
         the sanctuary
      3:45, the sanctuary also was trodden
         down, and the aliens

     hagia, "sanctuary, dedicated, hallowed"
I Macc. 3:51, For thy sanctuary is trodden down
         and profaned, and
      3:58, that are assembled...against us to
         destroy...our sanctuary
      3:59, to behold the calamities of...our
         sanctuary
      4:36, up to cleanse and dedicate the
         sanctuary
      4:38, And when they saw the sanctuary
         desolate, and the
      4:43, who cleansed the sanctuary, and bare
         out the defiled
      4:48, and made up the sanctuary, and the
         things that were
      5:1, that the altar was built, and the
         sanctuary renewed,
      6:7, also that they had...compassed about
         the sanctuary
      6:18, About this time they were in the...
         sanctuary, and
      6:26, this day are they besieging...the
         sanctuary also at
      6:51, As for the sanctuary, he besieged
         it many days:
      6:54, there were but a few left in the
         sanctuary, because
      7:33, and there came out of the sanctuary
         certain of the
      7:42, so destroy thou this host...against
         thy sanctuary,
      9:54, fifty and third year...the sanctuary
         should be pulled
    10:39, and the land...Igive it as a free
         gift to the sanctuary
    10:44, also and repairing of the works of
         the sanctuary,

```
I Macc. 13:3, Ye yourselves know...the laws and
              sanctuary, the
        13:6, Doubtless I will avenge my nation,
              and the sanctuary
       14:15, He beautified the sanctuary, and
              multiplied the
       14:29, for the maintenance of their
              sanctuary, and the
       14:31, their enemies purposed to...destroy
              ...the sanctuary
       14:36, they...polluted all about the sanc-
              tuary, and
       14:42, be their captain, and...take
              charge of the sanctuary
       14:48, this writing...be set up within...
              the sanctuary
        15:7, And as concerning Jerusalem and the
              sanctuary let
II Macc. 2:17, that God, that delivered...and
               gave...the sanctuary

              topos, "a place, spot"
II Macc. 4:33, him, and withdrew himself into a
               sanctuary
         4:34, persuaded him to come forth of the
               sanctuary:

              naos, "the dwelling of a god, a temple"
III Macc. 1:10, with the exact magnificence...of
                ...the sanctuary
```

SAND, ámmos, "sand, a sandy place"
```
Eccl. 1:2, Who can number the sand of the sea,
           and the drops of
     18:10, water unto the sea, and a gravel-stone
            ...of the sand
     22:15, Sand, and salt, and a mass of iron,
            are easier to
Song-Child. 1:12, thou wouldest multiply their
                  seed as...the sand
I Macc. 11:1, Egypt gathered together a great
              host, like the sand

              psammon, "a tract of sand, the sand"
Pr.-Mans. 1:9, I have sinned above the number of
               the sand of the
```

SANDAL, sandalion, "a small sandal, or slipper"
```
Judith 10:4, And she took sandals upon her feet,
             and put about her
```

Judith 16:9, Her sandals ravished his eyes, her
              beauty took his

SANDY, ảmmos, "a sandy place, race-course"
  Eccl. 25:20, As the climbing up a sandy way is to
               the feet of the

SANG, ảdō, "to sing"
  Judith 16:1, Begin unto my God with timbrels,
               sing, unto my Lord
         16:13, I will sing unto my God a new song:
                O Lord, thou

    humneō, "to sing, praise"
  Eccl. 47:8, In all his works...he sang songs, and
              loved him that

    psallō, "to sing to music, to sing praise"
  Eccl. 50:18, The singers also sang praises with
               their voices,

    humneō, "to sing a hymn, celebrate or worship
             with hymns"
  I Macc. 4:24, After this they went home, and sung
                a song of
  II Macc. 1:30, And the priests sung psalms of
                 thanksgiving

SARA, Sarra
  Tobit 3:7, It came to pass the same day, that...
             Sara the daughter
       6:10, he also hath one only daughter, named
             Sara;
       7:1, And he came to the house of Raguel,
            and Sara met him:
       7:8, And likewise Edna his wife and Sara
            his daughter went
       7:13, Then he called his daughter Sara, and
             she came to her
      10:11, Then Raguel arose, and gave him Sara
             his wife, and
      10:13, of heaven...grant that I may see...
             my daughter Sara
      11:17, And when he came near to Sara his
             daughter in law, he
      12:14, has sent me to heal thee and Sara my
             daughter in law

SATAN, Satanas, "Satan, an adversary, enemy"
  Eccl. 21:27, When the ungodly curseth Satan, he
               curseth his own

SATISFIED, árkeō, "satisfied, to be content, to
                    suffice"
    IV Macc. 6:28, Be merciful to thy people, and be
                    satisfied with

SAUL, Saoul
    I Macc. 4:30, and gavest the host of strangers
                    into the hands...of Saul

SAVAGE, barbaros, "a barbarian, one who is not a
                    proper Greek"
    II Macc. 4:25, king's mandate...and the rage of
                    a savage beast

SAVARAN, Savaran
    I Macc. 6:43, Eleazar also, surnamed Savaran, per-
                    ceiving that one

SAVE, sōzō, "to save, rescue"
    Wisd.-Sol. 16:7, turned himself toward it was not
                    saved by the
    III Macc. 6:36, a public ordinance...because God
                    had saved them
    IV Macc. 4:12, and that if he were saved, he
                    would celebrate to

SAVIOUR, sōtēr, "a saviour, deliverer, preserver"
    Wisd.-Sol. 16:7, turned himself toward...the
                    Saviour of all things
    Eccl. 51:1, I will thank thee, O Lord and King...
                    O God my Saviour:
    Bar. 4:22, For my hope is in...the Everlasting
                    your Saviour
    I Macc. 4:30, he prayed and said, Blessed art
                    thou, O Saviour of
    III Macc. 6:29, he said...and praised God their
                    holy Saviour

SCARECROW, sikuēratos, "a scarecrow"
    Epis.-Jer. 1:70, For as a scarecrow in a garden
                    of cucumbers

SCARLET, kokkos, "a kernel, a berry; esp. the kermes-
                    berry, used to dye scarlet"
    Eccl. 45:11, with twisted scarlet, the work of the
                    cunning

SCATTER, kiaskorpizō, "to disperse, scatter"
    Bar. 2:4, delivered them...where the Lord hath
                    scattered them
          2:13, we are but a few left...where thou hast
                    scattered us

Bar. 3:28, we are yet this day...where thou hast
         scattered us,

SCEPTRE, skeptros, "a sceptre"
Wisd.-Sol. 6:21, If your delight be then in thrones
                 and sceptres,
           7:8, I preferred her before sceptres
                 and thrones, and
          10:14, him not in bonds, till she
                 brought him the sceptre
Eccl. 32:18, will not be slack...till he have
             taken...the sceptre
Epis.-Jer. 1:14, one that offendeth him holdeth
                 a sceptre

SCHEDIA, Schedia
III Macc. 4:11, in this vessel, and ...it carried
                 at Schedia

SCORN, gelaō, "to laugh at, sneer at"
Wisd.-Sol. 4:18, shall see him...but God shall
                 laugh them to scorn

         katagelaō, "to laugh at"
Eccl. 7:11, Laugh no man to scorn in the bitter-
             ness of his soul:

SCORPION, skorpios, "a scorpion"
Eccl. 26:7, that hath hold of her is as though he
             had a scorpion
      39:30, teeth of wild beasts, and scorpions,
             serpents, and
IV Macc. 11:10, his body was then dismembered,
                 scorpion-fashion

SCOURGE, échthros, "hateful, hated, hostile"
Wisd.-Sol. 12:22, whereas thou dost chasten us,
                  thou scourgest

         mastix, "a whip, a scourge"
Eccl. 26:6, of heart...over another woman, and a
             scourge of the
      40:9, Death, and bloodshed...famine, tri-
             bulation, and the scourge
II Macc. 7:1, seven...were tormented with scourges
              and whips
         9:11, Here there, being plagued...by the
               scourge of God,

         mastizō, "to whip or flog"
III Macc. 2:21, At that time God...scourged the
                 man greatly

mastix
IV Macc. 6:6, high to heaven...was stripped off
            by the scourges
        9:12, they had laboured hard with effect
            in scourging

SCRIBE, grammateus, "a secretary, clerk, a scribe"

I Esd. 2:17, Thy servants Rathumus...the scribe,
            and the rest of
        2:25, again to Rathumus...to Semellius,
            the scribe, and to
        2:30, letters being read Rathumus, and
            Semellius, the scribe,
        8:3, This Esdras went up from Babylon, as
            a scribe, being
Eccl. 10:5, and upon the person of the scribe
            scribe shall he lay his
I Macc. 5:42, he caused the scribes of the people
            to remain by
II Macc. 6:18, Eleazar, one of the principal
            scribes, an aged man

SCRIPTURE, graphē, "The Holy Scripture, doctrines,
            declaration"
I Macc. 12:9, we also...have the holy books of the
            scripture in
IV Macc. 18:4, And he used to put you in mind of
            the scripture of

SCYTHIAN, Skuthēs, "a Scythian, a native of Scythia"
II Macc. 4:47, insomuch that he discharged...the
            Scythians
III Macc. 7:5, savage cruelty, worse than the
            Scythian custom

SCYTHOPOLIS, Skuthopolis
II Macc. 12:29, From thence they departed to
            Scythopolis, which

SCYTHOPOLITIANS, Skuthopolitai
II Macc. 12:30, had testified that the Scythopoli-
            tans dealt

SEA, thalassa, "the sea, a well of salt or brackish
            water"
I Esd. 4:2, in strength, that bear rule over the
            sea and land...?
Judith 1:12, inhabitants...till he come to the
            borders of the two seas
        1:28, fell upon the inhabitants of the sea
            coasts,

Judith 5:13, And God dried up the Red sea before
        them,
      5:22, these sayings...all that dwelt by the
        sea side...spake
Wisd.-Sol. 10:18, brought them through the Red
        sea, and led them
      14:13, But thy providence...governeth
        it...in the sea,
      14:4, yea, though a man went to the sea
        without art
      14:5, and passing the rough sea in a
        weak
      19:7, and out of the Red sea a way
        without
Eccl. 1:2, Who can number the sand of the sea,
        and the drops of
      18:10, As a drop of water unto the sea, and
        a gravel stone
      24:6, In the waves of the sea, and in all the
        earth...I got a
      24:29, For her thoughts are more than the sea,
        and her
      29:18, good estate, and shaken them as a wave
        of the sea:
      40:11, and that which is of the water doth
        return into the sea
      43:24, They that sail on the sea tell of the
        danger thereof
      44:21, stars...and cause them to inherit from
        sea to sea,
      50:3, to receive water, being in compass as
        the sea,
Bar. 3:30, Who hath gone over the sea, and found
        her...?
Song-Child. 1:55, O ye seas and rivers, bless ye
        the Lord:
I Macc. 4:9, how our fathers were delivered in
        the Red sea, when
      4:23, they got much gold...and purple of
        the sea,
      6:29, him from other kingdoms, and from
        isles of the sea,
      8:23, Romans, and to the people of the
        Jews, by the sea,
      8:32, and fight with thee by the sea and
        by land
      11:1, a great host, like the sand...upon
        the sea shore,

I Macc. 13:29, they might be seen of all that
            sail on the sea
        14:5, and made an entrance to the isle
            of the sea
        14:34, he fortified Joppe, which lieth
            upon the sea, and
        15:1, sent letters from the isles of the
            sea unto Simon
        15:11, king Antiochus, he fled unto Dora
            ...by the sea side:
        15:14, joined ships close to the towns by
            land and by sea,

  pelagos, "the deep, the open sea"
II Macc. 5:21, weening in his pride to make...the
            sea passable

  thalassa
II Macc. 9:8, afore thought he might command the
            waves of the sea
III Macc. 2:7, And thou rolledst the depths of
            the sea over him,
        7:30, They departed unharmed, free...
            by land, by sea, and
Pr.-Mans. 1:3, that hast bound the sea with the
            word of thy
        1:9, sinned above the number of the
            sand of the sea

SEACOAST, parathalassa, "by the sea"
  I Macc. 7:1, departed...unto a city of the sea
            coast
  II Macc. 8:11, Wherefore...he sent to the cities
            upon the sea coast

        paralios, "by the sea, on the sea shore"
  I Macc. 15:38, Then the king made Cendebeus cap-
            tain of the sea coast

SEAL, sphragis, "a seal to mark anything with,
            signet ring"
  Eccl. 38:27, every carpenter and workmaster...
            cut and grave seals,
        45:11, scarlet, the work...of the workman...
            graven like seals

      sphragizō, "to seal"
  Bel-Drag. 1:11, So Bel's priests said...shut the
            door...and seal it
        1:14, So when they were gone forth...
            they...sealed it

sphragis
Bel-Drag. 1:17, And the king said, Daniel, are
        the seals whole?

SEALED, sphragizō, "to close up, conceal, to seal"
Pr.-Mans. 1:3, that has closed the abyss and
        sealed it with thy

SEASHORE, aigialos, "seashore, beach, strand"
Eccl. 24:14, I was exalted like a palm tree on the
        sea shore

        thalassa, "the sea"
Song-Child. 1:12, seed...as the sand...upon the
        sea shore

SEASON, chronos, "time, a period, season, space of
        time"
Wisd.-Sol. 7:18, ending, and midst of times...and
        change of seasons
        8:8, much experience...and the events
        of seasons and
        10:17, and a light of stars in the
        night season;

        kairos, "due measure, right season, critical
        moment"
Eccl. 20:20, a fool's mouth; for he will not speak
        in due season

        ákairos, "not in season, unseasonable, ill-
        timed"
Eccl. 22:6, A tale out of season (is as) music
        in mourning:

        kairos
Eccl. 29:2, Lend to thy neighbour...and pay...
        again in due season
        36:8, By the knowledge of the Lord...they
        altered seasons
        39:16, good, and whatsoever he commandeth...
        in due season
        39:33, good: and he will give every needful
        thing in due season
        43:6, He made the moon also to serve her
        season for a

        chronos
Epis.-Jer. 1:3, Babylon, ye shall remain there...
        for a long season

kairos
I Macc. 4:59, the dedication...should be kept
        in their season

hēmera, "day, all day long, daily"
I Macc. 11:65, Bethsura, and fought against it a
        long season,

kairos
IV Macc. 14:19, The very bees at the season of
        honey-making,

SEAT, topos, "a place, spot, position"
Eccl. 12:12, Set him not by thee...lest he seek
        to take thy seat,

SECRET, kruphaios, "secret, hidden, clandestine"
Wisd.-Sol. 14:23, children in sacrifices, or used
        secret
        17:3, supposed to lie still in their
        secret sins,

kruptō, "to hide, cover, conceal, lie
        hidden"
Eccl. 3:11, for thee to see...the things that are
        in secret

kruptē, "a covered place, vault, crypt"
Eccl. 4:18, return the straight way...and shew
        him her secrets

apokruphos, "hidden, secret"
Eccl. 14:21, ways...shall also have understanding
        in her secrets
        23:19, the eyes of men...and considering
        the most secret
        39:3, He will seek out the secrets of grave
        sentences, and
        39:7, and knowledge, and on his secrets shall
        he meditate
        42:1, and speaking again...and of revealing
        of secrets
        48:25, what should come to pass for ever,
        and secret things

kruptos, "hidden, secret"
His.-Sus. 1:42, O Everlasting God, that knowest
        the secrets,

kruphaios
I Macc. 1:53, and drove the Israelites into secret
        places, and

I Macc. 2:31, Now...certain men...were gone down
            into secret places
         2:41, our brethren...were murdered in
            secret places

      musterion, "secret rite, a mystery"
II Macc. 13:21, But Rhodocus...disclosed the
            secrets to the

SEDECIAS, Sedekias
   I Esd. 1:46, And made Sedecias king of Judea and
            Jerusalem, when
   Bar. 1:1, Baruch the son of...Sedecias, the son
            of Asadias, the

SEDUCE, planaō, "to seduce, delude, mislead, deceive"
   Tobit 5:13, and they were not seduced by the error
            of our brethren

SEED, sperma, "that which is sown, a seed"
   Tobit 1:1, Tobit, the son of Tobiel...of the seed
            of Assel
   Wisd.-Sol. 3:16, adulterers...and the seed of an
            unrighteous bed
   Eccl. 1:15, foundation...and she shall continue
            with their seed
        10:19, They that fear the Lord are a sure
            seed, and they
        44:11, With their seed shall continually
            remain a good
        44:12, Their seed standeth fast, and their
            children for
        44:13, Their seed shall remain for ever, and
            their glory
        44:21, him by an oath, that he would bless...
            his seed,
        45:15, unto him by an everlasting covenant,
            and to his seed,
        45:21, sacrifices of the Lord, which he gave
            unto...his seed
        45:25, inheritance of Aaron should also be
            unto his seed
        46:9, gave strength also unto Caleb...and
            his seed obtained
        47:22, But the Lord will never leave...the
            seed of him that
        47:23, rested Solomon with his fathers, and
            of his seed he
   Song-Child. 1:12, that thou wouldest multiply
            their seed

I Macc. 5:62, Moreover these men came not of the
            seed of those by
        7:14, for said they, One that is a priest
            of the seed of
        10:30, unto me...for the third part of the
            seed,
IV Macc. 18:1, O Israelitish children, descendants
            of the seed of
Pr.-Mans. 1:1, God of...Jacob and of their
            righteous seed

SEIZURE, árpagē, "plunder, pillage, rapine"
    IV Macc. 4:10, with his armed force to the seizure
            of the treasure

SELEUCIA, Seleukeias
    I Macc. 11:8, gotten the dominion...by the sea
            unto Seleucia

SELEUCUS, Seleukos
    I Macc. 7:1, In the...fiftieth year Demetrius the
            son of Seleucus
    II Macc. 3:3, insomuch that Seleucus king of Asia
            of his own
        4:7, But after the death of Seleucus,
            when Antiochus,
        5:18, For had they not seen...Heliodorus
            ...whom Seleucus
        14:1, After three years...Demetrius the
            son of Seleucus,
    IV Macc. 4:3, will to the king's affairs...to
            king Seleucus
        4:4, Apollonius acquainting himself with
            ...Seleucus
        4:13, the high priest, induced by...king
            Seleucus should
        4:15, But on the death of Seleucus the
            king, his son

SEM, Sēm
    Eccl. 49:16, Sem and Seth were in great honour
            among men, and so

SENATE, gerousia, "a council of Elders, Senate, an
            embassy"
    Judith 11:14, they have sent some to Jerusalem...
            to...the senate

        bouleterion, "Council-chamber, court-house"
    I Macc. 8:19, They went therefore to Rome...into
            the senate, where

boulē, "the Council or Senate"
I Macc. 12:3, So they went unto Rome, and entered
the senate, and

gerousia
II Macc. 4:44, Now...three men that were sent
from the senate

SENNACHERIB, Sennachērim
Eccl. 48:18, In his time Sennacherib came up, and
sent Rabsaces,
II Macc. 8:19, Moreover he recounted unto...
Sennacherib an hundred
15:22, send thine angel...in the host of
Sennacherib

SENNACHERIM, Sennachēreim
III Macc. 6:5, When Sennacherim, the grievous
king of the

SENSUAL, hedupatheia, "pleasant living, luxury"
IV Macc. 2:4, And it is not merely the stimulus
of sensual

SENTENCE, pikros, "words, acts"
Eccl. 41:1, O death, acceptable is thy sentence
unto the needy,

krima, "a judgment, sentence"
Eccl. 41:3, Fear not the sentence of death, remember them that

SEPULCHRE, taphos, "a sepulchre"
I Esd. 1:31, and died, and was buried in his
father's sepulchre
I Macc. 2:70, and his sons buried him in the
sepulchres of his
9:19, Judas...and buried him in the sepulchre of his
13:27, Simon also built a monument upon
the sepulchre of
13:30, This is the sepulchre which he made
at Modin, and
II Macc. 5:10, and he...had none to mourn for him
...nor sepulchre

SERON, Serōn
I Macc. 3:13, Now when Seron, a prince of the
army of Syria heard
3:23, Now as soon as he had left off
speaking...Seron and

SERPENT, érpeton, "a creeping animal, a reptile"
  Wisd.-Sol. 11:15, they worshipped serpents void
                    of reason,

          éphis, "a serpent"
  Wisd.-Sol. 16:5, perished with the stings of
                   crooked serpents,
            17:9, yet being scared with...hissing
                  of serpents
  Eccl. 12:13, Who will pity a charmer that is
               bitten with a serpent
        21:2, Flee from sin as from the face of a
              serpent:
        25:15, There is no head above the head of
               a serpent;
        39:20, teeth of wild beasts, and scorpions,
               serpents, and

SERVANT, pais, "a maiden, a girl, a slave, servant"
  I Esd. 1:30, Then said the king unto his servant,
               Carry me away
         1:57, who became servants to him and his
               children, till

          oiketēs, "an inmate of one's house, a house
                   slave, menial domestic"
  I Esd. 4:59, victory...and thine is the glory,
               and I am thy servant

          pais
  I Esd. 6:13, So they gave us this answer, We are
               the servants of

          hierodoulos, "temple servant"
  I Esd. 8:49, And of the servants of the temple
               whom David had

          pais
  I Esd. 8:82, O Lord...thou gavest by the hand of
               thy servants, the

          oiketēs
  Tobit 8:18, Then Raguel bade his servants to fill
              the grave

          pais
  Tobit 9:2, Brother Azarias, take with thee a
             servant, and
  Judith 3:2, Behold, we the servants of Nabuchodo-
              nosor the great
         3:4, cities and the inhabitants thereof are
              thy servants;

<u>doulos</u>, "a slave, bondman"
Judith 5:5, my lord now hear a word from the
        mouth of thy servant
    6:3, but we his servants will destroy them
        as one man:
    6:7, Now therefore my servants shall bring
        thee back into
    6:10, Then Holofernes commanded his ser-
        vants, that waited
    6:11, So his servants took him, and brought
        him out of the

<u>pais</u>
Judith 7:12, Remain in thy camp...and let thy ser-
        vants get into

<u>therapōn</u>, "an attendant, servant"
Judith 7:16, words pleased Holofernes and all his
        servants, and

<u>doulos</u>
Judith 7:27, for we will be his servants, that
        our souls may live
    9:3, to be slain...and smotest the servants
        with their
    9:10, Smite by the deceit of my lips the
        servant with the

<u>therapōn</u>
Judith 10:20, near Holofernes went out, and all
        his servants, and
    10:23, when Judith was come before him
        and his servants,

<u>doulos</u>
Judith 11:4, shall hurt thee well, as they do the
        servants of
    11:5, unto him, Receive the words of thy
        servant, and
    11:17, For thy servant is religious, and
        serveth the God

<u>therapōn</u>
Judith 11:20, words pleased Holofernes and all
        his servants; and
    12:5, Then the servants of Holofernes
        brought her into the
    12:10, day Holofernes made a feast to his
        servants only,

<u>doulos</u>
Judith 13:1, Now when the evening was come, his

servants made

therapōn
Wisd.-Sol. 10:16, She entered into the soul of
the servant of the

doulos
Wisd.-Sol. 18:11, The master and the servant were
punished after

therapōn
Wisd.-Sol. 18:21, haste...declaring that he was
thy servant

pais
Bar. 1:20, curse, which the Lord appointed by
Moses his servant
2:24, would not hearken unto thy voice...by
thy servants the
2:28, as thou spakest by thy servant Moses
in the day when
3:36, all the way of knowledge, and hath
given...servant, and

doulos
Song-Child. 1:9, we cannot open our mouths, we
are...thy servants,
1:11, to depart from us...for thy
servant Isaac's
1:19, Deliver us...and let all them
that do thy servants hurt be
ashamed
1:62, O ye servants of the Lord, bless
ye the Lord:
His.-Sus. 1:27, declared their matter, the servants
were greatly

pais
Bel-Drag. 1:14, Now Daniel had commanded his servants to bring
I Macc. 1:6, Wherefore he called his servants,
such as were
1:8, And his servants bare rule every one
in his place
2:31, Now it was told the king's servants,
and the host
4:31, took silver and gold...with servants
and came into

doulos
I Macc. 4:30, quell the violence...by the hand of
thy servant

pais
I Macc. 16:16, and slew him...and certain of his
          servants

doulos
II Macc. 1:2, remember...Isaac, and Jacob, his
          faithful servants
      7:6, And he shall be comforted in his
          servants
      7:33, yet shall he be at one again with
          his servants

pais
II Macc. 8:28, they divided among themselves and
          their servants

doulos
II Macc. 8:29, merciful Lord to be reconciled with
          his servants

SETH, Sēth
  Eccl. 49:16, Sem and Seth were in great honour
          among men, and so

SEVEN, hepta
  Bel-Drag. And in the den there were seven lions,
          and they had
  I Macc. 13:28, Moreover he set up seven pyramids,
          one against
  II Macc. 7:1, It came to pass also, seven brethren
          with their
  IV Macc. 13:1, If then, the seven brethren de-
          spised troubles even
      13:22, sympathetically constituted the
          seven brethren,
      14:3, Sacred and harmonious concert of
          the seven brethren
      14:4, None of the seven youths turned
          cowardly, or

hebdomas, "seven"
  IV Macc. 14:7, harmonious brethren! for as the
          seven days of
      14:8, so the youths, circling around the
          number seven,

hepta
  IV Macc. 15:2, her...religion and the safety of
          her seven sons,
      15:6, And of all mothers the mother of
          the seven was the

IV Macc. 15:24, Although beholding the destruction
                of seven
        16:1, If, then, even a woman...and the
                mother of seven
        16:3, burned within her...when she be-
                held her seven sons
        16:6, many times miserable: who having
                borne seven sons
        16:7, O seven useless childbirths, and
                seven profitless
        17:2, O thou mother, who together with
                seven children
        17:7, shudder at...the mother of seven
                children enduring
        17:9, Here an aged priest, and an aged
                woman, and seven
      17:13, and the mother of the seven child-
                ren entered the
        18:7, And the righteous mother of the
                seven children
      18:20, brought with boiling rage the
                seven sons of the

SEVENFOLD, heptaplasion, "sevenfold"
Eccl. 20:12, much for a little, and repayeth it
              sevenfold

SEVENTH, hebdomos, "the seventh"
IV Macc. 12:1, When he...too...had been thrown,
              the seventh, the

SEXUAL, suneimi, "to have intercourse"
IV Macc. 2:3, For, although young, and ripe for
              sexual intercourse

SHADOW, skia, "a shadow or shade"
Wisd.-Sol. 2:5, For our time is a very shadow that
              passeth away;
        5:9, All those things are passed away
              like a shadow,
Eccl. 31:2, regardeth dreams is like him that
              catcheth at a shadow
Bar. 1:12, is strength...and we shall live under
              the shadow of

SHADOWING, skiazō, "to shade, overshadow, darken"
Wisd.-Sol. 19:7, as namely, a cloud shadowing
              the camp;

SHAME, aischunē, "shame done one, disgrace, dis-
              honour"
I Esd. 8:77, given up unto the kings...for a prey

with shame

Eccl. 4:21, and there is shame which is glory and
grace

6:1, not an enemy; for...thou shalt inherit
...shame, and

26:8, great anger, and she will not cover
her own shame

kataischune, "to shame, disgrace, dishonour"

Eccl. 42:14, churlishness of a man...which
bringeth shame and

aischune

Bar. 2:6, God appertaineth righteousness: but unto
us...shame, as

Song-Child. 1:9, cannot open our mouths, we are
become a shame

1:18, Put us not to shame: but deal
with us after

II Macc. 5:7, Howbeit for all this...received
shame for the reward

III Macc. 6:34, marked them out...were clothed
with shame,

SHAMEFACED, aischune, "shame done one, disgrace,
dishonour"

Eccl. 35:10, goeth lightning ; and before a shamefaced man goeth

entrepo, "to reprove, make ashamed"

Eccl. 41:16, Therefore be shamefaced according
to my word:

SHAMEFULLY, aischros, "shamefully"

II Macc. 11:12, and Lysias himself fled away shamefully, and so

SHAMELESS, anaides, "shameless, abashed, reckless"

Bar. 4:15, brought a nation upon them from far, a
shameless nation

SHEAVES, dragma, "as much as one can grasp, a hand-
ful, sheaf"

Judith 8:3, For as he stood overseeing them that
bound sheaves in

SHECHMITE, Sikimitas

IV Macc. 2:19, Jacob...having irrationally slain
...the Shechmites,

SHEEP, probaton, "a little sheep"

I Esd. 1:8, governors of the temple, gave the...
six hundred sheep

I Esd. 1:9, Jeconias...and Joram...gave...five
     thousand sheep,
Judith 8:26, what things he did to Abraham...when
     he kept the sheep
    11:19, and thou shalt drive them as sheep
     that have no
Bel-Drag. 1:3, had an idol...and there were spent
     upon him...forty sheep
    1:32, in the den there were seven lions
     ...and two sheep

SHEKEL, siklos, "a shekel"
I Macc. 10:40, I give every year fifteen thousand
     shekels of
    10:42, And beside this the five thousand
     shekels of

SHELTER, skepazo, "to shelter, cover"
III Macc. 3:29, Whatever place shall shelter a
     Jew, shall, when

SHEPHERD, poimen, "a herdsman, a shepherd"
Wisd.-Sol. 17:7, For whether he were husbandman,
     or shepherd, or
Eccl. 18:13, mercy of man is toward his neighbour
     ...as a shepherd

SHEWBREAD, prothesis, "a placing before, setting
                forth, the shewbread"
I Macc. 1:22, and the table of the shewbread, and
     the pouring
II Macc. 10:3, temple, they...set forth incense...
     and shewbread

SHIELD, aspis, "a round shield"
Judith 9:7, they trust in shield, and spear, and
     bow, and sling;
Eccl. 29:13, against thine enemies, better than a
     mighty shield,
I Macc. 4:57, of the temple with crowns of gold
     and with shields;

     hople, "a hoof, the solid hoof"
I Macc. 6:2, very rich temple...of gold, and
     breastplates and shields,

     aspis
I Macc. 15:20, seemed also good to us to receive
     the shield of
II Macc. 5:3, troops of horsemen in array...with
     shaking shields,
    15:11, not so much with defence of shields

and spears

skepas, "covering, shelter"
III Macc. 3:27, Whoever shall shield a Jew,
whether it be old man

asphalēs, "firm, steadfast, trusty"
III Macc. 7:6, Finding that the God of heaven
cast a shield of

SHINE, stilbō, "to shine, glitter"
Epis.-Jer. 1:24, except they wipe off the dust,
they will not shine

photizō, "shining brought, giving light"
Epis.-Jer. 1:67, they shew signs in the heavens
...nor shine as the

SHIP, ploion, "a floating vessel, a ship"
Eccl. 36:2, but he that is an hypocrite therein
is as a ship
I Macc. 8:26, they give any thing unto them, with
victuals...ships
8:28, or weapons, or money, or ships, as
it hath seemed
11:1, gathered together a great host...
and many ships,
13:29, made cunning devices...and by the
armour ships carved
15:3, certain pestilent men...have gathered
...ships of war
15:14, compassed the city round about, and
joined ships
15:37, In the meantime fled Tryphon by
ship unto Orthosias
III Macc. 4:7, they were hurried violently on
board ship

SHOE, hupodema, "a sandal, a shoe, boot"
Eccl. 46:19, made protestation...I have not taken
any man's shoe

SHOULDER, ōmos, "the shoulder"
Eccl. 6:25, Bow down thy shoulder, and bear her,
and be not
Epis.-Jer. 1:4, in Babylon gods of silver...borne
upon shoulders
1:26, They are borne upon shoulders,
having no feet,
II Macc. 12:35, Dositheus...coming upon him smote
off his shoulder

SICHEM, Sikimos
    Eccl. 50:26, and that foolish people that dwell
        in Sichem

SICK, nosos, "sickness, disease, affliction"
    Wisd.-Sol. 17:8, promised to drive away terrors...
        from a sick soul

        arrostos, "infirm, sick, an invalid"
    Eccl. 7:35, Be not slow to visit the sick:
        18:19, thou speak, and use physic or ever
            thou be sick

        pipto, "to fall dead, to fall in ruins, to
            fall"
    I Macc. 1:5, And after these things, he fell sick,
        and perceived

SICKNESS, arrostos
    Eccl. 34:22, me not...so shall there no sickness
        come unto thee
        38:9, My son, in thy sickness be not negli-
            gent: but pray

SIDON, Sidonos
    I Macc. 5:15, that they of Ptolemais, and of Tyrus,
        and Sidon,

SIGHT, horama, "a thing seen, sight, appearance"
    Epis.-Jer. 1:37, They cannot restore a blind
            man to his sight,

        enopion, "in the presence of"
    His.-Sus. 1:23, hands...than to sin in the sight
            of the Lord

SIGN, semeion, "a mark, sign, a trace"
    Wisd.-Sol. 10:16, and withstoood dreadful kings
            in wonders and signs;

        tekmerion, "a sign, clear proof"
    Wisd.-Sol. 19:13, came upon the sinners not with-
            out former signs

        semeion
    Eccl. 42:18, He seeketh out the deep...and he be-
            holdeth the signs
        43:6, the moon also to serve in her season
            ...and a sign of
        43:7, From the moon is the sign of feasts,
            a light that
    Bar. 2:11, hast brought thy people out of...
            Egypt with...signs,

Epis.-Jer. 1:67, neither can they shew signs in
the heavens among

kataseiō, "to sign silence by waving the hand,
to beckon"
I Macc. 6:38, the two parts of the host, giving
them signs what

epiphainō, "to manifest, to reveal"
II Macc. 2:21, and the manifest signs that came
from heaven unto

SIGNET, daktulios, "a ring, a seal-ring"
Tobit 1:22, and keeper of the signet, and steward,
and overseer,

sphragis, "a seal to mark anything with, a
signet-ring"
Eccl. 17:22, The alms of a man is as a signet with
him, and he
35:5, A concert of music in a banquet of
wine is as a signet
35:6, As a signet of an emerald set in a
work of gold, so
49:11, shall we magnify Zorobabel? he was
even a signet on

daktulios
Bar. 1:11, door fast, and seal it with thine own
signet
1:14, and shut the door, and sealed it with
the king's signet
I Macc. 6:15, And gave him the crown, and his robe,
and his signet

SILENCE, siōpē, "silence, a being silent, stillness"
Eccl. 20:5, There is one that keepeth silence,
and is found wise:
20:6, Some man holdeth his tongue, and some
keep silence,
41:20, and of silence before them that salute thee: and to

aphasia, "speechlessness"
II Macc. 14:17, was somewhat discomfited through
the sudden silence of his enemies

SILVER, argurios, "silver, of silver"
I Esd. 8:13, and carry the gifts...and all the
gold and silver
8:14, with that also...that silver and gold
mau be collected

I Esd. 8:20, to the sum of an hundred talents of
            silver, likewise
        8:55, and I weighed them the gold, and
            the silver, and the
        8:62, we had been there three days, the
            gold and silver
Tobit 1:14, I went into Media, and left...ten
            talents of silver
Judith 8:7, countenance...and her husband...left
            her...silver,
        10:22, shewed him of her; and she came out
            ...with silver

árguros, "silver"
Wisd.-Sol. 13:10, called them gods, which are the
            works...gold and silver,
Eccl. 26:18, As the golden pillars are upon the
            sockets of silver
        28:24, thou hedge thy possession...and bind
            up thy silver
        40:25, Gold and silver make the foot stand
            sure; but counsel
        47:18, thou didst gather gold as tin, and
            ...silver as lead
Bar. 1:8, he received the vessels...namely, silver
            vessels,
        3:17, pastime...and they that hoarded up
            silver and gold,
        3:18, For they that wrought in silver, and
            were so careful,
Epis.-Jer. 1:4, Now shall ye see in Babylon gods
            of silver, and
        1:10, priests convey from their gods
            gold and silver,
        1:11, thereof to the common harlots...
            gods of silver
        1:30, women set meat before the gods
            of silver,
        1:39, wood which are overlaid with
            gold and silver

árgurios
Epis.-Jer. 1:50, be but of wood, and overlaid with
            silver and
        1:55, wood, or laid over with gold or
            silver,
        1:57, gods of wood, or laid over with
            gold and silver,
        1:58, Whose gold and silver, and gar-
            ments wherewith

Epis.-Jer. 1:70, their gods of wood, and laid
          over with silver,
      1:71, gods of wood, and laid over with
          silver and gold
I Macc. 1:23, He took also the silver and the gold,
          and the
      2:18, children shall be honoured with
          silver and gold,
      4:23, where they got much gold, and silver,
          and blue silk
      6:1, Elymais...was a city...renowned for
          riches, silver, and
      6:12, I did...I took the vessels of gold
          and silver
     10:40, every year fifteen thousand shekels
          of silver
     10:42, the five thousand shekels of silver,
          which they
     10:60, met the two kings, and gave them...
          silver and gold,
     11:24, and took silver and gold, and rai-
          ment, and divers
     13:16, we now send an hundred talents of
          silver, and two
     15:26, At that time Simon sent him...silver
          also, and gold,
     15:31, else give me for them five hundred
          talents of silver
     15:32, Simon, and the cupboard of gold and
          silver plate,
     16:11, Moreover...Ptolemeus...had abundance
          of silver and
     16:19, that he might give them silver, and
          gold,
II Macc. 2:2, them not to...err...when they see
          images of silver
     3:11, whereof...was four thousand talents
          of silver
     4:8, unto the king...three hundred...ta-
          lents of silver,
     4:19, carry three hundred drachms of
          silver,
     4:24, offering...three hundred talents
          of silver
    12:43, to the sum of two thousand drachms
          of silver, he

SILVERSMITH, chrusourgos, "silversmith, melting or
            casting gold"

Wisd.-Sol. 15:9, his care...to excel goldsmiths
            and silversmiths,

SIMALCUE, Simalkouai
    I Macc. 11:39, there was one Tryphon...who...went
            to Simalcue the

SIMEON, Sumeōn
    I Macc. 2:1, Mattathias the son of John, the son
            of Simeon, a
    IV Macc. 2:19, our most wise father Jacob shame
            Simeon and Levi

SIMON, Simōn
    Eccl. 50:1, Simon the high priest, the son of Onias,
            who in his
    I Macc. 2:3, Simon, call Thassi:
            2:65, And behold, I know that your brother
                Simon is a man
            5:17, Then said Judas unto Simon...Choose
                thee out men,
            5:20, Now unto Simon were given three
                thousand men to go
            5:21, Then went Simon into Galilee, where
                he fought many
            5:55, and Jonathan...in...Galaad, and
                Simon...in Galilee,
            9:19, Then Jonathan and Simon took Judas
                their brother,
            9:33, Then Jonathan and Simon his brother,
                and all that
            9:37, After this came word to Jonathan
                and Simon...that
            9:62, Afterward Jonathan, and Simon...
                got them away to
            9:65, But Jonathan left his brother Simon
                in the city,
            9:67, them, and came up...Simon and his
                company went out
            10:74, these words...he went...where Simon
                his brother met
            10:82, Then brought Simon forth his host
                and set them
            11:59, His brother Simon also he made cap-
                tain from the
            11:64, he went to meet them, and left
                Simon his brother in
            11:65, Then Simon encamped against Bethsura,
                and fought

I Macc. 12:33, Simon also went forth, and passed through the

12:38, Simon also set up Adida in Sephela, and made it

13:1, Now when Simon heard that Tryphon had gathered...a

13:13, But Simon pitched his tents at Adida, over against

13:14, Now when Tryphon knew that Simon was risen up

13:17, Hereupon Simon, albeit he perceived that they spake

13:20, but Simon and his host marching against him in

13:25, Then sent Simon, and took the bones of Jonathan his

13:27, Simon also built a monument upon the sepulchre of

13:33, Then Simon built up the strong holds in Judea, and

13:34, Moreover Simon chose men, and sent to king

13:36, King Demetrius unto Simon the high priest, and

13:42, contracts, In the first year of Simon the high

13:43, In those days Simon camped against Gaza, and

13:45, upon the walls...beseeching Simon to grant them

13:47, So Simon was appeased toward them, and fought no

13:50, Then cried they to Simon, beseeching him to be at

13:53, And when Simon saw that John his son was a valiant

14:4, Judea, that was quiet all the days of Simon:

14:17, But as soon as they heard that his brother Simon

14:20, with the city, unto Simon the high priest

14:23, written a copy thereof unto Simon the high priest

14:24, After this Simon sent Numenius to Rome with a great

14:25, What thanks shall we give to Simon and his sons?

14:27, tables of brass...in the...third

year of Simon the

I Macc. 14:29, oftimes...Simon the son of Mattathias...with his

14:32, at which time Simon rose up, and
fought for his

14:35, The people therefore, seeing the
acts of Simon, and

14:46, Thus it liked all the people to
deal with Simon,

14:49, in the treasury, to the end that
Simon...might have

15:1, Moreover Antiochus...sent letters...
unto Simon the

15:2, King Antiochus to Simon the high
priest, and prince

15:17, The Jews' ambassadors...being sent
from Simon the

15:21, be any pestilent fellows...deliver
them unto Simon

15:24, And the copy thereof they wrote
to Simon the high

15:32, and when he saw the glory of Simon...
he was

15:36, the king, and made report...of the
glory of Simon,

16:1, Then came up John from Gazara, and
told Simon his

16:2, Wherefore Simon called his two eldest sons, Judas

16:13, consulted deceitfully against Simon
and his sons

16:14, Now Simon was visiting the cities
that were in the

16:16, So when Simon and his sons had
drunk largely,

II Macc. 3:4, But one Simon of the tribe of Benja-
min, who was the

3:11, to Hircanus...and not as that wicked Simon

4:1, This Simon now, of whom we spake
afore, having been

4:3, by one of Simon's factions murders
were committed,

4:6, for he saw that...Simon leave his
folly unless the

8:22, with himself his own brethren...to
wit, Simon, and

10:19, Maccabeus left Simon and Joseph,

and Zaccheus also
II Macc. 10:20, Now they that were with Simon,
being led with
14:17, Now when Simon, Judas' brother,
had joined battle
III Macc. 2:1, Now was it that the high priest
Simon bowed his
IV Macc. 4:1, For a certain man named Simon, who
was in opposition
4:4, Apollonius...praised Simon for his
care of the king's
4:5, and getting authority...with the
accursed Simon and

SIN, hamartia, "a failure, error, sin"
I Esd. 7:8, and twelve goats for the sin of all
Israel, according
8:75, for our sins are multiplied above
our heads, and our
8:76, since the time of our fathers we...
are in great sin,
8:77, and for our sins and for our fathers'
we with our
8:86, done unto us for our wicked works and
...sins:
9:7, unto them, Ye have...increased the
sins of Israel
9:11, But forasmuch as...our sin in these
things is spread
Tobit 3:3, Remember me...and punish me not for my
sins and
3:5, And now...deal with me according to my
sins and my
3:14, Thou knowest, Lord, that I am pure
from all sin with
4:5, My son...let not thy will be set to
sin, or to
4:21, And fear not, my son...and depart from
all sin, and do
12:9, deliver from death, and shall purge
away all sins
12:10, but they that sin are enemies to their
own life
Judith 5:20, be any error in this people, and they
sin against
7:28, you...our God and Lord...which pun-
isheth...our sins
11:10, nation shall not be punished...except
they sin against

Judith 11:11, is now fallen upon them, and their
            sin hath overtaken
       11:17, and he will tell me when they have
            committed...sins:
       13:16, deceived him, yet hath he not com-
            mitted sin with me,
Wisd.-Sol. 1:4, dwell in the body that is subject
            unto sin
        4:20, when they cast up the account of
            their sins,
       10:13, forsook him not, but delivered
            him from sin:
       11:23, mercy upon all...and winkest at
            the sins of men,
       12:19, hope that thou givest repentance
            for sins

  hamartanō, "to miss, miss the mark"
Wisd.-Sol. 15:2, For if we sin we are thine, know-
            ing thy power:

  hamartia
Wisd.-Sol. 17:3, they suppose to lie hid in their
            secret sins,
Eccl. 2:11, Lord is full of compassion...and for-
            giveth sins, and
      3:3, honoureth his father maketh an atone-
            ment for his sins:
      3:14, For...instead of sins it shall be
            added to build thee
      3:15, In the day of thine affliction...thy
            sins also shall
      3:27, And...the wicked man shall heap sin
            upon sin
      4:21, For there is a shame that bringeth
            sin;
      4:26, Be not ashamed to confess thy sins;

  hamartanō
Eccl. 5:4, Say not, I have sinned, and what harm
            hath happened

  hamartia
Eccl. 7:8, Bind not one sin upon another; for in
            one thou shalt
      8:5, Reproach not a man that turneth from
            sin, but remember
     10:13, For pride is the beginning of sin,
            and he that hath
     13:24, Riches are good unto him that hath no
            sin, and

Eccl. 15:20, He hath...neither...given any man
              licence to sin
       25:24, Of the woman came the beginning of
              sin, and through
       26:28, and one that returneth from right-
              eousness to sin
       26:29, a huckster shall not be turned from
              sin
       27:2, between the joinings of the stones:
              so doth sin stick
       27:10, As the lion lieth in wait for the
              prey: so sin for a
       28:1, shall find vengeance...and he will
              surely keep his sins
       28:2, Forgive thy neighbour...so shall thy
              sin also be
       28:4, and doth he ask forgiveness of his own
              sins?
       28:5, hatred, who will entreat for pardon
              for his sins?
       28:8, Abstain from strife, and thou shalt
              diminish thy sins:
       31:19, The most High is not...pacified for
              sin by the
       31:26, So it is with a man that fasteth for
              his sins, and
       35:12, take thy pastime, and do what thou
              wilt: but sin not
       38:10, Leave off for sin, and order thine
              hands aright, and
       39:5, heart...in prayer, and make supplica-
              tion for his sins
       42:1, things be not ashamed, and accept no
              person to sin
       46:7, the time of Moses...Caleb...withheld
              the people from sin
       47:11, The Lord took away his sins, and
              exalted his horn for
       47:23, There was also Jeroboam the son of
              Nebat, who causeth Israel to sin,
       47:24, and their sins were multiplied ex-
              ceedingly, that they
       48:16, that which was pleasing to God, and
              some multiplied sin
Bar. 1:10, And they said...buy you burnt offerings,
              and sin
       4:12, Let no man rejoice over me...who for
              the sins of my

307

Epis.-Jer. 1:2, Because of the sins which ye have
     committed
Song-Child. 1:4, all these things upon us because
     of our sins
    1:13, Lord, less than any nation...
     because of our sins
His.-Sus. 1:52, and said...thy sins which thou
     hast committed
II Macc. 5:17, not that the Lord was angry for...
     the sins of them
    5:18, For had they not been formerly
     wrapped in many sins
    6:14, till they become to the fulness of
     their sins,
    6:15, lest that, being come to the height
     of sin,
    7:32, For we suffer because of our sins
   12:45, perceived...that they might be
     delivered from sin
    13:8, for inasmuch as he had committed
     many sins about
III Macc. 2:13, see now, holy King, how through
     our many...sins
IV Macc. 17:22, For they became the antipoise to
     to the sin of the

SINAI, Sina
 Eccl. 48:7, who heardest the rebuke of the Lord
    in Sinai, and in

SINEW, sarx, "flesh, all the flesh or muscles in
    the body"
 IV Macc. 7:13, though the labours of his body...
    and his sinews

SINFUL, hamartōlos, "sinful, hardened in sin"
 Eccl. 10:23, neither is it convenient to magnify
    a sinful man
   11:32, coal is kindled: and a sinful man
    layeth wait for
   28:9, A sinful man disquieteth friends,
    and maketh debate
   35:17, A sinful man will not be reproved,
    but findeth an
 I Macc. 1:34, And they put therein a sinful nation,
    wicked men,
   2:44, So they joined their forces, and
    smote sinful men
   2:62, Fear not the words of a sinful man:
    for his glory

SINFULNESS, ádikos, "doing wrong, unjust, unright-
           eous"
  IV Macc. 5:8, is pleasant...and from notions of
           sinfulness

SING, exmologeŏ, "praise, celebrate, to confess in
           full"
  Judith 16:1, Then Judith began to sing this
           thanksgiving in all
  Eccl. 54:11, I will praise thy name continually,
           and will sing

SINGER, hieropsaltē,"a singer, consecrated singers"
  I Esd. 1:15, The holy singers also, the sons of
           Asaph, were in
      9:24, Of the holy singers: Eleasabus, and
           Tolbanes

      psallousēs, "one who sings to music"
  Eccl. 9:4, Use not much the company of a woman
           that is a singer,

SINNED, hamartanō, "to fail, to do wrong, err, sin"
  I Esd. 1:24, things that came to pass...concerning
           those that sinned,
  Judith 5:17, And whilst they sinned not before
           their God, they
  Wisd.-Sol. 12:11, cursed seed...for those things
           wherein they sinned
  Eccl. 10:29, Who will justify him that sinneth
           against his own
      19:4, credit is lightminded: and he that
           sinneth shall
      21:1, My son, hast thou sinned? do so no
           more, but ask
      27:1, Many have sinned for a small matter;
           and he that
      38:15, He that sinneth before his Maker,
           let him fall into
  Bar. 1:13, us also unto the Lord our God, for we
           have sinned
      1:17, for we have sinned before the Lord,
      2:5, Thus we are cast down...because we have
           sinned against
      2:12, O Lord our God, we have sinned, we
           have done ungodly,
      2:33, remember the way of their fathers,
           which sinned before
      3:2, O Lord, and have mercy...because we have
           sinned before

Bar. 3:4, now the prayers of the...Israelites...
        which have sinned
     3:7, all the iniquity of our forefathers,
        that sinned before
Song -Child. 1:5, For we have sinned and committed
        iniquity,
II Macc. 7:18, things for ourselves, having sinned
        against our
     10:4, but if they sinned any more against
        him, that he
Pr.-Mans. 1:7, proclaimed repentance..to those
        that have sinned
     1:8, repentance for...Jacob who have
        not sinned
     1:9, for I have sinned above the number
        of the sand of
     1:12, I have sinned, Lord, I have sinned,
        and I

SINNER, hamartolos, "sinful, a sinner"
Tobit 13:6, O ye sinners, turn and do justice be-
        fore him; who can
Wisd.-Sol. 4:10, so that living among sinners he
        was translated
     14:31, but it is the just vengeance of
        sinners,
     19:13, And punishments came upon the
        sinners not without former signs,
Eccl. 1:24, but godliness is an abomination to a
        sinner
     2:12, Woe be to fearful hearts...and the
        sinner that goeth
     6:1, even so shall a sinner that hath a
        double tongue
     7:16, Number not thyself among the multitude
        of sinners,
     8:10, Kindle not the coals of a sinner, lest
        thou be burnt
     9:11, Envy not the glory of a sinner, for
        thou knowest not
     11:9, and sit not in the judgment with sinners
     11:21, Marvel not at the works of sinners;
     12:4, Give to the godly man, and help not a
        sinner
     12:6, For the most High hateth sinners, and
        will repay
     12:7, Give unto the good, and help not the
        sinner

Eccl. 12:14, So one that goeth to a sinner, and is defiled with

15:7, foolish men shall not attain unto her, and sinners

15:9, Praise is not seemly in the mouth of a sinner, for it

16:13, The sinner shall not escape with his spoils: and the

19:22, not wisdom, neither...the counsel of sinners prudence

20:9, There is a sinner that hath good success in evil

21:6, He that hateth reproof is in the way of sinners: but

21:10, The way of sinners is made plain with stones, but at

23:8, The sinner shall be left in his foolishness:

25:19, let the portion of a sinner fall upon her

29:16, A sinner will overthrow the good estate of his surety

39:25, created from the beginning: so evil things for sinners

39:27, so to the sinners they are turned into evil

40:8, (Such things happen) unto all flesh ...and sevenfold more upon sinners

41:5, The children of sinners are abominable children, and

41:6 The inheritance of sinners' children shall perish, and

41:11, but an ill name of sinners shall be blotted out

I Macc. 2:48, hand of kings, neither suffered they the sinner to

Pr.-Mans. 1:5, of thy glory is...threatening sinners

SION, Sion

Judith 9:13, and against the top of Sion, and against the house

Eccl. 24:10, before him; and so was I established in Sion

48:18, Sennacherib came up...and lifted up his against...Sion,

48:24, should come to pass...and he comforted them...in Sion

311

Bar. 4:9, of God...she said, Hearken ye that dwell
         about Sion
     4:14, Like as now the neighbours of Sion
           have seen your
I Macc. 4:60, At that time also they builded up
             the mount Sion
         5:54, So they went up to mount Sion with
               joy and gladness
         6:48, king's army went up to Jerusalem...
               against mount Sion
         6:62, Then the king entered into mount
               Sion: but when he
         7:33, After this went Nicanor up to mount
               Sion, and
        10:11, workmen to build the walls and the
               mount Sion
        14:27, which they set upon pillars in mount
               Sion:

SIRACH, Sierach
   Eccl. 50:27, Jesus the son of Sirach of Jerusalem
               hath written in

SIREN, seirēnios, "a Siren, as in the case of a
                  deceitful woman"
   IV Macc. 15:21, Not so do siren melodies, or songs
                  of swans,

SISINNES, Sisinnes
   I Esd. 6:7, The copy of the letters which Sisinnes,
              governor of

SISTER, adelphē, "a sister"
   Tobit 5:20, Then said Tobit to her, Take no care,
               my sister; he
         7:16, called his wife Edna, and said unto
               her, Sister,
         8:4, Tobias rose up out of the bed, and
              said, Sister, arise
         8:7, And now, O Lord, I take not this my
              sister for lust,
   III Macc. 1:1, all his footmen and...took with
                  him his sister

SIT, kathiēmi, "to come down upon, to send down"
   Eccl. 9:9, Sit not at all with another man's wife,
              nor sit down
        11:1, Wisdom...maketh him to sit among great
              men
        11:9, concerneth thee not; and sit not in
              judgment with

Eccl. 12:12, neither let him sit at thy right
          hand, lest he seek

  anaklinō, "to lie back, to lean back"
III Macc. 5:16, to this, and then...commanded the
          guests to sit

SIVAN, Seioual
  Bar. 1:8, vessels of...the Lord...the tenth day
          of the month Sivan,

SKILL, epistemē, "skill, knowledge, experience"
  Eccl. 1:19, Wisdom raineth down skill and know-
          ledge of understanding, and
       10:30, The poor man is honoured for his
          skill, and the rich
       38:3, The skill of the physician shall lift
          up his head:
       38:6, And he hath given men skill, that he
          might be honoured

SKIN, kōdion, "a fleece, a sheep-skin"
  Judith 12:15, and her maid went out and laid soft
          skins on the

  derma, "the skink the hide of beasts"
II Macc. 7:7, So...when they had pulled off the
          skin of his head
IV Macc. 10:7, means to strangle him, they tore
          off his skin,

SLACK, brados, "slowness"
  Eccl 32:18, For the Lord will not be slack, neither
          will the

SLAIN, phoneuō, "to put to death, kill, slay"
  Judith 9:3, wherefore thou gavest their rulers to
          be slain, so

  apollumi, "to destroy, perish, put to death,
          die"
I Macc. 2:9, carried away into captivity, her
          infants are slain

  piptō, "to fall dead"
I Macc. 3:24, them from...Bethhoron unto the plain,
          where were slain
        4:15, Howbeit all the hindermost of them
          were slain with
        4:34, So they joined battle: and there
          were slain of the
        5:22, the gate of Ptolemais: and there
          were slain of the

I Macc. 6:42, his host drew near...and there were
        slain of the

    ʾapollumi
I Macc. 7:6, the people...saying Judas and his
        brethren have slain

    thuo, "to offer, slaughter, immolate"
I Macc. 7:19, Bacchides from Jerusalem...and when
        he had slain

    piptō
I Macc. 7:43, Nicanor's host...and he himself was
        first slain
      7:44, Now when Nicanor's host saw that he
        was slain, they
      7:46, out of all the towns of Judea...all
        slain with the
      9:1, Demetrius heard that Nicanor and his
        host were slain

    ʾapollumi
I Macc. 9:17, was a sore battle, insomuch as
        many were slain _____

    diaspō, "to tear asunder"
I Macc. 9:49, So there were slain of Bacchides'
        side that day

    piptō
I Macc. 10:50, the battle...and that day was
        Demetrius slain
      10:85, Thus there were burned and slain
        with the sword

    ʾapollumi
I Macc. 11:18, and they in the strong holds were
        slain one of

    ʾanaireō, "to put to death, kill, murder"
I Macc. 11:45, they that were of the city...would
        have slain the

    piptō
I Macc. 11:74, So there were slain of the heathen,
        that day about

    ʾapollumi
I Macc. 12:50, and they that were with him were...
        slain, they
      13:4, by reason whereof all my brethren
        are slain for

apokteinō, "to destroy, annihilate"
I Macc. 16:21, John that his father and brethren
          were slain

katapinō, "to destroy, annihilate"
II Macc. 1:13, into Persia...they were slain in
          the temple of Nanea

apokteinō
II Macc. 4:36,   certain of the Jews complained
          because Onias was slain

kataphtheirō, "to destroy, cause to perish"
II Macc. 5:14, score thousand, whereof forty
          thousand were slain,

apollumi
II Macc. 7:20, for when she saw her seven sons
          slain within the

aposphazō, "to cut the throat, to kill one-
          self"
IV Macc. 2:19, For...having irrationally slain
          the whole race of

apokteinō
IV Macc. 12:15, according to thy deserts for hav-
          ing slain without

sphazō, "to slaughter, kill, slay"
IV Macc. 13:12, the hand of Isaac endured to be
          slain for the sake

SLANDER, diabolos, "falsely accusing, slanderous"
Eccl. 26:5, things that mine heart feareth...the
          slander of a city

psegō, "to find fault with, to blame, dis-
          parage"
I Macc. 11:11, Thus did he slander him, because
          he was desirous

diabolos
III Macc. 6:7, when Daniel was hurled, through
          slander and envy,

basiniō, "to slander, to bewitch"
IV Macc. 2:15, of the...passions, as love of em-
          pire...and slander

SLAUGHTER, plēgē, "a blow, stroke, stripe, a wound"
I Macc. 5:34, wherefore he smote them with a
          great slaughter; so

315

trauma, "a wound"
I Macc. 9:40, Then Jonathan...lay in ambush, and
          made a slaughter

sphagē, "slaughter, butchery, a murderer"
II Macc. 12:16, will of God, and made unspeakable
          slaughters,

SLAVE, doulos, "a bondman, slave, subject"
  Judith 5:11, them low with labouring...and made
          them slaves
        14:13, for the slaves have been bold to come
          down upon us
        14:18, These slaves have dealt treacherously;
          one woman of

pais, "servant, slave, attendant"
I Macc. 3:41, servants...came into the camp...of
          Israel for slaves

douleuō, "to be a slave, be subject to"
IV Macc. 13:2, For just as if, had they as slaves
          to the passions

SLAY, phoneuō, "to murder, to slay, kill"
  Eccl. 31:22, He that taketh away his neighbour's
          living slayeth
        47:5, strength in his right hand to slay
          that mighty warrior

apokteinō, "to kill, slay, condemn to death"
His.-Sus. 1:53, The innocent and righteous shalt
          thou not slay
I Macc. 9:32, gat knowledge thereof, he sought for
          to slay him
        11:10, my daughter unto him, for he sought
          to slay me

SLAYING, thnēskō, "to be dead"
I Macc. 6:45, wherefore he ran upon him...slaying
          on the right

anaireō, "to kill, murder, put to death"
III Macc. 7:15, slaying thus, in that day, above
          three hundred

SLEEP, hupnos, "slumber, sleep"
  Wisd.-Sol. 7:2, blood...and the pleasure that came
          with sleep
  Eccl. 22:7, fool is...as he that waketh one from
          a sound sleep

316

Eccl. 34:1, the flesh, and the care thereof dri-
            veth away sleep
      34:2, a man slumber, as a sore disease
            breaketh sleep
      34:20, Sound sleep cometh of moderate
             eating:
      40:5, in the time of rest upon his bed his
            night sleep, do
      40:6, and afterward he is in his sleep as
            in a day
      42:9, a father; and the care of her taketh
            away sleep
      46:19, And before his long sleep he made
             protestation in
I Macc. 6:10, and said unto them, The sleep is
              gone from mine
III Macc. 5:11, He, however, who has sent his
                good creature sleep
          5:20, The king, then,...might thank his
                sleep of that
          5:22, Now did they employ the night in
                sleep, so much

SLEW, apokteinō, "to kill, murder, slay"
Eccl. 47:4, Slew he not a giant, when he was yet
            but young?

      spazō, "to slaughter, kill, slay"
I Macc. 1:2, many strongholds, and slew the kings
             of the earth

      thnēskō, "to be dead"
I Macc. 1:61, And they hanged the infants...and
              slew them that had

      spazō
I Macc. 2:24, when Mattathias saw...he ran and
              slew him upon the

      apothnēskō, "to die"
I Macc. 2:38, So they rose up against them...and
              slew them, with

      apokteinō
I Macc. 3:11, perceived, he went forth to meet
              him...and slew him:
        5:35, This done, Judas turned aside...and
              slew all the

      apollumi, "to destroy, perish, put to death"
I Macc. 5:51, who then slew all the males with
              the edge of the

I Macc. 6:24, for which cause they...could light
on they slew, and
7:4, So his host slew them

άποkteinō
I Macc. 7:16, howbeit he took of them threescore
men, and slew

traumatizō, "to wound"
I Macc. 8:10, and that they having knowledge...
slew many of them,

άpollumi
I Macc. 9:2, and after they had won it, they slew
much people

άpokteinō
I Macc. 9:61, they took of the men of the country
...and slew them
11:47, and dispersing themselves through
the city slew
12:48, Ptolemais...all of them that came
with him they slew
13:31, dealt deceitfully with the young
king...and slew him
16:16, Ptolemee and his men rose up...and
slew him
II Macc. 4:38, And being kindled with anger...
there slew he

spazō
II Macc. 5:6, but Jason slew his own citizens
without mercy, not

katasphazō, "to slaughter, slay"
II Macc. 8:24, And by the help of the Almighty
they slew above

άnaireō, "to put to death, kill, murder"
II Macc. 8:30, that were with Timotheus...they
slew above twenty
8:32, They slew also Philarches, that
wicked person, who
10:17, them strongly they won the holds...
and slew all

katastronnumi, "laid prostrate in death"
II Macc. 11:11, a charge upon their enemies like
lions, they slew

άpollumi
II Macc. 12:19, Howbeit Dositheus and Sosipater...
slew those that

SLOTHFUL, oknēros, "slothful, indolent, idle"
  Eccl. 22:1, A slothful man is compared to a fil-
        thy stone, and
      22:2, A slothful man is compared to the
        filth of a dunghill
      37:11, Neither consult with...the slothful
        for any work

SLUMBER, nustazō, "to nod, esp. in sleep; hence,
        slumber, sleep"
  Eccl. 22:8, a tale to a fool speaketh to one in
      a slumber
      34:2, Watching care will not let a man
      slumber, as a sore

SMITH, chalkeus, "a worker in copper, a coppersmith"
  Eccl. 38:28, The smith also sitting by the anvil,
      and considering

SMOKE, kapnē, "a smoke-hole, chimney"
  Tobit 6:7, And he said unto him...we must make a
      smoke thereof
      6:16, marriage chamber, thou...shalt make
      a smoke with it
      8:2, the liver of the fish thereupon, and
      made a smoke

      kapnos, "a smoke"
  Wisd.-Sol. 2:2, for the breath of our nostrils is
      as smoke
      5:14, like as the smoke which is dis-
      persed here
  Epis.-Jer. 1:21, Their faces are blacked through
      the smoke that
  I Macc. 4:20, their host to flight...for the
      smoke that was seen

SMOTE, suntribō, "to deprive of strength, to break,
      debilitate"
  Eccl. 33:10, Smite in sunder the heads of the
      rulers of the
  I Macc. 5:7, So he fought many battles...and he
      smote them

      patassō, aorist 1, epataxō, "to strike, kill,
             slay"
  I Macc. 5:65, Afterward went Judas forth...where
      he smote Hebron,
      7:41, O Lord...thine angel went out, and
      smote an hundred

319

aphaireō, "to take away, to cut off, remove"
I Macc. 7:47, Afterwards they took the spoils...
            and smote off

patassō
I Macc. 9:47, joined battle...and...stretched for-
            th his hand to smite
      9:66, And he smote Odonarres and his bre-
            thren, and the
     12:31, Wherefore Jonathan...smote them,
            and took their
     14:3, who went and smote the host of
            Demetrius and took

aphaireō
II Macc. 3:25, For...he ran fiercely, and smote
            at Heliodorus with

SNAKE, ophis, "snake, a serpent"
IV Macc. 18:8, injured me...nor did...the deceit-
            ful snake,

SNARE, pagis, "a snare, a trap, gin"
Eccl. 9:3, with an harlot, lest thou fall into
            her snares
      9:13, remember that thou goest in the midst
            of snare, and
     27:29, fall of the righteous shall be taken
            in the snare:
     51:2, and hast preserved my body from...the
            snare of the
I Macc. 5:4, of the children of Baean, who had
            been a snare,

SNOW, chion, "snow"
Wisd.-Sol. 16:22, But snow and ice endured the
            fire, and melted
Eccl. 43:13, By his commandment he maketh the
            snow to fall apace,
Eccl. 43:17, The noise of the thunder...scattereth
            the snow, and
Song-Child. 1:49, O ye frost and snow, bless ye
            the Lord: praise

SODOMITE, Sodomitas
Wisd.-Sol. 19:14, For the Sodomites did not re-
            ceive those, whom
III Macc. 2:5, It was thou who did make the Sodo-
            mites, those

SOJOURN, <u>paroikia</u>, "a sojourning"
  Wisd.-Sol. 19:10, For they...sojourned in the
                strange land, how

      <u>paroikeō</u>, "to sojourn, to reside in a
              place as a stranger"
  Eccl. 41:19, of theft in regard of the place where
              thou sojournest

        <u>paroikia</u>
  III Macc. 7:19, They...keep these days during
              their sojourn as

SOJOURNER, <u>paroikos</u>, "a sojourner, stranger, tempo-
              rary resident"
  III Macc. 6:36, ordinance...as long as they should
              be sojourners

SOLD, <u>pipraskō</u>, "to sell, to be devoted to"
  Judith 7:25, but God has sold us into their hands,
              that we should
  II Macc. 5:14, in the conflict; and no fewer sold
              than slain
       .10:21, that they had sold their brethren
              for money

SOLDIER, <u>dunamis</u>, "power, strength, might"
  I Macc. 3:28, also his treasure, and gave his
              soldiers pay for a

      <u>suntaxis</u>, "a putting together in order:
              of soldiers"
  I Macc. 4:35, put to flight, and the manliness of
              Judas' soldiers

      <u>dunamis</u>
  I Macc. 5:50, So the soldiers pitched, and assault-
              ed the city all
      6:29, unto him from other kingdom...bands
              of hired soldiers
      11:3, cities, he set...a garrison of sol-
              diers to keep it
      15:3, have gathered a multitude of foreign
              soldiers

      <u>gennaios</u>, "thorough-bred, high-born,
              genuine"
  II Macc. 13:14, and exhorted his soldiers to
              fight manfully,

      <u>dunamis</u>
  III Macc. 1:4, and...Arisnoe...begged the soldiers
              to fight

stratiotēs, "a soldier"
III Macc. 3:12, Philopater, to the commanders and
soldiers in
IV Macc. 3:7, attacking the Philistines...he with
the soldiers of
3:12, Wherefore his body-guards...two
valiant soldiers,
16:14, O woman, soldier of God for religion, thou aged
17:23, that endurance as an example to
his soldiers

SOLITARY, éremos, "lonely, desert"
Eccl. 9:7, Look not round about thee in the solitary places

SOLOMON, Salōmōn
I Esd. 1:3, in the house that king Solomon...had
built
1:5, prescribed...the magnificence of
Solomon his son
Eccl. 47:13, Solomon reigned in a peaceable time,
and was honoured
47:23, Thus rested Solomon with his fathers,
and of his
II Macc. 2:8, as when Solomon desired that the
place might be
2:12, So Solomon kept those eight days
IV Macc. 18:16, He declared the proverbs of Solomon, who saith,

SON, huios, "a son"
I Esd. 1:5, Israel prescribed, and according to...
Solomon his son
1:13, and set them before all the people;
and...the sons of
1:34, And the people took Joachaz the son
of Josias, and
8:47, hand of our Lord they brought...men
of the sons of
8:70, For both they and their sons have
married with their
8:84, shall ye not join your daughters unto
their sons,
9:19, of the sons of Jesus, the son of
Josedec, and his
9:21, And of the sons of Emmer; Ananias,
and Zabdeus, and
9:22, And of the sons of Phaisur; Elionais,
Massias, and

Tobit 1:7, part of all increase I gave to the sons
of Aaron,
1:15, was dead, Sennacherib his son reigned
in his stead;
1:20, goods were forcibly taken away...and
my son Tobias
2:2, saw abundance of meat, I said to my
son, Go and bring
3:9, let us never see of thee either son or
daughter
4:2, wherefore do I not call for my son
Tobias, that I may

paidion, "a young child"
Tobit 4:3, he had called him, he said, My son,
when I am dead,
4:5, My son, be mindful of the Lord our God
all thy days,
4:12, Beware of all whoredom, my son, and
chiefly take a
4:21, And fear not, my son, that we are made
poor:

huios
Tobit 5:14, I give thee? wilt thou a drachm a day
...my son?

paidion
Tobit 5:17, mother wept, and said...Why hast thou
sent away our son

huios
Tobit 7:3, From whence are ye...of the sons of
Nephthali...?
7:7, Thou art the son of an honest and good
man

paidion
Tobit 10:4, Then his wife said unto him, My son
is dead, seeing

teknon, "a child"
Tobit 10:5, Now I care for nothing, my son, since
I have let thee
10:7, But she said...my son is dead

paidion
Tobit 11:5, Now Anna sat looking about toward the
way for her son

huios
Tobit 11:6, spied him coming, she said...Behold
thy son cometh,

paidion
Tobit 11:9, ran forth, and fell upon the neck of
her son, and

huios
Tobit 11:15, scourged...me: for behold, I see my
son Tobias
12:1, Then Tobit called his son Tobias, and
said unto him, My son, see that
13:9, he will have mercy again on the sons
of the righteous
14:3, very aged, he called his son, and the
sons of his son,

teknon
Tobit 14:8, And now, my son, depart out of Nineve,
because that

paidion
Tobit 14:11, Wherefore now, my son, consider what
alms doeth, and

huios
Judith 1:6, And there came unto him...all the
sons of Chelpeul,
6:5, Ozias the son of Micha...and Chabris
the son of
8:1, Judith heard thereof...of Ox, the son
of Joseph,
8:16, for God is not man...neither is...as
the son of man
16:7, one did not fall...neither did the
sons of Titans
16:12, The sons of the damsels have pierced
them through,

teknon
Wisd.-Sol. 10:5, against his tender compassion
toward his son

huios
Wisd.-Sol. 12:21, circumspection didst thou judge
thine own sons
16:10, But thy sons not the very teeth
of venomous
18:4, they were worthy...who had kept
thy sons shut up,

teknon
Eccl. 2:1, My son, if thou come to serve the Lord
God, prepare thy
3:12, My son, help thy father in his age,

and grieve him

Eccl. 3:17, My son, go on with thy business in
meekness: so

4:1, My son, defraud not the poor of his
living, and make

huios
Eccl. 4:10, so shalt thou be as the son of the
most High,

teknon
Eccl. 6:18, My son, gather instruction from thy
youth up;

6:23, Give ear, my son, receive my advice,
and refuse not

6:32, My son, if thou wilt, thou shalt be
taught:

10:28, My son, glorify thy soul in meekness,
and give it

11:10, My son, meddle not with many matters:
for if thou

14:11, My son, according to thy ability do
good to thyself,

huios
Eccl. 16:1, unprofitable children, neither delight
in ungodly sons

teknon
Eccl. 16:24, My son, hearken unto me, and learn
knowledge, and

18:15, My son, blemish not thy good deeds,
neither use

apaideutos, "uneducated, ignorant, boorish"
Eccl. 22:3, An evil-nurtured son is the dishonour
of his father,

huios
Eccl. 30:1, He that loveth his son causeth him
oft to feel the

30:2, He that chastiseth his son shall have
joy in him, and

30:7, He that maketh too much of his son
bind up his

30:13, Train up thy son and exercise him
with work, lest by

teknon
Eccl. 34:22, My son, hear me, and despise me not,
and at the last

37:27, My son, prove thy soul in thy life,

325

                          and see what is
Eccl. 38:9, My son, in thy sickness be not negli-
              gent: but pray

  huios
Eccl. 40:1, every man, and an heavy yoke is upon
              the sons of Adam

  teknon
Eccl. 40:28, My son, lead not a beggar's life;
              for better it is

  huios
Eccl. 45:23, The third in glory is Phinees the
              son of Eleazar,
      46:1, Jesus the son of Nave was valiant in
              the wars, and
      46:7, he did a work of mercy...and Caleb
              the son of
      47:12, After him rose up a wise son, and for
              his sake he
      47:23, There was also Jeroboam the son of
              Nebat
      48:10, who was ordained for reproofs...unto
              thy son, and
      50:1, Simon the high priest, the son of
              Onias, who in his
      50:13, So were all the sons of Aaron in
              their glory, and
      50:16, Then shouted the sons of Aaron, and
              sounded the
      50:27, Jesus the son of Sirach of Jerusalem
              hath written in
Bar. 1:1, which Baruch the son of Nerias, the son
              of
      1:3, the words...in the hearing of Jechonias
              the son of
      1:7, it to Jerusalem unto Joachim...the son
              of Chelcias
      1:11, Nabuchodonosor...and for the life of
              Balthasar his son
      1:12, strength...under the shadow of Baltha-
              sar his son,
      2:3, that a man should eat the flesh of his
              own son, and the
      4:10, for I saw the captivity of my sons and
              daughters,
      4:14, dwell about Sion come, and remember...
              my sons and
      4:32, Miserable...is she that received thy

sons

Bar. 4:37, Lo, thy sons come whom thou sentest
        away...they come

His.-Sus. 1:48, said, Are ye such fools, ye sons
        of Israel, that

I Macc. 1:9, put crowns upon themselves; so did
        their sons

2:1, In those days arose Mattathias the
        son of John...a priest of the sons of

2:2, And he had five sons, Joannan, called
        Gaddis:

2:14, Then Mattathias and his sons rent
        their clothes,

2:16, came unto them, Mattathias also and
        his sons came

2:20, yet will I and my sons and my bre-
        thren walk in the

2:26, for the law...as did Phinees...the
        son of Salom

2:28, So he and his sons fled into the
        mountains, and

2:49, that Mattathias should die, he said
        unto his sons,

teknon

I Macc. 2:50, now therefore, my sons, be zealous
        for the law, and

2:64, Wherefore, ye my sons, be valiant,
        and shew

huios

I Macc. 2:70, And...his sons buried him in the
        sepulchres of his

3:33, and to bring up his son Antiochus,
        until he came

4:30, strangers into the hands of Jonathan
        the son of

6:15, to the end he should bring up his
        son Antiochus,

6:17, that the king was dead he set up
        Antiochus his son,

6:55, say, that Philip...bring up his son
        Antiochus

8:17, things, Judas chose Eupolemus the
        son of John,

9:53, Besides, he took the chief men's
        sons in the

10:57, and fifth year came Demetrius the
        son of

I Macc. 11:62, he made peace with them, and took the sons of their

paidarion, "a young child, a little boy or girl"
I Macc. 13:16, an hundred talents of silver, and two of his sons

13:53, And when Simon saw that John his son was a valiant

14:25, they said, What thanks shall we give...his sons?

14:29, Forasmuch as oftimes...Simon the son of Mattathias,

14:49, should be laid up...that Simon and his sons might

16:2, Wherefore Simon called his two eldest sons, Judas

16:13, he came down himself to Jericho with his sons,

16:14, was visiting the cities...with his sons, Mattathias

16:16, So when Simon and his sons had drunk largely,

II Macc. 2:20, against Antiochus Epiphanes, and Eupater his son,

7:20, for when she saw her seven sons slain within

7:27, But she bowing herself...spake... O my son, have pity

teknon
II Macc. 7:28, I beseech thee, my son, look upon the heaven and

huios
II Macc. 7:41, Last of all after the sons the mother died

9:26, every man will follow faithful to me and my son

10:10, Antiochus Eupater...the son of the wicked man,

III Macc. 6:28, Release the sons of the almighty living God of

7:6, for them as a father always fights for his sons;

IV Macc. 4:15, the king, his son Antiochus Epiphanes succeeds

12:6, that condoling with her for the loss of so many sons

teknon
IV Macc. 15:1, O reasoning of the sons, lord over
          the passions,

huios
IV Macc. 15:2, set before her...the safety of her
          seven sons for a
       15:9, on account of the excellent dis-
          position of her sons
       15:22, was the mother herself tortured,
          as her sons
       16:3, the lions...when she beheld her
          seven sons tortured

pais, "a child, a son or a daughter"
IV Macc. 16:6, I, and many times miserable; who
          have seven sons
       16:8, Vainly, for your sakes, O sons,
          have I endured

huios
IV Macc. 16:13, as one possessed with...her full
          number of sons

pais
IV Macc. 16:16, O sons, noble is the contest; to
          which you being

huios
IV Macc. 16:24, exhorting each of her sons, over-
          persuaded them

pais
IV Macc. 17:5, stars...and fixed in the firmament
          with thy sons
       17:9, aged priest, and an aged woman,
          and seven sons,
       18:20, brought with boiling rage the
          seven sons of the

SONG, humnos, "a hymn, a song, festive song or ode"
   Judith 15:13, followed in their armour, and with
          songs in their
       16:1, Then Judith began to sing...and all
          the people sang after her this song
          of praise

   ōdē, "song, lay, ode, strain"
Eccl. 39:14, a sweet saviour...and sing a song of
          praise, bless
       39:15, Magnify his name...with the songs of
          your lips,

Eccl. 47:8, the Holy One...with his whole heart
            he sang songs, and
      47:9, singers also...and daily sing praises
            in their song
      47:17, The countries marvelled at thee for
            thy songs, and

      humnos
I Macc. 4:24, After this they went home, and sung
            a song of

      ódē
I Macc. 4:54, that time and day....was it dedica-
            ted with songs, and

      humnos
I Macc. 13:47, So Simon...cleansed the houses...
            with songs and
      13:51, into it...with harps, and cymbals
            ...and hymns, and songs:

      ódē
II Macc. 7:6, Lord God looking upon us...as Moses
            in his song,

      humnos
III Macc. 7:16, uttering exclamations of joy, with
            songs of praise

      ódē
IV Macc. 18:18, For he did not forget the song
            which Moses taught

SORROW, lupē, "pain, distress, suffering"
  I Esd. 3:20, also...that a man remembereth neither
            sorrow nor debt

      ponos, "suffering, grief, pain"
  Eccl. 3:27, An obstinate heart shall be laden with
            sorrows; and

      ódis, "the pain of child-birth"
  Eccl. 7:27, with thy whole heart, and forget not
            the sorrows of

SOSIPATER, Sosipatros
  II Macc. 12:19, Howbeit Dositheus and Sosipater...
            Maccabeus'
      12:24, Timotheus himself fell into the
            hands of...Sosipater

SOSTRATUS, Sōstratos
  II Macc. 4:27, albeit Sostratus the ruler of the

castle required
II Macc. 4:29, in his stead...and Sostratus left
        Crates,

SOUL, psuchē, "breath, life, spirit, seat of the
        will, desire, appetite"
  Tobit 13:7, I will extol my God, and my soul shall
        praise the
        13:15, Let my soul bless God the great King
  Judith 7:27, For...we will be his servants, that
        our souls may
        12:24, Then said Judith unto him, As thy
        liveth, my
  Wisd.-Sol. 1:4, For unto a malicious soul wisdom
        shall not enter:
        1:11, and the mouth that belieth
        slayeth the soul
        2:22, not...nor discerned a reward for
        blameless souls
        3:1, But the souls of the righteous
        are in the hand of
        3:13, she shall have fruit in the visi-
        tation of souls
        4:11, that wickedness should...beguile
        his soul
        4:14, for his soul pleased the Lord;
        therefore hasted
        7:27, and in all ages entering into
        holy souls, she
        10:16, She entered into the soul of the
        servant of the
        11:26, for they are thine, O Lord, thou
        lover of souls
        14:11, they are become...stumblingblocks
        to the souls of
        15:11, and him that inspired into him
        an active soul,
        16:14, the spirit returneth not; neither
        the soul
        17:1, For great are thy judgments, and
        ...unnurtured souls have erred
        17:8, troubles from a sick soul, were
        sick
  Eccl. 1:30, thyself, lest thou...bring dishonour
        upon thy soul,
        2:1, My son, if thou come to serve the Lord,
        prepare thy soul for temptation
        2:17, They that fear the Lord will...humble
        their souls in

Eccl. 4:2, Make not a hungry soul sorrowful:
            neither provoke a
      4:6, for if he curse thee in the bitterness
            of his soul,
      4:17, walk with him...until she may trust
            his soul,
      4:20, Observe the opportunity...when it
            concerneth thy soul
      4:22, Accept no person against thy soul,
            and let not the
      6:2, counsel of thine own heart: that thy
            soul be torn
      6:4, A wicked soul shall destroy him that
            hath it, and
      7:11, Laugh no man to scorn in the bitter-
            ness of his soul:
      7:17, Humble thy soul greatly:
      7:21, Let not thy soul love a good servant,
            and defraud him
      7:29, Fear the Lord with all thy soul, and
            reverence his
      9:2, Give not thy soul unto a woman to set
            her foot upon
      10:9, for such an one setteth his own soul
            to sale
      10:28, My son, glorify thy soul in meekness,
            and give it
      10:29, will justify him that sinneth against
            his own soul?
      14:4, He that gathereth by defrauding his
            own soul gathereth
      14:9, A covetous man's eye...drieth up his
            soul
      14:16, Give, and take, and satisfy thy soul;
            for there is no
      16:17, Say not thou...what is my soul among
            such an infinite
      18:31, If thou givest thy soul the desire
            that please her,
      19:4, is lightminded; and...sinneth...
            against his own soul
      20:22, There is that destroyeth his own soul
            through
      21:2, Flee from sin...for...the teeth thereof
            are as the teeth of a lion, slaying the
            souls of men
      21:27, the ungodly curseth Satan he curseth
            his own soul

Eccl. 25:2, Three sorts of men my soul hateth,
           and I am greatly
      31:15, Blessed is the soul of him that fear-
             eth the Lord;
      31:17, he raiseth up the soul, and lighten-
             eth the eyes:
      35:23, In every good work trust thy own
             soul; for this is
      47:15, Thy soul covered the whole earth, and
             thou filledst
      48:5, Who didst raise up a dead man...and
            his soul from the
      51:6, By an accusation to the king...my
            soul drew near even
      51:19, My soul hath wrestled with her, and
             in my doing I was
      51:20, I directed my soul unto her, and I
             found her in
      51:26, Put my neck under the yoke, and let
             your soul receive
      51:29, Let your soul rejoice in his mercy,
             and be not

      pneuma, "life, spirit, breath, the breath of
              life"
Bar. 2:17, Open thy eyes and behold; for...the
           souls are taken

      psuchē
Bar. 2:18, but the soul that is greatly vexed,
           which goeth
      3:1, O Lord Almighty, God of Israel, the
           soul in anguish
Epis.-Jer. 1:7, with you, and I myself caring
                for your souls
I Macc. 1:48, children uncircumcised, and make
              their souls
II Macc. 6:30, But...in soul am well content to
               suffer these
IV Macc. 1:20, the passions...they also by nature
               refer to the soul
       1:26, In the soul it is arrogance, and
             love of money,
       1:28, therefore, two growths of the body
             and the soul,
       2:1, And what wonder? if the lusts of the
            soul, after
       3:3, One may not be able to root out
            anger from the soul
       3:15, But he...would terribly dangerous

333

                              to his soul
      IV Macc. 5:26, Those things which are convenient
                          to our souls, he
               7:4, as did that holy man when his pious
                          soul was tried

         karteropsuchia, "a courageous spirit or in-
                          dividual, patient person"
      IV Macc. 9:26, And when all admired his courageous
                          soul, the

         psuchē
      IV Macc. 10:4, of vengeance...ye are not able to
                          touch...my soul
               13:13, Let us sacrifice with all our
                          heart our souls to
               13:15, for great is the trial of our soul
                          and danger of
               13:20, their brotherly souls are rared
                          up lovingly
               14:6, are moved...with the directions of
                          the soul, so
               15:4, way can I describe...the...resem-
                          blance of soul and

         apopsuchē, "breathing out life"
      IV Macc. 15:18, expiring...the third breathing
                          out his soul

         psuchē
      IV Macc. 15:25, beholding in her own soul vehement
                          counsellors,

SOVEREIGNTY, kureia, "sovereignty"
   Bel-Drag. 1:5, the living God...hath sovereignty
                          over all

SOW, speirō, "to sow or plant a field"
   Eccl. 6:19, Come unto her as one that poweth and
                          soweth, and
          7:3, My son, sow not upon the furrows of
                          unrighteousness

SPACE, chronos, "time, an epoch, era, marked dura-
                          tion"
   IV Macc. 15:27, lean to that...for the safety of
                          a brief space

SPAIN, Hispania
   I Macc. 8:3, and what they had done in the country
                          of Spain, for

SPAKE, legō, "to speak, to say, to utter"
  I Esd. 1:3, And he spake unto the Levites, the
            holy ministers of

SPARK, spintheros, "a spark"
  Eccl. 11:32, Of a spark of fire a heap of coals
             is kindled;
        28:12, If thou blow the spark, it shall burn;
             if thou spit
        42:22, all his works! and...a man may see...
             a spark

SPARROW, strouthion, "a young sparrow"
  Tobit 2:10, mine eyes being open, the sparrow
             muted warm dung

SPARTA, Spartē
  I Macc. 14:16, when it was heard at Rome, and as
               far as Sparta,

SPEAR, gaisos, "a spear"
  Judith 9:7, For, behold...they trust in shield
             and spear

       doros, "the wood or shaft of a spear"
  Judith 11:2, therefore...I would not have lifted
             up my spear,
  Eccl. 29:13, better than a mighty shield and a
             strong spear

       logchē, "a spear-head, javelin-head"
  II Macc. 15:11, Thus he armed every one...with...
               shields and spears

SPEARBEARER, doruphoros, "spear-bearing"
  IV Macc. 6:1, answered the...tyrant, the spear-
               bearers came up, and
        6:23, Ye spearbearers of the tyrant, why
             do ye hunger?
        11:9, As he said this, the spearbearers
             bound him, and
        17:1, And some of the spearbearers said,
             that...she

SPEARMAN, doruphoros, "spear-bearing, body guard of
                        the king"
  IV Macc. 9:16, And when the spearmen said, Consent
               to eat, that
        9:26, admired his courageous soul, the
             spearmen brought

SPEECH, phoneō, "to speak aloud or clearly, to pro-
                 duce an articulate sound"

335

III Macc. 2:22, righteous judgment deprived of the
               faculty of speech

   lalia, "talking, chat, gossip"
III Macc. 4:16, gave glory to idols...and uttered
               unworthy speech

   phoneō
IV Macc. 10:18, Even if you take away the organ
               of speech, yet

SPEEDILY, tachus, "swiftly, quickly, fast"
   IV Macc. 10:21, But God shall speedily find you,
                  since you cut

SPIRIT, pneuma, "wind or air; spirit, inspiration"
   Tobit 3:6, Now therefore...command my spirit to
             be taken away from

      daimonion, "the Deity, Divinity, evil spirit"
   Tobit 3:16, and to bring Asmodeus the evil spirit;
              because she

      pneuma
   Tobit 6:7, he said unto him...if a devil or an
             evil spirit trouble

      daimonion
   Tobit 6:14, as the other before: for a wicked
              spirit loveth her,
         8:3, The which smell when the evil spirit
              had smelled, he

      pneuma
   Judith 16:14, thou didst send forth thy spirit,
                and it created
   Wisd.-Sol. 1:5, For the holy spirit of discipline
                  will flee deceit
              1:6, For wisdom is a loving spirit;
                  and will not
              1:7, For the Spirit of the Lord filleth
                  the world:
              5:3, repenting and groaning for anguish
                  of spirit

      psuchē, "life, soul, desire, appetite"
   Wisd.-Sol. 8:19, For I was a witty child, and had
                   a good spirit

      pneuma
   Wisd.-Sol. 12:1, For thine incorruptible Spirit
                   is in all things

336

Wisd.-Sol. 15:11, his Maker...and breathed in a
              living spirit
           15:16, made them and he that borrowed
              his own spirit
Eccl. 31:13, The spirit of those that fear the
              Lord shall live;
       38:23, be comforted for him when his spirit
              is departed
       39:6, he shall be filled with the spirit
              of understanding
       39:28, There be spirits that are created
              for vengeance,
       48:12, and Eliseus was filled with the
              spirit: whilst he
       48:24, He saw by an excellent spirit what
              should come to
Bar. 3:1, the soul in anguish, the troubled spirit,
              crieth
Song-Child. 1:15, in a contrite heart and an hum-
              ble spirit let us
            1:63, O ye spirits and souls of the
              righteous, bless
His.-Sus. 1:45, the Lord raised up the holy spirit
              of a youth,

    phronema, "the mind, the will, the spirit"
II Macc. 7:21, them in her own language, filled
              with courageous spirit

    psuchē
III Macc. 2:32, A nobler spirit, however, prompted
              the majority

    pneuma
IV Macc. 7:14, By the spirit of reasoning, and the
              reasoning of

SPOIL, diarpagē, "plunder"
Judith 8:19, which cause our fathers were given...
              for a spoil
         9:4, for a prey...and all their spoils to
              be divided

    arpagē, "plunder, pillage, rapine, prey,
              spoil"
Eccl. 16:13, The sinner shall not escape with his
              spoils: and

    skulon, "spoil, booty, prey"
I Macc. 1:3, to the ends of the earth, and took
              the spoils of many

I Macc. 1:19, strong cities in...Egypt...and took
the spoils thereof

1:31, And when he had the spoils of the
city, he set it

1:35, and when they had gathered together
the spoils of

2:10, had a part in her kingdom, and
gotten of her spoils

3:12, Wherefore Judas took their spoils,
and Apollonius'

skullō, "to trouble, vex, annoy"
I Macc. 3:20, us...and our wives and children,
and to spoil us

skulon
I Macc. 4:17, to the people, Be not greedy of the
spoils, inasmuch

skuleuō, "to strip or spoil a slain enemy"
I Macc. 4:23, Then Judas returned to spoil the
tents, where they

skulon
I Macc. 5:3, against the children of Esau...and
took their spoils

5:22, unto the gate of Ptolemais...whose
spoils he took

5:28, when he had won the city...took all
their spoils,

5:35, slew all the males...and received
the spoils thereof

5:51, who then slew all the males...and
took the spoils

pronomeuō, "to go out foraging, to forage"
I Macc. 6:3, he...sought to take the city, and
to spoil it;

skulon
I Macc. 6:6, and that they were made strong by...
store of spoils,

7:47, Afterwards they took the spoils and
the prey, and

9:40, rose up against them...and took all
their spoils

10:84, set fire on Azotus, and...took their
spoils

10:87, and his host unto Jerusalem, having
many spoils

11:48, they set fire on the city, and gat

                          many spoils
I Macc. 11:51, they cast away their weapons...
                    having great spoils
        12:31, Zabadeans, and smote them, and took
                    their spoils.
II Macc. 8:28, when they had given part of the
                    spoils to the
         8:31, and the remnant of the spoils they
                    brought to

SPOILED, skuleuō, "to strip or spoil an enemy"
I Macc. 5:68, the land of the Philistines...and
                    spoiled their cities
        6:24, for which cause they...spoiled our
                    inheritance
       11:61, From whence he went to Gaza...and
                    spoiled them
II Macc. 8:27, gathered their armour together,
                    and spoiled their
         9:16, which before he had spoiled, he
                    would garnish

SPOUSE, numphē, "a bride, a young wife, any married
                    woman"
Wisd.-Sol. 8:2, from my youth, I desired to make
                    her my spouse,

SPOUT, dromos, "a course, race, running"
II Macc. 14:45, though his blood gushed out like
                    spouts of water,

SPRING, aeros, "in mist or thick air, cloudy"
Wisd.-Sol. 2:7, ourselves...and let no flower of
                    the spring pass

        hēmera, "with dawn of day, daily"
Eccl. 50:8, and as the flower of roses in the
                    spring of the year,

        pēgē, "spring, origin of anything"
IV Macc 3:10, had numerous springs, could not by
                    their means

SPY, kataskopos, "a scout, a spy"
Eccl. 11:30, Like as a partridge taken...and like
                    as a spy,
I Macc. 12:26, He sent spies also unto their tents,
                    who came

SQUARE, tetragonos, "four-angled, quadrangular,
                    square"
I Macc. 10:11, workmen to build the walls...with

339

square stones

STAFF, hrabdos, "a rod, wand, a staff"
Bel-Drag. 1:26, and I shall slay the dragon without sword or staff

STAR, astēr, "a star, a luminous body, a meteor"
Wisd.-Sol. 7:19, the circuits of years, and posi-
tions of stars
7:29, more beautiful than the sun, and
above...the stars
10:17, by day, and a light of stars in
the night
13:2, either fire, or wind...or the
circle of the stars
17:5, neither could the bright flames
of the stars
Eccl. 43:9, the beauty of the heaven, the glory
of the stars, an

astron, "a star, constellation"
Eccl. 44:21, oath, that he would...exalt his seed
as the stars

astēr
Eccl. 50:6, He was as the morning star in the
midst of a cloud,
Bar. 3:34, The stars shined in their watches,
and rejoiced:
Epis.-Jer. 1:60, For sun, moon, and stars, being
bright, and sent
Song-Child. 1:12, and wouldst multiply their seed
as the stars of
1:40, O ye stars of heaven, bless ye
the Lord: praise
II Macc. 9:10, little afore he could reach to the
stars of
IV Macc. 17:5, does the moon appear with the stars
in heaven,

STATUTE, diathēkē, "a will and testament, a covenant"
Eccl. 45:17, his commandments...and authority in
the statutes

dikaioma, "an act of justice, an acquittal"
Bar. 4:13, They knew not his statutes, nor walked
in the ways of

STAY, sterigmos, "a setting firmly, propping fixed-
ness"
Tobit 8:6, gavest him Eve his wife for an helper
and stay:

STEP, <u>ichnos</u>, "foot-step, track"
  Eccl. 42:19, past, and for to come, and revealing
              the steps

STICK, <u>hrabdos</u>, "a rod, wand, stick, switch"
  Eccl. 30:24, Fodder, a stick, and burdens, are
              for the ass;

STIFFNECK, <u>sklerotrachelos</u>, "stiffneck"
  Bar. 2:30, not hear me, because it is a stiffneck-
            ed people

STIMULUS, <u>oistros</u>, "a gadfly, any vehement passion,
                  madness, frenzy"
  IV Macc. 2:3, ripe...he abrogated...the stimulus
               of his passions
           2:4, And it is not merely the stimulus
               of sensual

STING, <u>degma</u>, "a bite or sting"
  Wisd.-Sol. 16:5, fierceness came...they perished
                  with the stings

       <u>kentron</u>, "a point, sting"
  IV Macc. 14:19, The very bees...pierce with their
                 sting, as with a

STOCK, <u>hriza</u>, "a root, a stem, stock"
  Tobit 5:13, thou art my brother, of an honest and
             good stock:

       <u>xulon</u>, "firewood, timber, stick, tree, stock"
  Wisd.-Sol. 14:21, occasion to...ascribe unto
                   stones and stocks

       <u>genos</u>, "offspring, kindred, lineage, progeny"
  I Macc.12:21, in the writing...that they are of
               the stock of
  II Macc. 1:10, greeting...unto Aristobulus...who
                was of the stock

STONE, <u>lithos</u>, "a stone"
  Tobit 13:16, shall be built with sapphire...pre-
              cious stone:
  Judith 1:2, and stones hewn three cubits, and the
             broad, and a
         6:12, they...kept them from coming up by
              casting of stones
  Wisd.-Sol. 13:10, the works of men's hands...gold
                   ...or a stone good
             14:21, for men...did ascribe unto stones
                   and stocks the

Wisd.-Sol. 18:24, the four rows of the stones, was
                   the glory of
Eccl. 6:21, She will lie upon him as a mighty stone
            of trial; and
      21:8, is like one that gathereth himself stones
            for the tomb
      21:10, The way of sinners is made plain with
             stones, but at
      22:1, A slothful man is compared to a filthy
            stone, and
      22:20, Who casteth a stone at the birds frayeth
             them away:
      27:2, sticketh fast between the joinings of
            the stones;
      27:25, Whoso casteth a stone on high casteth
             it on his own
      29:10, from thy brother...and let it not rust
             under a stone
      35:20, way wherein thou mayest fall, and stum-
             ble not among stones
      45:11, with twisted scarlet...with precious
             stones graven
      47:4, when he lifted up his hand with the
            stone in the sling
      50:9, and as a vessel of beaten gold set with
            ...stones:
Epis.-Jer. 1:39, Their gods of wood...are like
                 the stones that be
I Macc. 2:36, answered them not, neither cast they
              a stone at
        4:43, and bare out the defiled stones into
              an unclean
        4:46, and laid up the stones in the moun-
              tain of the
        4:47, shut them out, and stopped up the
              gates with stones
        6:51, he besieged it...and...cast fire
              and stones, and
        10:11, the workmen to build the walls...
               with square stones
        13:27, upon the sepulchre...with hewn
               stones behind and
II Macc. 1:16, door of the roof, they threw stones
               like
         1:31, the water...to be poured on the
               great stones

      petros, "a piece of rock, a stone"
II Macc. 4:41, the attempt of Lysimachus, some

342

caught stones,

lithos
II Macc. 10:3, they made another altar and strik-
ing stones, they

STOOPING, badizo, "to go on foot, to go slowly,
pace"
Bar. 2:18, that is greatly vexed, which goeth
stooping and feeble

STOREHOUSE, tameion, "storehouse, granary, barn"
Eccl. 29:12, Shut up arms in thy storehouse: and
it shall

STORM, lailaps, "a tempest storm, hurricane"
Wisd.-Sol. 5:14, is...like a thin froth...driven
away by the storm,
5:23, stand up against them, and like
a storm shall

kataigis, "a storm"
Wisd.-Sol. 36:2, an hypocrite therein is as a ship
in a storm
43:17, to tremble: so doth the northern
storm

cheimon, "the season of winter, a storm of
rain"
IV Macc. 15:32, straitened by violent storms
which were

STORY, historia, "a learning by inquiry, knowledge
obtained by inquiry"
II Macc. 2:30, point...belongeth to the first
author of the story
2:32, Here then will we begin the story:
only adding

STRANGE, allotrios, "foreign, a foreigner, alien"
Bar. 4:3, Give not thine honour to another...to
a strange nation

alloglossos, "of a strange tongue, foreign"
Bar. 4:15, brought a nation upon them...of a
strange language

allotrios
I Macc. 6:13, I perceive...and, behold, I perish
...in a strange

STRANGER, allogenes, "of another race, a foreigner"
Judith 9:2, gavest a sword to take vengeance of

343

the strangers,

ǎllotrios, "of or belonging to another; hence strange, alien"
Wisd.-Sol. 19:15, And not only so, but...they used strangers not

paroikos, "a sojourning, temporary residence in a foreign land"
Eccl. 29:24, for where thou art thou art a stranger, thou darest
29:26, Come thou stranger, and furnish a table, and feed me
29:27, Give place, thou stranger, to an honourable man:

ǎllogenēs
Eccl. 45:13, neither did ever any stranger put them on,

ǎllotrios
Eccl. 45:18, Strangers conspired together against him, and

ǎllophulos, "of another race or nation"
Epis.-Jer. 1:5, Beware therefore that ye in no wise be like strangers,

ǎllotrios
I Macc. 1:38, the city was made an habitation of strangers,
2:7, city...and the sanctuary into the hand of strangers?
3:36, and that he should place strangers in all their

ǎllophulos
I Macc. 4:12, Then the strangers lifted up their eyes, and saw
4:22, they fled every one into the land of strangers
4:26, Now all the strangers that had escaped came and
4:30, and gavest the host of strangers into the hand of

ǎllogenēs
I Macc. 10:12, Then the strangers, that were in the fortresses

geneia, "a state of being a guest, the reception of a guest or stranger"
I Macc. 11:38, one to his own place, except certain

344

bands of strangers,

allophulos
I Macc. 11:68, And, behold, the host of strangers
met them in the
12:10, attempted to...become strangers
unto you altogether
II Macc. 10:5, Now upon the same day that the
strangers profaned

xenes, "a host, a stranger, strange or foreign"
III Macc. 6:3, now being wrongfully destroyed
as strangers

STRANGLE, straggo, "to draw tight, bind tight,
squeeze"
Tobit 2:3, and said, Father, one of our nation
is strangled,
3:8, Dost thou not know...that thou hast
strangled thine
3:10, these things...she thought to have
strangled herself:

STREAM, kludon, "a wave, billow, surge"
Wisd.-Sol. 19:7, land appeared...and out of the
violent stream

STREET, platus, "flat, wide, broad"
Tobit 13:17, And the streets of Jerusalem shall
be paved with
13:18, And all her streets shall say,
Alleluia; and they
Judith 1:14, and took the towers and spoiled the
streets thereof
7:14, come against them...in the streets
where they dwell
7:22, young children were...fell down in
the streets of the

hrume, "street, a narrow street"
Eccl. 9:7, Look not round about thee in the streets
of the city,

platus
Eccl. 23:21, This man shall be punished in the
streets, of the

hodos, "a path, road, highway"
Eccl. 49:6, They burnt the chosen city...and made
the streets

platus
I Macc. 1:55, incense at the doors of their
             homes, and in the streets
      2:9, carried away...her infants are slain
           in the streets
      14:9, The ancient men sat all in the
            streets, communing

hodos
II Macc. 3:19, women girt with sackcloth...abound-
              ed in the streets

platus
III Macc. 1:18, came out with their mothers...
               filling the streets

aguia, "a way or road, a street"
III Macc. 4:3, What home, or city...or what
              streets were there,

STRENGTH, ischus, "strength, force, might"
Bar. 1:12, and the Lord will give us strength,
          and lighten our
      3:14, Learn where is wisdom, where strength,
            and where is

hronnumi, "to strengthen, render firm"
III Macc. 7:1, to all who are set over affairs,
              joy and strength

STRIFE, mache, "battle, strife, combat"
Eccl. 38:8, Abstain from strife, and thou shalt
           diminish thy sins
      40:5, trouble, and unquietness, fear of
            death...and strife,
      40:9, Death, and bloodshed, strife, and
            sword, calamities,

STRIPE, masix, "a scourge, whip"
Eccl. 22:6, (is as) music in mourning: but
           stripes and correction

plege, "a blow, stroke, stripe"
II Macc. 3:26, before him...in apparel...and gave
              him...sore stripes
      6:30, But when he was ready to die with
            stripes, he

STRIVE, diamachomai, "to fight with, struggle
                     against"
Eccl. 8:1, Strive not with a mighty man, lest thou
          fall into his

346

Eccl. 8:3, Strive not with a man that is full
of tongue, and heap
8:16, Strive not with an angry man, and go
not with him
11:9, Strive not in a matter that concerneth
thee not; and

STROKE, plēgē, "a stroke, stripe"
Eccl. 28:17, The stroke of the whip maketh a
mark in the flesh:

mastix, "a scourge, a stripe"
Eccl. 39:28, created for vengeance, which...lay
on sore strokes

STRONGHOLD, ochurōma, "a stronghold, fortify"
I Macc. 6:61, king and the princes...went out of
the stronghold

ochuros, "firm and strong"
I Macc. 12:35, calling...them about building strong
holds in Judea
12:45, give it thee, and the rest of the
strong holds
13:33, Then Simon built strong holds in
Judea, and fenced
13:38, covenants we have made...and the
strong holds,
16:8, slain, and the remnant gat them to
the strong hold
II Macc. 8:30, were with Timotheus...got high and
strong holds

STUMBLE, proskoptō, "to strike one's foot, i.e., to
stumble against"
Eccl. 30:13, Train up thy son...lest by looseness
thou stumble
35:20, in a way wherein thou mayest fall,
and stumble not

STUMBLING, proskomma, "a stumbling, a shock"
Eccl. 31:16, cover from the sun...a preservation
from stumbling

STUMBLINGBLOCK, skandalon, "a stumblingblock, an
impediment, offence"
Wisd.-Sol. 14:11, are become an abomination, and
stumblingblocks
Eccl. 7:6, lest at any time thou...lay a stumblingblock in the way

proskomma, "a stumblingblock, an
occasion for sinning"

Eccl. 34:7, It is a stumblingblock unto them that
    sacrifice unto
    39:24, plain unto the holy; so are they
    stumblingblocks

SUBSTANCE, ischus, "strength, force, might, esp.
    bodily strength"
Eccl. 9:2, unto a woman to set her foot upon thy
    substance

SUBTIL, noeros, "intellectual"
Wisd.-Sol. 7:22, is the worker of all things...
    manifold, subtil,
    7:23, through all understanding...and
    most subtil

SUBTILTY, panourgia, "ready for all crimes, unscru-
    pulous"
Eccl. 19:25, There is an exquisite subtilty, and
    the same is

SUCKLING, nepios, "an infant, the young of an animal"
III Macc. 3:27, Jew, whether it be an old man...
    or suckling

SUD, Soud
Bar. 1:4, nobles...that dwelt at Babylon by the
    river Sud

SUFFER, eaō, "suffer to be done, allow"
I Macc. 15:14, the city...neither suffered he any
    to go out or in

    paschō, "to suffer, endure evil"
II Macc. 7:32, For we suffer because of our sins

    hupopheō, "to bear under, to endure patient-
    ly, undergo"
III Macc. 7:36, For our brethren who now have
    suffered a short

    pathetos, "having suffered, destined to
    suffer"
IV Macc. 13:16, If we suffer thus, Abraham, and
    Isaac, and Jacob

SUFFERING, pathē, "capable of suffering"
IV Macc. 7:8, of their own blood, and...sweat by
    sufferings even

    ponon, "pain, misery, anguish, travail"
IV Macc. 9:31, For I lighten my suffering by the
    pleasures which

IV Macc. 11:32, bestowest upon us...by means of
nobler sufferings

       pathēma, "a suffering, misfortune"
IV Macc. 15:23, strengthened her courage in the
midst of sufferings

SUN, hēlios, "toward the morn and rising sun, the
sun"
I Esd. 4:34, great is the eart...swift is the sun
in his course,
Tobit 2:4, I started up...until the going down of
the sun
    2:7, I wept: and after the going down of the
sun I went
Judith 14:2, as the morning shall appear, and the
sun shall come
Wisd.-Sol. 2:4, as a cloud...that is driven away
with...the sun
       7:29, For she is more beautiful than
the sun, and above
     16:28, that we must prevent the sun to
give thee thanks
Eccl. 17:31, What is brighter than the sun?
    23:19, the eyes of the Lord are...brighter
than the sun
    26:16, As the sun when it ariseth in the
high heaven; so is
    31:16, For the eyes of the Lord...cover from
the sun at noon
    36:7, one day excel another, when...the
light...is of the sun
    42:16, The sun that giveth light looketh
upon all things,
    43:2, the sun when it appeareth, declareth
at his rising a
    43:4, blowing a furnace is in works of heat,
but the sun
    46:4, Did not the sun go back by his means?
    48:23, In jis time the sun went backward,
and he lengthened
    50:7, as the sun shining upon the temple
of the most High,
Epis.-Jer. 1:60, For sun, moon, and stars, being
bright, and sent
    1:67, shew signs in the heavens...nor
shine as the sun,
I Macc. 6:39, Now when the sun shone upon the
shields of gold and

I Macc. 10:50, he continued the battle very sore
              until the sun
         12:27, Wherefore soon as the sun was down,
              Jonathan
II Macc. 1:22, was done, and the time came that
              the sun shone,
III Macc. 5:26, The sun's rays were not yet shed
              abroad, and the

SURETY, éggue, "a putting a pledge in one's hand;
              hence, surety, security"
   Eccl. 29:16, A sinner will overthrow the good
              estate of...surety

SURETYSHIP, éggue, "suretyship, security"
   Eccl. 29:18, Suretyship hath undone many of good
              estate, and
         29:19, A wicked man...shall fall into sure-
              tyship, and he

SURFEITING, áplestia, "insatiate desire"
   Eccl. 37:30, excess of meats bringeth sickness
              and surfeiting
         37:31, By surfeiting have many perished;
              but he that taketh

SURNAME, épikaleo, "to attach an additional name"
   I Esd. 2:25, Avaran: and Jonathan whose surname
              was Apphus

SUSANNA, Sosanna
   His.-Sus. 1:2, and he took a wife, whose name was
              Susanna, the
         1:7, when the people departed away at
              noon, Susanna
         1:22, Then Susanna sighed, and said, I
              am straitened on
         1:24, With that Susanna cried with a
              loud voice: and
         1:27, But when the elders had...a report
              made of Susanna
         1:28, two elders...full of imagination
              against Susanna
         1:29, and said before the people...Send
              for Susanna,
         1:31, Now Susanna was a very delicate
              woman, and
         1:42, Then Susanna cried out with a
              loud voice, and said
         1:63, Chelcias...praised God for their
              daughter Susanna,

SWADDLING, sparganon,   "swaddling or swathing band:
                          in plural, swaddling clothes"
  Wisd.-Sol. 7:4, I was nursed in swaddling clothes,
              and that with

SWALLOW, chelidon, "a swallow, the frog in the hol-
                    low of a horse's foot"
  Epis.-Jer. 1:22, Upon their bodies and heads sit
              bats, swallows,

SWAM, diakolumbao,   "to dive through or over"
  I Macc. 9:48, Then Jonathan...leapt into Jordan,
              and swam over

SWEAR, horkizo, "to put to an oath, to adjure,
                 conjure"
  I Esd. 1:48, had made him to swear by the name
              of the Lord

          omnuo,   "to swear, to promise with an oath"
  Wisd.-Sol. 14:29, insomuch as their trust is in
                     idols...they swear
              14:31, it is not the power of them by
                      whom they swear:
  Eccl. 23:10, is beaten...so he that sweareth and
              nameth God

          huperephaneo, "to be conspicious above others,
                          arrogant"
  Eccl. 27:14, The talk of him that sweareth much
              maketh the hair

          omnuo
  I Macc. 7:35, and swear in his wrath, saying,
              Unless Judas and

SWEARING, horkos, "an oath"
  Eccl. 23:9, Accustom not thy mouth to swearing;
              neither use

          anomia, "lawlessness"
  Eccl. 23:11, A man that useth much swearing shall
              be filled with

SWORD, hromphaia, "a large sword"
  I Esd. 1:53, who slew their young men with the
              sword, yea, even
              1:56, and the people that were not slain
                     with the sword h

          machaira, "a large knife, a sabre or scimitar"
  I Esd. 3:22, forget their love...and a little
              after draw out swords

hromphaia

I Esd. 4:23, Yea, a man taketh his sword, and
            goeth his way to
        8:77, our fathers' we...were given up...to
              the sword
Judith 1:12, was very angry...and...slay with the
             sword all the
        2:27, and smote all the young men with the
              edge of the sword

    sideros, "anything made of iron, a sword,
            spear, axe"
Judith 6:6, And then shall the sword of mine army,
            and the

    hromphaia

Judith 7:14, and their children shall be consumed
             with...the sword
        9:2, to whom thou gavest a sword to take
             vengeance,
        9:8, and...cast down with sword the horn
             of thy altar
        11:10, our nations shall not be punished,
               neither can the sword prevail
        16:5, he would...kill my young men with the
              sword, and dash
Wisd.-Sol. 5:20, His severe wrath shall he sharpen
                 for a sword,
Eccl. 21:3, All iniquity is as a two edged sword,
            the wounds
      26:28, the Lord prepareth such an one for
             the sword

    machaira
Eccl. 28:18, Many have fallen by the edge of the
             sword: but not

    hromphaia
Eccl. 39:30, of wild beasts, and scorpions...and
             the sword,
      40:9, Death, and bloodshed, strife, and
             sword, calamities,
      46:2, when he...stretched out his sword
             against the cities!
Bar. 2:25, cast out to the heat...and they died...
           by sword, and by
His.-Sus. 1:59, the angel of God waiteth with the
                sword to cut

    machaira
Bel-Drag. 1:25, and I shall slay this dragon

without sword or

hromphaia

I Macc. 2:9, are carried away...her young men
         with the sword
      3:3, great honour...protecting the host
         with his sword

machaira

I Macc. 3:12, Judas took their spoils, and
         Apollonius' sword also
      4:6, thousand men, who...had neither
         armour nor sword,

hromphaia

I Macc. 4:15, all the hindermost of them were
         slain with the sword
      4:33, cast them down with the sword of
         them that love
      5:28, he slew all the males with the edge
         of the sword,
      5:51, who then slew all the males with
         the edge of the sword, and rased
         the city,
      8:23, Good success be to the Romans...the
         sword also and
      9:73, Thus the sword ceased from Israel:
         but Jonathan

machaira

I Macc. 10:85, Thus there were burned and slain
         with the sword

hromphaia

I Macc. 12:48, they that came with him they slew
         with the sword

machaira

II Macc. 5:3, troops of horsemen in array...and
         drawing of swords,

xiphos, "a sword"

II Macc. 12:22, first band came...with the points
         of their...sword

hromphaia

II Macc. 15:15, forth his right hand gave to Judas
         a sword of
       15:16, Take this holy sword, a gift from
         God, with which

doru, "the wood or shaft of a spear"
III Macc. 5:43, and level its towns with fire
and the sword

sidēros
IV Macc. 14:19, season of honey-making, attack...
as withthe a sword,

TABERNACLE, skenē, "a tabernacle, a tent, booth"
I Esd. 1:50, God of their fathers...spared them
and his tabernacle
Tobit 13:10, Give praise to the Lord...that his
tabernacle be
Judith 2:26, children of Madian, and burned up
their tabernacles,
9:8, strength in thy power...and...pollute
the tabernacle
14:7, recovered him....Blessed art thou in
all the tabernacle
Eccl. 24:8, gave me a commandment...and caused
my tabernacle to
24:10, In the holy tabernacle I served before him; and so
24:15, and I yielded a pleasant odour...in
the tabernacle

skēnopegia, "a pitching of tents, the
feast of tabernacles"
I Macc. 10:21, at the feast of the tabernacles,
Jonathan put on
II Macc. 1:9, Now see that ye keep the feast of
tabernacles in
1:18, necessary to...keep it, as the
feast of the tabernacles,
2:4, that the prophet commanded the
tabernacles and the
2:5, And when Jeremy came thither...he
laid the tabernacle

skenē
II Macc. 10:6, And they kept...the feast of tabernacles, when as

TABLE, trapeza, "a table, an eating table"
Eccl. 6:10, Again, some friend at...is a companion
at the table,
14:10, (his) bread, and he is a niggard at
his table
29:26, Come, thou stranger, and furnish a
table, and feed me

Eccl. 34:12, If thou sit at a bountiful table, be
        not greedy upon
   40:29, The life of him that dependeth on
        another man's table
Bel-Drag. 1:13, And they little regarded it: for
        under the table
    1:18, the door, the king looked upon
        the table,
    1:21, consumed such things as were upon
        the table
I Macc. 1:22, And the table of the shewbread, and
        the pouring
    4:49, vessels...and the altars of incense,
        and the table
    4:51, Furthermore they set the loaves upon
        the table, and

   deltos, "a writing-table"
I Macc. 8:22, epistle which the senate wrote...
        in tables of brass,
   14:18, They wrote unto him in tables of
        brass, to renew
   14:27, So then they wrote it in tables of
        brass, which
   14:48, that this writing should be cut in
        tables of brass

TALE, muthos, "a tale, fable"
  Eccl. 20:19, An unseasonable tale will always be
        in the mouth of

   diagesis, "a narration, history"
  Eccl. 22:6, A tale out of season (is as) music
        in mourning:
   22:8, He that telleth a tale to a fool
        speaketh to one in a

TALENT, talanton, "a balance, anything weighed, of
        money or silver"
  I Esd. 1:36, set a tax upon the land of an hundred
        talents of
    3:21, it maketh to speak all things by
        talents:
    4:51, there should be yearly given twenty
        talents to the
    8:20, to the sum of an hundred talents of
        silver, likewise
    8:56, talents of silver, and silver vessels
        of an hundred talents, and an hundred
        talents of gold,

    Tobit 1:14, and left in trust with Gabael...ten
              talents of silver
         4:20, this to thee, that I committed ten
              talents to Gabael
    I Macc. 11:28, that he promised him three hundred
              talents
         13:16, Wherefore now send an hundred ta-
              lents of silver,
         13:19, he sent them the children and the
              hundred talents:
         15:31, or else give me for them five hun-
              dred talents of
         15:35, will we be given an hundred talents
              of them
    II Macc. 3:11, to Hircanus...in all was four hun-
              dred talents of
         4:24, presence of the king...got...three
              hundred talents
         5:21, carried out of the temple a thou-
              sand...talents, he
         8:10, should defray the tribute of two
              thousand talents
         8:11, they should have...and ten bodies
              for one talent,
    IV Macc. 4:17, to pay yearly three thousand...
              and sixty talents

TALK, legō, "to speak, to say, declare"
    Eccl. 11:8, hast heard the cause...in the midst
              of their talk

TAPHON, Tephon
    I Macc. 9:50, returned Bacchides to Jerusalem,
              and...Taphon, these

TARSUS, Tarseus
    II Macc. 4:30, while those things were in doing,
              they of Tarsus

TAX, zemioō, "to punish, to fine, do damage or hurt"
    I Esd. 1:36, And he set a tax upon the land of an
              hundred talents

TEACH, didaskō, "to teach, to learn"
    Eccl. 9:1, over the wife of thy bosom, and teach
              her not an evil
         22:7, Whoso teacheth a fool is as one that
              glueth a potsherd
    IV Macc. 5:24, And it instructs us in justice...
              and it teaches us
         18:10, And he used to teach you, when yet

                               with you, the

TEARS, diakru, "a tear, a drop, as of gum"
   Eccl. 22:19, He that pricketh the eye will make
               tears to fall:
        32:15, Do not the tears run down the widow's
               cheeks?
        38:16, My son, let tears fall down over the
               dead, and begin
   II Macc. 11:6, the holds...all the people with...
               tears besought the
   III Macc. 1:4, place; and...Arsinoe...with tears...
               begged the
        1:16, fell down...they filled the temple
               with...tears
        4:4, upon the uncertain issue of life,
               shed tears at
        5:7, the Almighty God, and...besought
               with tears their
        6:14, band of infants and their parents
               with tears he
        6:23, he heard the cry, and saw them...
               with tears he
   IV Macc. 4:11, dead...and implored the Hebrews,
               with tears,

TEETH, ódous, "a tooth"
   Wisd.-Sol. 16:10, But thy sons not the very teeth
               of venomous
   Eccl. 16:2, Flee from sin...for...it will bite
               thee: the teeth
        39:30, teeth of wild beasts, and scorpions,
               serpents, and

        brugmos, "a tooth"
   Eccl. 51:3, and hast delivered me...from the teeth
               of them that

        ódous
   IV Macc. 7:6, O priest...thou didst pollute thy
               sacred teeth;

TEMPERANCE, sóphrosuné, "sanity, soundness of mind"
   Wisd.-Sol. 8:7, And if...she teacheth temperance
               and prudence,
   IV Macc. 1:3, reasoning appears to hold the...way
               of temperance,
        1:6, For reasoning...and temperance, and
               prudence;
        1:18, forms of wisdom are prudence, and

                     justice...and temperance
IV Macc. 1:30, For reasoning...stand in the way
               of temperance,
          1:31, Now temperance consists of a com-
               mand over the
          5:23, Yet it instructs us in temperance,
               so that we are

TEMPERATE, sōphrōn, "temperate, sane, staid"
IV Macc. 2:2, on this ground, therefore the tem-
              perate Joseph is
          2:16, For the temperate understanding
               repels all these
          2:18, For the temperate mind is able, as
               I said, to be
          2:23, to which it maintain a temperate,
               and just...reign
          3:17, For the temperate mind has power
               to conquer the
          15:10, For they were both just and temper-
                ate, and manly,

TEMPEST, kataigis, "the aegis, or shield of Jupiter;
                    a rushing storm, hurricane"
Eccl. 16:21, It is a tempest which no man can see:
             for the most

TEMPLE, hieron, "hallowed, holy, divine, sacred
                rites"
I Esd. 1:2, according to their daily courses...in
            the temple
        1:5, as David...prescribed...standing in
            the temple
        1:8, Zacharias, and Syelus, the governors
            of the temple

        paos, "the dwelling of a god, a temple"
I Esd. 1:41, of the holy vessels...and set them
            in his own temple

        hieron
I Esd. 1:53, with the sword, yea, even within...
            their holy temple,
        2:7, with horses...and other things...for
            the temple of the
        2:18, that the Jews...lay the foundation
            of the temple

        naos
I Esd. 2:20, forasmuch as the things pertaining to
            the temple are

hieron
I Esd. 2:30, and the building of the temple in
Jerusalem ceased

naos
I Esd. 4:45, Thou also hast vowed to build up the
temple, which

hieron
I Esd. 4:51, be yearly given twenty talents to the
building of the temple,
5:44, the chief of their families...came
to the temple

naos
I Esd. 5:53, began to offer sacrifice...although
the temple of the

hieron
I Esd. 5:56, the second year...after his coming
to the temple of

naos
I Esd. 5:58, So the builders built the temple of
the Lord
5:67, that were of the captivity did build
the temple
6:18, Nabuchodonosor...set them in his own
temple,
6:19, he should...put them in the temple
at Jerusalem
7:2, holy works...of the Jews and governors
of the temple

hieron
I Esd. 8:14, which is given of the people for the
temple of the
8:22, ye require no tax...of any...ministers
of the temple,
8:49, And the servants of the temple whom
David had
8:67, and they honoured the people and the
temple of God
8:81, yea, and honoured the temple of our
Lord, and raised
8:91, in his prayer made his confession...
before the temple
9:1, Then Esdras rising from the court of
the temple went
9:6, multitude sat in the broad court of
the temple,

naos
Tobit 1:4, and where the temple of the habitation
          of the most

,
oikos, "a house, abode, dwelling, a temple"
Tobit 14:5, God will have mercy on them...they
           shall build a temple

naos
Wisd.-Sol. 3:14, shall be given...an inheritance
               in the temple
Eccl. 45:9, that he might be heard in the temple
            for a memorial

hagios, "devoted to the gods, a sanctuary"
Eccl. 47:10, they might praise his holy name, and
             that the temple
      49:12, the son of Josedec: who set up...an
             holy temple to

naos
Eccl. 50:1, his life repaired the house, and...
            fortified the temple

hieron
Eccl. 50:2, the foundation of the wall about the
            temple

naos
Eccl. 50:7, as the sun shining upon the temple of
            the most High,
      51:14, I prayed for her before the temple,
             and will seek

,
oikos
Epis.-Jer. 1:13, their faces because of the dust
                 of the temple,
           1:14, like as a vessel...even so it is
                 ...in the temple,
           1:18, even so the priests make fasts
                 their temples
           1:20, They are as one of the beams of
                 the temple, yet
           1:21, faces are black through the smoke
                 ...of the temple
           1:31, And the priests sit in their
                 temples, having

naos
Song-Child. 1:30, Blessed art thou in the temple
                  of thy holy

360

oíkos
Bel-Drag. 1:10, and the king went with Daniel into
              the temple of

naos
Bel-Drag. 1:14, forth...throughout all the temple
              in the presence

hieron
Bel-Drag. 1:22, king slew them, and...destroyed
              him and his temple

naos
I Macc. 1:22, the golden ornaments that were before
             the temple,

hagios, "the sanctuary,dedicated, hallowed"
I Macc. 1:45, and sacrifice, and drink offerings
             in the temple

naos
I Macc. 2:8, Her temple is become as a man without
            glory

oíkos
I Macc. 4:46, and laid up the stones in the moun-
             tain of the temple
        4:48, and the things that were within the
             temple
        4:49, made also new holy vessels, and into
             the temple

naos
I Macc. 4:50, burned...the candlestick...give light
             in the temple
        4:57, They decked also the forefront of
             the temple with

temenos, "a piece of land sacred to a god,
         the precincts of a temple"
I Macc. 5:44, But they took the city, and burned
             the temple with

hieron
I Macc. 6:2, and that there was a very rich temple,
            wherein were

naos
I Macc. 7:36, and stood before the altar and the
             temple,

hagios
I Macc. 10:42, they took from the uses of the
              temple out of

<u>hieron</u>
I Macc. 10:43, whosoever they be that flee unto
                the temple at
          10:84, took their spoils; and the temple
                of Dagon, with
          11:4, near to Azotus, they shewed him the
                temple of Dagon
          13:52, should be kept...Moreover the hill
                of the temple

<u>hagios</u>
I Macc. 14:15, and multiplied the vessels of the
                temple

<u>hieron</u>
I Macc. 15:9, obtained our kingdom, we will hon-
                our...thy temple,
II Macc. 1:13, Persia, and the army...they were
                slain in the temple
           1:15, set forth...he...entered...the
                compass of the temple
           1:18, purposed to keep the purification
                of the temple
           2:9, that he...offered the sacrifice...
                of the temple
           2:22, and recovered again the temple re-
                nowned and the
           3:2, the kings...did honour...and magnify
                the temple
           3:4, But one Simon...was made governor
                of the temple,
           3:12, inviolable sanctity of the temple,
           3:30, But they praised the Lord...for
                the temple, which
           4:14, courage to serve...at the altar,
                despising the temple
           4:32, stole certain vessels of gold out
                of the temple,
           5:15, this but...go into the most holy
                temple of all
           5:21, So when Antiochus had carried out
                of the temple a
           6:4, for the temple was filled with riot
                and revelling

<u>naos</u>
II Macc. 8:2, and also pity the temple profaned
                of ungodly men;

<u>hierosulos</u>, "robbing temple"
II Macc. 9:2, called Persipolis, and went about

362

to rob the temple

hieron

II Macc. 9:16, and the holy temple, which before
he had spoiled,

10:1, Maccabeus and his company...recover-
ed the temple and

11:3, and to make a gain of the temple,
as of the other

13:10, from their country, and from the
holy temple,

13:14, all to the Creator...the laws, the
temple, the city

13:23, Philip...offered sacrifice, honoured the temple,

14:4, palm...which were used solemnly in
the temple

14:13, to make Alcimus high priest of...
the temple

14:31, by Judas! policy, came into the
...holy temple

14:33, stretched out his right hand toward
the temple,

naos

II Macc. 15:33, hang up the reward of his madness
before the temple

hieron

III Macc. 1:10, with the exact magnificence of
the...temple, that

1:16, And when the priests...filled the
temple with

1:20, some there...swarmed into the Most
High temple

2:28, The entrance to their own temple
was to be

3:16, considerable sums of money upon
the temples of

naos

III Macc. 3:17, When we were eager to enter their
temple, and to

5:43, and destroy that temple which the
heathen

hieron

IV Macc. 4:3, affairs...which do not belong to
the temple

4:8, But Apollonius went away with threats
into the temple

4:20, erected a gymnasium...(but ne-

363

glected)...the temple

TEMPT, <u>peirazō</u>, "to tempt, make trial of, seek to
              seduce"
   Judith 8:12, And now who are ye that have tempted
               God this day,
   Wisd.-Sol. 1:12, For he will...found of them that
               tempt him not:
   Eccl. 18:23, thyself: and be not as one that
               tempteth the Lord

TEMPTATION, <u>peirasmos</u>, "trial, temptation, proof,
                   a putting to proof"
   Eccl. 2:1, My son...prepare thy soul for tempta-
      36:1, shall no evil happen unto him...but
            in temptation even
   I Macc. 2:52, Abraham found faithful in tempta-
               tion...?

TENT, <u>skenē</u>, "a tent, booth, a tabernacle"
   Judith 3:3, all our places...and all the lodges
               of our tents lie
      5:22, these sayings, all the people...
            about the tent
      6:10, commanded his servants, that waited
            in his tent,
      8:5, And she made her a tent upon the top
            of her house,
      8:36, So they returned from the tent, and
            went to their
     10:17, an hundred men...and they brought
            her to the tent,
     10:18, concourse...for her coming was noised
            among the tents
     10:22, and he came out before his tent with
            silver
     12:5, servants of Holofernes brought her
            into the tent,
     12:9, So she came in clean, and remained in
            the tent,
     13:1, evening was come...and Bagoas shut his
            tent without,
     13:2, And Judith was left alone in the tent,
            and Holofernes
     14:3, and they shall runto the tent of
            Holofernes,
     14:13, So they came to Holofernes' tent, and
            said to him
     14:14, in Bagoas, and knocked at the door
            of the tent;

Judith 14:17, After he went into the tent where
Judith lodged...he
15:1, And when they that were in the tents
heard, they were
15:11, And...they gave unto Judith Holofernes' tent, and all
Wisd.-Sol. 11:2, through the wilderness...and
pitched tents in
Eccl. 14:25, He shall pitch his tent nigh unto
her, and shall
I Macc. 4:20, perceived that the Jews...were
burning the tents;
4:23, Then Judas returned to spoil the
tents, where they
5:39, Arabians to help them, and...pitched
their tents
5:49, Judas commanded...that every man
should pitch is tent in the place
6:48, army went out...and the king pitched
his tents against
7:19, Bacchides from Jerusalem, and pitched his tents in
7:39, Nicanor went out of Jerusalem, and
pitched his tents
9:2, who went forth by the way...and pitched their tents
9:5, Now Judas pitched his tents at
Eleasa, and three

meris, "a part, a district, a division of a
country"
I Macc. 9:11, the host of Bacchides removed out
of their tents

skēnoma, "a dwelling place, nest, abode"
I Macc. 9:66, smote Odonarres and his brethren...
in their tent
II Macc. 12:12, granted them peace....so they departed to their tents
13:15, given the watchword...he went
into the king's tent
III Macc. 1:2, Theodotus...got through at night
to the tent of
IV Macc. 3:8, when evening came...he came to the
royal tent,about

TERRIBLE, tarachōdēs, "troublous, fond of troubling,
perplexing"
Wisd.-Sol. 17:9, For though no terrible thing did
fear them; yet

ktupos, "any loud noise, the crash of thunder"
Wisd.-Sol. 17:19, or a terrible sound of stones
cast down, or a

TERROR, phobos, "fear, terror, fright, dismay"
III Macc. 2:23, and body-guards...struck with
exceeding terror, and

TESTAMENT, diathēkē, "a covenant, a will or testament"
I Macc. 1:57, was found with any of the book
of the testament, or

TESTIFY, martuoō, "to testify, depose, to give evidence"
I Macc. 2:37, Let us die...heaven and earth shall
testify for us,

TESTIMONY, marturion, "testimony, proof, evidence"
Wisd.-Sol. 10:7, the waste land that smoketh is a
testimony,
Eccl. 34:24, and the testimonies of his niggard-
ness shall not be
45:17, He gave unto him...the testimonies,
and inform Israel
IV Macc. 12:17, will not forsake the testimony
of my brethren

THAMNATHA, Thamnatha
I Macc. 9:50, returned Bacchides to Jerusalem...
and Thamnatha,

THANKSGIVING, éxomologeō, "to agree, to praise,
celebrate"
Judith 16:1, Then Judith began to sing thanksgiving in all Israel
Eccl. 17:28, Thanksgiving perisheth from the dead,
as from one
51:11, thy name continually, and will sing
...thanksgiving;

eulogeō, "to bless, ascribe praise
and glorification"
I Macc. 4:24, went home, and sung a song of thanksgiving, and

humnos, "a song of praise, a hymn"
I Macc. 4:33, know thy name praise thee with
thanksgiving.

eulogia, "blessing, praise, divine
blessing"
I Macc. 13:47, houses...and so...with songs and

thanksgiving

ainesis, "praise"

I Macc. 13:51, and entered into it...with thanksgiving, and

humnos

II Macc. 1:30, And the priests sung psalms of
thanksgiving

eulogia

II Macc. 10:38, they praised the Lord with psalms
and thanksgiving

exomologeō

III Macc. 6:35, themselves up to feasting, and
glad thanksgiving

THEFT, klopē, "theft, a stealthy act"
Wisd.-Sol. 14:25, reigned in all men without exception...theft, and
Eccl. 41:19, and of theft regarding of the place
where thou

THEMAN, Thaiman
Bar. 3:22, heard of...neither hath it been seen
in Theman
3:23, The Agarenes...the merchants of Theman,
the

THEODOTUS, Theodoton
II Macc. 14:19, Wherefore he sent Posidonius, and
Theodotus, and
III Macc. 1:2, And one Theodotus, intending to
carry out his

THIEF, kleptē, "a thief, a rogue, deceiver"
Eccl. 20:25, A thief is better than a man that is
accustomed to
36:26, Who will trust a thief well appointed
that skippeth

lēsteia, "a course of plundering, robbery"
Epis.-Jer. 1:15, dagger...but cannot deliver himself from...thieves

kleptai, "thieves"
Epis.-Jer. 1:57, able to escape either from
thieves or robbers

THIGH, mēros, "the thigh"
Eccl. 19:12, As an arrow that sticketh in a man's
thigh, so is a

367

THIRSTY, dipsa, "to be thirsty"
  Wisd.-Sol. 11:4, When they were thirsty, they
                called upon thee,
          11:8, declaring by that thirst then
                how thou hadst
  Eccl. 26:12, She will open her mouth, as a thirsty
              traveller when
      51:24, are ye slow...seeing your souls are
              very thirsty?
  IV Macc. 3:10, But the king being very athirst,
              although he had
      3:15, But he, though parched up with
              thirst, reasoned

THONG, himas, "a leathern strap or thong"
  IV Macc. 9:11, the eldest of them...bound...on
              each side with thongs

THORN, akinthinos, "thorny, or thorns"
  Eccl. 28:24, Look that thou hedge thy possession
              with thorns, and

      hramnos, "a thorn or prickly shrub"
  Epis.-Jer. 1:71, their gods of wood...are like to
              a white thorn,

THOUGHT, dianoema, "a thought, notion"
  Eccl. 42:20, No thought escapeth him, neither any
              word is hidden

      logismos, "reckoning, consideration, rea-
              soning, reflection"
  IV Macc. 5:38, but thou shalt not lord it over my
              thoughts,

THOUSAND, chilioi, "a thousand"
  I Macc. 3:39, and with them he sent forty thousand
              footmen, and
      5:13, brethren...they have destroyed there-
              about a thousand
      5:20, Now unto Simon were given three
              thousand men to go

      trischilioi, "three thousand"
  I Macc. 5:22, pursued...the heathen about three
              thousand men,

      chilioi
  I Macc. 6:35, and for every elephant they appoint-
              ed a thousand

      chiliandros, "containing a thousand men"
  I Macc. 7:41, thine angel went out and smote...

                        five thousand of
I Macc. 10:36, I will further...enrolled...thirty
                        thousand men of
        10:40, Moreover I give every year fifteen
                        thousand shekels

        pentakischilioi, "five thousand"
I Macc. 10:42, Beside this, the five thousand
                        shekels of silver,

        chilioi
I Macc. 10:74, heard these words...choosing ten
                        thousand men he
        12:41, went out to meet him with forty
                        thousand men
        14:24, a great shield of gold of a thou-
                        sand pound
        15:18, and they brought a shield of gold
                        of a thousand

        dischilioi, "two thousand"
I Macc. 15:26, At that time Simon sent him two
                        thousand chosen

        chiliandros
I Macc. 16:4, So he chose out of the country
                        twenty thousand men
        16:10, that there were slain of them about
                        two thousand
II Macc. 5:21, carried out of the temple a thou-
                        sand and eight

        hexakischilioi, "six thousand"
II Macc. 8:1, Judas Maccabeus...assembled about
                        six thousand men

        oktakischilioi, "eight thousand"
II Macc. 8:20, battle...how they came but eight
                        thousand in all

        ennakisischilioi, "nine thousand"
II Macc. 8:24, they slew about nine thousand of
                        their enemies,

        chilioi
II Macc. 8:34, Nicanor, who had brought a thousand
                        merchants
        10:17, slew all that fell...and killed...
                        twenty thousand

        ennakischilioi
II Macc. 10:18, who were no less than nine thou-
                        sand, were fled

                        369

chilioi
II Macc. 11:4, power of God, but...his ten thou-
sands of footmen,
12:20, who had about...an hundred and
twenty thousand

THREATENING, apeile, "a threat, commination, harshness of language"
IV Macc. 8:18, Shall we not fear...the threaten-
ings of torment,
9:5, And you think to scare us, by
threatening us with
9:32, But thou art tortured with threat-
enings for impiety
Pr.-Mans. 1:5, because the...threatenings against
sinners

THRONE, thronos, "a seat, chair, the chair of a
judge, or teacher"
Judith 9:3, gavest their rulers...servants with...
their thrones
11:19, And I will lead thee...and I will set
thy throne in
Wisd.-Sol. 5:23, a mighty wind shall...overthrow
the throne of
6:21, If your delight be then in
thrones and sceptres,
7:8, I preferred her before sceptres
and thrones, and
18:15, words leapd from heaven out of
thy royal throne
Eccl. 1:8, There is one wise...sitting upon his
throne
10:14, The Lord hath cast down the thrones
of proud princes,
24:4, I dwelt in high places, and thy throne
is a cloudy
40:3, from him that sitteth on a throne of
glory,
47:11, The Lord took away his sins...and a
throne of glory in
Song-Child. 1:32, Blessed art thou on the glorious
throne of thy
I Macc. 2:57, David for being merciful possessed
the throne of
7:4, Now when Demetrius was on the throne
of his kingdom
10:52, and I am set in the throne of my
progenitors

I Macc. 10:53, for after...we sit in the throne
              of his kingdom
        10:55, gave answer...Happy be the...throne
              of their kingdom
        11:52, So king Demetrius sat on the throne
              of his kingdom,
IV Macc. 17:18, which, also, they now stand beside
              the divine throne,

THRONG, poreia, "a walking, mode of walking"
III Macc. 5:48, forces; and...saw the dust raised
              by the throng

THUNDER, brontē, "thunder"
Eccl. 35:10, Before the thunder goeth lightning;
            and before a
      40:13, unjust shall...vanish with noise,
            like a great thunder
      43:17, The noise of the thunder maketh the
            earth to tremble

      brontaō, "to thunder"
Eccl. 46:17, And the Lord thundered from heaven,
            and with a great

TIGRIS, Tigris
Judith 1:6, they that dwelt in the hill country...
            and Tigris
Eccl. 24:25, all things with his wisdom, as
            Phison and as Tigris

TIMBER, xulon, "a tree, wood, timber"
Wisd.-Sol. 13:11, Now a carpenter that felleth
                  timber, after he
Eccl. 22:16, As timber girt, and bound together
            in a building

TIMBREL, tumpanos, "with a kettle drum, a drum stick"
Judith 16:2, Begin unto my God with timbrels, sing
            unto my Lord

TIME, chronos, "time, a certain time, a period, space
              of time"
I Esd. 1:24, As for the things that came to pass in
            his time,
       8:76, For ever since the time of our fathers
            we have been
       8:79, a light...and to give us food in time
            of our servitude

      bios, "life, means of living, sustenance, sub-
            stance"
Wisd.-Sol. 2:5, For our time is a very shadow that

passeth away:

eukairos, "season, seasonable"
Eccl. 18:22, Let nothing hinder thee to pay thy
vow in due time,

kairos, "due measure, right season"
Eccl. 18:24, wrath that shall be at the end, and
the time of
18:25, When thou hast enough, remember the
time of hunger:
18:26, From the morning until the evening
the time is
19:9, For he heard and observed thee, when
time cometh he
22:6, and correction of wisdom are never
out of time
22:16, As time girt and bound...so...
council shall fear at no time
29:5, Till he hath received...he will pro-
long the time, and
32:20, the time of affliction, as cloud of
rain in the time
33:8, Make the time short, remember the
covenant, and let
35:4, not out words...and shew not forth
wisdom out of time
37:4, There is a companion, which rejoiceth
...in the time of
38:13, There is a time when in their hands
there is no good
39:17, For at time convenient they shall
all be sought out:
39:31, and when their time is come, they
shall not go
39:34, So that a man cannot say...for in
no time they shall
40:5, Wrath and envy...in the time of rest
upon his bed his
40:24, Brethren and help are against time
of trouble:
43:6, the moon also to serve...for a declar-
ation of times,
44:7, in their generations, and were the
glory of their times
44:17, found perfect and righteous: in the
time of wrath

hēmera, "day, the light of day"
Eccl. 47:1, after him rose up Nathan to prophesy

                    in the time of

kairos
Eccl. 47:10, and set in order the solemn times
            until the end,
      48:10, who wast ordained for reproofs in
            their times, to
      49:3, his heart unto the Lord, and in the
            time of the
      50:8, the branches of the frankincense tree
            in the time of
      50:24, his mercy with us, and deliver us at
            his time!
      51:10, I called upon the Lord...and in the
            time of the proud
      51:12, savest me from destruction, and...
            from the evil time
      51:30, Work your work betimes, and in his
            time he will give
Bar. 3:5, forefathers; but think upon...thy name
            at this time

chronos
Bar. 4:35, and shall be inhabited of devils for
            a great time

kairos
Song-Child. 1:14, Neither is there at this time,
                  prince or
His.-Sus. 1:14, gone out...they appointed they
                a time both
I Macc. 2:25, the king's commissioner...he killed
            at this time,

hēmera
I Macc. 2:49, Now when the time drew near that
            Mattathias should

genea, "a generation, descendant"
I Macc. 2:51, to remembrance what acts our fathers
            did in...time;

kairos
I Macc. 2:53, Joseph in the time of his distress
            kept the
      4:54, At what time and day the heathen
            had profaned it,
      4:60, At that time also they builded up
            the mount Sion

hēmera
I Macc. 5:55, Now what time as Judas and Jonathan

were in the land
I Macc. 5:67, At that time certain priests,
          desirous to shew

kairos
I Macc. 8:25, people of the Jews shall help them,
          as the time
      9:7, his host slipt away, he had not
          time to gether them
      9:10, Then Judas said, God forbid...if our
          time is come,
      9:56, And as he began to pull down, even
          at that time was
      10:41, overplus, which the officers paid...
          in former time,
      12:1, Now when Jonathan saw that the time
          served him, he
      12:10, for there is a long time passed
          since ye sent unto
      12:11, We therefore at times without ceas-
          ing, both in our
      13:5, far from me...spare mine own life in
          any time of

hēmera
I Macc. 14:36, For in his time things prospered
          in his hands, so

kairos
II Macc. 5:1, About the same time Antiochus pre-
          pared his second

chronos
III Macc. 4:17, At the end of the above mentioned
          interval of time

kairos
IV Macc. 1:10, with their mother at this time in
          behalf of
      6:20, be disgraceful if we should live
          on some short time

chronos
IV Macc. 13:19, In which these brothers having
          remained an equal time, and
          having been

TIMOTHEUS, Timotheon
I Macc. 5:6, passed over the children of Ammon...
          with Timotheus
      5:11, and they are preparing to come...
          Timotheus being

```
    I Macc. 5:34, Then the host of Timotheus, knowing
                  that it was
            5:37, After these things, gathered
                  Timotheus another host
            5:40, Then Timotheus said unto the captains
                  of his host,
   II Macc. 8:30, Moreover of those that were with
                  Timotheus and
            8:32, They also slew Philarches...who
                  was with Timotheus,
             9:3, was brought him what had happened
                  unto...Timotheus
           10:24, Now Timotheus, whom the Jews had
                  overcome before,
           10:32, As for Timotheus himself, he fled
                  into a very
           12:2, But of the governors...Timotheus and
                  Apollonius the
           12:10, in their journey toward Timotheus,
                  no fewer
           12:18, But as for Timotheus, they found
                  him not in the
           12:19, Dositheus and Sosipater...slew
                  those that Timotheus
           12:20, ranged his army by bands...and went
                  against Timotheus,
           12:21, Now when Timotheus had knowledge
                  of Judas'coming,
           12:24, Moreover Timotheus himself fell
                  into the hands of
```

TITANS, Titanōn
```
    Judith 16:7, did not fall...neither did the sons
                 of the Titans
```

TITHE, dekatos, "the tenth part, tithe"
```
    Eccl. 32:9, cheerful countenance, and dedicate thy
                tithes with
    I Macc. 3:49, brought also the priest's garments
                  ...and the tithes:
           11:35, things that belong unto us, of the
                  tithes and
```

TOBIAS, Tobias
```
    Tobit 2:1, my wife Anna was restored...with my
               son Tobias,
          5:7, Then Tobias said unto him, Tarry for me,
               till I tell
          5:16, So they were well pleased. Then said
```

                    he to Tobias,
    Tobit 6:17, Now when Tobias had heard these things,
                    he loved her,
        7:5, And they said...and Tobias said, He is
                    my father
        8:1, And when they had supped, they brought
                    Tobias in unto
        8:4, And after that...Tobias rose up out of
                    the bed, and
        9:6, And early in the morning...Tobias
                    blessed his wife
       10:7, Hold thy peace...and she...bewail her
                    son Tobias
       10:10, After these things Tobias went his way
                    praising God
       11:1, Then Raphael said to Tobias, Dost thou
                    not know...?
       11:15, hast scourged...for, behold, I see my
                    son Tobias
       12:1, Then Tobit called his son Tobias, and
                    said unto him,
       14:12, But Tobias departed with his wife and
                    children to
    II Macc. 3:11, some of it belonged to Hircanus son
                    of Tobias, a

TOBIE, Tobie
    I Macc. 5:13, yea, all our brethren were in the
                    places of Tobie

TOBIT, Tobit
    Tobit 5:10, Then Tobit said unto him, Brother shew
                    me of what
        5:11, Then Tobit said unto him, I would know,
                    brother, thy
        5:13, Then Tobit said, Thou art welcome,
                    brother:
        5:20, Then said Tobit to her, Take no care,
                    my sister;
        7:2, to Edna...How like is the young man to
                    Tobit my cousin?
        7:4, Then said he to them, Do you know Tobit
                    our kinsman?
       10:2, Then Tobit said, Are they detained?
                    or is Gabael dead
       10:6, To whom Tobit said, Hold thy peace,
                    take no care,
       11:10, Tobit also went forth toward the door,
                    and stumbled:

Tobit 11:16, Then Tobit went out to meet his daugh-
    ter in law at
11:17, But Tobit gave thanks before them,
    because...had mercy
12:1, Then Tobit called his son Tobias, and
    said unto him,
13:1, Then Tobit wrote a prayer of rejoicing
    and said,
14:1, So Tobit made an end of praising God
14:13, he inherited their substance, and
    his father Tobit's

TOMB, épitaphios, "on or over a tomb"
Eccl. 21:8, like one that gathereth himself stones
    for the tomb
IV Macc. 17:8, a worthy thing to have inscribed
    upon the tomb

TONGUE, glōssa, "a tongue, language or dialect"
Judith 3:8, and that all their tongues and should
    call upon him
Wisd.-Sol. 1:6, loving spirit...for God is...a
    hearer of his tongue
    1:11, Therefore...refrain thy tongue
    from backbiting:

    siagon, "the jawbone, cheek"
Wisd.-Sol. 8:12, When I hold my tongue, they shall
    bide my

    glōssa
Eccl. 4:24, wisdom shall be known: and learning by
    ...the tongue
    4:29, Be not hasty in thy tongue, and in thy
    deeds slack
    6:1, become not an enemy...that hath a double
    tongue
    8:3, Strive not with a man that is full of
    tongue, and heap
    9:18, A man of ill tongue is dangerous in his
    city;
    17:6, Counsel, and a tongue, and eyes, ears,
    and a heart,
    19:16, in his speech...and...offended with his
    tongue
    19:31, reproof that is not comely...some man
    holdeth his tongue
    20:6, Some man holdeth his tongue, because he
    hath not to
    20:7, A wise man holdeth his tongue till he
    see opportunity:

Eccl. 20:18, upon a pavement is better than to
            slip with the tongue
       25:7, have judged...the tenth I will utter
            with my tongue:
       25:8, with a wife...that hath not slipped his
            tongue,
       26:6, But a grief of heart...and a scourge
            of the tongue
       28:14, A backbiting tongue has disquieted
            many, and driven
       28:15, A backbiting tongue hath cast out
            virtuous women,
       28:18, edge of the sword; but not so many...
            by the tongue
       35:8, thy speech be short...be as one that
            ...holdeth his tongue
       36:23, If there be kindness...in her tongue,
            then is not her
       37:18, Four manners of things appear...but
            the tongue
       40:21, the psaltery make sweet melody: but
            a pleasant tongue is above them both
       51:2, preserved my body...from the snare of
            the slanderous tongue
       51:5, of the belly of hell, from an unclean
            tongue, and
       51:6, from an unrighteous tongue my soul drew
            near...unto
       51:22, The Lord hath given me a tongue for my
            reward, and I
Epis.-Jer. 1:8, As for their tongue, it is polished
            by the
II Macc. 7:4, being heated, he commanded to cut
            out the tongue,
         7:10, and when he was required to put out
            his tongue
        15:36, the...twelfth month, which in the
            Syrian tongue
III Macc. 6:4, Pharaoh, with...hardihood and loud-
            sounding tongue

       glōtta (Attic, in Attic Greek for glossa),
            "tongue"
IV Macc. 10:17, When he had said this...Antiochus
            ordered his tongue to be cut out
         10:19, Behold, my tongue is extended, cut
            it off;
         10:21, God shall...find you, since you cut
            off the tongue

phonē, "a sound, tone, language"
IV Macc. 12:7, his mother had urged him on in
              the Hebrew tongue,
        16:15, and saidst to thy sons in the
              Hebrew tongue

    glōssa
IV Macc. 18:21, the balls of their eyes, and cut
              out their tongues

TORMENT, basanos, "the touch-stone, torture, anguish,
              disease"
Wisd.-Sol. 3:1, in the hand of God, and there shall
              be no torment

    basanizō, "to try, to convict, to put to
              torture"
Wisd.-Sol. 11:9, ungodly were judged in wrath and
              tormented,
         12:23, Wherefore...thou hast tormented
              them with their
         17:13, And the expectation from within
              ...bringeth torment

    basanos
Wisd.-Sol. 19:4, this end...which was wanting to
              their torment

    basanizō
Eccl. 4:17, she will walk with him...and torment
              him with her

    basanos
Eccl. 30:26, yoke and a collar do bow the neck; so
              are the tortures
I Macc. 9:56, So Alcimus died at that time with
              great torment
II Macc. 7:8, Wherefore he also received the next
              torment in
        7:13, Now when this man was dead also,
              they tormented
        7:17, but abide awhile, and behold...how
              he will torment

    temnō, "to cut, to wound, maim, slaughter,
              sacrifice"
II Macc. 7:37, that thou by torments and plagues
              mayest confess,

    basanos
II Macc. 9:6, and that most justly: for he had tor-
              mented other

                        379

IV Macc. 6:30, noble as his torments, and even to
         the agonies

basanizō
IV Macc. 8:1, Then, indeed...he commanded...to
         torment them more

basanos
IV Macc. 9:18, For through all my torments I will
          convince you
        10:11, But thou...shalt endure indissoluble
          torments
        11:1, And when he had died, disfigured in
          his torments,
        11:2, to get accused from the torment
          which is in behalf
        11:6, But this is worthy of honours, not
          torments;
        11:16, So that if thou think proper to
          torment us for not

basanizō
IV Macc. 11:20, And he, while tormented, said, O
          period good and
        12:4, Thou seest the end of the...miser-
          ably tormented,

basanos
IV Macc. 12:12, divine vengeance is reserving you
          for...torments
        13:15, trial of soul and danger of eternal
          torment laid
        14:8, around the number seven, annulled
          the fear of torments.
        14:11, wonderful that...those men in
          their torments,
        15:18, first-born...looking miserable
          in his torments:
        15:21, do siren melodies...in the midst
          of torments!
        15:22, With what and what manner of tor-
          ments was the
        15:32, by violent storms which were the
          torments of thy
        16:1, endured to see her children's tor-
          ments even unto
        16:2, also that a woman despised the great-
          est torments
        16:15, thou stoodest looking upon Eleazar
          in torments,

IV Macc. 17:10, nation, looking unto God, and en-
                 during torments
          18:20, the seven sons...of Abraham...to
                 all his torments

TORMENTOR, demios, "the public executioner"
 II Macc. 9:29, Fear not this tormentor, but, being
                 worthy of thy

TORTURE, basanos, "torture, anguish, disease"
 Wisd.-Sol. 2:19, examine him with despitefulness
                   and torture,

          streblē, "instrument of torture"
 Eccl. 30:26, bow the neck: so are tortures and
               torments for an

          aikia, "injurious treatment, an outrage,
                 insult, blows,stripes"
 II Macc. 7:42, Let this be enough now...and the
                 extreme tortures

          basanos
 IV Macc. 5:6, I would counsel thee, old man, before
                thy tortures

          basanizō
 IV Macc. 6:5, high-minded, and truly noble, as one
                tortured in a

          aikizō, "to treat injuriously, to affront,'
                  torment, esp. by blows"
 IV Macc. 6:16, as though the advice more painfully
                 tortured him,

          basanos
 IV Macc. 6:27, I am slain for the sake of the law
                 by tortures,
           7:2, and overwhelmed with the breakers
                of tortures
          aikia
 IV Macc. 7:4, tried with the fiery trial of tor-
                tures and rackings

          basanos
 IV Macc. 7:10, O aged man of more power than tor-
                 tures, elder more
           7:16, then, an old man, through religion,
                 despised tortures even unto death
           7:24, reasoning, have conquered still more
                 bitter tortures

<u>probasanizō</u>, "to try or torture before"
IV Macc. 8:4, the madness of the old man who has
            been tortured

    <u>basanos</u>
IV Macc. 8:8, you will compel me to destroy you...
            by tortures

    <u>streblos</u>, "to wrench, dislocate; hence, to
            be racked or tortured"
IV Macc. 8:10, you not reason upon this...but to
            die in tortures?

    <u>basanismos</u>, "torturing, torture"
IV Macc. 8:11, he ordered the instruments of tor-
            ture to be
        8:18, O brethren, the instruments of tor-
            ture...?
        8:24, forward to put us to death, if we
            dread torture

    <u>basanizō</u>
IV Macc. 8:26, the young men say...when about to
            be tortured

    <u>basanos</u>
IV Macc. 9:5, us, by threatening us with death by
            tortures
        9:6, Hebrews have died...scorning your
            cruel tortures,
        9:9, But you...shall...endure eternal
            torture by fire

    <u>basanizō</u>
IV Macc. 9:27, whether he would eat before he was
            tortured
        9:30, tyrants, that thou art now tortured
            more than I...?
        9:32, But thou art tortured with threat-
            enings for

    <u>basanos</u>
IV Macc. 10:16, Invent, O tyrant, tortures; that
            you may learn,
        11:23, with me a great avenger, O deviser
            of tortures,

    <u>basanizō</u>
IV Macc. 12:4, the end of madness...for they have
            died in torture
        12:13, tongues...and having thus abused
            to torture them?

IV Macc. 13:26, And yet...were ill used for their
             religion, tortured

    basanos
IV Macc. 14:5, But all of them...hastened to death
             through tortures

    elkainō, "to be sore from a wound"
IV Macc. 15:11, the case of none of them were the
             various tortures

    basanos
IV Macc. 15:19, each of them looking sternly upon
             their tortures,

    basanizō
IV Macc. 16:3, Daniel...when she beheld her seven
             sons tortured

    basanos
IV Macc. 16:17, are younger should be afraid of
             the tortures
         17:3, bear without swaying the shock of
             tortures
         17:7, of religion various tortures even
             unto death
         17:23, to their endurance in torture pro-
             claimed
         18:21, and cut out their tongues...with
             varied tortures

TORTURER, basanistēs, "an inquisitor, tormentor,
             gaoler"
  IV Macc. 6:10, athlete, the old man...vanquished
             his torturers

    mastix, "a whip, scourge"
  IV Macc. 9:11, the torturers brought forth the
             eldest of them,

TORTURING, basanizō, "the act of torturing"
  IV Macc. 9:7, think not that thou harmest us by
             torturing us

TOWER, purgos, "a tower, a column"
  I Esd. 1:55, house of the Lord, they...set fire
             upon her towers
  Tobit 13:16, Jerusalem shall be built up with...
             walls and towers
  Judith 1:3, and set the towers thereof upon the
             gates of it, an
         1:14, his, and came upon Ecbatane, and took
             the towers,

383

Judith 7:32, the people...and they went into the
          walls and towers

   skopē, "a look-out tower, a watch-tower"
Eccl. 37:14, tell him more than seven watchmen...
          in an high tower

   purgos
I Macc. 1:33, they the city of David...with mighty
          towers, and
       4:60, builded mount Sion with high walls
          and strong towers
       5:5, He shut them up therefore in the
          towers, and
       5:65, and burned the towers thereof round
          about.

   akra, "a citadel, the end, the highest point"
I Macc. 6:18, About this time they that were in
          the tower shut up

   purgos
I Macc. 6:24, they of our nation besiege the tower,
          and are
       6:26, this day are they besieging the
          tower at Jerusalem,

   akra
I Macc. 6:32, Upon this Judas removed from the
          tower, and pitched

   purgos
I Macc. 6:37, And upon the beasts were their strong
          towers of
       9:52, Bethsura, and Gazara, and the tower,
          and put forces
       9:53, and put them into the tower at Jeru-
          salem to be kept
      10:6, gather together...the hostages that
          were in the tower
      10:7, Jerusalem...and of them that were in
          the tower:
      10:9, Whereupon they of the tower delivered
          their hostages
      10:32, And as for the tower which is at
          Jerusalem, I yield
      11:20, together them that were in Judea,
          to take the tower
      11:21, the king, and told him that Jonathan
          besieged the tower
      11:22, Jonathan, that he should not lay
          siege to the tower

I Macc. 11:41, Demetrius that he would cast those
of the tower

åkra
I Macc. 12:36, and raising a great mound between
the tower
13:21, Now they that were in the tower
sent messengers

purgos
I Macc. 13:33, in Judea, and fenced them about
with high towers,
13:43, camped against Gaza...and battered
a certain tower,

åkra
I Macc. 13:49, They also of the tower in Jerusalem
were kept so
13:50, to Simon...and when he had...clean-
sed the tower
13:52, that the hill of the temple that was
by the tower
14:7, together, a great number of captives
...and the tower
14:36, in the city of David...who had made
...a tower

purgos
I Macc. 16:10, So they fled even unto the towers
in the fields
II Macc. 14:41, when the multitude would have taken
the tower,

åkra
II Macc. 15:31, there...he sent for them that were
of the tower
15:35, He hanged also Nicanor's head upon
the tower, an
IV Macc. 13:6, For just as by means of towers,
projecting in
13:7, So that seven-towered right-reasoning of the young

TOWER-PORCH, purgos-stēlē, "an upright stone, grave-
stone, a boundary-post"
III Macc. 2:27, a stigma...wherefore he erected...
the tower-porch

TOWN, thugatēr, "a daughter; metaphorically, a city
or town"
I Macc. 5:8, And when he had taken Jazer, with the
towns belonging

385

I Macc. 5:65, Judas forth...in the land...where
he smote...the towns

komē, "a village, a country, a town"
I Macc. 7:46, Whereupon they came forth out of all
the towns of
II Macc. 8:1, Judas Maccabeus...went privily into
the towns,
8:6, Therefore he came at unawares, and
burnt up towns

chorios, "a place, country, land"
II Macc. 12:7, And when the town was shut up, he
went backward,
12:21, sent the women and children...for
the town was

TRAIN, paideuō, "to educate, teach, correct, to discipline"
Eccl. 30:13, Train up thy son, and exercise him
with work, lest

TRAMPLE, katapateō, "to trample down, trample under
foot"
III Macc. 2:18, We have trampled upon the holy
house, as

TRANSGRESS, parabainō, "to overstep, transgress,
offend"
I Esd. 8:24, And whosoever shall transgress the
law of thy God,
8:82, shall we say...? for we have transgressed thy
8:87, but we have turned back again and
transgress thy law
Tobit 4:5, let not thy will be set to sin, or to
transgress his
Judith 2:13, And take thou heed that thou transgress
none of the
19:24, He that hath small understanding...
and transgresseth
II Macc. 7:2, we are ready to die, rather than to
transgress the

parabainō
III Macc. 7:11, They alleged that men...transgress-
ed the ordinances
7:12, to destroy those who had transgressed the law of

paranomeō, "to transgress the law, act
illegally"

IV Macc. 5:17, we ought not in any point to transgress the law

parabainō
IV Macc. 5:29, nor will I transgress the sacred
oaths of my
9:1, Why...we are ready to die than to
transgress the
13:15, the eternal torment laid up for
those who transgress

TRANSGRESSING, empiptō, "to fall under the chastisement of, to fall into"
Eccl. 29:19, A wicked man transgressing the commandments of the

parabainō
IV Macc. 16:24, over-persuaded them from transgressing the

TRANSGRESSION, paranomia, "transgression of law,
habitual law-breaking"
IV Macc. 5:13, will pardon you for all your transgressions of the
5:20, For transgression of the law,
whether in small or

anomia, "lawlessness"
Pr.-Mans. 1:9, for I have sinned...My transgressions
are multiplied
1:12, sinned, Lord...I acknowledge my
transgressions
1:13, thee...destroy me not with my
transgressions

TRANSGRESSOR, parabas, "a transgressor"
Eccl. 40:14, his hand he shall rejoice: so shall
transgressors

TRANSLATED, metatithēmi,"to translate of the world,
transport"
Wisd.-Sol. 4:10, so that living among sinners he
was translated
Eccl. 44:16, Enoch pleased the Lord, and was translated, being an
II Macc. 11:23, Since our father is translated unto
the gods, our

TRAP, pagis, "a snare, a trap, gin"
Eccl. 27:26, shall fall therein: and he that set-
teth a trap

TRAVAIL, ōdis,"the throe of a woman, birth-pang"

Eccl. 31:5, and the heart fancieth, as a woman
    in travail

    áscholia, "occupation, a hindrance from other
        things"
Eccl. 40:1, Great travail is created for every
    man, and an heavy

    éphodos, "a way towards, approach, attack"
I Macc. 9:68, for his counsel and travail was in
    vain

TRAVEL, poreuomai, "to convey, transport, travel"
Eccl. 8:15, Travel not by the way with a bold
    fellow, lest he

    apoplazō,"to go astray, be driven off"
Eccl. 31:11, When I travelled, I saw many things;

    poreuomai
I Macc. 5:24, Judas Maccabeus also...travelled
    three days' journey

TRAVELLER, hodoiporos, "a wayfarer, foot-traveller"
Eccl. 26:12, She will open her mouth, as a thirsty
    traveller,
    42:3, of reckoning with thy partners and
    travellers;

TREASON, épiboulē, "conspiracy, plot"
II Macc. 5:7, he obtained...the reward of his trea-
    son, and fled

TREASURE, gazophulakion, "a treasury, the sacred
            treasury"
I Esd. 8:19, have also commanded the keepers of
    the treasures in

    thesauros, "a treasury, a store, treasure"
Tobit 4:9, for thou layest up a good treasure for
    thyself against
Eccl. 1:24, The parables of knowledge are in the
    treasures of

    apothesaurizō, "to lay up in store, trea-
           sure up, secure"
Eccl. 3:4, honoureth his mother, is as one that
    layeth up treasure

    thesauros, "treasure, precious deposit"
Eccl. 20:30, Wisdom that is hid, and treasure that
    is hoarded up,
    29:11, Lay up thy treasure according to
    the commandments of

Eccl. 40:18, he that findeth a treasure is above
           them both
      41:12, regard to thy name...above a thou-
           sand great treasures
      41:14, keep discipline in peace: for...a
           treasure that is
      43:14, Through this the treasures are opened:
           and clouds
Bar. 3:15, out her place? or who hath come into
           her treasures?
I Macc. 1:23, also he took the hidden treasures
           which he found

      gazophulakion
I Macc. 3:28, He opened also his treasure, and gave
           his soldiers
      3:29, when he saw that the money of his
           treasures failed,
IV Macc. 4:4, praised Simon for his care...of the
           treasure;

      chrēma, "goods, money, business transac-
           tion"
IV Macc. 4:10, with his armed force to the seizure
           of the treasure

TREASURER, gazophulakēs, "a treasurer"
I Esd. 2:11, delivered them to Mithridates his
           treasurer:

TREASURY, gazophulakios, "a treasury"
I Esd. 8:18, thou shalt give it out of the king's
           treasury
      8:45, I bade them...who was in the place
           of the treasury
I Macc. 14:49, copies thereof should be laid up in
           the treasury,

      chrēma
II Macc. 3:6, and told him that the treasury in
           Jerusalem was

      gazophulakion
II Macc. 3:24, present himself with his guard about
           the treasury,
      3:28, train...with...his guard into the
           said treasury,
      3:40, concerning Heliodorus, and the keep-
           ing of the treasury
      4:42, wounded...him they killed beside
           the treasury

II Macc. 5:18, sins...this man the king sent to
          view the treasury
IV Macc. 4:3, good will...wealth is laid up in
          the treasuries of

TREE, xulon, "wood, timber, a tree"
I Esd. 6:32, thou...out of his own house, should
          a tree be taken,
Eccl. 6:3, thy leaves...and leave thyself as a
          dry tree

     dendron, "an olive tree, a fruit-tree"
Eccl. 14:18, As of the green leaves on a thick tree,
          some fall,

     xulon
Eccl. 27:6, The fruit declareth if the tree have
          been dressed; so

     élaia, "the olive tree"
Eccl. 50:10, and as a fair olive tree budding
          forth fruit, and as

     stelechos, "the crown of the root, the stump"
Eccl. 50:12, the robe of honour...he himself stood
          ...as palm trees

     xulon
Bar. 5:8, even the woods and every sweetsmelling
          tree shall

     schinos, "mastick tree"
His.-Sus. 1:54, Now then...Under what tree sawest
          thou them...And

     dendron
His.-Sus. 1:58, Under what tree didst thou take
          them companying

     xulon
I Macc. 10:30, unto me...and the half of the fruit
          of the trees

     ákrodrua, "a fruit tree"
I Macc. 11:34, received...the fruits of the earth
          and of the trees

     xulon
I Macc. 14:8, and the earth gave her increase and
          the trees of

     dendron
IV Macc. 14:16, Others build their nests...in the
          tops...of trees,

xulon
IV Macc. 18:16, He is a tree of life to all those
who do his will

TREMBLE, odinō, "to have the throes of childbirth,
travail"
Eccl. 43:17, The noise of the thunder maketh the
earth to tremble

tremeō, "to tremble, quake, quiver"
I Macc. 2:24, Which thing, when Mattathias saw...
his reins trembled

TREMBLING, tromos, "trembling"
Eccl. 16:19, The mountains also...shall be shaken
with trembling
I Macc. 13:2, and saw that the people was in great
trembling

TRIAL, diaginoskō, "to distinguish, examine, inquire
into judicially"
Wisd.-Sol. 3:18, quickly, they have no hope...in
the day of trial

exetazō, "to inquire, examine, to interrogate"
Wisd.-Sol. 4:6, witnesses...against their parents
in their trial

dokimē, "proof, trial"
Eccl. 6:21, She will lie upon him like a mighty
stone of trial

dokimazō, "to prove, try, examine, test"
Eccl. 27:5, The furnace proveth...so the trial of
man is in his

pierasmos, "proof, trial, a putting to the
proof"
Eccl. 27:7, thou hearest him speak; for this is
the trial of men

kindunos, "danger, peril"
IV Macc. 13:15, for great is the trial of soul
and danger of

TRIBE, phulē, "a tribe, a clan or caste"
I Esd. 5:1, After this were the principal men of...
their tribes
5:4, And these are the names of...their
tribes

phularchon, "chief of the tribe"
I Esd. 7:8, of all Israel according to...the chief
of the tribes

phulē

I Esd. 9:5, And in three days were all they of the
            tribe of Juda
Tobit 1:1, book of the words of Tobit...of the
            tribe of Nephthali
      1:4, And when I was in my own country...all
            the tribes of
      1:5, Now all the tribes which together re-
            volted, and the
      4:12, a strange woman...which is not of thy
            father's tribe
      5:8, Call him unto me, that I may know of
            what tribe he is,
Judith 3:8, he...decreed...that all...that all ton-
            gues and tribes
      8:2, Manasses was her husband, of her tribe
            and kindred,
      8:18, now in these days, neither tribe, nor
            family, nor
      9:14, And make every nation and tribe to
            acknowledge that
Eccl. 33:11, Gather all the tribes of Jacob toge-
            ther
      44:23, gave him an heritage...among the
            twelve tribes
      45:6, like unto him, even his brother, of
            the tribe of Levi
      45:11, after the number of the tribes of
            Israel.
      45:25, made with David son of Jesse, of the
            tribe of Juda
      48:10, reproofs in their times...to restore
            the tribes of
II Macc. 3:4, But one Simon of the tribe of Benja-
            min, who was

TRIBULATION, suntrimma, "tribulation"
  Eccl. 40:9, Death, and bloodshed...tribulation
            and the scourge

            thlipsis, "pressure,compression, afflic-
            tion"
  I Macc. 6:11, I thought with myself, Into what
            tribulation am I

TRIBUNE, chiliarchos, "a legionary tribune"
  Judith 14:12, Assyrians saw them, they sent the...
            captains and tribunes
  I Macc. 16:19, also to Gazara to kill John: and
            unto the tribunes

TRIBUTARY, phoron, "that which is brought in"
  I Macc. 1:4, gathered a mighty strong host...who
          became tributaries

TRIBUTE, phoros, "tribute, tax"
  I Esd. 2:19, the walls thereof be made up again...
          give tribute
      4:6, no soldiers...compel one another to
          pay tribute

      aphilarguros, "not fond of money, not covet-
             ous"
  I Esd. 4:50, all the country...should be free with-
          out tribute:

      phorologos, "collector of tribute, tribute"
  I Macc. 1:29, the king sent his chief collector
          of tribute unto
      3:29, Nevertheless when he saw...that the
          tributes in the

      phoros
  I Macc. 3:31, Wherefore...take the tributes of
          the countries, and
      8:2, were men of great valour...brought...
          under tribute
      8:4, by their policy...the rest did give
          them tribute
      8:7, him alive...that he...should pay a
          great tribute
     10:29, And now do I free you...from tributes,
          and from

      telos, "an end, that which is paid to the
          state, tax"
  I Macc. 10:31, Jerusalem also be holy and free...
          from...tributes

      dorea, "a present, gift"
  I Macc. 10:33, I will that all my officers remit
          the tributes

      aphologetos, "without paying tributes"
  I Macc. 11:28, that he would make Judea free from
          tribute

      telones, "customs or taxes of a state"
  I Macc. 13:39, As for...any other tribute paid in
          Jerusalem, it

      phoros
  I Macc. 15:30, Now therefore deliver...the tributes
          of the places

II Macc. 8:10, So Nicanor undertook to...defray
      the tribute of two

TRIED, peirazō, "to tempt, to make proof of, an
      attempt"
IV Macc. 15:16, O thou mother, who wast tried at
      this time with

TRIPOLIS, Tripolis
II Macc. 14:1, years...Demetrius...entered by the
      haven of Tripolis

TROOP, parataxis, "an army in array"
I Esd. 2:30, removing in haste toward Jerusalem
      with a troop

     meros, "division, a part, portion"
I Macc. 9:11, the host...stood...being divided into
      two troops,

     hilē, "a troop of horses, company, squadron"
II Macc. 5:3, and troops of horsemen in array,
      encountering and

     strateuma, "troops, an army, corps, armed
      force"
IV Macc. 5:1, The tyrant Antiochus...with his armed
      troops standing

TROUBLE, thlipsis, "affliction, trial, pressure"
I Macc. 5:16, heard these words...their brethren...
      were in trouble

     kakos, "misery, evil, suffering, trouble"
I Macc. 6:13, perceive therefore that for this
      cause these troubles are come

     thlipsis
I Macc. 12:13, As for ourselves, we have had great
      troubles and

     ponēra, "wickedness, mischief, bad condi-
      tion"
II Macc. 1:5, prayers...and never forsake you in
      time of trouble

     thlipsis
II Macc. 1:7, What time Demetrius reigned...the
      extremity of trouble that came upon
      us

     kakos
II Macc. 2:18, he hath delivered us out of great
      troubles

taraché, "agitating, troubling, tumult"
II Macc. 3:30, which a little afore was full of
           fear and trouble,
      10:30, that being confounded...and full
             of trouble, they

ponos, "misery, anguish, pain"
IV Macc. 13:1, If then, the seven brethren despised
            troubles even
        13:4, impossible to overlook both passions
              and troubles

chalepainō, "to deal severely, harshly,
            grievous"
IV Macc. 16:22, having the same faith towards God,
             be not troubled

ponos
IV Macc. 16:23, unreasonable...not to stand up
             against troubles

TRUMPET, salpigx, "war-trumpet, signal by trumpet,
                  a trumpet"
I Esd. 5:59, stood arrayed...with musical instru-
           ments and trumpets
       5:64, But many with trumpets and joy shouted
             with loud
       5:65, insomuch that the trumpets might not
             be heard for
       5:66, enemies...knew what the noise of
             trumpets should mean
Eccl. 50:16, sons of Aaron, and sounded the silver
           trumpets, and
I Macc. 3:4, Then sounded they with trumpets, and
           cried with a
       4:13, they that were with Judas sounded
             their trumpets
       4:40, and fell down...and blew an alarm
             with the trumpets,
       5:31, the cry of the city went up to hea-
             ven with trumpets
       5:33, forth behind them...who sounded
             their trumpets, and
       6:33, rising very early marched...and
             sounded the trumpets
       7:45, sounding an alarm after them with
             their trumpets
       9:12, the hosts drew near...and shounded
             their trumpets,
       9:13, They also of Judas' side...sounded

395

                                   their trumpets
II Macc. 15:25, were with him came forward with
                   trumpets and

TRUTH, alḗtheia, "truth, frankness, sincerity"
 I Esd. 3:12, Truth beareth away the victory
          4:13, who had spoken of women, and of the
                 truth...began to
          4:35, Is he not great...? therefore great
                 is the truth and
          4:37, women are wicked...and there is no
                 truth in them:
          4:38, As for the truth, it endureth, and
                 is always strong,
          4:40, Blessed be the God of truth
          4:41, all the people then shouted...Great
                 is Truth, and
 Tobit 1:3, all the days of my life in the way of
                 truth and
          3:2, art just...and all thy ways are mercy
                 and truth, and
          7:10, is meet that...I will declare unto
                 thee the truth
         14:7, praise the Lord...and all those which
                 love...truth
 Judith 5:5, I will declare unto thee the truth
                 concerning this
 Wisd.-Sol. 3:9, their trust in him shall understand
                 the truth:
          6:22, of her...will not pass over the
                 truth
 Eccl. 1:30, because thou camest not in truth to
                 the fear of the
          4:25, In no wise speak against the truth;
                 but be abashed of
          4:28, Strive for the truth unto death, and
                 the Lord shall
         11:7, Blame not before thou hast examined the
                 truth:
         27:9, their like: so will truth return unto
                 them that
         31:4, Of...from that thing which is false
                 what truth can come
         37:15, the most High that he will direct thy
                 way in truth
         45:10, breast-plate of judgment, with the
                 revealers of truth
 Song-Child. 1:3, thou art righteous...and all thy

                              judgments truth
Song-Child. 1:4, In all thins...truth and judgment
                              didst thou
I Macc. 7:18, Wherefore...there is neither truth
                              nor righteousness
II Macc. 7:6, The Lord God looketh upon us, and
                              in truth hath

    ʾalēthēs, "true, sincere, truthful, honest"
IV Macc. 5:9, acting...if you follow vain conceits
                              about the truth
              5:11, Will you not awake...and...search
                              into the truth of
              6:18, if having lived up to old age in
                              all truth,

TRYPHON, Truphōn
I Macc. 11:39, Moreover there was one Tryphon, that
                              had been of
              11:54, After this returned Tryphon, and
                              with him the
              11:56, Moreover Tryphon took the elephants
                              and won Antioch
              12:39, Now Tryphon went about to get the
                              kingdom of Asia,
              12:42, Now when Tryphon saw that Jonathan
                              came with so
              12:49, Then sent Tryphon an host of foot-
                              men and horsemen
              13:1, Now when Simon heard that Tryphon
                              had gathered
              13:12, So Tryphon removed from Ptolemais
                              with a great
              13:14, Now when Tryphon knew that Simon
                              was risen up
              13:20, And after this came Tryphon to in-
                              vade the land,
              13:21, were in the tower sent messengers
                              unto Tryphon,
              13:22, Wherefore Tryphon made ready all
                              his horsemen to
              13:24, Afterward Tryphon returned and went
                              into his own
              13:31, Now Tryphon dealt deceitfully with
                              the young king
              13:34, Moreover Simon chose men...because
                              all that Tryphon
              14:1, his forces together...to fight again-
                              st Tryphon

I Macc. 15:10, at which time all the forces...
          left with Tryphon
        15:25, against Dora...by which means he
          shut up Tryphon
        15:37, In the mean time fled Tryphon by
          ship into
        15:39, but as for the king himself, he
          pursued Tryphon

TUBIENI, Toubbinos
II Macc. 12:17, and came...unto the Jews that are
          called Tubieni

TUNE, mousikos, "musician, poet, poetry set and sung
          to music"
Eccl. 44:5, such as found out musical tunes, and
          recited verses,

TUNIC, chitōn, "a tunic, vest"
IV Macc. 9:11, So that...tearing through his tunic,
          bound his

TURPENTINE, terebinthos, "the terebinth or turpentine-
          tree, turpentine"
Eccl. 24:16, As the turpentine tree I stretched
          out my branches,

TWO-EDGED, distomos, "double-mouthed, two-edged,
          double"
Eccl. 21:3, All iniquity is as a two-edged sword,
          the wounds

TYRANT, turannos, "lord and master; hence, an abso-
          lute sovereign"
Wisd.-Sol. 8:15, Horrible tyrants shall be afraid
          when they do
II Macc. 4:25, mandate...having rhe fury of a
          cruel tyrant,
        7:27, herself toward him, laughing the
          cruel tyrant to
III Macc. 6:24, Ye have governed badly; and have
          exceeded tyrants
IV Macc. 5:1, The tyrant Antiochus, therefore,
          sitting in public
        5:27, But, tyrant-like, thou not only
          forcest us to
        6:1, answered the exhortations of the
          tyrant the
        6:21, and be condemned by the tyrant for
          unmanliness, by
        6:23, Ye spearbearers of the tyrant, why
          do ye linger?

IV Macc. 7:2, and flouted by the threats of the
            tyrant, and
         7:25, for when the tyrant was manifestly
            vanquished in
         8:2, The tyrant having given this charge,
            seven brethren
         8:3, Whom, when the tyrant beheld, en-
            circling their
         8:12, and wedges, and bellows, the tyrant
            continued:
         8:14, having listened to thse words...of
            the tyrant, and
         8:27, So that as soon as the tyrant had
            ceased
         9:1, Why delayest thou, O tyrant?
         9:3, O tyrant, counsellor of law-breaking,
            do not, hating
         9:7, Make the attempt then, O tyrant;
            and if thou puttest
         9:10, When they had thus spoken, the
            tyrant was not only
         9:15, O most accursed tyrant, and enemy
            of heavenly
         9:24, nation, will punish the pestilent
            tyrant.
         9:29, sweet is every form of death...he
            said to the tyrant
         9:30, Thinkest thou not, most cruel of
            all tyrants, that
         9:32, But thou art tortured...most corrupt
            tyrant, the
         10:10, We, O accursed tyrant, suffer this
            for the sake of
         10:15, and the eternal punishment of the
            tyrant, and
         10:16, Invent, O tyrant, tortures; that
            thou may learn,
         11:2, I intend not, O tyrant, to get ex-
            cused from the
         11:12, A great favour thou bestowest upon
            us, O tyrant,
         11:13, being dead...was brought out; and
            on the tyrant
         11:21, For religious understanding, O ty-
            rant, is
         11:27, For the guards not of a tyrant but
            of a divine law
         12:2, whom the tyrant pitying, though he
            had been

IV Macc. 12:11, Impious tyrant, and most blasphe-
                mous man, wert
         15:2, were set...on the conditional pro-
                mise of a tyrant,
         16:14, hast conquered through endurance
                even a tyrant;
         17:2, with seven children didst destroy...
                the tyrant
         17:9, are buried through the violence of
                a tyrant,
         17:14, The tyrant was the opposite; and
                the world and
         17:17, The tyrant himself, and all their
                council, admired
         17:21, and that the tyrant was punished,
                and their
         17:23, For the tyrant Antiochus, looking
                to their manly
         18:5, And the tyrant Antiochus was both
                punished upon
         18:20, and yet not bitter day, when the
                bitter tyrant of

TYRIAN, Turion
Eccl. 46:18, And he destroyed the rulers of the
              Tyrians, and all

UNCIRCUMCISED, ákrobustia, "uncircumcised"
 I Macc. 1:15, and made themselves uncircumcised,
                and foosook the

               áperitmetos, "uncircumcised in respect
                             of untowardness and ob-
                             duracy"
 I Macc. 1:48, should also leave their children un-
                circumcised, and
         2:46, of Israel uncircumcised, those they
                circumcised

UNCLEAN, pseudos, "falsehood,perversion of religious
                   truth"
Eccl. 31:4, Of an unclean thing, what can be
             cleansed?

            ákathartos, "impure, unclean, lewd, foul"
Eccl. 40:15, The children of the ungodly...are as
              unclean roots
        51:5, from the depth of the belly of hell,
               from an unclean

koinos, "unclean, profane"
I Macc. 1:47, and groves...and sacrifice swine's
flesh, and unclean
1:62, resolved...in themselves, not to eat
any unclean
4:43, bare out the defiled stones into an
unclean place

miarophagein, "to eat things defiled with
blood"
IV Macc. 5:19, Think not eating the unclean, then,
a trifling
5:25, Wherefore it is that we eat not the
unclean:
7:25, for when the tyrant...force the old
man to eat the unclean thing
8:1, Then...if they would eat of the unclean thing, to
8:11, fear might prevail upon them to eat
unclean meat
8:27, tyrant had ceased counselling to eat
the unclean,
11:25, our reasoning, and to compel us to
eat the unclean

UNCLEANNESS, akathartos, "uncleanness, impure, un-
purified"
I Esd. 1:42, recorded of him, and of his uncleanness and impiety
8:83, the land...is a land polluted...with
their uncleanness
8:57, mingle ourselves with the uncleanness
of the nations

aselgeia, "intemperance, insolence,
lasciviousness"
Wisd.-Sol. 14:26, in marriages...and shameless
uncleanness

akathartos
I Macc. 1:48, leave their children...with all manner of uncleanness
13:48, Yea, he put all uncleanness out of
it, and placed
14:7, number...out of which he took all uncleanness,

koinos, "profane, ceremonially unclean"
III Macc. 2:17, Punish us not by means of the uncleanness of

401

UNCONQUERED, ánikētos, "unconquered, unconquerable"
IV Macc. 11:27, through this we keep our reasoning
           unconquered

UNDEFILED, ámiantos, "undefiled, pure"
Wisd.-Sol. 4:2, having gotten the victory, striving
           for undefiled
        8:20, rather, being good, I came into
           a body undefiled

UNDERMINED, huponoeo, "to think covertly, suspect,
                         conjecture"
II Macc. 4:26, Then Jason, who had undermined his
           own brother, being undermined by
           another,

UNDERSTANDING, sunēsis, "the faculty of apprehension,
                      intelligence, judgment"
Eccl. 3:13, And if his understanding fail, have
           patience with him
       6:33, If thou love to hear, thou shalt re-
           ceive understanding
       6:36, And if thou seest a man of understand-
           ing, get thee be
       8:9, the elders...and...thou shalt learn
           understanding
    10:23, to despise the poor man that hath under-
           standing;
    14:21, considereth her ways....shall have
           understanding
    15:3, With the bread of understanding shall
           she feed him,
    16:4, For by one that hath understanding shall
           the city be
    16:23, He that wanteth understanding will
           think upon vain
    17:7, filled them with the knowledge of
           understanding, and
    18:28, Every man of understanding knoweth
           wisdom, and will
    18:29, They that had understanding in sayings
           become also
    19:29, known by his look, and one that hath
           understanding

           phronismos, "understanding, sensible,
                     prudent"
Eccl. 20:27, to honour...and he that hath under-
           standing will please

noēma, "understanding, thought, design"
Eccl. 21:7, An eloquent man is known...but a man
of understanding

ennoeō, "to understand, to plan, devise, ponder"
Eccl. 21:11, that keepeth the law of the Lord get-
teth understanding

sunēsis
Eccl. 21:15, but when one of no understanding
heareth it,

phronismos
Eccl. 21:25, lips of talkers will be telling such...
understanding

sunēsis
Eccl. 22:13, and go not to him that hath no understanding
22:15, are easier to bear, than a man without
understanding
22:17, A heart settled upon a thought of understanding is as
24:26, He maketh the understanding to abound
25:5, the wisdom of old men, and understanding and counsel
25:8, is he that dwelleth with a wife of
understanding, and
26:28, There be two things...men of understanding that are
27:12, the indiscreet, observe...men of
understanding

phronesis, "thought-fulness, good
sense, wisdom"
Eccl. 29:28, These things are grievous to a man of
understanding:

asunesis, "want of understanding or
apprehension"
Eccl. 31:1, The hopes of a man void of understanding are vain and

sunetos, "quick at apprehending, intelligent, sagacious"
Eccl. 36:3, A man of understanding trusteth in the
law;

sunēsis
Eccl. 37:23, his people; and the fruits of his
understanding fail

403

Eccl. 39:6, he shall be filled with the spirit
            of understanding
       39:9, Many shall commend his understanding;
       47:14, youth, and as a flood,filled with
            understanding
       47:23, and...left behind him...one that had
            no understanding
       50:27, of Jerusalem hath...the instruction
            of understanding
Bar. 3:14, wisdom, where is strength, and where
            is understanding;
      3:23, seek wisdom...and searchers out of
            understanding;
      3:32, things...hath found her out with his
            understanding

            dianoia, "the mind, imagination, in-
                  sight, comprehension"
IV Macc. 11:14, younger than my brothers, but in
            understanding I

UNGODLINESS, dussebēs, "ungodly, impious"
  I Esd. 1:52, he being wroth with his people for
            their...ungodliness

UNGODLY, asebēs, "wickedly, ungodly, sinful"
  Wisd.-Sol. 1:9, shall be made into the counsels of
            the ungodly:
       1:16, but ungodly men with their works
            and words called
       3:10, But the ungodly shall be punished
            according to
       4:3, But the multiplying brood of the
            ungodly shall
       4:16, that is dead shall condemn the
            ungodly which are
       10:16, When the ungodly perished, she
            delivered the
       10:20, Therefore the righteous spoil the
            ungodly, and
       11:9, For when they were tried...they
            ...how the ungodly
       12:9, Not that thou wast able to bring
            the ungodly
       14:9, For the ungodly and his ungodli-
            ness are both
       14:16, Thus in a process of time an un-
            godly custom
       14:31, that punish always the offence of
            the ungodly

Wisd.-Sol. 16:16, For the ungodly, that denied to
                       know thee,were
              16:18, the flame was mitigated...again-
                       st the ungodly
              19:1, As for the ungodly, wrath came
                       upon them without
Eccl. 7:17, For the vengeance of the ungodly is
                       fire and worms
        9:12, Delight not in the thing that the un-
                       godly have
       12:5, unto him that is lowly, but give not to
                       the ungodly:
       16:1, unprofitable children, neither delight
                       in ungodly sons
       16:3, without children, than to have them
                       that are ungodly
       16:6, In the congregation of the ungodly shall
                       a fire be
       21:27, When the ungodly curseth Satan, he
                       curseth his own
       22:12, do men mourn...but for a fool and an
                       ungodly man all
       40:15, The children of the ungodly shall not
                       bring forth
       41:5, sinners are...conversant in the dwelling
                       of the ungodly
       41:7, The children will complain of an ungodly
                       father,
       41:8, Who be unto you, ungodly men, which have
                       forsaken the
       41:10, All...the ungodly shall go from a curse
                       to destruction
       42:2, most High, and...of judgment to justify
                       the ungodly
       49:3, unto the Lord, and in the time of the
                       ungodly he
Bar. 2:12, O Lord our God...we have done ungodly,
                       we have dealt
I Macc. 3:8, went through the cities...destroying
                       the ungodly
        3:15, there went with him a mighty host
                       of the ungodly to
        6:21, Howbeit certain of them...whom some
                       ungodly men of
        7:5, there came unto him all the wicked and
                       ungodly men
        9:58, Then all the ungodly men held a coun-
                       cil, saying,

I Macc. 9:73, from Israel: but Jonathan...de-
          stroyed the ungodly

     miseō, "to regard with less affection, to hate"
I Macc. 11:21, The certain ungodly persons...went
          unto the king,

UNHOLY, mierophagō, "to eat that which is defiled,
          polluted, abominable"
IV Macc. 13:2, as slaves to the passions eaten of
          of the unholy,

UNJUST, ádikos, "unjust, unrighteous, vicious"
Wisd.-Sol. 16:19, time, it burneth...the fruits
          of an unjust land
Eccl. 31:18, He that sacrificeth...the gifts of
          unjust men are not
     40:13, The goods of the unjust shall be dried
          up like a
     41:18, before a judge...of unjust dealing
          with thy partner
Song-Child. 1:8, And thou didst deliver us...to an
          unjust king,
II Macc. 4:35, were much grieved for the unjust
          murder of the man
     4:48, that followed the matter...did soon
          suffer unjust
III Macc. 6:27, Loose, loose the unjust bonds; send
          them to their

UNJUSTLY, ánomos, "wicked, lawless, violating law"
II Macc. 8:17, their eyes...the injury that they
          had unjustly done

UNLAWFUL, ánomos, "without law, impious, not subject
          to law"
Wisd.-Sol. 4:6, For the children begotten of unlaw-
          ful beds are

     paranomia, "violation of the law, trans-
          gression"
II Macc. 4:14, to be partakers of the unlawful al-
          lowance in the

     sarkophageō, "to eat flesh, devour"
II Macc. 4:14, While the tyrant excited him...to
          the unlawful

     paranomia
IV Macc. 9:4, your pity of us on the terms of un-
          lawful escape to

UNLEAVENED, azumos, "unleavened"
 I Esd. 1:10, priests and Levites, having the un-
            leavened bread,
        7:14, And they kept the feast of unleavened
            bread seven

UNMERCIFUL, aneleēmōn, "unmerciful, uncompassionate"
 Eccl. 32:18, he have smitten in sunder the loins
            of the unmerciful
        37:11, Neither consult with a woman...nor
            with an unmerciful

UNPUNISHED, athōos, "innocent, unpunished"
 II Macc. 7:19, think not thou, that...thou shalt
            escape unpunished

UNRIGHTEOUS, adikos, "unjust, unrighteous, vicious"
 I Esd. 4:36, tremble at it, and with it is no
            unrighteous thing.
 Wisd.-Sol. 1:8, Therefore he that speaketh unright-
            eous things

            paranomia, "violation of the law, trans-
                        gression"
 Wisd.-Sol. 3:16, adulterers...and the seed of an
            unrighteous bed

            adikos
 Wisd.-Sol. 3:19, For horrible is the end of the
            unrighteous
        4:16, shall condemn...the many years...
            of the unrighteous
        10:3, But the unrighteous went away from
            her in his
        16:24, against the unrighteous for their
            punishment
 Eccl. 10:8, Because of unrighteous dealings, in-
            juries, and riches
        17:20, None of their unrighteous deeds are
            hid from him,
        32:12, with gifts...and trust not to unright-
            eous sacrifice,
        32:18, neither will the Mighty be patient...
            with the unrighteous
        51:6, By an accusation to the king from an
            unrighteous

            adikia, "a wrong, offence, injustice"
 III Macc. 2:4, who didst destroy the former workers
            of unrighteous

UNRIGHTEOUSLY, ádikos, "unrighteous, unjust, doing
    wrong"
Wisd.-Sol. 12:23, men have lived dissolutely and
    unrighteously,

        ádikeō, "to do wrong, to wrong, in-
        jure"
Bar. 2:12, our God, we have sinned, we have done...
    unrighteously
UNRIGHTEOUSNESS, ádikos, "unjust, unrighteous, vi-
        cious"
I Esd. 4:37, in their unrighteousness also they
    shall perish.

        ádikia, "a wrong, offence, injustice"
Tobit 4:5, My son...follow not the ways of unright-
    eousness
   12:8, righteousness is better than much with
    unrighteousness
Eccl. 7:3, My son, sow not upon the furrows of
    unrighteousness
   17:14, And he said unto them, Beware of all
    unrighteousness;

UNWISE, áphrōn, "unwise, inconsiderate, simple"
Wisd.-Sol. 1:3, from God...when it tried, reproveth
    the unwise

        ásunetos, "void of understanding, stupid"
Eccl. 21:18, is wisdom to a fool; and the knowledge
    of the unwise

        mōros, "dull, heavy, stupid"
Eccl. 42:8, Be not ashamed to inform the unwise and
    foolish

UPBRAID, óneidizō, "reproach, report, character; dis-
    grace"
Eccl. 41:22, or to be overbusy...and after thou
    hast given, upbraid

UPBRAIDING, óneidismos, "reproach, reviling"
Eccl. 41:22, be overbusy with his maid...or of up-
    braiding speeches

UPRIGHTNESS, euthutēs, "rectitude, equity, righteous-
    ness"
Eccl. 7:6, stumblingblock in the way of thy up-
    rightness

VAIN, kenos, "empty, empty-handed, void, fruitless"
    Wisd.-Sol. 3:11, wisdom...is miserable, and their
        hope is vain,

    matēn, "fruitless, without profit, vain"
    Wisd.-Sol. 13:1, Surely vain are all men by nature,
        who are

    kenos
    Eccl. 31:1, The hopes of a man void of understand-
        ing are vain and
        31:5, Divinations, and soothsayings, and
        dreams are vain:
    I Macc. 9:68, Bacchides...for his counsel and tra-
        vail was in vain
    III Macc. 6:6, three friends...of their own will...
        serve vain

    matēn
    III Macc. 6:11, Let not the vain-minded congratu-
        late vain idols

    kenodoxos, "vain-glorious, desirous of vain-
        glory"
    IV Macc. 5:9, I think, still more senseless, if you
        follow vain

    kenos
    IV Macc. 8:17, Why do we cheer ourselves with
        vain counsels, and

VAIN-GLORY, kenodoxos, "vain-glorious, desirous of
        vain-glory"
    IV Macc. 8:23, Let us not oppose necessity, nor
        seek vain-glory

VAINLY, matēn, "fruitless, vain"
    IV Macc. 16:8, Vainly, for your sakes, O sons,
        have I endured

VAIN-MINDED, mataios, "vain, ineffective, deceptive"
    III Macc. 6:11, Let not the vain-minded congratu-
        late vain idols

VALIANT, andreia, "manliness, courage, manly spirit"
    Wisd.-Sol. 8:15, found good among the multitude,
        and valiant in

    krataios, "mighty, strong, resistless"
    Eccl. 46:1, Jesus the son of Nave was valiant in
        the wars, and

andreia
I Macc. 2:64, Wherefore, ye my sons, be valiant,
and shew

dunatos, "strong, mighty, powerful"
I Macc. 3:58, And Judas said, Arm yourselves, and
be valiant men,

andragatheō, "to be or behave like a brave
man"
I Macc. 5:61, they were not obedient...but thought
to do some valiant act

ischus, "mighty, strong, powerful"
I Macc. 8:1, the fame of the Romans, that they were
...valiant men,

dunatos
I Macc. 9:21, How is the valiant man fallen, that
delivered Israel

karteros, "strong, staunch, brave"
IV Macc. 3:12, Wherefore his body-guards...two
valiant soldiers,

VALIANTLY, ischus, "mighty, strong, powerful, valiant,
brave"
I Macc. 2:46, children soever they found...they
circumcised valiantly

androdēs, "like a man, manly"
I Macc. 6:31, Idumea...and Bethsura...and fought
valiantly

VALLEY, aulōn, "a hollow way, a channel, strait"
Judith 7:3, And they camped in the valley near
unto Bethulia, by

pharagx, "a mountain cleft, a deep chasm,
gully, ravine"
Judith 7:4, said every one to his neighbour...for..
the valleys,

aulōn
Judith 7:17, of the children of Ammon departed...
in the valley,
10:10, And when they had done so...she
passed the valley,
10:11, Thus they went straight forth in the
valley: and

pharagx
Judith 11:17, with thee...and thy servant will go
...into the valley

Judith 13:10, And...they compassed the valley,
and went up the

hupsēlos, "highland country, towering"
I Macc. 6:40, spread upon the high mountains, and
...on the valleys

aulōn
III Macc. 6:17, uttered a loud cry...so that the
adjacent valleys

VAPOUR, atmis, "an exhalation, vapour, smoke"
Eccl. 38:28, The smith sitting also by the anvil...
the vapour of
43:4, man blowing a furnace...breathing
out fiery vapours,
II Macc. 7:5, Now...as the vapour of the pan was
for a good space

VEHEMENCE, baruthumos, "indignant, sullen"
III Macc. 6:20, the person...and...paralysed the
vehemence of his

VEHEMENT, labros, "furious, vehement, boisterous"
IV Macc. 16:3, fierce were the lions...nor the...
most vehement fire

VEIL, katapetasma, "veil, curtain"
I Macc. 1:22, the table of the shewbread...and the
veil, and the
4:51, loaves upon the table, and spread
out the veils,

VENGEANCE, ekdikēsis, "vengeance, punishment, retri-
butive justice"
Judith 8:27, in the fire...neither hath he taken
vengeance on us
8:35, Then said Ozias...Go in peace...to
take vengeance on
9:2, O Lord God of my father Simeon...take
vengeance of the
16:17, Woe to the nations that...will take
vengeance of them

dikē, "justice, judicial punishment, vengeance"
Wisd.-Sol. 1:8, cannot be hidden: neither shall
vengeance,

ekdikēsis
Eccl. 7:16, for the vengeance of the ungodly is
fire and worms

Eccl. 18:24, shall be at the end, and the time of
           vengeance, when
       27:28, and reproach are from the proud; but
           vengeance, as a
       28:1, He that revengeth shall find vengeance
           from the Lord,
       32:18, till he have...repayed vengeance to
           the heathen
       39:28, There be spirits, that are created
           for vengeance,
       46:1, Jesus the son of Nave...taking vengeance
           of the enemies
       47:25, they sought out all wickedness, till
           the vengeance
       48:7, Lord...and in Horeb the judgment of
           vengeance
I Macc. 7:9, And him he sent...that he should take
           vengeance of
       7:24, all the coasts of Judea...and took
           vengeance of them
       9:26, And they made inquiry...and took
           vengeance of them,
II Macc. 6:15, lest that...afterwards he should
           take vengeance of

           diké
II Macc. 8:11, immediately...not expecting the ven-
           geance that was
IV Macc. 4:21, At which Divine vengeance being
           grieved, instigated
       9:9, But you...from Divine vengeance,
           endure eternal
       9:32, thou shalt not escape...the vengeance
           of Divine
       10:4, Now then, whatever instrument of ven-
           geance ye have,
       11:3, you may owe heavenly vengeance a
           punishment
       12:12, Wherefore the divine vengeance is
           reserving for

VENISON, broma, "that which is eaten, food"
Eccl. 36:19, As the palate tasteth divers kinds of
           venison:

VERMILION, miltos, "red earth, red chalk, vermilion"
Wisd.-Sol. 13:14, vile beast, laying it over with
           vermilion,

VESSEL, skeuos, "a vessel"

I Esd. 1:41, Nabuchodonosor also took of the holy
            vessels of the
       1:45, sent and...brought into Babylon...
            the holy vessels

       skeuē, "apparatus, tackle"
I Esd. 2:10, King Cyrus also brought forth the
            holy vessels which
       2:13, golden cups...and a thousand other
            vessels
       2:14, So all the vessels of gold and silver,
            which were
       4:41, and to send away all the vessels that
            were taken
       4:57, He sent away also all the vessels
            from Babylon, that
       8:17, And the holy vessels of the Lord,
            which are given
       8:57, and I weighed them in gold...and the
            holy vessels of
       8:58, Both ye are holy unto the Lord, and
            the vessels are

       aggeion, "a vessel, pail"
Judith 7:20, Thus...all their vessels of water
            failed all the

       holkē, "trading vessel, a ship which is towed"
Judith 15:11, the people spoiled the camp...and
            beds, and vessels,

       skeuē, "tackling of a ship"
Wisd.-Sol. 15:7, the same clay maketh both the
            vessels that serve
       15:13, that of earthly matter maketh
            brittle vessels
Eccl. 13:11, and made a vessel thereof fit for the
            service of

       ploion, "a floating vessel, a ship of any
            kind"
Eccl. 14:1, calleth upon a piece of wood more rot-
            ten than the vessel

       skeuē
Eccl. 27:5, The furnace proveth the potter's ves-
            sels;
       50:9, as fire and incense in the censer,and
            as a vessel of
Bar. 1:8, at the same time when he received the
            vessels of the

Epis.-Jer. 1:17, For like a vessel that a man
            useth is nothing
      1:59, a king...or a profitable vessel
            in an house,
I Macc. 1:21, the sanctuary and took away...all
            the vessels
      1:23, the silver and the gold, and the
            precious vessels:
      2:9, Her glorious vessels are carried away
            into captivity
      4:49, They made also holy vessels, and
            into the temple
      6:12, But now I remember...that I took all
            the vessels of

    aggeion
I Macc. 6:53, Yet at the last, their vessels being
            without

    skeuē
I Macc. 14:15, beautified the sanctuary, and mul-
            tiplied the vessels
II Macc. 4:48, the matter for the city...and for
            the holy vessels
      5:16, and taking the holy vessels with
            polluted hands,
      9:16, and restored all the holy vessels
            with many more,
VESTMENT, stolē, "a garment, robe, dress, clothing"
  I Esd. 5:45, the holy treasury...an hundred priest-
          ly vestments

      stolisma, "an equipment, dress, garment"
I Esd. 5:59, And the priests stood arrayed in
            their vestments
      7:9, also and the Levites stood arrayed in
            their vestments

     stolē
II Macc. 3:15, before the altar in their priests'
            vestments,

     esthēsis, "a robe, vestment, raiment"
III Macc. 1:16, And when the priests fell down in
            their vestments

VEXED, lupē, "pain, distress, grief, sorrow"
  Bar. 2:18, but the soul that greatly vexed, which
         goeth stooping

tarassō, "to agitate, trouble, to terrify"
I Macc. 3:5, and sought...those that vexed his
people

VIAL, phialē, "a flat shallow cup or bowl"
I Macc. 1:22, and the table of the shewbread...and
the vials, and

VICE, kakia, "badness, gaseness, cowardice"
Wisd.-Sol. 7:30, But after this cometh night: but
vice shall not
IV Macc. 2:12, it over...parents toward their children...for vice;

VICTIM, talaiporia, "toil, difficulty, calamity,
bodily hardships"
III Macc. 4:12, brethren lamented the...distress
of these victims,
5:5, The underlings...bound the hands
of the...victims

VICTORIOUS, nikē, "victory, victorious principle"
III Macc. 3:20, madness of these persons, and our
victorious

alophoros, "bearing away the prize,
victorious"
IV Macc. 18:23, with their victorious mother, are
assembled

VICTORY, epinikios, "of victory"
I Esd. 3:5, every one of us speak a sentence...in
token of victory

nikos, "victory"
I Esd. 3:9, and said that...to him shall the victory be given, as
4:59, and said, From thee cometh victory,
from thee cometh

ischus, "strength, force, might, a force
of soldiers"
Wisd.-Sol. 10:12, and in a sore conflict she gave
him the victory

nikē, "victory, victorious principle"
I Macc. 3:19, for the victory of battle standeth
not in the

epinikos
II Macc. 8:33, such time as they kept the feast
for the victory

415

nikē
II Macc. 10:28, virtue their refuge also...pledge
...their success and victory

10:38, praised the Lord...who...gave
them the victory

12:11, sore battle, but Judas' side...
got the victory

13:15, and having given the watchword...
victory is of God

15:21, his hand toward heaven...knowing
that victory

IV Macc. 7:3, of piety till it sailed into the
harbour of victory

17:12, For at that time virtue...approv-
ing the victory

VICTUALS, episitismos, "a furnishing oneself with
provisions, a stock of pro-
vision"
Judith 2:18, and plenty of victuals for every man
of the army,

brōma, "that which is eaten, food"
Judith 11:12, for their victuals failed them, and
all their water

trophē, "nourishment, food, victuals"
I Macc. 1:35, They stored it also with armour and
victuals, and

diatrophē, "sustenance, support"
I Macc. 6:49, were in Bethsura...they had no
victuals there

brōma
I Macc. 6:53, at the last, their vessels being
without victuals

trophē
I Macc. 6:57, Wherefore...we decay daily, and our
victuals are but

siton, "wheat, corn, grain, bread"
I Macc. 8:26, anything unto them...or aid them with
victuals

8:28, neither shall victuals be given to
them that take

9:52, and put forces in them with provision of victuals

trophē
I Macc. 13:21, Now they that were in the tower

416

sent...victuals

broma

I Macc. 13:33, built up the strong holds...and
laid up victuals
14:10, He provided victuals for the cities,
and set in
III Macc. 12:14, it, put such trust in...provision
of victuals,

VILE, hubris, "wanton, violence, lewdness, insolence"
Wisd.-Sol. 4:18, him...but...they shall hereafter
be a vile carcase
15:10, His heart is ashes, his hope is
more vile than

VILLAGE, kome, "an unwalled village or country town"
I Esd. 4:50, all the country...should give over
the villages of
Judith 15:7, that returned from...the villages
and the towns,

VINE, ampelos, "a vine"
Eccl. 24:17, As the vine brought I forth pleasant
savour, and my
I Macc. 14:12, for every man sat under his vine
and his fig tree,

VINEYARD, ampelon, "vineyard"
I Esd. 4:16, Even of them came they...that planted
the vineyards,
I Macc. 3:56, as were building house...or were
planting vineyards

VIOLENCE, dunamis, "strength, mighty, power"
I Macc. 6:47, seeing the strength of the king,
and the violence

horme, "an assault, attack, violence,
passion"
III Macc. 1:16, to avert the violence of the fierce
aggressor,

bia, "bodily strength, force, might"
IV Macc. 11:26, Your fire is cold...and your violence harmless
17:2, O thou mother, who...didst destroy
the violence of
17:9, sons, are buried through the violence of a tyrant,

VIOLENT, biaios, "strength, forcible, acting with
violence"

417

Wisd.-Sol. 19:7, shadowing the camp...and out of
    the violent stream

    bia
III Macc. 4:5, urged onward by the impulse of a
    violent,

    karteros, "strong, staunch, brave"
IV Macc. 15:32, of the law...straitened by violent
    storms which

VIOLENTLY, krataios, "mighty, strong, resistless"
Eccl. 46:6, of mighty power he made the battle
    to fall violently

    bia, bodily strength, force, might"
III Macc. 4:7, exposed to public gaze, they were
    hurried violently

VIRGIN, parthenos, "a virgin, a maid, maiden, pure,
    chaste"
Judith 16:5, burn up borders...and make...my vir-
    gins as a spoil
Eccl. 15:2, him, and receive him as a wife married
    of a virgin
    20:4, As is the lust of an eunuch to de-
    flower a virgin; so
Epis.-Jer. 1:9, And taking gold, as it were for
    a virgin that
I Macc. 1:26, so that the princes and elders mourn-
    ed, the virgins
II Macc. 3:19, And the women, girt with sackcloth
    ...and the virgins
    5:13, of young and old...children, slay-
    ing of virgins
III Macc. 1:18, Virgins who had been shut up
    within their
IV Macc. 18:7, the righteous mother...spake...I
    was a virgin, and

VIRGINITY, mētra, "womb"
Judith 9:2, vengeance of strangers, who...polluted
    her virginity

    parthenia, "virginity"
Eccl. 42:10, in her virginity, lest she should be
    defiled and
IV Macc. 18:8, of the desert...make spoil of my
    chaste virginity;

VIRTUE, áretēs, "goodness, excellence"
Wisd.-Sol. 4:1, it is to have no children, and to
            have virtue:
        7:20, the diversities of plant, and the
            virtues of
        8:7, a man love righteousness, her
            labours are virtues
        13:4, they were astonished at their
            power and virtue,
        19:20, had power in the water, forgetting
            his...virtue:

    ischus,"strength, force, might"
Eccl. 38:5, water made sweet with wood, that the
            virtue thereof

    áretēs
II Macc. 10:28, the one part having together with
            their virtue
        15:12, vision...from a child in all
            points of virtue,
III Macc. 6:1, Eleazar...whose life had been adorn-
            ed with virtue,
IV Macc. 1:2, especially does it embrace...the
            highest virtue
        1:8, but I shall prove it...in defence
            of virtue
        1:10, For their virtues, then, it is
            right that I should
        2:10, For the law conquers...not surren-
            dering virtue
        7:22, that it is a blessed thing to en-
            dure...for virtue
        9:8, ill-treatment...shall bear off the
            rewards of virtue
        9:18, Hebrews are alone unconquered in
            behalf of virtue
        9:31, my suffering...which are connected
            with virtue
        10:10, suffer this for the sake of Divine
            ...virtue
        11:2, O tyrant, to get excused...in be-
            half of virtue
        11:4, O thou hater of virtue and of men,
            what have we
        12:15, desert...without cause the champion
            of virtue
        13:23, in the same law, and practising the
            same virtues

IV Macc. 17:12, For at that time virtue presided
over the contest
17:23, tyrant Antiochus, looking to their
manly virtue,

VIRTUOUS, áretēs, "skill, character of virtue, re-
putation"
IV Macc. 13:26, although nature and intercourse
and virtuous

VISION, horama, "that which is seen, a view, sight"
Tobit 12:19, did appear unto you...but ye did see
a vision

prosōpon, "face, visage, outward appearance"
Wisd.-Sol. 17:4, that held them...and sad visions
appeared unto

phantasia, "making visible, the power of the
mind by which it places objects
before it"
Wisd.-Sol. 18:17, Then suddenly visions of horrible dreams

horasis, "seeing, the sense of sight"
Eccl. 31:3, The vision of dreams is the resemblance
of one thing
40:6, Little or nothing...troubled in the
vision of his
46:15, faithfulness...he was known to be
faithful in vision
48:22, For Ezekias...was great and faithful
in his vision,
49:8, It was Ezekiel who saw the glorious
vision, which was

theoria, "a beholding, a sight, spectacle"
II Macc. 15:12, And this was the vision: That
Onias, who had

VOICE, phōnē, "sound, tone, the voice, a cry"
I Esd. 5:61, And they sung with loud voices songs
to the praise
5:62, the trumpets, and shouted with a loud
voice,
9:10, the whole multitude, and said with a
loud voice,
Judith 7:23, Then all the people...cried with a
loud voice, and
7:29, and they cried unto the Lord God with
a loud voice

Judith 8:17, the salvation of him...and he will
          hear our voice,
      13:12, Now when the men of her city heard
          her voice, they
      13:14, Then she said to them with a loud
          voice, Praise,
      14:9, speaking, the people shouted with a
          loud voice,
      14:16, Therefore she cried with a loud
          voice, with weeping
      16:11, shouted for joy...these lifted up
          their voices, but
Wisd.-Sol. 1:7, the Lord...containeth all things
          ...of the voice
      17:19, sound of stones...or a roaring
          voice of most
      18:1, had a very great light, whose
          voice they hearing,
Eccl. 17:13, majesty...and their ears heard his
          glorious voice
      21:20, A fool lifteth up his voice with
          laughter; but a wise
      31:24, one prayeth, and another curseth,
          whose voice will
      45:5, He made him to hear his voice, and
          brought him into
      46:17, and with a great noise made his voice
          to be heard
      46:20, death he prophesied...and lifted up
          his voice from
      47:9, singers also before the altar, that
          by their voices
      50:18, The singers sang praises with their
          voices, with
Bar. 1:18, disobeyed him, and have not hearkened
          unto the voice
      1:19, Egypt...we have been negligent in not
          hearing his voice
      1:21, Nevertheless we have not hearkened unto
          the voice of
      2:6, cast down...and have not been obedient
          unto his voice
      2:10, Yet we have not hearkened unto his
          voice, to walk in
      2:22, But if ye will not hear the voice of
          the Lord, to
      2:23, to cease out of the cities...the voice
          of joy

Bar. 2:24, But we would not hearken unto the
          voice, to serve the
     2:29, If ye will not hear my voice, surely
          this very great
     3:4, have sinned...and not hearkened unto
          the voice of thee
His.-Sus. 1:24, With that Susanna cried with a
          loud voice: and
Bel-Drag. 1:18, the door, the king...cried with a
          loud voice,
I Macc. 2:19, Then Mattathias answered and spake
          with a loud voice
     2:27, cried throughout the city with a
          loud voice, saying
     3:50, Then cried they with a loud voice
          toward heaven,
     3:54, they the trumpets, and cried with a
          loud voice
     13:8, And they answered with a loud voice,
          saying, Thou
     13:45, the people of the city...cried with
          a loud voice,
IV Macc. 8:27, For they...altogether with one
          voice, as from the
     15:21, siren melodies...O voices of child-
          ren, calling upon

VOID, ákuroŏ, "to deprive of authority, abrogate,
          to cancel"
IV Macc. 17:2, O thou mother...render void his
          wicked intentions,

VOLUME, suntagma, "that which is put together in
          order"
II Macc. 2:23, declared...will assay to abridge
          in one volume

VOTE, psephos, "a pebble variously employed, esp.
          in a ballot"
IV Macc. 15:26, she holding two votes, one for
          death, the other

VOW, euchě, "a prayer, wish or a vow"
I Esd. 2:7, and other things, which have been set
          forth by vow,
     4:43, Then said he unto the king, Remember
          thy vow, which
     4:46, And now...I desire therefore thou
          make good the vow,

I Esd. 5:53, And all they that had made any vow
         to God began to

euchomai, "to pray, pay one's vows"
I Esd. 8:13, the Lord...which I and my friends
         have vowed
      8:50, And there I vowed a fast unto the
         young man before
      8:58, the vessels are holy...and the silver
         is a vow unto
Eccl. 18:22, Let nothing hinder thee to pay thy
         vow in due time,
Epis.-Jer. 1:35, In like manner...though a man
         make a vow unto
II Macc. 3:35, So Heliodorus...made great vows
         unto him that had

VOYAGE, ephodos, "a way towards, a means of reaching,
         access"
II Macc. 5:1, same time Antiochus prepared his
         second voyage into

      katapleō, "to sail towards land, to come
         to land"
III Macc. 4:10, the deck above them barred...
         during the whole voyage

WAGES, misthos, "wages, pay, hire"
Tobit 2:12, when she had sent them home...they
         paid her wages,
      2:14, she replied upon me, It was...more
         than the wages
      4:14, Let not the wages of any man, which
         hath wrought for
      5:3, him the handwriting, and said...I will
         give him wages
      5:14, But tell me, what wages shall I give
         thee?
      5:15, Yea, moreover...I will add something
         to thy wages
      12:1, Tobias, and said...see that the man
         have his wages
Wisd.-Sol. 2:22, of God...neither hoped they for
         the wages of

WAITER, parestōtē, (derived from paristemi,"to at-
         tend, to stand in attendance);
         hence, "one who waits on another"
Judith 13:1, evening was come...Bagoas...dismissed
         the waiters

WAKEFUL, ágrupnia, "sleeplessness, waking, watching"
  Eccl. 42:9, A daughter is a wakeful care to a
          father;

WALK, poreuomai, "to transport, go away, travel,
          journey"
  Eccl. 4:17, For at the first she will walk with
          him by crooked
     5:2, Follow not thine own mind...to walk
          in the ways of thy
  Bar. 1:18, and disobeyed him, and have not
          hearkened...to walk in
     2:10, Yet we have not hearkened unto his
          voice to walk in
     3:13, For if thou hast walked in the way of
          God, thou
     4:2, Turn thou, O Jacob...walk in the light
          of the presence
     4:13, They knew not his statutes, nor walked
          in the ways of
  His.-Sus. 1:7, Susanna went into her husband's
          garden to walk
       1:8, And the two elders saw her...
          walking; so that their
       1:36, And the elders said, As we walked
          in the garden
  I Macc. 2:20, yet will I and my sons and my bre-
          thren walk in the

WALL, teichē, "a wall, esp. of a town"
  I Esd. 1:55, the house of the Lord, they...brake
          down the walls of
     2:19, Now if this city and the walls there-
          of be made up
     2:24, if this city be built again, and
          the walls thereof

    teichos, "a wall, mostly of private building"
  Tobit 1:17, and my clothes to the naked...or cast
          about the walls
     2:9, I returned from the burial, and slept
          by the wall
     2:10, I knew not that there were sparrows
          in the wall, and
    13:16, built up with sapphire, and...thy
          walls and towers

    teichē
  Judith 1:2, and built in Ecbatane walls round about
          of stones

Judith 7:32, dispersed the people...and they went
    unto the walls
  14:1, unto them, Hear me...and hang it upon
    the...walls
  14:11, arose, they hanged the head of Holo-
    fernes upon the wall,
Wisd.-Sol. 13:15, made a convenient room for it,
    set it in a wall
Eccl. 14:24, her house shall also fasten a pin in
    her walls

 toichos, "the wall of a house or court"
Eccl. 22:17, a thought...is as fair plaistering
    on the wall of

 teichē
Eccl. 49:13, elect was Neemias...who raised up
    for us the walls
I Macc. 1:31, of the city...and pulled down the
    houses and walls
  4:60, also they builded up the mount
    .Sion with high walls
  6:7, also that they had pulled down the
    ...high walls, as

 teichos
I Macc. 6:62, into mount Sion...to pull down the
    wall round about
  9:50, strong cities...these did he
    strengthen with...walls,
  9:54, Moreover...Alcimus commanded that
    the wall of the
  10:11, And he commanded the workmen to
    build the walls and
  10:45, Yea, for the building of the walls
    of Jerusalem,

 teichē
I Macc. 12:36, and making the walls of Jerusalem
    higher, raising
  13:10, the men of war, and made haste to
    finish the walls
  13:33, Simon built up the strong holds...
    and great walls,
  13:45, the people of the city...climbed
    upon the walls
  14:37, placed Jews therein, and fortified
    ...the walls of
  16:23, of the acts of John...the building
    of the walls

II Macc. 3:19, abounded in the streets...and some
to the walls
5:5, Now when...they that were upon the
walls being put
10:17, they...kept off all that fought
upon the wall,
11:9, praised the merciful God...to
pierce through walls
12:13, strong city, which was fenced about
with walls,
12:14, it put such trust in the strength
of the walls
12:15, Judas...gave a fierce assault
against the wall,
12:27, destroyed them...the strong young
men kept the walls
14:43, missing his stroke...he ran boldly
up to the wall,
III Macc. 1:29, Now the men only, the very walls
and floor seemed

WAR, polemos, "a battle, fight: generally war"
I Esd. 1:25, after all...Pharaoh the king of Egypt
came to raise war
1:27, out from the Lord God against thee;
for my war is

poliorkia, "a beleaguering or besieging of a
city, a siege"
I Esd. 2:23, the Jews were rebellious, and raised
always wars

polemos
I Esd. 4:4, If he bid them make war the one against
the other
4:6, for those that...have not to do with
wars, but use
Judith 1:5, in those days Nabuchodonosor made war
with Arphaxad
1:16, being a very great multitude of men
of war,
2:16, he ranged them, as a great army is
ordered for...war
5:1, the children of Israel had prepared
for war,
6:2, And who art thou...that we should not
make war with

polemistēs, "a warrior, combatant"
Judith 7:2, their strong men...and the army of the

men of war was

polemikos, "of or belonging to war, warlike"
Judith 7:5, Then every man took up his weapons of
war, and when

polemistēs
Judith 7:7, viewed the passages...and set garri-
sons of men of war

polemos
Judith 11:8, have heard of thy wisdom...and wonderful feats of war
Wisd.-Sol. 8:15, tyrants...shall be found good...
and valiant in war
14:22, for them...in the great war of
ignorance,

polemistēs
Wisd.-Sol. 18:15, word leaped from heaven...as a
fierce man of war
Eccl. 26:28, two things that grieve my heart...a
man of war that

polemos
Eccl. 46:1, Jesus the son of Nave was valiant in
the wars, and
Bar. 3:26, There were the giants famous...and so
expert in war
Epis.-Jer. 1:15, dagger...but he cannot deliver
himself from war
1:48, For when there cometh any war of
plague upon
1:49, that they...neither save themselves from war,
I Macc. 1:2, and made many wars, and won many
strong holds, and
1:18, and made war against Ptolemee king
of Egypt:
2:32, they pursued after them...and made
war against them
3:13, of the faithful...goout with him
to war
4:7, camp of the heathen...and these were
expert of war
5:19, Take ye the charge...and see that
ye make not war
5:30, an innumerable people bearing...
engines of war
8:2, of...valour...It was told him also
of their wars

I Macc. 8:24, If there come first any war upon the
              Romans or any
        8:26, shall they give any thing unto them
              that make war
        8:27, In the same manner also, if war comes
              first upon the
        9:22, the other things concerning Judas
              and his wars, and
        9:67, Simon and his company...burned up
              the engines of war
       11:15, when Alexander heard of this, he
              came to war
       11:20, same time Jonathan...made an engine
              of war against
       12:13, we have had great troubles and wars
              on every side,
       12:44, to great a trouble seeing there is
              no war betwixt
       12:53, Then all the heathen...said...let
              us make war upon

    polemistēs
I Macc. 13:10, So then he gathered together all
               the men of war,

    polemos
I Macc. 14:29, Forasmuch as oftentimes there have
               been wars in

    polemikos, "in hostile fashion"
I Macc. 15:3, certain pestilent men have...pre-
              pared ships for war

    polemistēs
I Macc. 16:4, chose out of the country twenty thou-
              sand men of war

    polemos
I Macc. 16:23, the rest of the acts of John, and
               his wars, and
II Macc. 2:14, together all those things...lost
               by reason of...war
         2:20, And the wars against Antiochus
               Epiphanes, and

    polemikos
II Macc. 8:9, who in matters of war had great
              experience

    polemos
II Macc. 10:10, Antiochus...gathering briefly the
                calamities of the wars

II Macc. 10:15, therewithal the Idumeans...went
about to nourish war
14:6, Jews that be called Assideans...
nourish war, and
III Macc. 1:2, his own responsibility, and so
to end the war

polemios , "of or belonging to war"
IV Macc. 4:22, For being at war with Ptolemy in
Egypt, he heard

polemos
IV Macc. 11:8, being alien from God, those makest
war against

stratopedeusis, "an encamping, the station of
a fleet"
IV Macc. 18:6, then, departing from Jerusalem, he
made war against

WARLIKE, polemos, "a battle, fight, war"
I Macc. 3:3, and girt his warlike harness about
him, and he made
5:56, heard of the valiant acts and warlike deeds which
14:9, young men put on glorious and warlike
apparel.

WARM, thermē, "heat, warmth"
Tobit 2:10, not that...the sparrows muted warm
dung into mine eyes

WARNED, chrematismos, "a response from God, a divine
communication"
II Macc. 2:4, same writing that the prophet, being
warned of God,

WARRIOR, polemistēs, "a warrior, combatant"
Judith 15:3, the children of Israel, every one
that was a warrior

polemos
Eccl. 47:5, the most high Lord...to slay that
mighty warrior,

WASH, baptizō, "to dip repeatedly, to dip under,
baptize"
Judith 10:3, and washed her body all over with
water, and anointed
12:7, and washed herself in a fountain of
water by the
Eccl. 31:25, He that washeth himself after the

429

touching of a dead

louō, "to bathe the body, to wash"
His.-Sus. 1:15, as they watched...she was desirous to wash herself
     1:17, to her maids...Bring me oil... that I may wash

WASHING, **loutron**, "a bathing, washing, ablution"
Eccl. 31:25, if he touch it again, what availeth his washing?
His.-Sus. 1:17, to her maids, Bring me oil and washing balls,

WASP, **sphekia**, "a wasp's nest"
Wisd.-Sol. 12:8, those sparedst as men, and didst send wasps,

WATCH, **skopos**, "a watcher, a mark, goal"
Eccl. 40:6, nothing is his rest...as in a day of keeping watch,

       phulakē, "a watching or guarding, keeping watch or guard"
Eccl. 42:11, Keep a sure watch over a shameless daughter, lest

       phulax, "watchmen, guard, sentinel"
Eccl. 40:10, of the Holy One they...never faint in their watches

       gregoreō, "to be awake, watch, attentive"
Bar. 2:9, Wherefore the Lord watched over us for evil, and the

       phulax
Bar. 3:34, The stars shined in their watches, and rejoiced:

WATCHED, **paratereō**, "to watch narrowly, to observe"
His.-Sus. 1:16, nobody there save the two elders, that...watched

WATCHMAN, **phulax**, "a watcher, a guard, a sentinel"
Judith 13:11, Then said Judith afar off to the watchmen at the

       skopos, "a watcher"
Eccl. 37:14, sometime wont to tell him more than seven watchmen,

WATER, **hudōr**, "water"
Judith 2:7, them, that they prepare for me earth and water:

Judith 7:7, passages...and came to the fountains
            of their waters,
        7:12, let thy servants get into...the foun-
            tain of water,
        7:13, the inhabitants of Bethulia have
            their water hence;
        7:17, the children of Ammon departed...and
            took the waters
        7:21, the cisterns were emptied, and they
            had not water to
        8:9, Now...they fainted for lack of water;
        9:12, Lord God of the heavens...Creator
            of the waters, King
        10:3, and washed her body all over with wa-
            ter, and anointed
        11:12, their victuals fail them, and all
            their water scant,
        12:7, and went out and washed...in a foun-
            tain of water
Wisd.-Sol. 5:10, ship that passeth over the
            waves of the water,
        5:22, cast as out of a stone bow, and
            the water of the
        10:18, through the Red Sea, and led them
            through...water
        11:4, they called upon thee, and water
            was given them
        11:7, the commandment...thou gavest unto
            them...water
        13:2, either fire, or wind...or the' vio-
            lent water, or
        16:17, most to be wondered at, the...
            force in the water
        16:19, time it burneth even in the midst
            of water
        16:29, the unthankful shall melt...as
            unprofitable water
        17:18, a whistling wind...or a pleasing
            fall of water
        18:5, destroyedst them all together in
            a mighty water
        19:7, a cloud shadowing the camp; and
            where water stood
        19:19, For earthly things were turned
            into...water,
        19:20, The fire had power in the water,
            forgetting his
Eccl. 3:30, Water will quench a flaming fire; and
            alms maketh

Eccl. 15:3, she feed him, and give him the water
           of wisdom
      15:16, He hath set fire and water before
           thee: stretch forth
      18:10, As a drop of water unto the sea, and
           a gravel stone
      25:25, Give the water no passage; neither
           a wicked woman
      26:12, will open her mouth...and drink of
           every water near
      29:21, The chief thing for life is water,
           and bread, and
      38:5, Was not the water made sweet with
           wood, that the
      39:17, For at time convenient...the water
           stood as an heap,

     katakluzō, "to inundate, deluge"
Eccl. 39:23, His blessing covered the dry land
           as a river...watered

     hudōr
Eccl. 39:26, things for the whole use of man's
           life are water,
      40:11, and that which is of the waters
           doth return
      43:20, When the cold north wind bloweth,
           and the water is
      48:17, Ezekias fortified his city and
           brought in water into
      50:3, in his days the cisterns to receive
           water, being in
      50:8, flower of roses...as lilies by the
           rivers of waters,
Song-Child. 1:37, O all ye waters that be above
           the heaven, bless
      1:56, O ye whales, and all that move
           in the waters,
I Macc. 9:45, and behind us, and the water of the
           Jordan

     potamos, "a river, stream"
I Macc. 11:60, and passed through the cities be-
           yong the water

     hudōr
II Macc. 1:20, many years...Neemias...found no
           fire, but thick water
      1:31, consumed, Neemias commanded the
           water that was

432

II Macc. 1:33, So when this matter was known...
    there appeared water
    15:39, For as it is hurtful to drink wine
    or water alone;
IV Macc. 3:11, but a certain irrational longing
    for the water in

WATER-BROOK, <u>cheimarhros</u>, "a stream which flows in
    winter, a brook"
I Macc. 16:5, in the morning...there was a water
    brook between
    16:6, So he and his people pitched over
    the water brook,

WAVE, <u>kuma</u>, "the swell of the sea, a wave, billow,
    surge"
Wisd.-Sol. 14:1, and about to pass through the
    raging waves,
    14:3, for thou hast made...a safe path
    in the waves
Eccl. 24:6, In the waves of the sea, and in all
    the earth, and in
    29:18, of good estate, and shaken them as a
    wave of the sea
II Macc. 9:8, he might command the waves of the
    sea;
IV Macc. 13:6, means of towers projecting...the
    towering waves,

    <u>kludōn</u>, "a wave, a billow, surge"
IV Macc. 15:31, For as the ark of Noah...bore up
    against the waves

WAX, <u>kēros</u>, "bees-wax, wax"
Judith 16:15, moved...the rocks shall melt as wax
    at thy presence
    16:23, she increased more and more in hon-
    our and waxed old
Eccl. 8:6, Dishonour not a man in his old age:
    for even some of us wax old

    <u>palaiō</u>, "to wrestle with, struggle against"
Eccl. 14:17, All flesh waxeth old as a garment:
    for the covenent
Bar. 3:10, How happeneth it, Israel...that thou
    art waxen old in a
His.-Sus. 1:52, and said...O thou that art waxen
    old in wickedness

ginomai, "to come into a particular state or
condition"
II Macc. 10:29, But when the battle waxed strong,
there appeared

WAY, hodos, "a path, road, entrance, track"
Wisd.-Sol. 5:7, We wearied ourselves in the way
of wickedness and
14:3, governeth it: for thou has made
a way in the
18:23, fallen down...he...stayed the
way of the living
19:5, and that thy people might pass
through a...way:
Eccl. 2:6, Believe in him...order thy way aright,
and trust in him
2:15, They that fear the Lord...will keep
his ways

poreuma, "a passage, way, carriage"
Eccl. 4:17, at the first she will walk with him
by crooked ways,
5:2, Follow not thine own mind...to walk
in the ways of thy

euthutēs, "rectitude, equity"
Eccl. 7:6, to lay a stumblingblock in the way of
thy uprightness

poreuō, "to bring, to carry, go, walk"
Eccl. 8:15, Travel not by the way with a bold
fellow, lest he

hodos
Eccl. 11:26, unto the Lord...to reward a man according to his ways
14:21, He that considereth her ways in his
heart shall also

eisodos, "a way into, entry"
Eccl. 14:22, after her as one that traceth, and
lie in wait in her ways.

hodos
Eccl. 16:20, these things...and who is able to
receive his ways?
17:15, Their ways are ever before him, and
shall not be hid
17:19, their works are...before...his eyes
...upon their ways
21:10, The way of sinners is made plain

434

with stones, but at
Eccl. 21:16, The talking of a fool is like a burden
in the way:
23:19, the eyes of men...beholding all the
ways of men,

anabasis, "a going up, a way up, the ascent of
a mountain"
Eccl. 25:20, As the climbing up a sandy way is
to the feet of the

hodos
Eccl. 35:20, Go in a way wherein thou mayest fall,
and stumble
35:21, Be not confident in a plain way
36:11, Lord hath divided them, and made
their ways diverse
39:24, As his ways are plain unto the holy;
so are they
47:22, pleased the Lord, and was strong in
the ways of David

euthutes
Eccl. 51:15, flower till the grape...my foot went
the right way,

hodos
Bar. 2:33, from their stiff neck...for they shall
remember the way
3:13, For if thou hadst walk in the way of
God, thou
3:20, Young men have seen light...but the way
of knowledge
3:23, that seek wisdom upon earth...have
known the way of
3:27, did not the Lord choose, neither gave
he the way of
3:31, No man knoweth her way, nor thinketh
of her path
3:36, He hath found out all the way of
knowledge, and hath
4:13, They knew not his statutes, nor walk
in the ways of
4:26, My delicate ones have gone rough ways,
and were taken
Epis.-Jer. 1:43, also with cords about them, sitting in the ways,
Song-Child. 1:3, yea true are all thy works, thy
ways are right,
I Macc. 5:4, remembered...that they lay in wait

for them in the ways
I Macc. 5:28, Judas and his host turned suddenly
by the way of the
5:53, Judas gathered together...the people
all the way,
9:2, who went forth by the way that
leadeth to Galgala,
II Macc. 2:6, of those that followed him came to
mark the way,

WEALTH, ólbos, "happiness, bliss, wealth"
Eccl. 30:15, estate of body are above all gold
and infinite wealth

chrēma, "a thing that one uses or needs,
esp. money, goods"
IV Macc. 4:3, I am come to inform thee that...
private wealth is

WEAPON, hoplon, "weapon, armour"
Judith 6:12, of the city saw them, they took up
their weapons,
7:5, Then every man took up his weapons of
war, and when
14:11, the morning arose...every man took
his weapons, and

hoplopoieō, "to arm, equip, to arm one's
self"
Wisd.-Sol. 5:17, He shall take to him...his weapon
for the revenge

hoplon
I Macc. 5:43, first over unto them, and all...cast
away their weapons
7:44, host saw that...they cast away their
weapons,
8:26, shall they give anything unto them
...weapons, money,
8:28, neither shall victuals...or weapons,
or money, or
9:39, lifted up...their instruments of
music, and...weapons
10:6, Wherefore he gave him authority...to
provide weapons,
11:53, With that they cast away their weapons, and made
16:16, largely, Ptolemee and his men...took
their weapons,
II Macc. 5:26, them...and running through the city

with weapons
II Macc. 8:18, For they, said he, trust in their
· weapons and
9:2, the city...to defend themselves
with their weapons
10:23, And having good success with their
weapons in all
10:27, So after the prayer he took their
weapons, and

panoplia, "a complete suit of armour, as the
shield"
II Macc. 10:30, and took Maccabeus betwixt them...
with...weapons

hoplon
II Macc. 11:7, Then Maccabeus himself first of all
took weapons,

WEATHER, eudia, "a cloudless sky, fair or fine
weather"
Eccl. 3:15, shall melt away, as the ice in the
fair...weather

WEDDING, gamos, "a wedding, marriage"
Tobit 8:19, And he kept the wedding feast fourteen
days
·9:2, Brother Azarias...said...bring him to
the wedding
9:6, in the morning they went forth...and
came to the wedding
10:7, thy peace...until the fourteen days of
the wedding

WEED, chortos, "a feeding-place, fodder, grass"
Eccl. 40:16, The weed growing upon every water and
bank of a river

WEEP, klaiō, "to weep for, bewail"
Tobit 3:1, Then I being grieved did weep, and in
my sorrow prayed
Eccl. 7:34, Fail not to be with them that weep,
and mourn with
22:11, Weep for the dead, for he hath lost
the light: and weep for the fool

dakruō, "to shed tears, weep"
Eccl. 34:13, therefore it weepeth upon every occasion

klaiō
Eccl. 38:17, Weep bitterly, and make great moan,
and use

437

WEEPING, klauthmos, "weeping"
Bar. 4:11, joy did I nourish them, but sent them
          away with weeping
     4:23, For I sent you out with mourning and
           weeping:
His.-Sus. 1:35, And she weeping looked up toward
               heaven:

     klaiō
I Macc. 7:36, priest entered in, and stood before
              the altar...weeping

WEIGHT, stathmos, "weight, a balance, pair of scales"
Eccl. 42:4, of exactness of balance and weights:
            or of getting
      42:7, Deliver all things in number and
            weight

WEPT, klaiō, "to weep for"
Tobit 7:6, Then Raguel leaped up and kissed him,
           and wept
      7:7, and blessed him...he was sorrowful,
           and wept
      7:17, Which when she had done...she wept,
            and she received
      11:9, and fell upon the neck of her son...
             and they wept
      11:14, And he wept, and said, Blessed art
             thou, O God, and
Bar. 1:5, Whereupon they wept, fasted, and prayed
          before the Lord
His.-Sus. 1:33, Therefore her friends and all that
               saw her wept

     dakruon, "to shed tears, weep"
III Macc. 4:2, Jews suffered great throes of sor-
               row, and wept

WEST, dusmē, "the setting of the sun; hence, the
             west"
Bar. 4:37, thy sons...gathered together from the
           east to the west
      5:5, and stand on high, and look...toward...
           the west unto the

WHALE, kētos, "any sea monster, a huge fish"
Eccl. 43:25, and wondrous works, variety of all
             kinds...of whales
Song.-Child. 1:56, O ye whales, and all that move
                  in the waters,

WHEAT, puros, "grains of wheat"
 Judith 3:3, houses, and all our places, and all
    our fields of wheat,
 Eccl. 39:26, the use of man's life are water...
    flour of wheat,

WHEEL, trochon, "a wheel, arunner, anything orbicu-
    lar"
 Eccl. 39:29, the potter sitting at his work and
    turning the wheel
 IV Macc. 5:32, Now then: prepare your wheels, and
    kindle a
    8:12, And when the spearman brought for-
    ward the wheels,
    9:12, without effect...they hurled him
    upon the wheel

  tropos, "a twisted leather thong"
 IV Macc. 9:17, he answered...O accursed ministers,
    is your wheel,

  trochon
 IV Macc. 10:7, to strangle him...they hauled him
    to the wheel;
    11:17, As he said this, they brought him
    to the wheel
    15:22, her sons were undergoing the
    wheel and the

WHIP, mastix, "a whip, scourge"
 Eccl. 28:17, The stroke of the whip maketh marks
    in the flesh:
 II Macc. 7:1, were tormented with scourges and
    whips

WHIRLWIND, pneuma, "wind, air in motion"
 Eccl. 43:17, noise of the thunder...the storm and
    the whirlwind

  lailaps, "a tempest, a storm, hurricane"
 Eccl. 48:9, who wast taken up in a whirlwind of
    fire, and in a
    48:12, Elias it was, who was covered with
    a whirlwind;

WHISPERER, psithuros, "whispering, slanderous"
 Eccl. 28:13, Curse the whisperer and double-ton-
    gued; for such

WHITENESS, leukos, "light, brilliant, white, grey"
 Eccl. 43:18, the eye marvelleth at the whiteness
    thereof, and the

WHORE, porneia, "fornication, prostitution"
  Eccl. 23:23, first, she hath disobeyed the law...
        she hath played the whore

WHOREDOM, porneia, "fornication, whoredom"
  Tobit 4:12, Beware of all whoredom, my son, and
        chiefly take a
  Eccl. 26:9, The whoredom of a woman may be known
        in her haughty
      41:17, Be ashamed of whoredom before father
        and mother:

WHOREMONGER, pornē, "a prostitute, unchaste female"
  Eccl. 23:17, All bread is sweet to a whoremonger,
        he will not

WICKED, poneros, "causing pain or hardship, bad,
        evil, wickedness"
  I Esd. 2:18, known to the Lord...that the rebel-
        lious and wicked

      kakia, "malice, wickedness, depravity"
  I Esd. 2:29, and that those wicked workers pro-
        ceed no further to

      adikos, "unrighteous, unjust, lawless"
  I Esd. 4:37, Wine is wicked, the king is wicked,
        women are wicked

      poneros
  I Esd. 8:86, all that is befallen is done unto
        us for our wicked

      hamartolos, "one who deviates from the path
        of virtue, sinful"
  Tobit 4:17, of the just, but give nothing to the
        wicked

      adikia, "wrong, offence"
  Tobit 6:14, I am the only son...if I go in unto
        her...a wicked

      ponēra, "bad, unsound, evil, wicked, im-
        pious"
  Wisd.-Sol. 3:12, their wives are foolish, and
        their children wicked
        3:14, is the eunuch, which...hath
        wrought no...wicked
        4:14, hasted he to take away...the
        wicked
      10:5, Moreover, the nations in their
        wicked conspiracy

ánosios, "unholy, wicked"
Wisd.-Sol. 12:4, whom thou hatedst for...wicked
        sacrifices

    hamartolos
Eccl. 3:27, An obstinate heart...and the wicked
        man shall heap sin

    ponēra
Eccl. 6:4, A wicked soul shall destroy him that
        hath it, and

    ádikia
Eccl. 14:9, not satisfied with the portion...of
        the wicked

    ponēros
Eccl. 14:10, A wicked eye envieth (his) bread, and
        he is a

    ánomia
Eccl. 16:4, that hath understanding...the wicked
        shall speedily

    ponereuomai, "to be evil or wicked, to deal
                wickedly"
Eccl. 19:26, There is a wicked man that hangeth
        down his head

    kakia
Eccl. 20:18, so the fall of the wicked shall come
        speedily

    ánomia
Eccl. 21:9, The congregation of the wicked is like
        tow wrapped

    ponēra
Eccl. 25:16, with a lion...than to keep house with
        a wicked woman

    hamartolos
Eccl. 29:19, A wicked man transgressing the com-
        mandments of the

    ásebēs, "wicked, ungodly, sinful"
Eccl. 31:19, is not pleased with the offerings of
        the wicked;

    ponēros
Eccl. 34:13, Remember that a wicked eye is an evil
        thing:
    37:3, O ye wicked imagination, whence camest
        thou...with

441

ánomos, "without law, impious"
Eccl. 39:24, are plain...so are they stumblingblocks to the wicked

ásebēs
Eccl. 39:30, and the sword punishing the wicked to
destruction

mastix
Eccl. 40:10, these things are created for the wicked, and through

ponēros
Eccl. 46:7, they withstood the enemy...and appeased
the wicked
Bar. 1:22, every man followed the imagination of
his own wicked
2:8, that we might turn every one from....his
wicked heart
2:33, return from their stiff neck, and from
their wicked

ádikos
Song-Child. 1:8, thou didst deliver us into...the
most wicked in

paranomia, "violation of the law, transgression"
His.-Sus. 1:32, And these wicked men commanded to
uncover her
hamartōlos, "a sinner, depraved, sinful, detestable"
I Macc. 1:10, And there came out of them a wicked
root, Antiochus

paranomos, "contrary to law and custom, unlaw-
ful, illegal"
I Macc. 1:11, In those days went there out of
Israel wicked men,

hamartōlos
I Macc. 1:34, And they put therein a sinful nation,
wicked men,

ánomos
I Macc. 2:44, So they joined their forces, and
smote...wicked men
3:6, Wherefore the wicked shrunk for fear
of him, and all
7:5, there came unto him all the wicked
and ungodly men

áse̅bēs
I Macc. 7:9, And him he sent with the wicked Al-
             cimus, whom he

ánomos
I Macc. 9:23, Now after the death of Judas the
              wicked began to

áse̅bēs
I Macc. 9:25, Then Bacchides chose wicked men, and
              made them

ánomos
I Macc. 9:69, Wherefore he was very wroth at the
              wicked men that

dusse̅bēs, "impious, ungodly"
II Macc. 3:11, and that some of it belonged to...
               that wicked Simon
           6:13, a token of his great goodness, when
                 wicked doers

paranomia, "violation of the law, transgress"
II Macc. 8:4, and remember the wicked slaughter
              of harmless

dusse̅bēs
II Macc. 9:9, the worms rose up out of the body
              of this wicked

áse̅bēs
II Macc. 10:10, we declare the acts of...the son
                of this wicked

áthemitos, "unlawful, criminal, wicked"
II Macc. 10:34, And they that were within...utter-
                ed wicked words

diabolos, "a traitor, informer, slanderer"
II Macc. 14:27, rage...with the accusations of
                the most wicked man

ánosios, "impious, unholy"
III Macc. 2:2, give ear to us who are oppressed
               by wicked and

pone̅ria, "badness, ill condition, wickedness"
IV Macc. 2:12, over the love of parents...reprov-
               ing them when wicked

kakia
IV Macc. 17:2, O thou mother...render void his
               wicked intentions,

WICKEDLY, ásebeō, "to be impious, to act wickedly"
  I Esd. 1:24, As for the things...those that...do
              wickedly against
  II Macc. 4:17, For it is not a light thing...to
              do wickedly against

WICKEDNESS, ánomia, "lawlessness, iniquity"
  Wisd.-Sol. 1:9, Lord for the manifestation of his
              wicked deeds

           kakia, "malice, malignity, depravity"
  Wisd.-Sol. 2:21, they did imagine...for their own
              wickedness hath

           porneia
  Wisd.-Sol. 4:6, For the children...are witnesses
              of wickedness

           kakia
  Wisd.-Sol. 5:13, like manner...were consumed in
              our own wickedness

           adikia, "wrong, offence"
  Wisd.-Sol. 11:15, But for the foolish devices of
              their wickedness

           kakia
  Wisd.-Sol. 12:2, chastenest thou them...that leav-
              ing their wickedness
         17:11, For wickedness, condemned by
              her own witness,
         19:13, the sinners...according to their
              own wickedness,

           ponēria, "badness, wickedness, ill con-
              dition"
  Eccl. 3:28, punishment of the proud...the plant
              of wickedness hath
      11:33, of a mischievous man, for he worketh
              wickedness:
      12:10, enemy: for like as iron rusteth, so
              is his wickedness
      14:6, and this is a recompence of his
              wickedness

           kakia
  Eccl. 14:7, And if he doeth good...he will de-
              clare his wickedness
      19:5, Whoso taketh pleasure in wickedness
              shall be condemned

           ponēria
  Eccl. 19:22, The knowledge of wickedness is not

wisdom,

Eccl. 19:23, There is a wicked ness, and the same
an abomination;

25:13, any plague...and any wickedness, but
the wickedness

25:17, The wickedness of a woman changeth
her face, and

kakia

Eccl. 25:19, All wickedness is but little to the
wickedness of a

poneria

Eccl. 32:3, To depart from wickedness is a thing
pleasing to the

plemeleia, "mistake, a fault, error,
offence"

Eccl. 38:10, sin...and cleanse your heart from
all wickedness

poneria

Eccl. 42:13, from garments cometh a moth and from
women wickedness

anomia

Eccl. 46:20, in prophecy, to blot out the wickedness of the

47:25, For they sought out all wickedness,
till the

poneria

Bar. 2:26, house which is called by thy name...
seen this...wickedness

anomia

His.-Sus. 1:5, appointed two...judges...that wickedness came from

1:38, a corner of the garden, seeing
this wickedness

kakia

His.-Sus. 1:52, said, O thou that art waxen old
in wickedness

anomia

His.-Sus. 1:57, daughter of Judea would not abide
your wickedness

kakia

III Macc. 2:25, proceeded to Egypt, grew worse in
wickedness

445

WIDOW, chēra, "a widow"
  Judith 8:4, So Judith was a widow in her house
               three years and
       9:4, hast given their wives for a prey...
            also a widow
       9:9, pride...give into mine hand, which
            am a widow,
  Wisd.-Sol. 2:10, oppress the poor...let us not
            spare the widow,
  Eccl. 32:14, nor the widow, when she poureth out
            her complaint.
     32:15, Do not the tears run down the widow's
            cheeks? and is
  Bar. 4:12, Let no man rejoice over me, a widow,
            and forsaken of
     4:16, and they have carried away the...child-
            ren of widow, and
  Epis.-Jer. 1:38, They can shew no mercy to the
            widow, nor do good
  II Macc. 3:10, high priest...laid up for the re-
            lief of widows and
      8:28, And after the sabbath...the widows,
            and orphans,
      8:30, of those...they slew...and...maimed,
            orphans, widows,
  IV Macc. 16:10, and fair children, should be a
            lone widow

WIFE, gunē, "a woman, a wife, spouse, a married
      woman"
  I Esd. 4:20, his own country, and cleaveth unto
            his wife
     4:21, He sticketh not to spend his life
            with his wife, and
     9:7, transgressed the law in marrying
            strange wives,
     9:12, that have strange wives come at the
            time appointed,
     9:17, So their cause that held strange
            wives was brought
     9:18, come together, and had strange wives,
            there were
     9:20, to put away their wives, and to offer
            rans to make
     9:36, All these had taken strange wives,
            and they put then
  Tobit 1:20, Then all my goods were...left me, be-
            side my wife Anna

Tobit 2:1, Now when I was come home again, and
       my wife Anna was
    3:15, I never polluted my name...I...keep
       myself for a wife:
    4:12, of all whoredom, my son, and chiefly
       take a wife of
    4:13, despise not...thy people, in not tak-
       ing a wife of them
    6:10, speak for her, that she may be given
       thee for a wife
    6:15, remember the precepts...thy father
       gave thee...marry a wife
    7:8, And likewise Edna his wife and Sara
       his daughter wept
    7:14, and called Edna his wife, and took
       paper, and did
    8:6, Thou madest Adam and gavest him Eve
       his wife for an
    8:21, then he sould...have the rest when I
       and my wife be
    9:6, morning they went forth...and Tobias
       blessed his wife
    10:4, Then his wife said unto him, My son
       is dead,
    10:11, Then Raguel arose, and gave him Sara
       his wife, and
    11:1, things Tobias...blessed Raguel and Edna
       his wife, and
    12:3, me again to thee in safety, and made
       whole my wife,
Judith 7:14, So they and their wives and their
       children shall be
    7:27, not to see the death of our...wives
       nor our children,
    9:4, and hast given their wives for a prey,
       and their

    gamos, "a wedding, a marriage festival, the
       marriage state"
Wisd.-Sol. 13:17, maketh he prayer for his goods,
       for his wife
Eccl. 7:26, Hast thou a wife after thy mind? for-
       sake thou her not
    9:1, Be not jealous over the wife of thy
       bosom, and teach
    9:9, Sit not at all with another man's wife,
       nor sit down
    15:2, shall she meet him, and receive him as
       a wife

Eccl. 23:22, Thus shall it go also with the wife
            that leaveth her
       25:1, the love of neighbours, a man and a
            wife,
       25:8, Well is he that dwelleth with a wife
            of understanding,
       25:20, As the climbing up a sandy way...
            so is a wife full of
       26:1, Blessed is the man that hath a vir-
            tuous wife, for the
       26:3, A good wife is a good portion, which
            shall be given in
       26:7, An evil wife is a yoke shaken to and
            fro:
       26:16, when it ariseth...so is the beauty
            of a good wife
       30:19, Give not thy son and wife, thy bro-
            ther and friend,
       36:24, He that getteth a wife beginneth a
            possession, a
       36:25, Where no hedge is...he that hath no
            wife will wander
       40:19, of a city continue...but a blameless
            wife is counted
       40:23, companion never meet amiss: but above
            both is a wife
       41:21, away thy face...or to gaze upon
            another man's wife;
       42:6, Sure keeping is good, where an evil
            wife is; and
Epis.-Jer. 1:28, that are sacrificed unto them...
            their wives lay
       1:33, take off their garments, and
            clothe their wives
His.-Sus. 1:2, and he took a wife, whose name was
            Susanna, the
       1:29, the people, Send for Susanna...
            Joacim's wife
Bel-Drag. 1:10, Bel were three score and ten, be-
            side their wives
       1:15, in the night came the priests with
            their wives
       1:21, and took the priests with their
            wives and children
I Macc. 2:30, both they and their children, and
            their wives, and
       2:38, So they rose up against them...with
            their wives and

448

I Macc. 3:20, They came up against us...and our
             wives and children
       3:56, But as for such as were...betrothed
             wives, or were
       5:13, yea, all our brethren...their wives
             and their
       5:23, And those that were in Galilee...
             with their wives
       5:45, Then Judas gathered together all...
             their wives, and
       8:10, and that they...carried away cap-
             tives their wives
      10:54, a league...and give now thy daugh-
             ter to wife:
       13:6, I will avenge my nation...and our
             wives, and our
      13:45, city...climbed upon the walls with
             their wives,
II Macc. 12:3, The men of Joppe...with their wives
             and children
      15:18, For...they took for their wives,
             and their children
III Macc. 1:4, fight manfully for...their children,
             and wives:
       3:25, as the Jews, who dwell among you,
             with wives and

WILDERNESS, erēma, "a solitude, desert, wilderness"
   Judith 5:14, and cast forth all that dwelt in the
             wilderness

             erēmos, "a lonely place, a desert, so-
             litary"
Wisd.-Sol. 11:2, They went through the wilderness
             that was not
      18:20, tasting of death...and destruc-
             tion...in the wilderness
Eccl. 43:21, devoureth the mountains,and burneth
             the wilderness,
      45:18, together against him...maligned him
             in the wilderness
I Macc. 1:39, Her sanctuary was laid waste like a
             wilderness, her
       2:29, after justice...went down into the
             wilderness
       2:31, that certain men...were gone down
             ...in the wilderness
       3:45, Now Jerusalem was laid void as a
             wilderness

I Macc. 5:24, and his brother Jonathan, went...
in the wilderness
5:28, turned suddenly by the way of the
wilderness
9:33, Then Jonathan, and Simon...fled into
the wilderness
9:62, Jonathan, and Simon...got them
away...in the wilderness
13:21, **in the tower**...hasten...unto them
by the wilderness
II Macc. 5:27, Judas Maccabeus...withdrew himself
into the wilderness

WIND, anemos, "wind, a whirlwind"
Wisd.-Sol. 4:4, flourish...they shall be shaken
with the wind,
5:14, like dust that is blown away with
the wind
5:23, Yea, a mighty wind shall stand up
against them,
7:20, living creatures, and...the
violence of winds,

pneuma, "wind, air, breath, spirit, life"
Wisd.-Sol. 17:18, Whether it were a whistling
wind, or a

anemos
Eccl. 22:18, on an high place will...stand against
the wind:
31:2, dreams is like him that...followeth
after the wind
34:19, sufficient for a man...and he fetch-
eth not his wind
43:16, mountains are shaken, and...the south
wind bloweth
43:20, When the cold north wind bloweth, and
the water is

pneuma
Song-Child. 1:26, furnace as it had been a moist
whistling wind,
1:42, O all ye winds, bless ye the
Lord: praise and

anemos
III Macc. 2:22, and fro as a reed is shaken with
the wind, he

WINDOW, thuris, "a small door, a window"
Tobit 3:11, Then he prayed toward the window,

and said, Blessed
Tobit 14:23, He that prieth in at her windows
           shall also hearken
II Macc. 3:19, girt with sackcloth...looked out
           at the windows

WINE, oinos, "wine"
I Esd. 4:16, the vineyards, from whence the wine
           cometh.
    4:37, Wine is wicked, the king is wicked,
           women are
Judith 10:5, Then she gave her maid a bottle of
           wine, and a cruse
    11:13, Spend the firstfruits...and the
           tenths of wine and
    12:1, that they should prepare...drink
           of his own wine
    12:13, from the presence of Holofernes
           ...and drink wine,
    13:2, alone in the tent...for he was filled
           with wine
Wisd.-Sol. 2:7, Let us fill ourselves with costly
           wine and
Eccl. 9:9, and spend not thy money with her at
           the wine
    9:10, not an old friend; for the new...is
           new wine
    19:2, Wine and women will make men of under-
           standing to fall
    34:25, Shew not thy valiantness in wine; for
           wine hath
    34:26, proveth the edge by dipping; so doth
           wine the heart
    34:27, Wine is as good as life to a man, if
           it be not drunk
    34:28, Wine measurably drunk and in season
           bringeth gladness
    34:29, but wine drunken with excess maketh
           bitterness of the
    34:31, Rebuke not thy neighbour at the wine ,
           and despise him
    35:36, set in a work of gold, so...is plea-
           sant wine
    40:20, Wine and music rejoice the heart; but
           love of
    49:1, in all mouths, and as music at a
           banquet of wine
Bel-Drag. 1:3, spent upon him every day...six vessels

Bel-Drag. 1:11, So Vel's priests said...make ready the wine, and
II Macc. 15:39, For as it is hurtful to drink
or water alone

sumponion,"a drinking together , a feast, banquet"
III Macc. 2:25, to Egypt, grew worse...through...
companions in wine

oinos
III Macc. 5:2, commanded him with a quantity of
unmixed wine, and
5:45, elephants urged the beasts...with
incense and wine
6:30, bade him provide a seven days'
quantity of wine

WING, _keros_, "wing of an army or fleet"
I Macc. 9:12, As for Bacchides, he was in the right
wing:
9:15, who discomforted the right wing,
and pursued them
9:16, But when they of the left wing saw
that they of the right wing, were

WIPE, _ekmasso_, "to wipe off, wipe dry"
Epis.-Jer. 1:13, They wipe ther faces because of
the dust of the
1:24, Notwithstanding...they wipe off
the rust, they

WISDOM, _sophia_ "cleverness or skill in art, prudence, wisdom in common things."
I Esd. 3:7, he shall sit next to Darius because
of his wisdom
4:59, thee cometh victory, and from thee
cometh wisdom,
4:60, Blessed art thou, who hast given me
wisdom:
8:23, And thou, Esdras, according to the
wisdom of God
Judith 8:29, not the first day wherein thy wisdom
is manifested;
11:8, For we have heard of thy wisdom and
thy policies, and
11:20, pleased Holofernes...and they marvelled at her wisdom
11:21. both for beauty of face, and wisdom
of words

Wisd.-Sol. 1:6, For wisdom is a loving spirit;
                and will not acquit
           3:11, For whoso despiseth wisdom and
                 nurture, he is

phronēsis, "a thoughtful frame, intelligence,
            sense"
Wisd.-Sol. 3:15, the fruit of good labours: and
                 the root of wisdom

sophia
Wisd.-Sol. 4:9, But wisdom is the grey hair unto
                men, and an
           6:9, O kings, do I speak that ye may
                learn wisdom,
           6:12, Wisdom is glorious, and never
                 fadeth away; yea,
           6:15, Therefore upon her is the perfec-
                 tion of wisdom:
           6:22, As for wisdom, what she is, and
                 how she came up,
           6:23, Neither will I...have...fellow-
                 ship with wisdom
           7:7, and understanding...and the spirit
                of wisdom came
           7:12, And I rejoiced in them all, be-
                 cause wisdom goeth
           7:15, God hath granted me...wisdom, and
                 directeth the
           7:16, For in his hand are both we and
                 our words: also wisdom
           7:22, For wisdom, which is the worker
                 of all things
           7:24, For wisdom is more moving than
                 any motion:
           7:28, God loveth none but him that
                 dwelleth with wisdom
           7:30, But vice shall not prevail against
                 wisdom
           8:1, Wisdom reacheth from one and to
                another mightily:
           8:5, a possession...what is richer than
                wisdom...?
           8:17, how that to be allied with wisdom
                 is immortality
           8:21, Now...that was a point of wisdom
                 also to know
           9:2, and ordained man through thy wis-
                dom, that he

Wisd.-Sol. 9:17, And thy counsel...giveth wisdom, and send thy

9:18, that are pleasing unto thee... through wisdom

10:4, being drowned with the flood, wisdom again

10:8, For regarding not wisdom, they gat not only this

10:9, But wisdom delivered from pain those that

10:21, For wisdom opened the mouth of the dumb, and

14:5, wouldest not that the works of thy wisdom

17:7, allusions of art magic, they were put down...wisdom

Eccl. 1:1, All wisdom cometh from the Lord, and is with him for

1:3, Who can find out the...the deep, and wisdom?'

1:4, Wisdom hath been created before all things, and the

1:6, To whom hath the root of wisdom been revealed?

1:14, The fear of the Lord is the beginning of wisdom:

1:16, To fear the Lord is the fulness of wisdom, and filleth

1:18, The fear of the Lord is a crown of wisdom, making

1:19, Wisdom raineth down skill and knowledge of understanding

1:20, The root of wisdom is to fear the Lord, and the

1:25, If thou desire wisdom, keep the commandments,

1:26, For the fear of the Lord is wisdom and instruction:

4:11, Wisdom exalteth her children, and layeth hold of them

4:23, And refrain not to speak, when...there is wisdom in

4:24, For by speech wisdom shall be known; and learning by

6:18, instruction from thy youth...so shalt thou find wisdom

6:22, For wisdom is according to her name, and she is not

Eccl. 6:37, ordinances of the Lord...he shall...
give thee wisdom
11:1, Wisdom lifteth up the head of him that
is of low degree
14:20. the man that doth meditate good things
in wisdom,
15:3, understanding...feed him, and give
him...wisdom
15:10, For praise shall be uttered in wisdom,
and the Lord
15:18, For the wisdom of the Lord is great
and he is mighty
18:28, Every man of understanding knoweth
wisdom, and will
19:20, The fear of the Lord is all wisdom;
19:22, The knowledge of wickedness is not
wisdom, neither at
19:23, and there is a fool wanting in wisdom
19:24, is better than one that hath much
wisdom
20:30, Wisdom that is hid, and treasure
that is hoarded up,
20:31, his folly, than a man that hideth his
wisdom
21:11, He that keepeth the law...getteth...
wisdom
21:12, will not be taught; but there is a
wisdom which
21:18, As a house that is destroyed, so is
wisdom to a fool:
22:6, but stripes and correction of wisdom
are never out of
23:2, will set scourges...and the discipline
of wisdom over
24:1, Wisdom shall praise herself, and shall
glory in the
24:25, He filleth all things with his wisdom,
as Phison, and
24:34, have...laboured...for all them that
seek wisdom
25:5, O how comely is the wisdom of old men,
and understanding and counsel
25:10, O how great is he that findeth wisdom!
31:8, wisdom is perfection to a faithful
mouth
31:9, A man that hath travelled...will declare wisdom
35:4, Pour not out words where there is...not

...wisdom

Eccl. 37:20, There is one that sheweth wisdom in words, and is

37:21, given him...because he is deprived of all wisdom

38:24, The wisdom of a learned man cometh by opportunity of

38:25, How can he get wisdom that holdeth the plough, and

39:1, his mind to the law...will seek out wisdom of all

39:10, Nations shall shew forth his wisdom, and the

40:20, rejoice the heart: but the love of wisdom is above

41:14, children keep discipline in peace: for wisdom that

42:21, garnished the excellent works of his wisdom, and he

43:33, things; and to the godly hath he given wisdom

44:15, The people will tell of their wisdom, and the

45:26, God give you wisdom in your heart to judge his

50:27, understanding and knowledge...out of his...wisdom

51:13, When I was yet young...I desired wisdom openly in my

51:17, I ascribe the glory unto him that giveth me wisdom

phronēsis

Bar. 3:9, commandments of life; give ear to understanding wisdom

3:12, Thou hast forsaken the fountain of wisdom

3:14, Learn where is wisdom, where is strength, where is

sophia

Bar. 3:23, The Agarenes that seek wisdom upon earth, the merchants

phronēsis

Bar. 3:28, they were destroyed, because they had no wisdom, and

sophia

IV Macc. 1:15, is putting foremost the considera-

       tion of wisdom
IV Macc. 1:16, And wisdom is a knowledge of divine
      and human
    1:18, And the forms of wisdom are pru-
      dence, and justice,

WISE, <u>phronimos</u>, "understanding, prudence, practical
      wisdom, wise"
 Tobit 4:18, Ask counsel of all that are wise, and
     despise not any
   6:12, And the maid is fair and wise: now
     therefore hear me

  <u>sophos,</u> "clever or skilful in any art, abtruse,
     wise, prudent"
Wisd.-Sol. 6:17, For they shall see the end of the
     wise, and
   6:24, But the multitude of the wise is
     the welfare of.

  <u>panourgos</u>, "crafty, cunning, artful, wily"
Eccl. 1:6, wisdom been revealed? or who hath known
   her wise

  <u>sophos</u>
Eccl. 1:8, There is one wise and greatly to be
    feared, the Lord
   6:33, and if thou bow thing ear, thou shalt
   6:34, of the elders, and cleave unto him
    that is wise
   6:8, Despise not the discourse of the wise,
    but acauaint
   9:14, As near as thou canst...consult with
    the wise
   9:15, Let thy talk be with the wise, and
    all thy
   9:17, For the hand of the artificer...and
    the wise ruler of
   10:1, A wise judge will instruct his people;
    and the
   10:25, Unto the servant that is wise shall
    they that are
   18:27, A wise man will fear in every thing,
    and in the day
   19:31, some man holdeth his tongue, and he
    is wise
   20:5, There is one that keepeth silence,
    and is found wise:
   20:7, A wise man will hold his tongue till
    he see.

Eccl. 20:13, A wise man by his words maketh him-
            self beloved:
      21:13, The knowledge of a wise man shall
            abound like a

  phronismos, "understanding, discreet, thought-
            ful, practically wise"
Eccl. 21:15, A skilful man hear a wise word, he
            will commend it,

  ponourgos
Eccl. 21:20, A fool lifteth up his voice...but a
            wise man doth

  phronismos
Eccl. 21:21, Learning is unto a wise man as an
            ornament of gold,

  sophos
Eccl. 21:26, is in their mouths: but the mouth
            of the wise is in

  phronismos
Eccl. 22:4, A wise daughter shall bring an in-
            heritance to her

  sophos
Eccl. 36:2, A wise man hateth not the law, but
            he that is an

  ponourgos
Eccl. 37:19, There is one that is wise and teach-
            eth many, and yet

  sophos
Eccl. 37:22, Another is wise to himself: and the
            fruits of
      37:23, A wise man instructeth his people;
            and the fruits of
      37:24, A wise man shall be filled with
            blessing; and all
      37:26, A wise man shall inherit glory among
            his people, and
      38:24, and he that hath little business
            shall become wise
      38:31, trust to their hands; and every one
            is wise in his
      44:4, by their counsels...wise and eloquent
            in their

  sophistes, "a master of one's craft, learned,
            wise"
Eccl. 47:14, How wise was thou in thy youth, and,

458

as a flood,

<u>sophia</u>, "cleverness or skill in art, prudence,
        wisdom"
II Macc. 2:9, It was also declared that he being
        wise offered the

<u>pansophos</u>, "all-wise, very wise
IV Macc. 1:12, proceed...giving glory to the all
        wise God
        2:19, For, why else, does our most wise
        father Jacob

<u>sophia</u>
IV Macc. 7:23, For the wise and brave man only is
        lord over his

WITHER, <u>marainō</u>, "to quench, cause to decay, fade
        or wither"
· Wisd.-Sol. 2:8, ourselves with rosebuds, before
        they be withered:

WITNESS, <u>martus</u>, "a judicial witness, a testifier
        of a doctrine"
Wisd.-Sol. 4:6, begotten of unlawful beds are
        witnesses of

<u>katamartureō</u>, "to bear witness against"
His.-Sus. 1:21, If thou wilt not, we will bear
        witness against
        1:43, thou knowest that they have borne
        false witness
        1:49, for they have borne false witness
        against her

<u>pseudomartureō</u>,"to be a false witness, bear
        false witness"
His.-Sus. 1:61, elders, for Daniel had convicted
        them of false witness

<u>epimartureō</u>,"to bear false witness"
I Macc. 2:56, Caleb for bearing witness before the
        congregation·

<u>antimartureō</u>, "to witness against"
II Macc. 7:6, The Lord God looketh upon us...which
        witnessed to

<u>diamartureō</u>, "to call for or against an ob-
        jection, to be affirmed on
        evidence"
IV Macc. 16:16, contest: to which you being called
        as a witness

WOMAN, gunē, "a woman, mistress, lady, a female"
 I Esd. 1:32, And in all Jewry...the women made
               lamentation for him

      gunaikeia, "pertaining to a woman, female"
 I Esd. 3:12, Women are strongest: but above all
              things Truth
        4:13, The third, who had spoken of women,
              and of truth
        4:15, men...who is it that ruleth them...
              are they not women?
        4:17, also...bring glory unto men; and
              without women cannot
        4:26, there be...that have run out of their
              wits for women
        4:27, Many also have perished...and sinned,
              for women
        4:34, O ye men, are not women strong?
        8:91, confession...a very...multitude of
              men and women and
        9:9, and separate yourselves...from the
              strange women
        9:41, from morning unto midday, before
              both men and women;

      gunē
 Judith 6:16, And they called together all...their
              women, to the
        7:23, all the people assembled...both
              young men, and women,
        8:31, pray thou for us, because thou art
              a godly woman,
        9:10, the deceit of my lips...and...by the
              hand of a woman
       11:1, Holofernes unto her, Woman, be of
              good comfort,
       11:21, There is not such a woman from one
              end of the earth
       12:15, So she arose...with all her woman's
              attire, and her

      thelus, "a female, a woman"
 Judith 13:15, So...the Lord hath smitten him by
              the hand of a woman

      gunē
 Judith 13:18, blessed art thou...above all women
              upon the earth
        14:18, slaves have dealt treacherously;
               one woman of the

Judith 15:12, Then all the women of Israel ran
together to see
15:13, And...all the people in the dance,
leading all the women: and all the
men
16:16, hath disappointed them by the
hand of a woman
Eccl. 7:19, Forego not a wise and good woman: for
her grace is
9:2, Give not thy soul unto a woman to set
her foot upon
9:8, Turn away thine eye from a beautiful
woman, and look
10:18 nor...anger for them that are born of
a woman
19:2, Wine and women will make men of understanding to fall
25:13, plague...any wickedness, but the
wickedness of a woman
25:16, I rather dwell with a lion...than...
with a wicked woman
25:17, The wickedness of a woman changeth
her face, and
25:21, Stumble not upon the beauty of a woman, and desire
25:22, A woman, if she maintain her husband,
is full of anger
25:23, A wicked woman abateth the courage,
maketh an heavy
25:24, Of the woman came the beginning of
sin, and through
25:25, Give the water no passage; neither
a wicked woman
26:2, A virtuous woman rejoiceth her husband,
and he shall
26:6, But a grief of heart and sorrow is a
woman that is
26:8, A drunken woman and a gadder abroad
causeth great
26:9, The whoredom of a woman may be known
in her haughty
26:14, A silent and loving woman is a gift
of the Lord;
28:15, A backbiting tongue hath cast out
virtuous women, and
36:21, A woman will receive every man, yet
is one daughter
36:22, The beauty of a woman cheereth the

the countenance and
Eccl. 42:12, beauty; and sit not in the midst of
women
42:13, For from garments cometh a moth,
and from women
42:14, the churlishness of a man than a
courteous woman,
47:19, Thou didst bow thy loins unto women,
and by thy body
48:19, Then trembled their hearts and hands
...as women in
Epis-Jer. 1:30, can they be called gods? because
women set meat
1:43. The women also with cords about
them, sitting
His.=Sus. 1:2, and took a wife...a very fair woman, and one that
1:36, said, As we walked in the garden
alone, this woman
1:40, But having taken this woman, we
asked who the
Bel-Drag. 1:20, I see the footsteps of, men, woman and children
I Macc. 1:26, and elders mourned...and the beauty
of women was
1:32, But the women and children took
they captive and
1:60, the commandment they put to death
certain woman,
II Macc. 3:19, And the woman girt with sackcloth
under their
5:13, was killing of young and old...
women, and children,
5:24, He sent also...to sell the women
and the younger
6:4, filled...with harlots, and...women
within the circuit
6:10, For there were two men brought,
who had
12:21, had knowledge of Judas' coming,
he sent the women
IV Macc. 4:9, And the priests, with the women
children
4:25, For even women, because they
continued to circumscise
14:11, And think it not wonderful that...
even a woman's
15:17, O thou only woman who hast brought

forth perfect
IV Macc. 16:1, If, then, even a woman, and that
an aged one, and
16:2, I have proved...that a woman di-
spised the greatest
16:5, For we must consider also this;
that had the woman
16:14, O woman, soldier of God for religion, thou, aged

WOMB, kolia, "a cavity, belly, womb"
Tobit 4:4, Remember, my son...when thou wast in
her womb; and when

metra, "the womb"
Eccl. 1:14, Lord is...wisdom...it was created...
in the womb
40:1, from the day they go out of their
mother's womb
49:7, nevertheless was...sanctified in his
mother's womb

kolia
II Macc. 7:22, I cannot tell how we came in my
womb; for I
7:27, have pity upon me that bare thee...
in my womb

metra
IV Macc. 13:18, the Divine...engender through
the mother'womb

WONDER, thaumasios, "marvellous, wonder, admirable"
Eccl. 33:6, Shew new signs, and make other strange
wonders:
45:3, By his words he caused the wonders
to cease, and he

WOOD, xulon, "wood ready for use, firewood"
Wisd.-Sol. 13:13, the very refuse...being a
crooked piece of wood
14:1, himself to sail...calleth upon
a piece of wood
14:5, men commit their lives to a
small piece of wood
14:7, For blessed is the wood which
wjereby righteousness cometh
Eccl. 8:3, Strive not with a man...and heap not
wood upon his fire
38:5, Was not the water made sweet with wood?
Bar. 5:8, Moreover even the woods and every sweet

smelling tree

xulinos, "of wood, wooden"
Epis.-Jer. 1:4, shall ye see in Babylon gods of
             silver and of wood
        1:11, deck them as men with garments...
             and wood
        1:30, For...women set meat before the
             gods of...wood
        1:38, Their gods of wood, and which
             are overlaid with
        1:50, For seeing that they be but of
             wood, and overlaid
        1:55, fire falleth upon the house of
             gods of wood or
        1:57, Neither are those gods of wood,
             and laid over
        1:59, the owner shall have use of
             ...a pillar of wood in
        1:63, fire sent from above to consume
             hills and woods
        1:70. acarecrow in a garden...so are
             their gods of wood
        1:71, And likewise their gods of wood,
             and laid over

klema, "a shoot or twig"
Song-Child. 1:22, ceased not to make the oven hot
             with....wood

xulinos
I Macc. 6:37, the beasts were there strong towers
             of wood,

drumos, "an oak-coppice, wood"
I Macc. 9:45, for, behold...the marsh likewise
             and wood

xulon
II Macc. 1:21, then commanded he...to sprinkle
             the wood and the

WORD, logos, "a word, a thing uttered, speech,
             language', talk"
I Esd. 1:24, the things that came to pass...the
             word of the Lord

hrema, "that which is spoken, saying, speech,
             word"
I Esd. 1:28, Josias did not turn back...regarding
             the words of the

logos
I Esd. 1:47, and cared not for the words that
          were spoken

hrēma
I Esd. 2:1, king of the Persians, that the word
          of the Lord might
      9:55, because they understood the words
          wherein they were
Tobit 8:2, And as he went, he remembered the words
          of Raphael,
Judith 5:5, Let my lord now hear a word from the
          mouth of thy
       6:4, For with them...he said: none of my
          words shall be in
       6:9, And if thou persuade thyself...none
          of my words will
       6:17, And he answered and declared unto
          him the words of
       7:31, days passed...I will do according
          to your word
       8:8, And there was none that gave her an
          ill word; for she
       8:9, Now when she heard the evil words of
          the people

logos
Judith 8:28, to her...there is none that may
           gainsay thy words
        10:1, to cry...and had made an end of all
           these words

hrēma
Judith 10:13, before Holofernes...to declare words
           of truth
         10:16, before him...shew unto him according
           to thy words
         11:5, Then Judith said unto him, Receive
           the words of thy
         11:9, concerning the matter...we have heard
           his words:

logos
Judith 11:20, Then her words pleased Holofernes
           and all his
         11:21, both for beauty of face, and wisdom
           of words
Wisd.-Sol. 1:9, and the sound of his words shall
              come unto the
             1:16, but ungodly men with their works

and words
Wisd.-Sol 2:17, Let us see if his words be true:
and let us
6:11, wherefore set your affection upon
my words

hrēna
Wisd.-Sol. 6:25, Receive therefore instruction
through   through my words,

logos
Judith 10:13, before Holofernes.. to declare words
of truth

10:16, before him.. shew unto him according
to thy words

11:5, Then Judith said unto him, Receive
the words of thy

11:9, concerning the matter.. we have heard
his words;

logos
Judith 11:20, Then her words pleased Holofernes
and all his

11:21, both for beauty of face, and wisdom
of words

Wisd.-Sol. 1:9, and the sound of his words shall
come unto the

1:16, but ubgodly men with their works
and words

2:17, Let us see if his words be true,
and let us

6:11, Wherefore set your affection upon
my words:

hrēna
Wisd.-Sol. 6:25, Receive therefore instruction
through my words,

logos
Wisd.-Sol. 9:1, fathers..who hast made all things
with thy word,

16:11, were pricked, that they should
remember thy words

16:12, neither herb, nor .. plaister..
but thy word,

hrēna
Wisd.-Sol. 16:26, that it is thy word which pre-
serveth

18:15, thine Almighty word leaped from
heaven out of

466

Wisd.-Sol. 18:22, the destroyer,not with might,
                  but with a word

Eccl. 1:23, He will hide his words for a time,and
            the lips of
      2:15, They that fear the Lord will not dis-
            obey his words;
logos
Eccl. 3:8, Honour thy father and mother both in
           word and deed,
      4:24,shall be known, and learning by the
           word of the
      7:14, Use not many words in a multitude of
            elders, and make
      8:11, injurious person,lest he..entrap thee
            in thy words
      12:12, thy seat, and..at the last remember my
             words
      16:24, My son,hearken unto me..and mark my
             words with thy
      18:15, My son, blemish not thy good deeds,
             neither use uncomfortable words
      18:16, Shall not the dew assuage the heat?
             so is a word
      18:17, Lo, is not a word better than a gift?
      19:10, If thou hast heard a word, let it die
             with thee;
      19:11, A fool travaileth with a word, as a
             woman in labour
      19:12, sticketh in a man's thigh,so is a word
             within a
      20:8, He that useth many words shall be ab-
            horred:
      20:13, A wise man by his words maketh himself
             beloved:
      20:27, A wise man shall promote himself to
             honour with .. words
      21:15, If a skilful man hear a wise word, he
             will commend it
      21:25, will be telling..the words of such as
             have
      23:12, There is a word that is clothed about
             with death:
      23:13, thy mouth to..swearing, for therein is
             the word of
      25:20, way..so is a wife full of words to a
             quiet man
      27:23, he will speak sweetly,and will admire
             thy words

467

Eccl. 28:25, and weigh thy words in a balance,and
              make a door
       29:3, Keep thy word and deal faithfully
              with him, and thou
       29:5, he will prolong the time, and return
              words of grief,
       34:31,neighbour at the wine..give him no
              despiteful words,
lalia, "talk,language,dialect"
Eccl. 35:4, Pour not out where there is a musician,
              and

logos
Eccl. 35:8, be short,comprehending much.in few
              words
       37:20,There is one that sheweth wisdom in
              words, and is
       42:15, I will not remember..the words of his
              mouth,
       43:26, and by his word all things consist

hrema
Eccl. 47:8, he praised the Holy One..with words of
              of glory;

logos
Eccl. 48:3, By the word of the Lord he shut up the
              heaven, and
       48:5, Who didst raise up a dead man..by the
              word of the
       48:13, No word could overcome him; and after
              his death
       51:5, from the depth of the belly..and lying
              words
Bar. 1:1, And these are the words of the book,
              which Baruch
       1:3, And Baruch did read the words of this
              book in the
       1:21, we have not hearkened ..unto all the
              words of the
       2:1, Therefore the Lord hath made good his
              word, which he
       2:24, therefore hast thou made good the words
              that thou
hrema
Bar. 4:37, thy sons come..to the west by the word
              of the Holy One
       5:5, children gather from the west..by the
              word of the Holy

logos
His.-Sus. 1:47, What mean these words that thou
                   hast spoken?

hrēma
Bel-Drag. 1:9, can certify me...Let it be according to thy word

logos
I Macc. 1:30, and spake peaceable words unto them, but all was

2:22, We will not hearken to the king's words, to go from

2:23, Now when he had left speaking these words, there

2:55, Jesus for fulfilling the word was made a judge in

2:62, Fear not then the words of a sinful man: for his

lalos, "talkative, chattering"
I Macc. 4:19, As Judas was yet speaking these words, there

logos
I Macc. 5:16, when Judas and the people heard these words, there

6:8, Now when the king heard these words, he was

7:10, sent messengers to Judas...with peaceable words

7:11, But they gave no heed to their words; for they saw

7:27, Jerusalem...and sent unto Judas... friendly words,

9:37, After this came word to Jonathan and Simon his

10:3, Demetrius sent letters unto Jonathan with loving words,

10:17, he wrote a letter...according to these words, saying

10:24, I also will write unto them words of encouragement,

10:46, when Jonathan and the people heard these words,

10:74, So when Jonathan heard these words of Apollonius,

13:7, Now as soon as the people heard these words, their

15:53, Hereunto Athenobius answered him not a word

II Macc. 7:24, Now Antiochus...did not only exhort him by words,

II Macc. 9:5, smote him...as soon as he had
          spoken these words
        10:34, And they that were within...uttered
          wicked words
        15:11, every one of them...as with com-
          fortable and good words
        15:17, Thus being well comforted by the
          words of Judas
IV Macc. 4:13, Onias the high priest, induced
          these words,
         7:9, Thou, father, hast...made credible
          the words of
        16:14, hast been found more powerful in
          deeds and words
Pr.-Mans. 1:3, that hast bound the sea with the
          word of thy

WORK, ergon, "a deed, work, action, duty enjoined"
I Esd. 1:23, And the works of Josias were upright
          before the Lord
         6:10, And those works are done with great
          speed, and the work goeth on
         7:2, did very carefully oversee the holy
          works, assisting
         7:3, And so the holy works prospered, when
          Aggeus and
Tobit 3:2, O Lord, thou art just, and all thy
          works and all thy
       3:11, prayed toward the window...let all
          thy works praise
      12:6, he took them both apart...to shew
          forth the works of
      12:11, nothing from you...but...to reveal the
          works of God
      12:22, Then they confessed the great and
          wonderful works of
      13:9, he will scourge thee for thy children's
          works,
Judith 13:4, So all went forth, and...look upon
          the work of mine
Wisd.-Sol. 1:12, of your life...pull not...the
          works of
         2:4, and no man shall have our works
          in remembrance,
         3:11, nurture...their hope is vain,
          and their works
         6:3, given you of the Lord...who shall
          try your works,

Wisd.-Sol. 8:4, For she is privy to the mysteries
...of his works

ergazomai, "to work, to labour, to perform"
Wisd.-Sol. 8:6, And if prudence work; who of all
that are is a
11:1, She prospered their works in the
hand of the holy
12:4, Whom thou hatedst for doing most
odious works of
12:19, But by such works hast thou
taught thy people
13:1, all men by nature...who...by considering the works
13:7, For being conversant in his works
they searched
13:10, and in dead things...are the works
of men's hands

ergasia, "work, toil, labour"
Wisd.-Sol. 13:12, and after spending the refuse
of his work to
14:5, Nevertheless thou wouldest not
that the works of
14:20, multitude, allured by the grace
of the work

ergon
Eccl. 1:9, He created her...and poured her out
upon all his works
5:3, and say not, Who shall control me for
my works?
7:15, Hate not laborious work, neither hus-
bandry, which the
9:17, For the hand of the artificer the
work shall be
11:4, Boast not of thy clothing...for the
works of the Lord
11:20, in thy covenant...and wax old in thy
works
11:21, Marvel not at the works of sinners;
14:19, Every work rotteth and consumeth away,
and the worker
15:19, eyes are upon them...and he knoweth
every work of man
16:12, so...also: he judgeth a man according
to his works
16:14, Make way for every work of mercy: for
every man shall find according to his
works

471

Eccl. 16:21, for the most part of his works are
              hid
      16:22, Who can declare the works of his
              justice?
      16:26, The works of the Lord are done in
              judgment from the
      16:27, He garnished his works for ever, and
              the chief of them
      17:9, and they shall praise his...his
              marvellous works
      17:19, Therefore all their works are as
              the sun before him,
      18:4, To none hath he given power to declare
              his works:
      18:6, As for the wondrous works of the Lord,
              there may

      ergazomai
Eccl. 24:22, He that obeyeth me...and they that
              work by me shall
      30:13, Train up thy son, and exercise him
              with work, lest
      30:28, Set him to work, as is fit for him:
              if he be not

      ergon
Eccl. 32:19, to every man according to his deeds,
              and to the works
      34:22, My son...in all thy works be quick,
              so shall there be

      ergasia
Eccl. 37:11, a woman...nor with an hireling for
              a year of...work
      38:8, apothecary make a confection; and of
              his works there
      38:27, carpenter and workmaster...watch to
              finish a work
      38:29, So doth the potter sitting at his
              work, and turning
      38:31, to their hands; and every one is wise
              in his work
      38:34, But they will maintain the state...
              as in the work of
      39:14, sweet savour...and bless the Lord in
              all his works
      39:16, All the works of the Lord are exceed-
              ing good, and
      39:19, The works of all flesh are before him,
              and nothing

472

Eccl. 39:33, All the works of the Lord are good:
            and he will give
      42:15, I willnow remember the works of the
            Lord, and
      42:16, The sun giveth light...and the work
            thereof is full
      42:17, The Lord hath...given power...to de-
            clare all his...works
      42:22, Oh how desirable are all his works!
      43:2, the sun when it appeareth, declaring
            ...the work of the
      43:4, A man bloweth a furnace is in works
            of heat, but the
      43:25, For therein be strange and wondrous
            works, variety

   ergon
Eccl. 43:28, we be able to magnify him? for...all
            his works
      43:32, things than these be, for we have
            seen...his works
      45:10, with a holy garment...and purple,
            the work of the
      45:11, with twisted scarlet, the work of
            the cunning
      45:12, He set a crown of gold...of...costly
            work, the desire
      47:8, In all his works he praised the Holy
            One most high
      47:22, But the Lord will never leave...any
            of his works
      48:14, and at his death were his works mar-
            vellous
      51:30, Work your work betimes, and in all his
            time he will
Bar. 2:9, watched over us; for the Lord is right-
            eous in...his works
      3:18, For they that wrought in silver...and
            whose works are
Epis.-Jer. 1:51, and...the works of men's hands...
            there is no work of
Song-Child. 1:3, thou art righteous...yea, true
            are all thy works,
            1:34, O all ye works of the Lord,
            bless ye the Lord:
I Macc. 4:51, the loaves...and finished all the
            works which
      9:51, garrison, that they might work ma-
            lice upon Israel

    I Macc. 10:41, shall be given toward the works
                   of the temple
            10:44, For the building also and repairing
                   of the works of
            14:42, that he should...set them over their
                   works, and over
   II Macc. 3:36, The testified he to all men the
                   works of the
  III Macc. 2:8, These saw and felt the work of
                   thine hands, and
            3:5, as they adorned their conversation
                   with works of

WORKER, poiema, "a work, workmanship, creation"
  III Macc. 2:4, It was he who didst destroy the
                 former workers of
            2:5, It was thou who didst make...those
                 workers of

WORKMAN, technitēs, "an artificer, a workman, crafts-
                     man"
  Wisd.-Sol. 8:6, if prudence work; who...is a more
                  cunning workman
            14:2, of gain devised that, and the work-
                  man built it
  Eccl. 45:11, twisted scarlet, the work of the cun-
               ning workman,

          tekton, "an artisan, a carpenter"
  Epis.-Jer. 1:8, As for their tongue, it is polish-
                  ed by the workman
             1:45, they can be nothing else than the
                  workmen

WORKMANSHIP, ergatēs, "a workman, labourer"
  Wisd.-Sol. 7:16, are...all wisdom...and knowledge
                   of workmanship

WORKMASTER, architekton, "an architect, head or mas-
                          ter-builder"
  Eccl. 38:27, So every carpenter and workmaster,
               that laboureth

WORLD, kosmos, "order, regular, the world, the ma-
                terial universe"
  Judith 5:21, in their nation...we become a reproach
               before all the world
  Wisd.-Sol. 1:14, created all things...and the gen-
                   erations of the world
            2:24, through envy of the devil came
                  death into the world

Wisd.-Sol. 5:20, he sharpen for a sword, and the
world shall
    10:1, She preserved the first formed
father of the world, that was
created alone,
    11:22, For the whole world before thee
is as a little
    13:2, of heaven to be the gods which
govern the world

aiōn, "an age, the world, eternity"
Wisd.-Sol. 13:9, that they could aim at the world;
    14:6, For in the old time also...the
hope of the world
    14:14, vain glory of men they entered
into the world,
    14:21, And this was an occasion to
deceive the world:
    16:17, For...the world fighteth for the
righteous
    17:20, For the whole world shine with
clear light, and
    18:4, light..of the law...to be given
unto the world
    18:24, For in the long garment was the
whole world,

aiōn
Eccl. 24:9, He created me from the beginning before the world,
    38:34, But they will maintain the state of
the world, and
    39:9, his understanding; and so long as the
world endureth
    42:18, the deep...and he beholdeth the signs
of the world
    43:6, also to serve in her season...and a
sign of the world

gē, "earth or land"
Song-Child. 1:8, hands of...the most wicked in all
the world
    1:13, O Lord, are...kept under this
day in all the world

oikoumenē, "the civilised world, the whole
habitable globe"
Song-Child. 1:21, them know that thou art Lord...
over the...world

    gē
I Macc. 14:10, name was renowned unto the end of
               the world
      15:9, your honour shall be known through-
               out the world

    kosmos
II Macc. 3:12, inviolable sanctity of the temple,
               honoured over...the world

    gē
II Macc. 5:15, content with this...holy temple of
               all the world

    aiōn
II Macc. 7:9, the King of the world shall raise
               us up,

    kosmos
II Macc. 7:23, but doubtless the Creator of the
               world, who
      8:18, said he...come against us, and also
               all the world
     12:15, company, calling upon the Lord of
               the world,
     13:14, he had committed all to the Creator
               of the world,
IV Macc. 5:25, established by God...the Creator
               of the world
      8:22, and deprived ourselves of this
               pleasant world?

    kosmosphoros, "world-destroying"
IV Macc. 15:31, For as the ark of Noah, bearing
               the world in the

    kosmos
IV Macc. 17:14, The tyrant was the opposite; and
               the world and

WORM, skolex, "a worm"
Judith 16:17, in putting fire and worms in their
               flesh; and they
Eccl. 10:11, he shall inherit creeping things,
               beasts, and worms.
     19:3, Moths and worms shall have him to
               heritage, and a
I Macc. 2:62, for his glory shall be dung and
               worms.
II Macc. 9:9, So that the worms rose up out of the
               body of this

WORSHIP, <u>proskuneō</u>, "to prostrate oneself, to wor-
                    ship"
  Tobit 5:13, said, Thou art welcome...to Jerusalem
                    to worship,

          <u>latreuō</u>, "to serve, to work for hire, to
                    serve the gods"
  Judith 3:8, Yet...all nations should worship
                    Nabuchodonosor only,

          <u>proskuneō</u>
  Judith 5:8, the way of their ancestors, and wor-
                    shipped the God of
          6:18, Then the people fell down and wor-
                    shipped God, and
          8:18, For there arose none in our age...
                    which worship gods
         13:17, all the people...bowed themselves,
                    and worshipped God
         16:18, they entered into Jerusalem, they
                    worshipped the

          <u>threskeuō</u>, "to observe religiously"
  Wisd.-Sol. 11:15, their wickedness, wherewith...
                    they worshipped
         14:16, process of time...graven images
                    were worshipped

          <u>sebomai</u>,"to feel awe or fear, to worship"
  Wisd.-Sol. 15:6, Both they that make them...and
                    they that worship
         15:17, he worketh a dead thing...which
                    he worshippeth
         15:18, Yea, they worshipped those beasts
                    also that are

          <u>proskuneō</u>
  Eccl. 50:21, And they bowed themselves down to
                    worship the second

          <u>theosebeia</u>, "the worship or fear of God"
  Bar. 5:4, called of God for ever, The...glory of
                    God's worship

          <u>proskuneō</u>
  Epis.-Jer. 1:6, But say ye in your hearts, O Lord,
                    we must worship

          <u>therapeuō</u>, "to wait on, to worship, to serve"
  Epis.-Jer. 1:39, are like stones...they that wor-
                    ship them shall be

sebomai
Song-Child. 1:9, cannot open our mouths...to them
that worship
1:67, O all ye that worship the Lord,
bless the God
Bel-Drag. 1:4, And the king worshipped it, and
went daily to
1:5, Who answered and said, Because I
may not worship
1:23, there was a great dragon, which
they...worshipped
1:24, And the king said to Daniel...
therefore worship

proskuneō
Bel-Drag. 1:25, Daniel unto the king, I will
worship the Lord my
1:27, Daniel said, Lo, these are the
gods ye worship

sebomai
III Macc. 3:4, yet, as they worshipped God, and
observed his law,

proskuneō
III Macc. 3:7, who said much...with regard to
their worship and

sebomai
IV Macc. 5:24, instructs us in justice...so that
we worship the
8:13, Fear, young men, and Righteousness
which ye worship
11:5, Does it seem evil to thee that we
worship the

WORSHIPPING, threskeuō, "to observe religiously,
hold scrupulously"
Wisd.-Sol. 14:27, For the worshipping of idols not
to be named is

proskuneō
Epis.-Jer. 1:5, when ye see the multitude...wor-
shipping them
I Macc. 4:55, all the people fell upon their faces,
worshipping

WOUND, plēgē, "a blow, stroke, stripe, a wound"
Eccl. 21:3, All iniquity is as two-edged sword,
the wounds whereof

trauma, "wound"
Eccl. 30:7, maketh too much of his son shall bind
         up his wounds;
    34:30, increaseth...diminisheth strength,
         and maketh wounds

WOUNDED, plēgē, "a blow, strike, a wound"
Eccl. 25:23, woman abateth the courage, maketh...
         a wounded heart

traumatizō, "to wound"
I Macc. 16:9, At that time was Judas John's bro-
         ther wounded; but
II Macc. 4:42, Thus many of them they wounded, and
         some they
    8:24, help of the Almighty they...wounded
         and maimed the
    11:12, Many of them also being wounded
         escaped naked:

WRATH, órgē, "anger, indignation, vengeance"
I Esd. 8:21, that wrath come not upon the kingdom
         of the king and
    9:13, till we turn away the wrath of the
         Lord from us for
Tobit 1:18, And...in his wrath he killed many;
         but the bodies were

dunamis, "might, power, force"
Judith 2:7, declare unto them, that...I will go
         forth in my wrath

thumos, "any vehement passion, wrath, anger"
Judith 9:8, strength in thy power, and...their
         force in thy wrath

órgē
Wisd.-Sol. 5:20, His severe wrath shall he sharpen
         for a sword,

thumos
Wisd.-Sol. 5:22, And hailstones full of wrath
         shall be cast as

órgē
Wisd.-Sol. 10:10, the righteous fled from his
         brother's wrath,
    11:9, they knew how the ungodly were
         judged in wrath,
    16:5, of beasts came upon these...thy
         wrath endured not
    18:20, touched not the righteous...but

the wrath endured

thumos

Wisd.-Sol. 18:21, blameless man...set himself
against the wrath,

òrgē

Wisd.-Sol. 18:23, dead were fallen down...he stay-
ed the wrath, and

18:25, gave place...that they only
tasted of the wrath

thumos

Wisd.-Sol. 19:1, As for the ungodly, wrath came
upon them without

òrgē

Eccl. 7:16, thyself among...sinners, but remember
that wrath will

16:6, ungodly...and in a rebellious nation,
wrath is set on

16:11, And if...he escape unpunished...mercy
and wrath are

thumos

Eccl. 18:24, Think upon the wrath that shall be
at the end, and

25:15, There is no head above...and there
is not wrath above

òrgē

Eccl. 27:30, Malice and wrath, even these are
abominations:

thumos

Eccl. 28:10, As the matter of the fire is...so is
his wrath;

òrgē

Eccl. 39:23, into saltness: so shall the heathen
inherit his wrath

thumos

Eccl. 39:28, There be spirits that...appease the
wrath of him that

40:5, Wrath, and envy, trouble, and unquiet-
ness, fear of

òrgē

Eccl. 44:17, found perfect and righteous: in time
of wrath he

45:18, Strangers conspired together...with
fury and wrath

Eccl. 47:20, stain thine honour...so that thou
          broughtest wrath
     48:10, who wast ordained...to pacify the
          wrath of the Lord's
Bar. 1:13, unto this day the fury of the Lord and
          his wrath is

thumos
Bar. 2:13, Let thy wrath turn from us: for we
          are but a few left
     2:20, For thou hast sent thy wrath and indig-
          nation upon us,
     4:9, For when she saw the wrath of God coming
          upon you, she
     4:25, My children, suffer patiently the wrath
          that is come

orgē
I Macc. 1:64, And there was great wrath upon Israel
        2:49, Now when the time drew near...the
            time of wrath of
        3:8, through the cities of Juda...turning
            away wrath from

thumos
I Macc. 7:35, and sware in his wrath, saying, un-
            less Judas and

orgē
II Macc. 5:20, itself...was forsaken in the wrath
             of the Almighty,
         7:38, and that in me and my brethren,
             the wrath of the
         8:5, Now when Maccabeus had his company
             wrath of the Lord
III Macc. 6:22, The king's wrath was converted into
              compassion:

thumos
IV Macc. 1:4, manifestly has the rule over affec-
            tion...as wrath and
         1:24, Wrath is an affection, common to
             pleasure and to
         9:32, corrupt tyrant, the vengeance of
             Divine wrath
Pr.-Mans. 1:5, magnificence of thy glory is...the
              wrath thy

WRITE, graphō, "to inscribe, write down, register, en-
          roll"
Tobit 12:20, Now therefore give God thanks...but

write all things

Bar. 2:28, servant Moses...when thou didst command
        him to write

I Macc. 10:24, I also will write unto them words
        of encouragement

      11:31, a copy of the letter which we did
        write unto our

      12:22, come to our knowledge, ye shall do
        well to write

      12:23, We do write back again to you, that
        your cattle

I Macc. 13:37, received: and we are ready...to
        write unto our

      13:42, The people of Israel began to write
        in their

WRITING, graphē, "writing, representation by means
        of lines, drawing, painting"

I Esd. 2:2, spirit of Cyrus...and he made procla-
        mation...by writing

      gramma, "that which is drawn or written,
        an inscription"

I Esd. 3:13, when the king was risen up, they took
        their writings

      3:15, down in the royal seat of judgment;
        and the writing

      graphē "writing, representation by means
Eccl. 42:7, number...and put all in writing that
        thou givest out,

      44:5, out musical tunes, and recited verses
        in writing:

      45:11, with twisted scarlet...with a writing
        engraved for a

I Macc. 12:21, It is found in writing, that the
        Lacedemonians and

      14:43, should be obeyed...and that all the
        writings in the

II Macc. 2:4, It was also contained in the same
        writing, that

WRITTEN, graphomai, "to be written"
I Esd. 1:11, to the several dignities...as it is
        written in the

      1:24, the things that came to pass...they
        were written in

      1:33, These things are written in the book
        of the stories

      1:42, But those things that are recorded...

                            are written in
I Esd. 6:32, And he commanded that...anything
            herein written, out
        8:64, And all the weight of them was writ-
            ten up the same
I Macc. 10:56, now I will do to thee, as thou
            hast written:
        14:23, furthermore we have written a copy
            thereof unto
        15:15, having letters...wherein were
            written these things:
        16:24, behold, these are written in the
            chronicles of his
II Macc. 2:16, then are about to celebrate...we
            have written unto
        9:25, many of you...to whom I have writ-
            ten as followeth:
        11:16, For there were letters written unto
            the Jews from

WRONG, adikia, "a wrong, offence"
II Macc. 10:12, choosing to do justice unto the
            Jews...for the wrong that had been
            done

WROTE, graphō, "to engrave, write or enact in
            writing"
I Esd. 2:25, Then the king wrote back again to
            Rathumus the
        6:17, But in the first year...the king
            wrote to build this
Bar. 1:1, And these are the words...which Baruch
        ...wrote in
I Macc. 1:41, Moreover king Antiochus wrote to his
            whole kingdom,
        1:51, In the selfsame manner wrote he to
            his whole
        10:17, Upon this he wrote a letter, and
            sent it unto him,
        10:65, So the king honoured him, and wrote
            him among his
        13:35, Unto whom king Demetrius answered
            and wrote after
        14:18, they wrote unto him in tables of
            brass, to renew
        14:27, So then they wrote it in tables of
            brass, which
        15:22, The same things wrote he likewise
            unto Demetrius

I Macc. 15:24, And the copy hereof they wrote
     to Simon the high
   16:18, Then Ptolemee wrote these things,
     and sent to the
II Macc. 1:7, we the Jews wrote unto you in the
     extremity
   8:8, So when Philip saw that...he wrote
     unto Ptolemeus,
III Macc. 3:11, Now the king...wrote the following
     letter to the
   6:41, The king commended them and wrote
     the subjoined

WROTH, thumoō, "to be wroth or angry"
I Esd. 1:52, so far forth, that he being wroth
     with his people

XANTHICUS, Xanthikos
II Macc. 11:30, depart shall have...the thirtieth
     day of Xanthicus
   11:33, and the fifteenth day of the month
     Xanthicus
   11:38, and the fifteenth day of the month
     Xanthicus

YEAR, etos, "a year, every year"
I Esd. 1:39, Five and twenty years old was Joacim
     when he was
   1:43, reigned in his stead: he was...eigh-
     teen years old;
   1:46, king...when he was one and twenty
     years old;
   1:58, rest, until the full term of seventy
     years
   5:57, they laid the foundation...in the
     second year after
Tobit 14:2, And he was eight and fifty years old
     when he lost
Judith 1:1, In the twelth year of the reign of
     Nabuchodonosor,
   2:1, And in the eighteenth year, the two
     and twentieth day
   8:4, So Judith was a widow in her home three
     years and
   16:23, and...being hundred and five years
     old
Wisd.-Sol. 4:8, age is not that which...is measured
     by...years

poluetēs, "many years, full of years"
Wisd.-Sol. 4:16, youth that is soon perfected the
            many years
Eccl. 18:9, of a man's days at the most is an
            hundred years
Bar. 1:2, in the fifth year, and in the seventh
            day of the month,
Epis.-Jer. 1:3, unto Babylon, ye shall remain
            there many years,
I Macc. 1:7, So Alexander reigned twelve years,
            and then died
        1:20, And after...the hundred forty and
            third year...Israel
        1:29, And after two years full expired,
            the king sent
        1:54, day...in the hundred forty and fifth
            year, they set
        2:70, And he died in the hundred forty and
            sixth year,

eniautos, "a year or cycle of season"
I Macc. 3:28, treasure, and gave his soldiers pay
            for a year,

etos
I Macc. 3:37, departed...the hundred forty and
            seventh year;
        4:52, day...in the hundred forty and eighth
            year,

eniautos
I Macc. 4:59, brethren...kept their season from
            year to year,

etos
I Macc. 6:16, died there in the hundred forty and
            ninth year
        6:20, came together...in the hundred and
            fiftieth year,

sabbaton, "the seventh day of rest"
I Macc. 6:49, they came out of the city...it being
            a year of rest

etos
I Macc. 7:1, In the hundred and one and fiftieth
            year Demetrius

eniautos
I Macc. 8:4, patience they...did give them tribute
            every year

I Macc. 9:3, first month of the hundred fifty and
            second year
        9:57, that...the land of Juda was in rest
              for two years
        10:21, seventh month of the hundred and
               sixtieth year, at

éniautos
I Macc. 10:40, Moreover I give every year fifteen
               thousand
         10:42, thousand shekels...out of the ac-
                counts year by year

étos
I Macc. 13:51, into it...the hundred seventy and
               first year, with

éniautos
I Macc. 13:52, that that day should be kept every
               year with
         16:14, was visiting...in the hundred...
                and seventeenth year

étos
II Macc. 1:7, as Demetrius reigned, in the hun-
              dred...and ninth year
          1:20, Now after many years, when it
                pleased, Neemias,

chronos, "space of time, a period, a season"
II Macc. 4:23, Three years afterward Jason sent
               Menelaus...to bear

étos
II Macc. 7:27, have pity upon me that...gave thee
               suck three years
          11:3, and to set the high priesthood to
                sale every year
          11:21, The hundred and eight and fortieth
                 year, the four

chronos
II Macc. 14:1, After three years was Judas inform-
               ed, that

géras, "old age, grow aged"
IV Macc. 5:12, kindly admonition, have pity upon
               your own years?
           8:19, compassion...and relent over the
                 years of our

YOKE, hupozeugnumi, "to yoke under, put under the
                    yoke"

I Esd. 5:43, five camels...and five beasts used
the yoke

__zugos__, "a yoke, a cross bar or band"
Eccl. 26:7, An evil wife is a yoke shaken to and
fro: he that
28:19, Well is he...who hath not drawn the
yoke thereof, nor
28:20, For the yoke thereof is a yoke of
iron, and the
30:26, A yoke and a collar do bow the neck:
40:1, created for every man, and an heavy
yoke is upon the
51:26, Put your neck under the yoke, and
let your soul
I Macc. 8:18, entreat them that they would take
the yoke from
8:31, Wherefore hast thou made thy yoke
heavy upon our
13:41, Thus the yoke of the heathen was
taken away from

YOUNG, (man, maiden, woman, child) __neaniskos__,"a
young man, youth"
I Esd. 1:53, who slew their young men with the
sword, yea, even
3:4, Then three young men, that were of the
guard kept the
3:16, And he said, Call the young men, and
they shall
4:58, Now when this young man was gone
forth, he lift up
Judith 16:5, he would burn up my borders, and kill
my young men,
Eccl. 35:7, Speak young man, if there be need of
thee:

__neos__, "recent, young, fresh, youthful"
Eccl. 42:8, aged that contendeth with those that
are young:

__neōteros__, "younger, more youthful"
Eccl. 51:13, When I was yet young, or ever I went
abroad, I
Bar. 3:20, Young men have seen light, and dwelt
upon the earth:

__neaniskos__
His.-Sus. 1:21, we will bear witness...that a
young man was with

neaniskos
His.-Sus. 1:37, Then a young man, who there was
                hid, came unto
          1:40, taken this woman, we asked who
                the young man was,
          1:45, led to be put to death...the holy
                spirit of a young
I Macc. 1:26, princes and elders mourned, the vir-
                gins and young
          2:9, her young men with the sword of the
                enemy
         14:9, sat all in the streets...and the
                young men put on

neanias, "a young man, youth"
II Macc. 3:26, Moreover two young men appeared
                before him,
          3:33, was making an atonement, the same
                young men in the

neos
II Macc. 5:13, Thus there was killing of young and
                old, making

neaniskos
II Macc. 7:12, that the king...marvelled at the
                young man's

neanias
II Macc. 7:25, But when the young man would in no
                case hearken
          7:30, she was yet speaking...the young
                man said, Whom
         10:35, Nevertheless...twenty young men of
                Maccabeus' company
         12:27, flight...the strong young men kept
                the walls,

neaniskos
II Macc. 13:15, and...the most valiant and choice
                young men...went

neos
IV Macc. 2:3, For, although young and ripe for
                sexual intercourse

neaniskos
IV Macc. 3:12, two valiant young soldiers, rever-
                encing the desire

neos
IV Macc. 6:19, should become a pattern of impiety
                to the young,

IV Macc. 9:6, But...more rightly should we younger
       men die,

neanias
IV Macc. 8:26, But nothing of this kind did the
       young men say or

neoteros
IV Macc. 11:14, I am indeed younger than my broth-
       ers, but in
       12:1, When he...the seventh, the youngest
       of all, came

neaniskos
IV Macc. 13:7, seven-towered right-reasoning of
       the young men,
       13:9, Let us imitate the three young men
       in Assyria who

neanias
IV Maccl 14:9, at the recital of the affliction
       of those young
       14:20, But sympathy with...the young men,
       who had a spirit

neoteros
IV Macc. 16:17, that you who are younger should
       be afraid of

YOUTH, neanikos, "a youth, young man"
  Judith 6:16, all the ancients of the city, and all
       their youth

neotes, "youth"
Wisd.-Sol. 2:6, us speedily use the creatures like
       as in youth
       4:16, Thus the righteous that is dead...
       and youth that
       8:2, I loved her, and sought her out
       from my youth, I
Eccl. 6:18, My son, gather instruction from thy
       youth up:
    7:23, Hast thou children? instruct them...
       from their youth
    25:3, If thou hast gathered nothing in thy
       youth, how canst
    30:11, Give him not liberty in youth
    30:12, Bow down his neck in his youth
    47:14, How wise wast thou in thy youth, and
       as a flood,
    51:15, Even...from my youth up I sought after
       her

<u>paidarion</u>, "a young child, a little boy or girl"

His.-Sus. 1:45, led to be put to death, the Lord raised up...a young youth

<u>neotēs</u>

I Macc. 1:6, he called his servants...with him from his youth, and

2:66, Maccabeus, he hath been mighty...even from his youth

II Macc. 4:9, for the training up of youth in the fashions of the

<u>neanias</u>

IV Macc. 8:4, O youths, with favourable feelings, I admire the

9:13, And the noble youth, extended upon this, became

9:21, bones was now destroyed, the high-minded...youth

<u>meirakion</u>, "a lad, stripling"

IV Macc. 11:24, We six youths have destroyed thy tyranny

<u>pais</u>, "a child, a son or a daughter"

IV Macc. 12:9, rejoicing exceedingly at the promise of the youth,

<u>meirakion</u>

IV Macc. 14:6, directions of the soul, so those holy youths agreed

14:8, so the youths, circling around the number seven

<u>neaniskos</u>

IV Macc. 14:12, For the mother of those seven youths endured the

ZABADEANS, <u>Zabedaios</u>

I Macc. 12:31, turned to the Arabians, who were called Zabadeans

ZABDIEL, <u>Zabdiēl</u>

I Macc. 11:17, for Zabdiel the Arabian took off Alexander's head,

ZACCHEUS, <u>Zakchaion</u>

II Macc. 10:19, Maccabeus left Simon and Joseph, and Zaccheus also

ZACHARIAS, Zacharias
  I Esd. 1:8, And Hilkias, Zacharias, and Syelus,
        the governors of
      1:15, were in their order...Asaph,
        Zacharias, and
  I Macc. 5:18, So he left Joseph the son of
        Zacharias, and Azarias
      5:56, Joseph the son of Zacharias, and
        Azarias, captains

ZAMBRI, Zambri
  I Macc. 2:26, for the law of God, like Phinees did
        unto Zambri

ZARACES, Zarakēn
  I Esd. 1:38, And he bound Joacim and the nobles;
        but Zaraces his

ZEAL, zēlos, "good sense, zeal, generous rivalry"
  Eccl. 45:23, is Phinees the son of Eleazar, because
        he had zeal

    zēloō, "to have strong affection toward, to
        be zealous"
  I Macc. 2:24, he was inflamed with zeal and his
        reins trembled,

ZEALOUS, zēlos, "noble aspiration, zeal, ardour in
        behalf of"
  I Macc. 2:27, the city...saying, Whosoever is
        zealous of the law,

    zēloō, "to have strong affection toward,
        to be zealous"
  I Macc. 2:50, now therefore, my sons, be ye zeal-
        ous for the law,

    zēlos
  I Macc. 2:54, Phinees our father in being zealous
        and fervent

    zēloō
  I Macc. 2:58, Elias for being zealous and fervent
        for the law was

    zēlotēs, "a generous rival, a zealot"
  II Macc. 4:2, Thus was he bold...and was so zeal-
        ous of the law

ZEALOUSLY, zēloō, "be ardently devoted, aspire
        eagerly after"
  I Macc. 2:26, Thus dealt he zealously for the law
        of God, like as

491

ZIDON, Zidonion
  I Esd. 5:55, Unto them of Zidon also Tyre they gave
           carrs, that

ZOROBABEL, Zorobabel
  I Esd. 5:48, stood up Jesus the son of Josedec...
           and Zorobabel, the
        5:56, And in the second year...began
           Zorobabel the son of
        5:68, So they went to Zorobabel and Jesus,
           and to the
        5:70, Then Zorobabel and Jesus and the chief
           of the families
        6:2, Then stood up Zorobabel the son of
           Salathiel, and
        6:27, And also he commanded that...Zorobabel
           the servant of
        6:29, a portion carefully to be given...to
           Zorobabel the

BIBLIOGRAPHY

Arndt, William F. and F. Wilbur Gingrich. A Greek-
English Lexicon of the New Testament and
Other Early Christian Literature.
Chicago: The University of Chicago Press, 1957.

Linddell and Scott's. Greek-English Lexicon, 28th
edition. Oxford: At the Clarendon Press,
1903.

Short, Charles. The Order of Words in Greek Prose:
An Essay. New York: Harper and Brother
Publishers, 1899.

THE ANALYTICAL GREEK LEXICON. Grand Rapids, Michi-
gan: Zondervan Publishing House, 3rd. print-
ing, 1968.

ABOUT THE AUTHOR

Dr. Lester T. Whitelocke, a native of Jamaica, West Indies, is a naturalized citizen of the United States of America. Dr. Whitelocke holds the B.S. degree from Florida Memorial College, St. Augustine, Florida, graduating cum laude. He received the B.D. degree from Berkeley Baptist Divinity School, Berkeley, California, and the Ph.D. degree from Boston University Graduate School of Theology, Boston, Massachusetts. He has done further studies at Virginia Commonwealth University, Richmond, Virginia, Oxford University, and The Hebrew University of Jerusalem, Jerusalem, Israel. He is a member of the Association of Baptist Professors of Religion, the American Academy of Religion, the Alpha Kappa Mu Honor Society, and the Baptist Ministers Conference of Richmond. He is listed in the Dictionary of American Scholars, the International Dictionary of Biography, and Who's Who: Distinguished Citizens of North America.

Dr. Whitelocke has served as pastor of St. John's Baptist Church, Woburn, Massachusetts, Second Mount Olive Baptist Church, Little Plymouth, Virginia and is currently serving as pastor, Bethesda Baptist Church, Colonial Heights, Virginia. His publications include several articles and Book Reviews in outstanding Journals. He is the author of The Development of Jewish Religious Thought in the Intertestamental Period.

Dr. Whitelocke is currently serving as Professor of Old Testament Studies and Hebrew at Virginia Union University School of Theology, Richmond, Virginia.

DATE DUE

OCT 3 1 '83			
APR 30 '84			
MR 4 '91			

DEMCO 38-297